CLASSROOM BEHAVIOUR

SAGE was founded in 1965 by Sara Miller McCune to
support the dissemination of usable knowledge by publishing
innovative and high-quality research and teaching content.
Today, we publish more than 750 journals, including those
of more than 300 learned societies, more than 800 new
books per year, and a growing range of library products
including archives, data, case studies, reports, conference
highlights, and video. SAGE remains majority-owned by our
founder, and after Sara's lifetime will become owned by a
charitable trust that secures our continued independence.

Los Angeles | London | Washington DC | New Delhi | Singapore

4th Edition

CLASSROOM BEHAVIOUR

A PRACTICAL GUIDE TO EFFECTIVE
TEACHING, BEHAVIOUR MANAGEMENT
AND COLLEAGUE SUPPORT

BILL ROGERS

Los Angeles | London | New Delhi
Singapore | Washington DC

Los Angeles | London | New Delhi
Singapore | Washington DC

SAGE Publications Ltd
1 Oliver's Yard
55 City Road
London EC1Y 1SP

SAGE Publications Inc.
2455 Teller Road
Thousand Oaks, California 91320

SAGE Publications India Pvt Ltd
B 1/I 1 Mohan Cooperative Industrial Area
Mathura Road
New Delhi 110 044

SAGE Publications Asia-Pacific Pte Ltd
3 Church Street
#10-04 Samsung Hub
Singapore 049483

Editor: Jude Bowen
Development editor: Amy Jarrold
Editorial assistant: George Knowles
Production editor: Nicola Marshall
Proofreader: Rosemary Morlin
Indexer: Silvia Benvenuto
Marketing manager: Lorna Patkai
Cover design: Wendy Scott
Typeset by: C&M Digitals (P) Ltd, Chennai, India
Printed by: CPI Group (UK) Ltd, Croydon, CR0 4YY

Previous edition info – Third edition published 2011. Reprinted 2012,2013 and 2014. Second edition published 2006. Reprinted 2006, 2007, 2008 and 2009. First edition published by Books Education, 2000.Re-issued by Paul Chapman Publishing, 2002.

Library of Congress Control Number: 2014951351

British Library Cataloguing in Publication data

A catalogue record for this book is available from the British Library

ISBN 978-1-44629-519-9
ISBN 978-1-44629-533-5 (pbk)

MIX
Paper from
responsible sources
FSC
www.fsc.org   FSC® C013604

At SAGE we take sustainability seriously. Most of our products are printed in the UK using FSC papers and boards. When we print overseas we ensure sustainable papers are used as measured by the Egmont grading system. We undertake an annual audit to monitor our sustainability.

Memory is the scribe of the soul.

Aristotle

What reviewers have said about *Classroom Behaviour*
(first, second and third editions)

"Bill Rogers offers individual teachers a wide repertoire of relational management skills. He provides clear guidance for putting professional integrity and emotional literacy into practice from early, minimal intervention to responding to the most difficult student and the most challenging situation. He also suggests ways staff groups might develop a more supportive environment for each other – including mentoring. I cannot speak highly enough of *Classroom Behaviour*. All educators will identify with the situations Bill describes. He does not duck the realities in today's schools and classrooms. He manages, however, to find the balance between acknowledging the difficulties and demands on teachers, whilst also being supportive of students by responding to their needs, competencies and their right to respectful interactions. He does this with clarity, vitality and humour. Every teacher needs this book, and every student needs them to have read it."

Sue Roffey
University of Western Sydney and University of London

"Any book by Bill Rogers is eagerly grasped by classroom teachers and other professionals concerned with the behaviour and pastoral care of pupils.

Bill Rogers writes in a candid style with humour and wit. After a stressful day in the classroom this book can give you the strength to go on. It is full of practical suggestions and anecdotal stories which relate to real situations.

This book should be read by every teacher in training and NQT (newly qualified teachers) as well as the experienced teacher."

Chris Stansfield
North Lincolnshire LES, UK

"He presents with vivid authenticity – his stories are always a potent cocktail of pain and humour – tales of classroom and school challenge with which any practising teacher immediately identifies. He has that uncanny and rare knack of throwing a sharp focus on everyday classroom instances which all of us intuitively knew all along, but which we had never realised with such clarity and precision. Having read *Classroom Behaviour* (published last year but available only at events until recently) I am seeing teachers – and my own managing and parenting skills – with such a sharp focus that it is like putting on my first set of glasses. That is the book's effect: it empowers and energises teachers, and it is a must for every department and school."

Professor Tim Brighouse
Chief Education Officer, Birmingham
Times Educational Supplement, 19 April 2002

"As a newly qualified teacher, I found this text extremely helpful in developing some of my key teaching skills, especially reflecting on the behaviour and practice of both teachers and students in the more 'challenging' classes."

Bill Harris
Scottish Support For Learning

"This book is a must for those entering the teaching profession and it would be really useful in a professional development programme for existing teachers."

Support For Learning

"To review a book by Bill Rogers is definitely difficult! I would put it in the class of reviewing a Bentley for a motoring magazine. Rogers is a giant in the world of behavioural management. Reviewing the third edition of what is turning out to be an indispensable reference for those working with young people has been a pleasure.

When I began teaching, 'back in the day' as is the modern term, guides that actually gave you a head start on good practice in the classroom were few and far between. What is good about this book is that it gives you not only the theory, but also advice on how that theory transfers to practice. Due to his own classroom experiences, Rogers can empathise with the reader. He empathises the fact that a good rapport with students can support good classroom practice.

There are a number of new additions here, with sections that deal with bullying, working with students on the autistic spectrum, and working with very challenging youngsters.

What I found most beneficial was that this piece of work is very 'user friendly' and very readable. It is also set out in a way which allows the reader to look at actual situations that Rogers has been in, how he dealt with them and then the theory of what actually occurred.

New features included in the text are a wider range of case studies, covering students within the 4–18 age range, questions for discussion and, most helpful of all, a glossary of relevant terms.

I would recommend this book to anyone in the teaching profession, from those who are starting out to those who are more experienced. We should constantly be evaluating our performance and how we can improve it. Bill Rogers definitely points the way."

John Wagstaff
Head Teacher, Vale of Glamorgan Local Authority, UK
Journal of Emotional and Behavioural Difficulties
Sept.1.(2012) Vol. 17 No. 3–4. p 216

Contents

About the author

Bill Rogers taught for many years before becoming an education consultant and author; he lectures widely on behaviour management, discipline, effective teaching, stress management and teacher welfare across the UK and Europe, Australia and New Zealand. Bill also works as a mentor-teacher, team-teaching in challenging schools. He is well aware of the challenges of teacher leadership in schools today.

Dr Bill Rogers read theology at Ridley College Melbourne University, then psychology and education also at Melbourne University. He is a Fellow of the Australian College of Education, Honorary Life Fellow of All Saints and Trinity College, Leeds University and Honorary Fellow at Melbourne University Graduate School of Education. He has written many books for SAGE Publications. This particular book, *Classroom Behaviour*, has been translated into several languages in its various editions.

To find out more about Bill's work, visit his website www.billrogers.com.au where you will find full details of how to book him for a workshop or training event.

Acknowledgements

Putting a book together is time-consuming for more than the author. I want to thank my wife Lora – closest friend and fellow teacher – who gave ongoing support and tolerated an overly papered dining-room table replete with endless cups of tea and coffee… (we often share our work at this table). Thanks, too, to our daughter Sarah; we shared the dining-room table many, many times (homework and book writing). Thanks also, Sarah, for the drawing in the Epilogue in the first edition.

To all my colleagues whose stories and accounts are detailed herein and to all the students who (although names are changed) would be surprised to read that their behaviour has been the subject of the many cases studies utilised in this book.

To all the team at SAGE Publications (London) who encouraged me through each edition of this book. My particular thanks to Jude Bowen, Amy Jarrold Marianne Lagrange and Nicola Marshall. Thank you, too, to Jennifer Crisp and Wendy Scott for the design motifs on each edition.

To Professor, Sir Tim Brighouse for his kind and generous review of the first edition of *Classroom Behaviour* (in the *Times Educational Supplement*).

My thanks, also, to those other reviewers who patiently waded through the book and their gave feedback: Sue Roffey, Mike O'Connor, Chris Stanfield and Bill Harris.

To Dr John Robertson, friend and colleague, for advice, wisdom and support over the years.

My thanks yet again, too, to Felicia Schmidt who patiently transcribed my handwriting (yes – *handwriting*) into readable text. A task undertaken with generosity of spirit and – always – goodwill.

My thanks, lastly, to my many colleagues who put up with me as a mentor-teacher in their classrooms and whose accounts form the interactive examples about teaching, behaviour and behaviour management in this book.

All the best to my first-year colleagues embarking on their teaching journey.

We chose our profession; we chose teaching (I hope) to "make a difference" with our students – a positive difference – in the teaching and learning journey. I hope this book supports, and enables, that choice.

Bill Rogers

Preface to the fourth edition

My purpose in writing *Classroom Behaviour* was to share practical skills for effective teaching, behaviour management and discipline.

As well as the research that bears on these issues, my work has always been critically informed by my work as a mentor-teacher in challenging schools in Australia and the UK. This role includes *direct team-teaching*, with colleagues often struggling with hard-to-manage classes (see Chapter 8).

In this fourth edition I have thoroughly revised the text, adding several case studies – particularly with reference to highly attentional and power-seeking students.

I have revisited and extended the sections that address discipline issues from the perspective of *group dynamics* – how distracting and disruptive behaviour is affected by how the peer audience affects and is affected by distracting students.

I do hope this fourth edition will inform, encourage, equip and enable you in your teaching journey.

Scope

Chapter 1 explores the dynamics of children's behaviour; how both student(s) and teacher behaviour affect each other, for good or ill. The issue of teacher "control" and management, as contrasted with *behaviour leadership*, is developed as it relates to the aims and purposes of management, teaching and discipline.

Chapter 2 addresses the critical phase of the year, the "establishment phase". Those first meetings that help define and shape our leadership, authority, discipline and our relationship with the class (as a group); the beginnings of workable cohesion as a class. Particular emphasis is given to the importance of a "classroom agreement" for behaviour and learning; developed with the students and based in essential rights and representation.

Chapter 3 develops a framework for behaviour management and explores key behaviour leadership and discipline skills within that framework. A number of case examples are noted to illustrate those skills.

Chapter 4 explores the fundamentals of effective teaching and outlines core understandings and skills. Case studies are, again, noted to illustrate aspects, features and skills of effective teaching.

Chapter 5 discusses behaviour management in terms of behaviour consequences and "punishment". A framework for planning and utilising consequences is developed. School-wide consequences, such as detention and time-out, are also discussed and suggested practices developed.

This chapter also addresses the crucial role of a teacher in enabling repairing and rebuilding with students.

Chapter 6 addresses challenging behaviours and children who present with emotional and behavioural difficulties. A school-wide framework for supporting teachers and students is developed with an emphasis on an educational model of support for children with symptomatic or diagnosed behaviour disorders.

Chapter 7 addresses the issue of anger: our own anger as teachers and how we better communicate with and support others when they are angry. The issue of communicating with angry parents is also addressed.

Chapter 8 discusses how we can support each other, as teachers, particularly when things get difficult. Issues such as the hard-to-manage class, harassment (of teachers *by* students!), stress and coping are discussed in the context of colleague support. Practical strategies are explored for each of these issues with a particular emphasis on supportive collegial mentoring.

NB   Case examples and case studies are an essential feature of this text. All the practices and skills discussed are illustrated within (and from) case studies drawn from mentor-teaching with colleagues in Australian and English schools.

The case studies traverse early years to secondary school settings (with some parent–teacher examples). These case studies are listed with a brief description and page allocation in the text on p. 313–314. Also throughout the text case samples are cross-referenced across chapters, look for (p.). Thanks.

More than just a book

As well as reading what Bill has to say you can now see and hear him in action, too!
Visit https://study.sagepub.com/rogers4e for free access to interactive online materials.

What you'll find

 Videos of classroom scenarios where you'll see Bill in action

 Podcasts of Bill discussing common behaviour scenarios and answering teachers' most frequently asked questions

 Tools to use with your students and in your classroom

 Further Reading that provides extra information on key topics.

Introduction: "I never thought I'd become a teacher"

"There's some corner of a foreign field that is forever England … a dust whom England bore … gave once … a pulse in the eternal mind … gives somewhere back the thoughts England by England given …"

Rupert Brooke (The Soldier)

"The thoughts of England" … given "somewhere back …"

My formative schooling was in England. I never thought I'd become a teacher; I had mixed success at school. It wasn't the work; I could handle that (by and large) – it was the culture of control and authority. Few teachers encouraged or allowed students much expression of their views or ideas. I also had many "run-ins" with petty, mean-spirited and, at times, cruel teachers: "shades of the prison house begin to close upon the growing boy". Being chastised – even hit and caned – was an occupational hazard in those days (the mid-1950s to the early 1960s). On one occasion, at the age of 11, I was caned for breaking a pencil that another pupil had snatched from me. I had snatched it back, he wailed and I got "caught". I was blamed in the ensuing fracas, and later caned. I was also caned for "answering back" on a number of occasions, for drawing pictures in my work-books instead of listening to the teacher and for sneaking off to the shops at lunchtime (a major crime in those days). When a teacher was unfair, unjust, I'd try to make – what I thought – was a just point. I was punished yet again.

I survived – we all did – but I never thought I'd become a teacher.

In the 1950s (after the Second World War) many of the male teachers in my school would have served in the armed forces, and they didn't take kindly to students appearing as even mildly challenging to adult authority. I suppose I was heralding the view that I had basic rights. At the heart of these rights was the desire to be treated with fundamental dignity and respect; strangely, I had no problems with the teachers who gave such respect. Thankfully there were a few …

I can recall one particular teacher walking up to me (1961), in front of the class, and grabbing my shirt. (I'd been whispering something to a friend behind me.) He then pushed me with his fingers in my chest and said, "Were you brought up or dragged up, Rogers?" He didn't like me. I stood up, heart thumping, and said, "It's none of your bloody business!" (I was a little taller than him, even at 15.) No one was going to "have a go" at my parents or their parenting. I then turned and walked out of the class. The class was hushed – *waiting*; it was all very dramatic. As I walked out of the classroom several students gave me a knowing and "thank you" look … I didn't see "the git" (as we'd nicknamed him) for a week. He didn't even put me on detention, surprisingly – he must have realised he'd gone too far (even then). He merely kept out of my way until the end of term.

I recall, as a student at school, looking out of classroom windows many, many, times (particularly when bored or when the teacher droned on and on). I could see, in the distance, the green fields and trees and gentle low hills of Hertfordshire. The window seemed to say, "Come!" I couldn't.

I left school at 15; I ran away. I left because I'd been caught putting up a large picture of all the teachers I disliked on the central school noticeboard. It was 1962, just two days to go until the end of term. I'd spent a long time on this painting – in oils on a very large canvas – the faces painted in the manner of Salvador Dali; the faces of the teachers "melting", merging into the darker, swirling, background. I had come into school early, that particular day, with the unsigned painting rolled up hidden under my blazer. It was my message, my "statement"; a parting *coup de grâce*. I was observed by a prefect as I surreptitiously pinned up the painting. He reported me, although he didn't have to. I hadn't signed it, though my friends knew … At the form assembly our senior master held up the painting (thereby giving it a second public viewing), looked at me and said, "You know what is going to happen to you, don't you, Rogers?" Well, I'd been caned before. I sighed, frowned, shrugged my shoulders looking suitably mollified. He hadn't seen any humour in my actions …

He rolled up the painting and as he dismissed the class I had seen him put it on the desk in his office area adjacent to the form classroom. I hid, a little way up the corridor and when he wasn't looking, I sneaked in and retrieved my property, stuck it under my school jumper and – *en route* to Period One – put it back on the notice-board yet again (surreptitiously). Later that morning the Form 4 students were watching a film in the upstairs double classroom; a black and white nature film (*Otters in Canada* or something like that). It was probably a "filler activity", it being within the last two days of summer term. We were whispering in the darkness, pretending to be absorbed in the film, when a knock on the door heralded yet another prefect. The teacher turned off the projector, a beam of light from the opened door fell across the front of the darkened classroom and a voice said, "Mr Smith wants to see Billy Rogers *immediately*". The teacher said something like, "Alright, if he's here I'll send him as soon as the film has finished". He didn't seem to take the prefect's words particularly seriously – at least the "immediacy" part. The door closed, and the darkness and the noise of the film gave me enough "cover" to sneak out. I whispered to my friend, "Don't say anything, I'm off – home". I tip-toed quietly, my back pressed along the wall, moving carefully in the darkness. I opened the door as quietly as I could, "escaped" and found partial freedom.

We had a letter a week later, from the headmaster (after school closure for the summer term – we didn't have a phone). "We are deeply disappointed with your son's behaviour …" it went on, or words to that effect. My parents asked me what I wanted them to do about "all this". Wisely, they let me go to another school – for six months or so. Just before my sixteenth birthday my family migrated to Austra-lia (for ten English pounds). Excellent value. I didn't know (how could we) what future would await us as the ocean liner left England's green and chalky cliffs …

Many years later, on one of my many trips back to England to conduct seminars, and lectures, on behaviour management and discipline issues in schools and uni-versities, I met a teacher whose father had taught me at the high school where I had painted "*the* picture". I relayed the account of the painting episode and he shared it with the local press (I didn't know he had passed on the story). The article detailed me as a self-proclaimed academic failure, who failed his 11-plus exam and whose strongest schoolday memories were of canings received for rebel-lious behaviour but who is now an education consultant on that very topic.

I was a little annoyed at the line in the press "self-proclaimed academic failure …" (I've never said that or believed that): annoying journalistic licence I suppose. But there is a lesson in this trip down memory lane. You can't predict where a student will go or what he or she may become. Some of my teachers had said – in effect – and sometimes in words, "You won't amount to anything …", and then had added the *because* statement of the day: "because you didn't listen" or "won't listen", or "because you won't concentrate or apply yourself". There is also the lesson that *learning is lifelong*, that education doesn't finish at school, or with school. There is, obviously, a difference between *schooling* and *education*.

I eventually became a teacher – many years later. Some of my teachers way back at least taught me how *not* to discipline: how not to embarrass, criticise and shame children. They also taught me how *not* to teach. Of course, thankfully, I had a few good, kind and generous teachers too. We always remember such teachers. They affirmed, encouraged and believed in me and enabled me to continue learning and value learning and education to this day. They also enhanced an early, and positive, belief that "I could do it".

It was Haim Ginnot[1] who spoke of the crucial consequences of teachers' actions which have the power to affect children's lives for better or worse. Being able to open, or close, the minds and hearts of children is a responsibility for all teachers to reflect upon. In my journey as a teacher I have had to rethink many aspects of classroom behaviour, teacher behaviour, the purposes and limitations of discipline and management, and how we can establish and sustain more cooperative classrooms, where rights and responsibilities work together for the benefit of all.

This book is the outcome of many years of in-service training with teachers and countless hours in the classroom with colleagues as a mentor-teacher in Australian and British schools.

Having made over 40 visits to the UK (and Europe) to conduct seminars, and professional development, in schools and with education authorities and universities, I hope the link between my Australian teaching and consultancy experiences and my in-service work in the UK will continue to find a receptive (and useful) audience here.

A few important prefacing notes to the text from here on …

Tactical pausing (…)

This book has many case examples and case studies illustrating distracting and disruptive behaviours. These are drawn directly from my work with colleagues as a mentor-teacher. All the practices and skills explored in this book are drawn primarily from those mentoring experiences (as well as supported by research in these areas).

In many of the dialogue exchanges between teachers and students – within those case studies – throughout the book, you will find a set of brackets with an "ellipsis" (…). This signals (in the text) a typical teacher behaviour I choose to describe as "tactical pausing". This is a conscious behaviour whereby the teacher *briefly* pauses in their communication to emphasise the need for student attention, or allow some processing by the student of what the teacher has just said. It can also communicate (to older children) a sense of expectant "calming".

For example, if we beckon, or direct, a student to come across to us, in the playground, from several yards away, we need to get eye contact first; a cue to "attention". This is easier (obviously) if we know the student's name. If we don't, we probably lift our voice (as we look in their direction) – without shouting – and say, "EXCUSE ME (…)! EXCUSE ME (…)" (Do we want to be excused?) Or we may say, "Oi (…)! Oi (…)" We might use a generic, "FELLAS (…)! Fellas (…)", or "Guys (…)". Having "called" them, we – then – tactically pause … The tactical pausing (…), in directional language, is our attempt to initiate and sustain some attention and focus.

In the classroom we frequently include tactical pausing when engaged in management and discipline. Several students are chatting away as the teacher seeks to settle the class at the beginning of a lesson. She scans the room with her eyes (saying nothing). As the restlessness settles she says, "Looking this way and listening (…) …"; she tactically pauses. Lowering her voice she repeats, "Looking this way and listening, thanks (…)". Again she tactically pauses to engage student take-up … Sensing the class attention and focus, she *then* says: "Good morning everyone …" and begins another teaching session. Tactical pausing is a small aspect – but an important small aspect – of overall teacher behaviour.

No disclaimers

There are books whose disclaimer reads: "All characters are fictitious … any resemblance to …." It's the opposite in this book. Every example and case study, even the briefer "snatches" of teacher–student dialogue, are drawn directly from my teaching/mentoring role in schools. My own teaching, these days, comes out of periodic peer-mentoring – working directly in a team-teaching role with primary and secondary teachers who are seeking to be more consciously reflective of their day-to-day teaching, behaviour leadership and discipline. Mentoring is a joint professional journey: there is no superior–inferior relationship. The aim is to build *reflective* professional practice (see Chapter 8).

In this book each skill or approach suggested is supported by case examples (and case studies) taken from recent teaching situations that I have been involved in as a mentor-teacher. I have been engaged in such mentorship (often in very "challenging schools") over the past 15 years.

I have changed the names of colleagues (teachers) and students wherever ethical probity demands. I have even changed grade and subject allocations and gender where I thought necessary, without changing the behavioural context and meanings of the real examples and situations noted. As I wrote each case example, each "snatch" of teacher–student(s) dialogue, the memories of particular classes, and particular students – even particular days – came back – easily, quickly. I could even "relive" some of the emotion that occasioned some of the more difficult discipline situations my colleagues and I have had to address.

In sharing these case examples with you, my aim is always to draw forth concepts, approaches, principles, practices and skills of effective teaching, management and discipline. As I write, I am also acutely aware of the fact that, as a teacher, you are constantly on the go from the moment you walk in the school gates. Being acutely aware of what the day after day after day of teaching can be like, I have sought to address ineffective as well as effective teacher practice, always distinguishing between what one *characteristically* does and what one does as a result of bad-day syndrome (p. 22f).

There is never a stage when we stop being a reflective teacher (or learner). I hope this book enables your own professional reflection and supports and encourages you in your teaching journey.

Theories, positions and this book

There are a number of well-established theoretical positions addressing behaviour management and discipline in schools. Like any theoretical approaches, these range across a continuum, normally categorised (in the literature) as ranging from explicit teacher control (for example, particular forms of assertive discipline) to "non-directive" approaches (for example, "teacher effectiveness training"). These theoretical "positions" – on a continuum – are in part philosophic, in part pedagogic and in part psychological, and they all have implications for one's values and practices as a teacher. This book is not a discussion of differing theoretical approaches, positions or "models". When "my" approach has been noted and discussed in different behaviour management texts I am portrayed as somewhere in the middle of a theoretical continuum – broadly described as "democratic discipline" or "positive behaviour leadership" or "interactionist" or "referent power". If readers are interested to peruse theoretical models, I would suggest the excellent texts of Edwards and Watts (2008), Charles (2005), Wolfgang (1999), Tauber (1995) and McInerney and McInerney (1998).

There is, fundamentally, nothing new in these theoretical "models". At base they delineate the degree, and kind, of teacher leadership exercised in behaviour management and discipline. They also highlight the degree, and kind, of leadership intervention a teacher should exercise in matters of discipline. While I have found many theorists very helpful in my practice as a teacher, and in my research as university lecturer and writer, my interest has always been focused on how to bring our "philosophy", our values, our delineation of ourselves as teacher-leader *within the practicalities of day-to-day* teaching. And, further, how we utilise our behaviour leadership to build positive, working, relationships with our students.

In writing this text I have sought – at every point – to ask not just *why* I should lead and discipline in a given way (the value question), but *what* and *how* I should lead, guide, enable, manage, correct and support students (the utility question).

Note

1   Haim Ginott was a professor of Psychology at New York Graduate School (1922–73). He did much to develop a model of discipline that advocates dignified, respectful and congruent communication with one's students. His emphasis on the positive power of teacher leadership has always been a source of great encouragement and assistance in my own journey of teaching and mentoring.

1

The dynamics of classroom behaviour

Day-to-day school teaching normally takes place in a rather unusual setting: a small room (for what we seek to enable and do), often inadequate furniture and space to move, a 50-minute time slot (or less) to cover set curriculum objectives, and 25–30 distinct, and unique, personalities, some of whom may not even want to be there. Some of our students come from very supportive homes, some go home to frequent shouting, arguing, poor diet, family dysfunction and worse … There may be diagnosed behaviour disorders in some of our students; there will certainly be students with significant learning needs.

The ability and motivation to learn by students in this formal setting of school varies enormously. It also doesn't take long for students to work out what their teachers are like and whether the teacher can "make it work …" in this place; and whether the teacher can lead and manage this space, the time we spend, the curriculum and the widely different personalities, temperaments, abilities … Why would there not be some natural, normative, stresses and strains associated with a teacher's day-to-day role?

We teach each other

Into that rather unusual setting, where students and teachers bring personal agendas, feelings and needs, and where certain obligations and rights have to be balanced, both teacher and student are "teaching" each other through their daily relational behaviours. Also, an individual student's distracting, disruptive behaviour is significantly affected by the audience of peers and vice versa (p. 15).

It is not simply enough to detail distracting and disruptive student behaviour as a discrete issue only pertaining to the student. In any school the same students may behave differently in different settings, with different teachers over a school day. The teacher's behaviour and the student's behaviour have a reciprocal effect on each other and on the ever present "audience" of peers. *Every discipline transaction is a social transaction.*

The case examples that follow (as noted earlier) are taken directly from my work with colleagues as a mentor-teacher. These shared observations are the basis of our professional self-reflection that enable and support, and call forth the necessary skills of our behaviour leadership.

As you read these case examples I encourage you to reflect on how teacher behaviour and student behaviour act reciprocally on each other. The nature, extent and effect of disruptive behaviour, in this sense, is not simply the result of students acting disruptively; *behaviour is also learned within its context.*

"Overly vigilant" management

Corey has been described by some of his teachers as "a bit of a lazy lad", a "bit of a pain!" and worse ... Any support from home for basic organisational skills and the application of day-to-day responsibility at school is limited and sporadic. In the classroom he is leaning back in his seat, a vacant look in his eyes – he's looking out of the window (to partial freedom perhaps?). His attention is hardly gripped by the task requirement in his maths class. It's his third lesson with this teacher.

The teacher walks over to him and, standing next to his table, asks, "Why haven't you started work?"

"I haven't got a pen, have I?" Corey, at least, is honest at this point.

"Don't talk to me like that!" The teacher doesn't like Corey's tone and manner ("lazy and disrespectful sod"). "Well I haven't got a pen, have I? What d'you expect me to say?" Corey folds his arms sulkily, averting his eyes from his teacher.

"Well get a pen then!" At this, Corey gets up and walks out of the classroom. The teacher hurriedly catches up with him.

"Where do you think you're going? Get back in here!"

Corey, with feigned exasperation, says, "You asked me to get a pen! – I'm just going to get one from my locker." He clicks his tongue and sighs indulgently.

"I meant get one from another student – you just don't walk out of my class." Corey slopes off towards the back of the classroom to a mate. "Hey Craig, give us a pen." Craig answers, "I'm not giving you a pen – gees I didn't get the last one back." Corey walks back to the teacher (most of the class is now enjoying this little *contretemps*). "He won't give me a pen." He grins.

Corey's teacher says, "Look I'm sick of this. You know you're supposed to bring pens and paper ..." Corey butts in, "Yeah well people forget sometimes y'know!"

"Look if you can't come to my class prepared to work, you can leave and go to Mr Smith (the year head)."

"Yeah – well I'm leaving. It's a shit class anyway!!" Corey storms out.

The teacher calls after him. "Right! I'll see you in detention!" Corey (now half-way dawn the corridor) calls back. "I don't care!"

A small incident like this, a student without a pen, becomes a major fracas. I've seen this happen with some teachers. Maybe the teacher is having a bad day (maybe the student is too) though a good deal of Corey's behaviour is about attention and "the theatre of his peers ...". Maybe the teacher is characteristically petty, churlish, pedantic, sarcastic ... What can be seen, though, is that the teacher's behaviour contributes as much to this incident – and its management – as that of the student.

In another classroom a similar incident is taking place. The teacher walks across to a student who has been un-engaged in his learning task for several minutes. She has given him some take-up time – after all, he may be thinking, he may just need a few minutes to get his ideas formed and focused, he may be another lad "with" ADSD (attention deficit spectrum disorder).

She greets him and says, "Bradley, I notice you're not working ... can I help?" She avoids asking why he hasn't started work yet.

He says, "I haven't got a pen."

"You can have one of mine," replies his teacher.

As it is still the first few lessons of term one, the teacher still has not sorted out which students are genuinely forgetful, or maybe lazy, or maybe just seeking attention or indulging in some "game-playing" or even struggling with the classwork ... She has a box of blue pens and red pens, some rulers, some spare erasers and some pencils (all taped with a 1cm band of yellow electrical tape around the tip – to track them back to the box – itself yellow). On the box, in large letters, it reads: RETURN HERE – THANKS IN ADVANCE Ms Brown.

The offer of a pen is met with "Yeah – but I haven't got a *red* pen have I?"

"There's one in my yellow box" (she points back to the teacher's table).

"Yeah, but I haven't got any paper" (he grins).

"Bradley – there's A4 lined and plain paper next to the yellow box." "OK, Bradley? – I'll come and see how you're going a little later." She finishes with a wink and she walks away giving Bradley some "take-up time". Her tone and manner indicate that she is aware of Bradley's avoidance "game-playing" but is confident that he will get what he needs and actually start some work. She comes back, a little later in the lesson, to chat with Bradley, to re-establish and check on the progress of his work and to give some encouragement and support.

> **NB**   Some teachers argue that in "giving" such students pens (and so on) we only perpetuate their irresponsibility. Would they rather simply argue? – punish? It is normally the case that only a few students come to class without pens/paper/books (and so on). My colleagues and I would rather provide such – in those critical first meetings – as we establish our leadership and relationship with the class. If the student continues to come to class without equipment (say three times in close succession), we have a one-to-one meeting to ask questions and offer support. With some students we've found it beneficial to provide a small "table pencil-case" that the student picks up at the start of the day from (say) the tutor teacher (with red and blue pen, eraser, pencil, ruler ...) and then returns at the close of the day.

A Year 3 student (diagnosed as "special needs") has a small soft toy giraffe on her table next to her daily diary-writing task. The teacher walks over and in an unnecessarily stern voice says, "You know you're not supposed to bring toys to your table, don't you?" He snatches it up and walks off. The girl (naturally) protests and he adds, "Get on with your work or you'll finish it at recess …". Who would speak to a student like that? He did. This is even more disconcerting as he has been informed she has special needs.

He could have walked over, looked at the toy, even smiled (miserable sod), and given a fair and simple "directed choice". For example:

"Danielle, that's a nice little giraffe you've got there (...), it's work time now though and I want you to put it in your locker tray or on my table" (here he could use a softer directional voice) "and carry on with your writing. I'll come and see how you're getting on soon …"

This leaves her with both a behavioural choice, a "task-focus" and expectation of cooperation by her teacher.

A female student walks into class a few minutes late. Melissa, a Year 9 student, likes a bit of attention, she's grinning at a few of her friends as she enters. She is wearing long, "dangly" earrings (non-regulation). She is quickly noticed by her teacher.

Teacher: "Right – come here [in a sharpish voice – visibly frustrated with Melissa's lateness and '*grand dame* entrance']. Why are you late?"
Student: "I'm just a *few* minutes late."
Teacher: "Why are you wearing those … things?"
Student: "What? What things?"
Teacher: "*Those* things – you know what I'm talking about – those earrings."
Student: "Mrs Daniels [her form teacher] didn't say anything!" [Melissa's tone is sulky, indifferent – she averts her eyes. The teacher senses – yet annoyingly "creates" – a challenge.]

Teacher: "Listen, I don't care *what* Mrs Daniels did or didn't do – get them off now. You know you're not supposed to wear them!" [He's clearly getting rattled now. He believes it's an issue on which he has not only to exercise discipline – he has to *win*.]

Student: "Yeah – well how come other teachers don't hassle us about it, eh?"

Teacher: "Who do you think you're talking to?! Get them off now or you're on detention!"

Petty as this was, it happened; it still does. Some teachers believe that such teacher behaviour is "legitimate" in that it shows who is "in control" *and* it enforces the school rules. However, what message do the peer audience, and Melissa, really get from the way this teacher dealt with this "uniform misdemeanour"?

If a teacher's management style is this "vigilant" – unnecessarily and overly vigilant – there are many students who will naturally challenge and even "bait" the teacher (I was often tempted to myself, at that age!). Such a management stance often proceeds from the teacher's belief that they should be in *control* of the student. Not, of course, that we can "control" students; we can lead, guide, encourage, assert, even command, but the ease with which some teachers use the word *control* may well indicate a *characteristically* demanding leadership approach (see later, p. 29f, 144f).

Non-vigilance and relaxed vigilance

Walking across the playground at the end of Period Six, I noticed a couple of students riding their bikes towards the school gate doing mini-wheelies on the gravel (most students – in this school – most times, walk their bikes on school property, as per the school rule). I also noticed a colleague on end-of-day duty who couldn't have failed to see the two lads. In the brief glance (*en route* to the staff room) I noticed he looked wistful and, no doubt, tired; seemingly oblivious to the bike riders. Perhaps he was singing (to himself) one of the favourite ditties of teachers, "How many days till the end of term …?" I was about 20 yards away from the lads and I called them over.

"Fellas (...), Fellas (...)" – eventually getting some eye contact; from distance. "See you for a few minutes over here (...) Thanks."

They stopped – akimbo their bikes – near the school gate. I thought they might just ride off (that's happened before).

"What? What d'you want?!"

They looked annoyed with a "we're-in-a-hurry-don't-hassle-us" look. I wanted them to come across to me so that I could briefly chat with them away from their immediate peer audience. This approach is often preferable in playground settings. It minimises the "theatre" of the immediate peer audience.

"Gees, what?! What d' we do?!" they called back.

"You're not in trouble – a brief chat (...) now. Thanks."

I turned aside, walked a few paces and stopped facing away from them, to convey expectation (from distance) – take-up time (p. 118f, cf. p. 98).

The whole "episode" hadn't taken long at all.

I saw them walking across the playground in my direction (out of the corner of my eye).

I didn't want to message a visual stand-off; I've seen teachers call students over, and standing with fists curled on hips, legs astride, messaging (no doubt) a kind of "showdown". This was not a "showdown" issue.

They came over and stood nearby, with their bikes. They were frowning, averting their eyes, sulking ... A muttered "What ...?"

I tactically ignored the sighs (the sulky look, the marginal eye contact), I wanted to keep the immediate focus on the main issue (at this point) – bike-riding in school grounds. I introduced myself and asked their names.

"Adam (...) Lukas" (still sulking and sighing).

"Fellas (...) I know you're on your way home. Just a brief chat. Adam and Lukas (...) what's the school rule for bike-riding in school grounds?" (Avoid asking *why* they were riding their bikes ...).

"What?" Adam wasn't sure what I was getting at initially.

I repeated the question. "What's the school rule ...?"

"Other teachers don't hassle us ..."

He now knew what I was on about.

"Maybe they don't." I smiled – adding a brief "partial agreement" (p. 104). I had a last go ...

"What's our school rule?"

This time Adam looked at me, grinned, adding "It depends who's here ..."

That's the point.

Students know which teachers are "non-vigilant".

NB   Not all students will answer a "rule-directed question" (expressed as "What's our rule for ...?"). If they don't, we'll "answer" it for them – making clear (and fair) what the school rule is. It is a way of raising "behaviour awareness" (p. 93f). It does make it harder to exercise reasonable consistency in a school when some teachers ignore or choose not to address these sorts of behaviours.

It is easy to fall into a kind of jaded tiredness when it comes to behaviour management, particularly in corridors and playgrounds. If such "non-vigilance" is typical across a school it makes it doubly hard for others in the team to exercise "relaxed vigilance".

Some students will "argue the toss" with the teacher when "called over" for a reminder about school rules (and so on). Some students will "do a runner". Rather than get into a heated argument, my colleagues and I have found it very helpful to use our small "behaviour monitoring book" (yellow cover; like the yellow card in soccer ...). We record their names, incident, date, and so on. We can find the names from the photo chart (or from student feedback nearby). That information is then passed on to a senior colleague. In 24 to 48 hours, the initiating teacher – who was on playground duty (who recorded the issue) – will then follow up with the said student(s) concerned with a senior teacher present to heighten the seriousness and give support. We don't normally chase students (unless it is a major safety issue with young children). We have learned that it is not the severity of the consequence but *the fair certainty* of the consequence that matters. It enables a school-wide consciousness to students when teachers *will* follow up and follow through when students "do a runner".

All of us have been "non-vigilant" (in corridors, and playgrounds ...) from time to time; on those days when we're tired, rushed off our feet ... We don't *intentionally* mean to "ignore" inappropriate, unacceptable, behaviours; it's bad-day syndrome. What *is* disconcerting is those teachers who characteristically walk past ... don't engage or address ... inappropriate disruptive behaviours in these non-class settings.

Relaxed "vigilance"

As Melissa (Year 9) enters the classroom (late), to a little coterie of grins, her teacher briefly cues the class, "Excuse me class" – this acknowledges they are being inconvenienced by Melissa's lateness. She turns to Melissa and welcomes her; a passing frown is replaced by a smile: "Welcome Melissa" (her friends laugh). "I notice you're late; please take a seat." The teacher does not make an issue of the lateness or the fact that she is wearing dangling earrings at this point in the lesson. As Melissa walks to her seat (was that the gait of a supermodel?) the teacher is reclaiming whole-class attention and focusing on the lesson "as if nothing significant had happened at all", which is, of course, the case. The teacher's confident calmness and focus has minimised Melissa's initial audience-seeking entry. The teacher will address the issue of Melissa's lateness during the on-task phase of the lesson; not now, in the middle of whole-class teaching time ...

Later in the on-task phase of the lesson, she calls Melissa aside (quietly) from her immediate peer audience. "Melissa – you were late last period and today ... we'll need to have a brief chat after class."

Melissa moans, "Why? I couldn't help it!"

"Well perhaps you can explain that to me after class – I won't keep you long. Nice earrings."

She quickly changes the focus.

"What?" "Nice earrings ..." Melissa grins with ill-concealed "suspicion".

"Yeah?"

"What's the school rule about earrings, Melissa?"

The teacher avoids the pointless interrogative "*Why* are you ...?" or "*Are you* wearing earrings?" What's the point of asking a student "why" they're doing something inappropriate if we, and they, know they're doing it?

Melissa appeals to a well-worn student ploy, "But Mrs Daniels didn't say anything in form-group about them." Here Melissa sighs, folds her arms and gives a sulky, frowning, look.

"Maybe she didn't." The teacher doesn't call Melissa a liar, nor does she pass judgement on her colleague's possible ignoring of jewellery rules. "I can check that with her." The teacher's tone is pleasant, not sarcastic or in any way provocative. She repeats the question. "What's our school rule about earrings?" By using a direct question ("what?") the teacher is directing the ownership of behaviour back to Melissa who – again – mentions Mrs Daniels. The teacher "partially agrees" (briefly) "Yes – you said that" but refocuses to the rule question.

"What's the rule for ...?"

Melissa sighs, "Yeah – well ... we're not supposed to." She says it, sighing, in an "I-can't-believe-why-we've-got-this-petty-rule ..." kind of voice.

The teacher then says, "Alright Melissa, it's my job to remind you; you know what to do." She smiles, "I'll come and see how your work is going later."

The teacher becomes task oriented now. She signals an end to this brief rule reminder, conveying the expectation that Melissa will take the earrings off. By giving the student some take-up time (p. 98, 118f) she also minimises any forced "showdown" such as forcing Melissa to hand over the jewellery. If Melissa doesn't take them off, then the teacher knows the underlying issue is a potential power-struggle, and rather than force her to take them off will use a deferred consequence (p. 102, 190f).

The "student tribal tom-toms" convey the message around the class that this teacher will address issues that relate to school rules (even earrings) but they also appreciate the *way* this teacher does it.

Is it worth the teacher's brief effort to address the student's lateness and earrings in *this* way? The "simple" answer is yes. *Relaxed* vigilance enables workable consistency – we'll never get perfect consistency across teacher leadership, just reasonable and workable consistency. This teacher sends the clear (fair) messages about arriving to class on time and jewellery rules but in a least intrusive way that keeps the workable and respectful relationship between teacher and student intact. She also addresses the lateness at a time of *her* choosing instead of overreacting *at the point of attentional entrance*.

NB   If the student is late to class, say three times in close succession, the teacher is better served setting up a one-to-one meeting with the student (say at lunch time) to check for reasons and offer support. It is also worth checking if this student is also late to other classes so that a year-level collegial response can be considered.

Inappropriate language

I was mentor-teaching in a maths class a few years ago. My colleague and I had finished the whole-class teaching phase of the lesson and we were moving around the room to encourage, assist, refocus students during on-task learning time.

Out of the corner of my eye I saw a student throw an eraser, parabolically, to another student who missed the catch. Cassie called across the room – loudly – to the student who had dropped it.

"Gees, you silly bitch!" She said this in a laughing, "matey", kind of way (had she meant her friend to catch it?).

The other girl laughed – as did many in the class. My colleague was closer to the fracas than I was but hadn't taken any action regarding the student's language so I called to Cassie, across the room, to come over to me (away from her immediate coterie). She stayed seated.

"What? What do you want?!" She gave me a sulky, frowning, look across the room.

I repeated, "See you for a minute over here thanks."

I had said this in a firm (but relaxed) way while working with another group of students. She stood up, arms folded.

"What did I do then, eh?"

I wasn't going to discuss anything across the distance of several rows of students. I had directed her away from her immediate classmates to avoid unnecessary embarrassment (to her), also to distract and divert from her coterie and also to speak to her (briefly) about her behaviour. Cassie certainly knew how to "play to the gallery".

I added for a third (and last time), "I want to see you over here. Now (...). Thanks." I turned my eyes away from Cassie (yet again), and turned aside to the group I was working with to convey "expectation" and give take-up time. (...) If she had refused to come over I would have communicated a deferred consequence (see later, p. 102, 190f).

She came over and stood next to me, with folded arms, averted eye contact, eyes raised to the ceiling and sighing ... "What do you want?" she said, in a careworn voice.

It's hard to keep the focus on the "primary" issue or behaviour. *Tactically* ignoring the sulky non-verbals, I said, "I called you over so I wouldn't embarrass you in front of your classmates."

"What?" She seemed oblivious as to any "reason" why I'd need to speak to her.

"You threw an eraser at Melinda ... and called across the room to her that she was a silly bitch." I'd said all this quietly. She looked at me, askance (with feigned credulity?).

"What!? She doesn't care if I call her that. She's my friend anyway....!!"

Should we simply accept this kind of "street" language, as some social commentators suggest we should? Should we accept "friendly banter" expressed in language that includes words like bitch, slut, a—hole, d—head, wanker, and so on? If I do let such language go I've tacitly said, "I don't care if you speak to each other like that in our class" (and I do care) (see later, p. 239f).

I said, "I don't know if Melissa cares ... I do." (I meant it.) She sighed and said, "So-reee!" (sorry). I briefly reminded her of our classroom agreement about respectful language. "Can I go back to my seat now?" Her tone and manner continued to evidence sulky indifference.

It would have been pointless at this point to add, "Look, you don't really mean you're sorry! Say it properly, as if you mean it!" (I've seen teachers force students, like Cassie, into face-losing or verbal slanging matches because of the tone of voice in which an "apology" is given). It's tempting to want to confront, even embarrass, students in order to "win" – but win what? All we end up doing is over-servicing the student's attentional goal.

With students like Cassie we will need to make our point with respectful assertion *in front of her peer audience* (p. 257f). This is always the issue – the social dynamics. We avoid over-servicing the student's goal of attention of power (p. 217f). In Cassie's case we also follow-up (one-to-one) after class to address her behaviour (p. 122f).

As Cassie was leaving the class later that morning she said to me, "This class was OK till you came". That was probably true (as her version of "OK" goes). The class had got used to being *very* noisy, with frequent calling out, talking loudly across the classroom, and the sort of banter I'd heard from Cassie that morning. Above all, there was clearly a lack of focus by many students during "on-task learning" time. There were several students like Cassie who hadn't had the issue of "friendly banter" addressed until this occasion. I also had a brief chat with her after class (p. 122f). She was more amenable in the following lessons. We developed a basic, respectful understanding about expectations, about learning and behaviour. It took time, effort and continued goodwill and patient communication of our expectations. The issue of disrespectful language and swearing is addressed later (pp. 239f).

NB When addressing thoughtless, inconsiderate, disrespectful, mean-spirited behaviour ... *we focus on the behaviour itself*. We do so clearly, assertively (without aggressive hostility), according – obviously – to the context.

"When you say things like (be specific) that shows (be specific) disrespect, discourtesy, offence ...".

"That's not sportsmanlike behaviour – it stops now."

Or even the direct, "That's a put-down; it stops now."

The student needs to hear the intensity of our "moral weight" relative to the issue, with a brief, clear, unambiguous "I" statement: "I am disgusted by ... appalled by ... (be briefly specific but clear about the *behaviour*) ..." (see p. 257f). Or, "That is offensive (disgusting, distasteful, cruel, cowardly totally unacceptable, unnecessary ...)". Use an appropriate degree of, and clarity of, description (regarding the behaviour).

If a student continues to speak or act in discourteous, disrespectful or derogatory ways, we will need to make the immediate (or deferred) consequences clear. This may need to occasion time-out (see pp. 180f).

Being a reflective practitioner

However many years we have been teaching, we can always benefit from some reflection on our teaching and management practice. I once had a teacher say to me, "You can't teach an old dog new tricks". My colleague was in a small group of teachers discussing behaviour management practices and skills. I knew my colleague had management concerns, and challenges, in a number of classes (but unfortunately found it hard to share those concerns). The discussion group was a collegial forum we had established to enable a general sharing of concerns and look for collegial solutions. When she had said this, a little too defensively ("You can't teach an old dog new tricks"), I replied, "But you're not a dog; you're a human being". I respectfully noted that what we were discussing were not "tricks" but, rather, well-established practices, approaches and skills ... My wry smile was returned by my colleague. "If we're willing, and see a need for fine-tuning, even change, in our management practice and if we are aware of more effective management practice, we *can* always learn ... with support ...". The discussion continued on about the nature of, and challenge of, change in our teacher leadership practice.

"Primary" and "secondary" behaviours

In many of the exchanges between teacher and students in this book, you will note a frequently recurring theme: that of a student's non-verbal and verbal behaviour potentially increasing the stress a teacher faces when seeking to address distracting and disruptive student behaviour. Elsewhere I have described such behaviours as "*secondary* behaviours". The student's pouting, sighing, sulking, tut-tutting, raising eyes to ceiling, and huffing behaviours and their procrastination and argumentative stance are *secondary* to the *primary* issue that the teacher addresses (Rogers 2011). These "secondary behaviours" are often as stressful – sometimes more stressfully annoying than the "primary" issue or behaviour the teacher is addressing.

A student has not cleaned up his work area and it is getting close to the "bell" (breaktime). The teacher reminds the student to clean up. The student says, "Alright, alright ..." but sighs as he says it, rolls his eyes to the ceiling, leans back in his seat, leans forward again, but makes no initial move to start cleaning up. It is as if he's "saying", "Here-we-go-again"; "blah-blah-blah".

The *primary* issue (litter on the floor) is not a major discipline issue; it is however a necessary class reminder for all students. Even the words the student uses ("alright") are barely "amenable". It is the *tone* of the voice, the expelled sigh, the upward turn of the eyes; his body language appears to say, "I don't care – don't hassle me!" It is these *secondary* behaviours that appear (quickly) as more disconcerting or frustrating to the teacher than the issue of the litter itself.

These behaviours are often an expression of the student's attentional behaviour, or at times power seeking. "You can't *really* make me …" (p. 217f).

I was teaching a Year 10 social studies class a few years back (as mentor-teacher). It was my first session with this group. During the whole-class teaching phase of the lesson a student in the back row leaned back in her seat and sprayed a small can of what looked like perfume around the room. It had clearly annoyed some of the class. (I could smell the deafening, cloying, scent from the front of the classroom.) Several students (her friends) laughed. Several boys started to join in the feigned "Ahhr!! – it stinks!" It was behaviour that couldn't be ignored. I called across the room to her, by name.

"Anne (…) Anne (…)" – I'd remembered her name from roll call. She looked across the room at me with a look of (feigned?) surprise.

"Yes – what?". She leaned back in her chair, grinning, the can of perfume spray still on the desk.

"You've got a can of Impulse (that's what I thought the brand was) and you've sprayed it around the room." It helps to be specific and briefly "describe the reality of the situation" (a sort of "wavelength check"). "I want you to put it on my desk or put it away in your bag. Thanks." I gave her a directed choice rather than walk to the back of the room and either tell her to "hand it over" or just take it.

"It's not Impulse, it's Evoke," was her response. No doubt she said it to garner more group attention ("Notice me, everyone!"). Her tone of voice seemed to suggest: "Let's play verbal ping-pong shall we?"

These kinds of "secondary behaviours" are much more annoying to teachers than the "primary behaviours" that trigger them: the sighs, the head movements, the averted eyes or the eyes to the ceiling, the supercilious grin and, of course, the annoying time-wasting things that some students say.

It's tempting to argue: "I don't care if it's Chanel number bleedin' 9!! Put it away now or … !!" I said, "I want you to put it in your bag or on my desk", repeating the "directed choice" (p. 103, 191f). Her bag was under her table.

"But it stinks in here!" She still wanted to play verbal ping-pong. A bit of brief, partial agreement can help avoid pointless argument.

"I know it stinks." She was actually right on that score. Local factories produce some awful smells that – on a hot day – waft, almost palpably, into the classrooms at this school. I repeated the directed choice.

At that point I took the minimal risk of leaving Anne with the directed "choice", as it were, and reclaimed group attention by saying something like, "Looking up here everyone (…). Thanks." and going back to the diagram and topic I had started to address earlier. Out of the corner of my eye I noticed her slowly (ever so slowly) put the perfume in her bag.

If she had refused, full stop, to put it away, a deferred consequence would have been made clear to her (see pp. 102).

The naturally stressful challenge always, in such situations, is to communicate a sense of "calmness" and personal self-control when dealing with such "secondary behaviours". Yes, there are times when it is appropriate and necessary to communicate one's frustration and anger (Chapter 7), and to assert, but in this case, with this kind of silly attentional "game-playing", a directed choice, avoiding argument and refocusing the class are more effective. Of course, I could have:

- walked over and grabbed the perfume off the table, "Right! I'll have that!"
- demanded she hand the perfume over, "Right … give it to me … give it to me now!" What if she doesn't, what if she says, "No!! – can't make me!" and she's right.
- said "Don't you ever speak to me like that! Who the hell do you think you are?" (or words to that effect)
- been sarcastic or rude, in order to embarrass her in front of the class
- told her to leave the room.

Some of these options (above) are no doubt transitionally tempting! What I am trying to say is that we, in effect, teach each other in these episodic transactions. Anne is learning something about *appropriate* teacher authority and leadership and (where necessary) about facing the consequences of her behaviour. So are the audience of her peers.

NB   Every discipline transaction is a social *transaction*. When we discipline one, or a few, students in front of their peers, whatever we say is obviously heard by, and has an impact on, the audience of peers. We are not simply speaking to the individual/s who are being distracting or disruptive. There is a sense in which we are speaking to everyone about how an individual's behaviour affects others *in our class*. This is why our corrective language needs thoughtful planning (p. 97f). Merely reacting to behaviour incidents as they arise is the least effective way to exercise our behaviour leadership. It is also the least effective way to invite and engage student cooperation.

There are always many things I *could* do or say. There are always many "ifs", "could-bes" and "what-ifs" in behaviour management, particularly with challenging students (Chapter 6). There is also no guarantee that any approach will always "work" in all situations.

There needs to be, however, practices and skills that reflect our values about how we lead, guide, encourage and support young people. Later, in Chapter 3, the practices and skills of behaviour leadership are explored in some detail. This first chapter explores the natural, daily, dynamic within which we need to exercise our behaviour leadership. Behaviour is complex at times; situational and relational behaviour also has its audience-seeking effect, which can either work for the teacher's (and class's) benefit or work against the teacher.

We can ill afford to lose the goodwill of the 70 per cent (or so) of cooperative students by forcing the challenging student to lose face and thereby making it easy for the 70–80 per cent to "side" with the disruptive student or, conversely, allow ourselves to be "backed-into-a-psychological-corner".

In one of my Year 10 classes recently, I was moving around the room during on-task learning time and noticed a student with a smart phone (something I come across frequently these days) – tiny earphones in his ears and clearly enjoying the music that I could also hear, faintly, even as I worked with students nearby. Walking over to him I made eye contact and beckoned with my fingers for him to take the earphones out. He did. I could hear the pulsating, musical buzz more intensely now.

"It'll help if you turn it off," I suggested. He did. I then asked him how his work was going ...

> **NB** This is important. The first response (in an on-task learning context like this) is not to immediately ask him to hand over his smart phone. We keep such a transaction *least intrusive* by entering into the student's workspace invitationally and being task/encouragement focused. We talked about the work, I made a few suggestions, asked a few questions to extend his thinking about the task ... *then* had a quiet word about the phone.

"Brock," I asked, "What's the school rule about phones in class?" Students are allowed to bring iPods or hand-held electronic games or mobile phones to this particular school but they're not supposed to use them in class – for obvious reasons one would think. It's hard to communicate to a student who, in Brock's case, has loud music going on "upstairs". And these days a student's phone, is not merely a phone, it is their "third hand" *and* it's effectively a computer that is able to access the world-wide graffiti or social media board in several seconds ... Some students are not merely listening to music, or texting, they are engaging the world-wide graffiti board ... The classroom is not the place for this kind of "social media".

Instead of answering the question I had asked ("What's the school rule about mobile phones in class?") Brock pointed to his regular teacher and said, "Ms Smith doesn't mind if we have them on – long as we're doing our work ..." He didn't say this disrespectfully (some do); he was stating it as a matter of fact.

In my team-teaching-mentoring role in this school, I had noticed that a few teachers didn't seem to care if students brought, and played, their music from their phones or iPods (in class time) as long as they got their classwork done as well. No doubt at all – of course students can work with music coursing in their ears (even head-banging music ...); that's not the issue. The school rule is clear (and fair) and there for a reason – "no phones or iPods in class time". Students have plenty of time (outside class time) to play music and text and ...

Some teachers "over-service" a student's verbal "secondary behaviour" by entering into a pointless discussion about the veracity of what the student has said about "other teachers letting them", or they will argue against the student's view of "how stupid and unfair the rules are ...". Some teachers try to defend the reasons for the rule (generally an unwise course); "Brock ... look ... I don't make the rules do I?" Some teachers almost sound like they are "pleading". They present with a 'defeated', if affable and well-meaning tone. Students often read – from such "reasoning" – that whatever happens the student will have their way, despite what the *school-wide* fair rules may say. "Other teachers might let you play iPods but they're not really supposed to, *are they?*" It is pointless *asking the student to reason* (*at this point in the lesson*) about something they may see as unfair; besides it is a time-wasting exercise distracting away from the business of teaching and learning.

Some teachers become overly vigilant and defensive, and will cast aspersions on other colleagues. "Look I don't care what Ms Smith does or doesn't do! In my class you don't have personal music on – *full stop!* Now – give it to me." When students want to appeal to "what other teachers do (or let us do)" a *brief* partial agreement is helpful followed by a refocusing to the right or rule affected, or a refocusing to the task:

"Miss Donkin lets us have music on in social studies."

"Even if she does (partial agreement; it doesn't help to call the student a liar) (...) however in this class the school rule is clear. I want you to turn it off and put your phone on my table or, if you like, in your bag (or pencil case) ...". The teacher beckons to the teacher's table. "You'll get it back at the end of the lesson."

Whenever I've given this *directed choice* (at primary or secondary level), I've never had a student say (yet), "OK, I'll put my expensive phone, or iPod" (or other *objet d'art*) "on your table". If the student refuses to put it away, we will need to make the consequence (the *deferred consequence)* clear (p. 102).

Residual "secondary behaviour"

Jaydon is chewing a largish, viscous, fruity-smelling chewing gum during on-task learning time. The teacher is moving around the room, micro-teaching, encouraging, reminding, and (where necessary) giving quiet reminders about appropriate behaviour ... The teacher walks over and quietly says, "Jaydon (...)". Brief eye-contact is established.

  "What?" (He looks up ...). "Good morning again".

"Oh yeah. Morning."

The teacher asks how his work is going, has a brief chat about the student's progress and adds: "The bin is over there."

"What?" he asks.

"Tropical?" (She suggests the chewing gum's flavour ...).

"Eh? – Yeah ..."

"The bin is over there." This quiet incidental direction in part "describes the reality" (there is a bin) and invites some basic connective "behaviour awareness" (put the chewing gum in the bin) by reminding the student where the bin is. It is said respectfully, a little tongue-in-cheek, as if to say "You know that I know that you know what you should do ...".

If the student engages in secondary dialogue "But other teachers don't hassle us about chewing gum. C'mon ...!" (blah, time-wasting, blah), the teacher will *briefly* acknowledge and refocus.

"In this class, the school rule is clear and the bin is near ... Ta." The teacher walks off expecting cooperation (or, at least, compliance) by giving the student some take-up-time (p. 118f).

Ten seconds or so later the student shuffles off to the bin sighing and muttering. "I'll put it in the bin, I'll put it in the bin, n'yah, n'yah (in a sotto voce whine) ..."

The teacher *tactically* ignores this "residual secondary behaviour" and observes (out of the corner of his eye) that the student has slumped in his seat, drawn-out sigh, and slowly restarted work (more residual "secondary behaviour"). A little later he goes over to the student and re-establishes the working relationship by focusing on the task. "So, how's it going then? Let's have a look. Where are you up to?"

You can imagine what could happen if the teacher over-services all those residual "secondary" behaviours. "Look!! When you put chewing gum in the bin, you put it in the bin *without* a fanfare – alright?!" or, "Why can't you do a simple thing like put chewing gum in the bin without making a song-and-dance about it?!" That would unnecessarily re-escalate any residual tension as well as over-servicing this kind of attentional behaviour. I have seen many teachers overly engage such behaviours, ending up arguing or even threatening students with detention.

Some teachers try to ameliorate what they see as the perceived upsetness of the student. They take the huffing and puffing and muttering as an indication they've upset the student; they take it *personally*. "Troy, Troy, I don't make the rules do I ... be reasonable ... *please*". This kind of "intended goodwill" only over-services the sulkiness and pouting. It is generally better to *tactically* ignore such "secondary" behaviours *until* the student is back on task, as it were, and then have a brief "re-establishing" that focuses on the task (the classwork) at hand (p. 116f).

If a student"s "secondary behaviour" is overly disrespectful, or disturbingly distracting, in tone or manner, it will need to be addressed, briefly and firmly, and with a focus on the unacceptable *behaviour* and then refocus the student back to the task or expected behaviour: "I'm not speaking to you disrespectfully, I don't expect you to speak to me like that". This to a student whose tone of voice is cocky or arrogant. At this point it is also prudent to give "take-up time" as the student sulks off back to his seat.

It will also be helpful to follow-up with the student, after class, one-to-one (away from his peer audience) to speak with him about the tone/manner ... of his behaviour (p. 122f). In this one-to-one context we can make clear to the student what we see in their "secondary behaviour". Some students are not always aware of how their tone of voice, manner, body language "come across". If such follow-up is carried out early in the teacher–student relationship – with supportive respect – it can go a long way to seeing a reduction in residual "secondary behaviours".

We will also come across students who, through their behaviour, say (in effect), "You can't make me!" or "I don't have to do what you say ...". I have seen some infant students really upset their teachers by turning aside and refusing to look at them after the teacher has specifically given a direction: "Bronson (...) Bronson (...) Look at me. Look-at-me!!" I've seen teachers put their hand under a child's chin and force it up to engage attentional eye contact. I've seen teachers bodily turn young children around so they are facing their teacher. If the teacher is getting frustrated and *forcing* the child's head up, the resistant child may well be saying (through his/her behaviour) "You can't make me!", or "I can do what I want and you can't stop me". The child's "private logic" is for him – at this point – "true". *Who is controlling whom?* The issue of this kind of challenging children is addressed more fully in Chapter 6.

- At younger primary age, children are not always aware of their "secondary" behaviours. It will help to have a chat with them later (one-to-one) to explain and even briefly "model" such behaviours to them (see p. 128/235f).[1]
- Sometimes "secondary behaviours" are the result of habit; the student may be unaware that their non-verbal behaviours appears as sulky, pouty, indifferent, testy – displaying a "chip on the shoulder" (with some students there is "a bucket of attitudinal chips"!). In these cases, early and thoughtful follow-up to acknowledge the teacher's concern and gain some shared understanding, and then working with the student to support behaviour change, are crucial (p. 122f).
- Sometimes such behaviour is the student's bad-day syndrome; sensitivity by the teacher will acknowledge this (privately) and encourage the student to be more aware of their behaviour in the future.
- Sometimes such behaviour is provoked by the teacher through their own insensitive, petty, even confrontational behaviour

- Sometimes the student, too, will use their secondary behaviours in a provocative way to "test" out the psychological, relational, "territory" of the classroom and their teacher. Such behaviour is sometimes used as a territorial posturing, particularly in males.
- For some students their secondary behaviour may be a form of "exitatory stimulation", where the student uses his attentional behaviour as a form of "conditioned stimulation" – the "theatre" of attention and power (p. 217f).[2]

One of the harder messages I had to learn as a younger teacher was that I cannot simply and easily "control" others' behaviour. Nor can I simply decide what students will do regarding their behaviour ... I can decide what I will do in response; I can control myself *in* the teaching and management situation (although that, too, is not always easy ...). To the extent that I thoughtfully control myself, my language, my "manner" and my approach to the students, is the degree to which I can invite cooperation or, conversely, finding my students becoming difficult, or even resistant. The skills addressed later in Chapters 2, 3 and 4 specifically address the issue of effective teaching, behaviour leadership and discipline.

I have also learned not to make demands on the daily reality of teaching that reality won't bear.

Our "explanatory style" in behaviour management: creating or managing stress

Some teachers bring an *overly* demanding "explanatory style" to classroom management and discipline; a *characteristic* way of defining and explaining social, relational, reality. One's explanatory style cannot only affect how one relates to others, but can also affect one's emotional state and well-being (Bernard 1990; Seligman 1991; Rogers 2012).

When stressful events come to us, it is not only – or *simply* – the stressful event that directly causes how we feel, and how effectively we cope and manage. Our "explanatory style", our "working beliefs" about behaviour – what students *should* and *shouldn't* do – also contribute significantly to how effectively we manage stressful situations.

Unhelpful, demandingly assumptive, beliefs, of themselves, can actually increase one's stress and impede one's ability to engage student cooperation. Such beliefs are directly related to *how we perceive and explain* what is happening when a student is attentionally demanding, rude, arrogant, lazy or indifferent. "Secondary behaviour" is a typical case in point. When a student slouches, sighs, rolls his eyes to the ceiling or gives a malevolent grin, some teachers will "automatically" react to such "secondary behaviours" in a stressful way, often saying (later) that "Children *must not* question, or disagree or argue with their teachers" (their superiors), or "Children *should* do what I say the *first time*", or "Children *should not* answer back". The most common belief statement I hear is, "Children *should not* be rude, they *should* respect their teachers. I *deserve* respect" (full stop).

The "should" and "must" and *deserve* part of the explanatory style is often the problem. There is an imperative here; a demand on reality that is often unrealistic – and unrewarded in daily reality, particularly in more challenging schools. There are many children who show disrespect, who do not respond, comply, or "obey" the first time, who answer back, who are *uncivil*. It is unpleasant of course, and frustrating when this happens and – yes – we need to address such behaviours. However, when we say, "students *must* obey me …", "*must* not answer back …" or "*must* respect me … I *deserve* respect …", we are making *absolute demands* that, if not met, contribute directly to the level of our stress and also to how effectively we handle distracting, disruptive behaviour situations. If we say, "He *shouldn't* answer back to me" when he did (in reality), the internal self-speech can increase the amount of stress one feels at that point, particularly if the intensity of cognitive demand (shouldn't!) is a *characteristic* way that one explains such naturally stressful reality.

I have seen different teachers managing the same challenging behaviour issues, in much the same situations and contexts, and seen quite different degrees of effectiveness in management and teacher coping. This is not explained simply through personality style alone (Rogers 2012). A more *realistic* belief avoids *absolutistic* imperatives: "*I can't stand it when …!!*" is different – in kind – from statements such as "*It's annoying, frustrating, unpleasant* when … *but I can cope when* I do X, Y, Z". We might still feel stressed holding this belief (it's *annoying* rather than "I can't stand it.") *and* explaining difficult events in this way, but we won't be *as* stressed for *as* long. Of course our beliefs need to be buttressed and supported by skills of coping, and leadership, in management contexts. It is the *balance* between realistic beliefs and management skill that enables less stressful, more positive, coping day after day.

A *cognitive fixation* about receiving (indeed, demanding) respect can alter how we perceive, interpret and manage the sorts of "secondary behaviours" noted earlier. Whether we like it or not, we have to "earn" respect from our students by the effectiveness of our teaching (Chapter 4), our confident leadership and by the effort we make to build and sustain workable relationships with our students. It is self-defeating to simply, or merely, *demand* respect.

Beliefs and standards

The belief "Children *must* not swear …" is not the same as having a standard about respectful language. Having a more realistic and appropriately flexible belief about inappropriate language, including swearing – "I *don't like most swearing*, however I won't let it unnecessarily stress me, while at the same time I will need to address it accordingly to situation, and circumstance" – will occasion a less stressful state of mind and (with some prior skill) enable a more effective management of inappropriate student language, including swearing (see p. 239f).

It can help to learn to "tune into" and "dispute" unhelpful, self-defeating beliefs and explanatory styles that are often couched in "must" and "should" language ("I *should* be able to control these kids!!"). By "reframing" the demands to preferences based on reality, we tune into workable reality without "dropping our standards". We also reduce insistence-focused statements about reality ("He *must* …", "I *must* …", "Others *must* …") that can increase emotional stress levels. At the end of the day, social reality has no obligation to simply obey our *demands*.

This is not mere badinage. Talking, even self-talking, is an action, and actions have effects. If I characteristically say to myself "I'm no good", that is over-generalising. If I have an insistent cognitive demand behind such thoughts ("I *must* get it right all the time"), I'll set an impossible personal standard. If, however, I say "Look, I'm having difficulty with (a given student or class group)" and "What skills and support do I need?", that is *accurate* self-talk. It is also honestly realistic. Being more accurate, reasonable and realistic about our daily social and professional reality will help me in addressing my goals and managing inevitable, natural, stress in my day-to-day teaching and behaviour leadership.

Inaccurate, inflexible, demanding and negative self-talk can become an unreflective habit. If not addressed, it may become so *characteristic* that it is no longer a conscious activity. And while past performance and past experience may have interred our characteristic self-talk, it is in the present that we are using it and in the present that changes need to be made. By consciously reflecting on our characteristic self-talk (in stressful contexts) we can learn to reframe *unrealistic demands* to enable realistic self-talk that is *preferential*, and realistic, rather than demanding.

The bad-day syndrome

There will be days (naturally) when normative tiredness and concerns arising from one's personal life, the issues of the day and one's state of health will affect the quality of our day-to-day teaching and behaviour management. Even those days when we just feel "out-of-sorts" will have this effect. It is easy on those days for *our* frustration to spill over into our behaviour. We may become short-tempered, snappy and even angry.

It is important to telegraph to students when we're having a bad day. "You can probably tell I'm not feeling the best today. It's not your fault. ["Well it is a bit", you might be tempted to say!] I don't want to go into it all – but I'm a bit annoyed (or cheesed off). If you see me getting a bit "snappier" today you'll know why …".

If we are unwell, it will be important to explain briefly "I've got a bad headache, or …". If it is a more personal issue, it is normally unwise to share details; it is generally enough to just telegraph the fact we're having a bad day. Most students cannot really cope with such personal information (nor should they have to). I am amazed at how much private and personal information some teachers are apparently willing (and comfortable) to share with children – even primary-aged children: information about a teacher's relationships, their divorce details, their financial hassles and even concerns they have about their fellow teachers!

Children enjoy the sort of sharing about a teacher's childhood experiences ("When I was a boy we did …") but it is inappropriate to use the teacher–student relationship to either "offload" one's personal frustrations or to make students inappropriate confidantes.

We don't need to go into details on our bad days; it is enough to let them know so that they can have some basic awareness of how we're feeling, even on occasion some sympathy with our shared humanity! Children understand that *everybody* has bad days.

There are also those bad days where we might say something inappropriate, or thoughtless, to a student; a throwaway line that we didn't intend to use; a sharper tone; even an insensitive, churlish or petty comment. Tiredness, stress, being rushed and hurried (and harried) by others can easily chip away at our goodwill and patience. On such days we are wise and professional – human – to remember to acknowledge and apologise. Having done so, it will then be important not to engage in self-blame and to move on.

This is to be distinguished from teachers who *characteristically* discipline and manage in petulant, petty, mean-spirited ways; destined (it seems) to create, even sustain, unnecessary anxiety and unacceptable control over their students. While such teachers may still (in some schools) get "results", they do so at a great cost to student well-being and self-esteem. I have worked with teachers who have refused to forgive students (even students who have made an attempt to apologise). I have seen teachers refuse to apologise when it was the right and proper thing to do, or who nurse a grudge against a student for a long, long time. They forget that we are all fallible. Such teaching and management behaviour – where characteristic – in a teacher's practice, will need to be professionally confronted.

It is also important to remember that teaching is our profession not our life. Yes, it is a profession that will have a significant impact on the lives of the children we teach and it carries significant responsibilities. It will also naturally bring frustration, tiredness and anger at times.

Many first-year teachers, well over half my age, say how tired they get as beginning teachers. This is natural as we begin the teaching journey and deal with the challenges of preparation, differentiation, marking, discipline and its follow-up, students with significant learning needs and behaviour disorders ... and monitoring of students' work and the looming incursion of OFSTED ...

Colleague support enables us to see beyond our own resources, to know, and receive assurances, from shared experience, knowledge and skill. Our colleagues' moral support ("We're all in the same boat ..." "It's not just me ..." We've all been there ..."); their professionalism, goodwill; the way in which we give direct support (as in time-out situations) can all help ameliorate the bad-day syndrome.

Coping with our personal, psychological, junk mail

Bad days, failure and self-criticism often seem to go together. We can at times be quite hard on ourselves, unfairly hard, when we don't perform well or as well as we think we should.

I've sat and talked with many teachers who, having got angry with a student or a class, say things like "I *shouldn't* have got angry like that ...". Why ever not? There are many situations where we will get frustrated – even angry – with our students. The problem may well be the "like that" aspect of our anger. Frustration and anger are normal, natural in the stressful dynamic of behaviour management and discipline. Yes, there are more effective ways of managing anger than shouting or yelling, but we *did* get angry. We are not a failure for that. We can always do something about poorly expressed anger (Chapter 7).

Psychological junk mail comes loaded with global, "stable", self-talk: "I *shouldn't* have!" (we did); "It's *not fair!*" (really?); "I *always* get it wrong!" (always?); "I'll *never* get through to them" (never?). Maybe we *shouldn't* have done, or said, X, Y, Z, *but we did*; that's the reality. If we add to such self-talk repetitions of, and ruminations about, our failure ("I *shouldn't!*", or comments such as, "*I'm an idiot*", "*I'm* stupid, a *total failure*" – total?, "I *never* get a fair deal") we will naturally feel worse and cope less effectively with our failure, and our struggle.

I'm not suggesting a kind of cognitive "shrugging it off" by saying it doesn't really matter when it does; *our struggle and real (or perceived) failure can and does hurt at times*. It *does* matter when we fail, when we get things wrong; but *repetitive self-talk* (like that above) acts like psychological junk mail and we will feel worse than we need to feel.

Feelings of failure are normal, natural and even appropriate. Learning to fail meaningfully means we acknowledge our fallibility (in ourselves *and* others). It will help to label the failure for what it is – a mistake, a lapse in judgement (even a lack of skills) – and instead of excusing the failure we ask what can be learned from it: "Do I need to apologise to anyone?" (probably); "What do I need to do?" (specifically); "Do I need support or help to move beyond this?" Colleague support will always help ...We can learn as much, at times, from what goes wrong as what goes right a message we frequently tell our students.

By *relabelling* failure and *refocusing* – "OK, I *did* get it wrong. I should have done X, Y, Z" – and then asking "*What* can I do now and what can I do *next time* in a similar situation?", we *redirect the emotional energy* that can easily be eaten up by "mentally kicking oneself" (Edwards 1997). Tuning into negative self-talk is not easy; like any skill it needs to be acknowledged and practised as a kind of inner self-checking "mechanism" – whenever we catch ourselves "posting psychological junk mail upstairs". Maybe we can't take control of the first negative and self-defeating thought that comes into our head but we can *learn* to take control of *subsequent* thinking and our internal dialogue. We're likely to be using negative self-talk when we're experiencing emotions such as frustration, anger or ongoing anxiety, a sense of "powerlessness", or residual jadedness towards someone or about some situation or circumstance. The reason for disputing erroneous and self-defeating thinking is that it can bring about a more effective way of coping; both emotional and practical coping. We will need to ask ourselves if our current thoughts – the way we explain hurtful or bad and stressful events to ourselves – is actually helping to deal with our struggle, our failure. What are the consequences, the outcome, of *this* kind of thinking? How can I reframe my characteristic thinking about the natural stresses I face ...?

Professor Martin Seligman, a leading researcher on *learned* helplessness and *learned* optimism has said:

Failure makes everyone at least *momentarily* helpless. It's like a punch in the stomach. It hurts, but the hurt goes away – for some people almost instantly ... for others the hurt lasts, it seethes, it roils, it congeals into a grudge ... they remain helpless for days or perhaps months, even after only small setbacks. After major defeats they may never come back. (1991: 45)

According to Seligman *learned* helplessness derives from an explanatory style that believes, and explains, difficult and bad events in several dimensions: permanence, pervasiveness and personalisation. "It's *me* …" (or, "It's *them*!"), "I *never* get it right … it will last *forever* … it will affect *everything* I do …".

An *optimistic explanatory style* acknowledges the annoyance, even pain, in failure, but avoids using abiding traits to explain the failure and bad events. Using honest, and realistic, qualifiers helps to reorient: "Yes, I do *sometimes* get it wrong", "*lately* I haven't been up to scratch with my lesson plans" and "it is *annoying* that I missed out on my promotion, so what do I need to do to improve or change?" The more optimistic explanatory style *acknowledges frustrating reality, but reframes* it, seeing the failure as having transient rather than permanent and pervasive causes. Further, the optimistic explanatory style avoids recumbent self-blame, or other blame: "It's *me* …", "I'll *never* change …" and "I'll *never* get it right …". Acknowledging one's *temporary* stupidity, ineptness, laziness, lack of forethought and planning is, in short, acknowledging one's humanity (Rogers 2012)!

It is the *habits* of explanation that lie at the heart of "explanatory styles" and personal self-talk. It is not simply the explanation we make in interpreting our episodic stresses; it is the *characteristic residual* explanatory style one falls back on in seeking to cope with, understand and manage stressful events. Seligman's research into learned helplessness and learned optimism is a positive and very practical resource in stress management and coping.

Contrast "I *never* …", "I *always* …", "I *can't* stand it …" and "*Everybody* in this class is …", with "I *sometimes* fail; *however* …", "*Some* people *are difficult* to work, with while others are not …", "It may be *difficult* (rather than "I *can't stand it*") … *but* when I …", "It *will* get better *when* …", "If I do X and Y, things will improve …" and "Even if *I've failed, I am not a failure* …". Private (internal) speech clearly has a self-guiding and self-regulatory function.

Failure doesn't mean we *are* a failure. Defining failure in global and stable terms, rather than in situational and specific terms, changes our perception of both ourselves and those situations and relationships in which we experience stress and a significant sense of failure.

Adaptive, and maladaptive, thinking behaviours *are learned as well as habituated* from our personal history (Rogers 2012). These thinking skills (and self-talk skills) when matched with behaviour leadership and teacher skills enable effective coping and even enjoyable and effective teaching (bad days notwithstanding p. 22f).

You control us! Who controls whom and what?

Working with a new Year 9 class once, I struggled to communicate the difficult message that it was *their* job to control *their* behaviour. Apparently their previous teacher (on stress leave) had battled with this class, week in and week out, and now it was my turn.

At the classroom meeting I conducted with this class, I raised the issue of their perception of "control" (p. 29f). Many students had said that it was "the teacher's job to control the class", "It's the teacher's job to make us behave".

I asked "how?", and in the ensuing (and lively) discussion students' comments about teacher control ranged from "shouting" behaviours through to "intimidation" and "detentions". I further asked if they *liked* that kind of teacher behaviour, and if they believed such behaviour was fair and helpful. As we teased this out they agreed that it wasn't helpful to anyone really – being *forced* to behave through the "controlling" behaviour of teachers. What it amounted to is that these students effectively wanted the teachers to "control us" but part of *that* arrangement meant that they would make it a challenge for the teachers to control them: "you've got to prove you can control us". When students talk like this there is also the more important underlying message of security: they expect their teachers to be able to lead, manage and direct the day-to-day complexities of 25–30 students in a small room, engaged in teaching, learning and socialisation. To this extent their "cry of control" is valid; but our role is also to lead the students beyond mere simplistic, external, control to appropriate "self" and "shared" control.

It took a while but we finally managed to shift their thinking and (in part) their "game-playing" towards a new understanding: "As students … we control ourselves … You (our teacher) lead, guide and support us to manage ourselves. We give you that right and that responsibility to lead us in that way." This was the understanding I was trying to develop with them.

This shift in thinking in our students is not merely a teaching exercise. Teachers need to be able to call on student cooperation through:

- shared understandings of core rights and responsibilities. This was expressed through a collaborative classroom agreement (see Chapter 2 and Appendix A)
- the teacher's effort to teach with some enthusiasm, skill and willingness to address a wide range of student ability and to consider a range of teaching approaches (Chapter 4)

- the teacher's effort to communicate respect and care, particularly when they discipline (Chapter 3)
- the teacher's willingness to reach individuals as well as class groups; even a brief effort to get to know, and assist, an individual has a powerful effect on teacher–student cooperation.

I have many, many, times discussed the issue of teacher management and discipline with students. They are able to sum up how confident, sure, "together", able, (and so on) a teacher is. They seem to gain this knowledge by *how* a teacher *initially* expresses themselves in their management and their discipline, and how effectively the teacher manages to teach (Chapters 2 and 3). Those first impressions, in those first meetings with the class, significantly determine how the class group defines the teacher's subsequent role. As one student wrote about taking teachers on the first impression (he passed the note on to me – it was a class where I had been mentoring a colleague …):

> When you can see that you can get away with things with a teacher you often be stupid [sic] and go to other people's desks and don't take any notice of them [the teacher …]

This student is saying, in effect, that a "good" teacher needs to control the classroom environment and *situation* in which students behave. They normally then discuss (as this student does) how and why students do (or don't) "take notice" of teachers. Having notice taken of one's leadership and authority is primarily related to how relaxed one appears, how confident one's leadership style appears when *encouraging and directing* group *and individual behaviour* (see Chapters 3 and 4). One's confidence is significantly increased by having a plan for those first meetings with our class(es). This is discussed in the section on the establishment phase and in the later section on language skills of behaviour management (Chapter 3) and effective teaching (Chapter 4).

Don't smile until Christmas

This is not the clearest, most helpful, maxim in teaching! I remember being told a version of this many years ago. Imagine standing in front of a group (in the corridor before you lead your class in or in the classroom) with a tense, frowning, face – perhaps impatient breathing – rocking back and forth on the toes, frowning, "expecting" trouble …(?) … Such non-verbal behaviour will – more than anything – indicate a lack of confidence in one's authority and "status". It may even provoke unnecessary, contestable, behaviour in some of our students. If a teacher stands in front of a class group looking anxious, arms folded in a protective – closed – body language, or a hesitant and sheepish smile that says, in effect, "please be nice to me ...", students may well read "indecisiveness", and, again, a lack of confidence.

A confident, pleasant, relaxed smile, *while we are communicating* (not a sycophantic smile) can telegraph a potential confidence in student cooperation. Of course, what we *then* do, *and say,* is essential to how we are able to *initiate and sustain* class attention and focus ... This is addressed at length in Chapter 3.

Of course, what the maxim is meant to say is that one needs to be firm and clear in our leadership at the outset of our ongoing relationship with a new class about behaviour and learning. There is truth in this. It is much harder to reclaim unfocused, off-task, distracting behaviours than to establish positive, clear norms from day one and reinforce that by positive and confident behaviour leadership – the first meetings are crucial (p. 37f, 55f).

I have heard teachers say that they, in effect, "lost" the class because they tried to be "too friendly"; in effect trying to be their "buddy"/"mate" from the first meeting with the class. We are their teacher/leader; we are not their "mate" or "buddy"; we can, and should, be friendly, kind and generous of spirit, *respectful*, but we are their *teacher*, we are not a "substitute" parent, or carer ...

The 70–80 per cent

I have seen teachers lose the goodwill and potential cooperation of a significant percentage of the class by the way they treat certain individuals and the group. Some teachers are surprised when the bulk of the class becomes resentful if the teacher treats any *one* individual with characteristic disrespect or fosters unresolved conflict. I have seen teachers use whole-class detentions to seek to put pressure on several disruptive students only to initially frustrate and then alienate the 70–80 per cent of cooperative students when they continue to use such detentions.

While it is natural to get frustrated by some individuals in a class group, we need the cooperation of the 70–80 per cent to successfully manage and support the 20–30 per cent of more attentional, difficult or challenging students.

What we can, and can't, "control"

When I write, here in this book, about managing or leading students, I'm not speaking about *controlling* our students; it's surprising the ease, the facility, with which we say, "I *made* the student put his hand up ...", or "I *took* the student aside and told him to ...". We can't simply *make* a student do anything, or *take* a student anywhere, unless of course he or she is either naturally cooperative, highly compliant or obedient, or unquestioningly compliant or obedient (which are not necessarily healthy personality behaviour traits at all). I have always discouraged our own children to "*simply* obey your teacher *because* they are a teacher". (Mind you, I've taught them skilful ways to address unfair or even unjust teacher behaviour as well.)

Rather than asking myself how can I more effectively "control my students", it is more appropriate – and much more constructive – to ask "How can I be a more effective teacher leader?" and "What can I do to bring more effective control *to* the teaching and learning context?" The way I manage myself and my thinking and attitude have a significant (even lasting) effect on how students behave (cooperatively or uncooperatively) when I am with them.

The approaches, and skills, developed in this book are a means to *that* end.

Intent and relationships

Students hear and see the teacher's intention in a teacher's discipline and management of behaviour – beyond the words. If the *intention* read is one where the teacher is perceived as wanting to *merely* control, embarrass, shame or cause emotional "hurt" to the child, then the acceptance of such discipline will be (naturally) resented and often lead to an unworkable teacher–student relationship. For example, where a teacher emphasises the intentional severity of the consequence, rather than the certainty, then that is all the child will focus on (p. 127) – where the teacher uses the one-to-one follow-up consequential time (behaviour interview/detention, etc.) to "get back at" the student. It is very unfortunate to have to address such teacher behaviour but I've seen it happen.

If it is our intention to enable a student to take responsibility for his or her behaviour and to actively consider others' rights, and if our discipline has that as its aim, the child will more likely hear and see that intention in the kind of language and manner we use when we address their behaviour in the "public" domain of the classroom and in any one-to-one behaviour consequence time. The degree of cooperation, even compliance, in student behaviour, also depends on the kind of relationship existing between teacher and student.

In the establishment phase of the year, the teacher is seeking to build a workable relationship with the whole class, as a group, and also with the individuals. Even deceptively mundane expressions of humanity, such as learning (and using) a student's name (at all times), positive greetings to the group and individuals (even out of class), remembering aspects and details of their individuality (a student's hobbies, special interests, events and birthdays) are all indicators of a teacher's effort to build and sustain positive working relationships.

Being pleasant and respectful (not sycophantic) to "unlikeable" students; going out of one's way to say "hello" (even, at times, to an unreturned or muttered response); not holding grudges and starting each day afresh are all aspects of relational teacher behaviour that children soon acknowledge, affirm and respond to in a positive way.

When students get to know that we care about them as individuals (as persons with needs, concerns, feelings), then our discipline is judged and accepted within the understanding that their teacher cares about, and for them.

Building relationships

It is, generally speaking, the positive relationships we develop with our students that we remember long after they have forgotten the history of the Tudors, or positive and negative integers. When I used to ask our own children, "What was maths (or French, or history) like today?" Sometimes they would talk about the subject matter, but more often they talked about the *kind* of teacher they had and what happened in the relational dynamics of the classroom. Our children quickly "sorted" out which teachers could manage which classes (and why); which teachers taught well (and interestingly); which were fair and considerate; and which were normally patient, had a sense of humour and, above all, cared.

I went to a high school in St Albans (England) for six months (aged 15). I was running late for my science class one morning. The bus was late. I arrived at the classroom door huffing and puffing, anxious because Mr Brown was not the most empathetic teacher in the school. Entering the classroom I saw a *new* teacher; a supply teacher? (I wasn't sure). He approached me at the door, smiling, and said, "You look a bit puffed out …" (I'd been running). "I'm Mr Ryland. What's your name?" His tone and manner immediately put me at ease. He spoke to me quietly, away from the class (and the immediate hearing of others). "Who do you normally sit next to?" Having told him I sat next to Roger (a friend), he explained we were doing an experiment on Archimedes' principle (displacement of mass in water; Eureka!). "Roger will fill you in, eh? Catch your breath Billy. I'll come over and see how you're going later." Not only did I feel better (less anxious and less embarrassed), but I was also more motivated (in a subject that wasn't a favourite). Not only did I remember Archimedes' principle, but I remembered the difference a teacher can make to how one feels and "works" as a student.

Contrast Mr Ryland's treatment of my lateness and this personal account written by our eldest daughter when she was in high school (Year 9).

Vicki and I were sitting on the wall (where we usually wait for the lift home from Vicki's grandpa) at the end of the school day. Miss Brown (Vicki's maths teacher) came over to us and said, "Have you made any effort to get that maths book yet?" And before Vicki could answer she said, "No, I don't think you have. I told you to wait behind on Friday and someone told me you only waited five minutes!"

"I couldn't wait because my grandpa didn't know I was staying behind and he would be worried."

I chipped in at this point, trying to help out. "And it's a bit hard to stay behind because we go home in a car pool."

And Miss Brown said, "I don't think this has anything to do with you! I don't think you know what this is about so I think you should just keep out of this!"

Well I just shut up (being the generally angelic and compliant student I am) but the truth is I knew a damn sight more than she did and instantly made up my mind I did not like this teacher.

Respect:

- means respecting the essential dignity of the individual.
- is based on equality and mutuality of rights; this is at the core of the UN Charter on the rights of the child (and on human rights generally). Respect is intrinsically related to fundamental human rights. It is the basis for building cooperative classrooms and schools. In being aware of, and considering, others' rights, we (in effect) affirm and acknowledge our own rights. We can stand up for our rights – firmly and respectfully – without trampling on others' rights. The teacher's modelling of mutual respect is essential in building a rights-enhancing and rights-protecting school community.
- means recognising the equality of human beings (in gender, race, background, individual differences, knowledge, position …).
- means that even when we need to discipline a student we do not reject him as a person. This is probably the most challenging belief and practice we seek to hold as teachers. It means we can (and should) balance firmness with kindness; assertion with not holding grudges. It means (and this is also very difficult) starting each day afresh with the student as it were. I would further argue that we don't have to *like* all our students (some students will be much easier to *like* than others …). Respect is about our behaviour towards others, the way we

treat them ... It is pointless *trying to force* ourselves to like a student whose behaviour (at times) can be obnoxious ... Respect is about a mindset and *one's behaviour* towards the "unlikeable".
(For a sustained discussion on respect with the teacher–student/s relationship see Rogers 2011: 225–7.)

The conveying of respect does not mean the excusing of a student's irresponsible and wrong behaviour; it is an essential prerequisite in resolving conflict and initiating restitution.

How might he have felt ...?

A colleague of mine found this missive on the worldwide graffiti board (you know – the Internet). It describes so well the normative frustrations of a teacher; frustrations that even Jesus must have felt:

The joy of teaching

Then Jesus took his disciples up the mountain and gathering them around him, He taught them saying: "Blessed are the poor in spirit, for theirs is the kingdom of heaven. Blessed are the meek. Blessed are they that mourn. Blessed are the merciful. Blessed are they that thirst for justice. Blessed are you when persecuted. Blessed are you when you suffer. Be glad and rejoice for your reward is great in heaven." Then Simon Peter said, "Are we supposed to know this?" And Andrew said, "Do we have to write this down?" And James said, "Will we have a test on this?" And Phillip said, "I don't have any paper!" And Bartholomew said, "Do we have to turn this in?" And John said, "The other disciples didn't have to learn this!" And Matthew said, "May I go to the toilet?" Then one of the Pharisees who was present asked to see Jesus's lesson plan and inquired of Jesus, "Where is your anticipatory set and your objectives in the cognitive domain?" And Jesus wept.

(Anon)

Reflection

- When you reflect on your own experiences at school, as a student, what qualities, attributes, of any of your teachers, do you remember with affection (or disaffection and pain!)?

- When you look at the dynamics of your classes how does the concept of "relaxed vigilance" relate to your *characteristic* behaviour leadership (p.7f)? How do you respond to the concept of "control" noted in this chapter (p. 29f)?
- How aware are you of "primary" and "secondary" behaviours in some of your students (p. 12f)? How do you conceive this "secondary behaviour" reality? What skills and practices enable you when you address such behaviours in your students?
- In reflecting on your normative stress – how aware are you of your "characteristic explanatory style" in coping with and managing stress (p. 20f)?

Notes

1   The issue of *briefly* modelling or "behaviour mirroring" (Rogers 2003a) a student's behaviour back to them (*only* in a one-to-one relationship and in non-classroom time) should always be prefaced by a request "Do you mind if I show you what it looks (or sounds) like when you …?" Also, such "mirroring" should not be conducted with children with autism spectrum disorder – it may only confuse or unnecessarily upset them.
2   This is an interesting theory proposed by Mills (in Robertson 1997). Some children, according to Mills, use such behaviours to "ward off" feelings of depression or stress. In their home background they may well be in a situation of high arousal (a loud home – quarrelling and shouting, significant sibling tension, television blaring …). The "excitation" sought at school may well be compensatory. Robertson notes that the crucial factor in *any* effectiveness in dealing with such pupils is the calm attitude a teacher conveys (Chapter 5, see also pp. 60–62).

 Visit https://study.sagepub.com/rogers4e for additional resources to help you better manage classroom behaviour. You'll also be able to hear from Bill himself as he talks you through common behaviour management scenarios.

CHAPTER 2

New class, new year: the establishment phase of behaviour management

"Habits change into characters."

Ovid (45 BC–AD 17, author of the *Metamorphoses*)

New year, new class, new start

As you stand in your classroom on that pupil-free day, before Day One, Term One, you scan the room and furniture (sometimes inadequate and uncomfortable), you think, "Tomorrow there will be 25–30 students in here, each with their unique personality, temperament and needs. Phew!" For some of you it will be your first class as a teacher, you will be "on your own" as it were; for others it will be another fresh new year that (at times) will soon develop into the daily, hourly, minute-by-minute juggle of demands that make up normative teaching and learning and relationships.

Most teachers can remember their first class – and even their first day.

One of the important, fundamental, questions at this stage of the year is "What can I do (and what can *we* do as a collegial team) to *minimise*, and prevent (where possible), unnecessary hassles or problems in establishing positive behaviours in our classes and a cooperative learning culture?" The answer to this question will focus on the necessary procedures, routines and rules to enable the smooth running of quite a complex community. It will be important to integrate routines and rules into a workable "system" and then *consciously teach* that "system" through discussion, modelling, encouragement and teacher-management.

There is ample and extensive research to show that effective and positive teachers are acutely conscious of the importance of the first lesson, the first few days, the first few weeks and how they establish the shared rights and responsibilities of classroom behaviour with their students (see Doyle 1986; Kyriacou 1986, 1991; McInerney and McInerney 1998; Rogers and McPherson 2014; Robertson 1997; Rogers 2011, 2006b).

In those first meetings our behaviour leadership will be assessed and challenged – this is normal. *How* we establish our leadership and relationship within expectations of behaviour and rights *and* responsibilities is crucial to the building of positive relationships and a cooperative learning culture.

"Establishment phase" (practices and skills)

The establishment phase of the year is foundational in the development of a class group (and even the school as community). In terms of basic group dynamics there is a psychological and developmental readiness in the students for their teachers to explain, discuss and *teach* how things will be *this* particular year with regard to expectations about behaviour and learning, in *this* class with *this* teacher. The basic phases in the "developmental *life*" of a classroom community are set out in Figure 2.1.

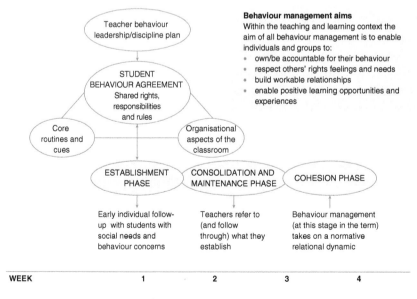

Figure 2.1   The fundamental phases in the development

At the first meeting(s) with their teacher(s), students should expect their teacher to clarify:

- lining up and room entry procedures, teaching the important distinction between "social time" (outside classroom time) and our teaching and learning time (in our classroom). We will emphasise a calm and considerate entry (without any "testosteronic-bonding" by some male students!).
- seating plans and student grouping for Week One, and possibly Term One. Such planning needs to include whether seating should occur in rows, pairs or table groups. It will also need to address "who sits with whom". It normally does not help to just let students simply sit with their "best mates"(see, p. 52/54).
- student entry to class and settling at workplaces or "carpet space" for early years. Routines and cues will need to be explained, modelled and monitored. With early years, it will also be important not only to explain but to model: "personal space/place" when "on the carpet area" and keeping hands and feet to oneself and "listening with eyes and ears"; taking your turn; hands-up without calling-out and waiting for the teacher to "call" on you (so we all get a fair go …) (see Rogers and McPherson 2014).
- organisation of locker space/place. At primary-age level, where locker trays are in the classroom, consideration needs to be given to how they are sited for ease of student movement. This is a crucial organisational aspect in early years. I have seen too many classes where early years seating and tables were sited impossibly close to one another, where movement patterns *themselves* create distraction and disruption to learning and interpersonal behaviour patterns.
- use of cues for whole-class discussion and questions and use of teacher cue(s) to initiate *whole-class attention* at any stage. This essential teacher leadership "cue" enables students' understanding of *whole-class attention and focus*. This is addressed at some length later (p. 58f, 55f, 70f, 108f).
- appropriate movement patterns between whole-class teaching time and on-task learning time (transitions between whole-class teaching time and on-task (small group) learning phase/time).
- use of appropriate cues to receive teacher assistance and support during the on-task phase of the lesson/phase/activity.
- routines for tidying work space/place.
- cues and procedures for lesson closure and exit from the classroom.

These routines/cue/procedures are addressed in some detail later in this chapter and in Chapter 3. These are, of course, the core – foundational – routines/cues. Teachers also need to establish routines for lunch (dinner times); for monitor systems; for homework procedures, distribution of notices; use of school diaries; quiet reading time procedures; toilet/drink rules; dealing with students who are frequently (rather than incidentally) late to class; and so on. Such routines and procedures need to be developed collegially on a team, or faculty, basis rather than left to personal preference alone.

When raising student awareness about behaviour and learning (and their impact on each other) we need to emphasise the fundamental RIGHTS AND RESPONSIBILITIES of our learning community:

> - "We share the same place, time, space, resources, every day. We have to learn to get on with each other for our own good and the good of others and to help each other in our learning here ..."
> - "Everyone here is individual – we have our own feelings, needs, concerns ..."
> - "As we would want others to think about us and our feelings, so we, in turn, we think about and behave towards them..."
> - "There are rights and responsibilities we *all* share here: the right to be treated with respect and fairness, the right to learn (without distraction or disruption from others ..., the right to feel safe here ..." (see also Appendix A)

It can help to discuss with students the common issues and concerns about shared space, time and resources, and basic, respectful relationships (including civility and manners). With younger children, a practical discussion on basic manners will be important initially (and revisited many times in the first few weeks): "please"; "thank-you"; "excuse me"; "asking if you want to borrow ..."; "giving/putting things back where we borrowed ..."; "sharing and cooperative behaviour ..."; "saying 'excuse me', if someone is in your way ...". For some children the classroom environment (notably at early years level) presents expectations and norms of behaviour some children are not used to, or that they do not easily accommodate to; it can help to conduct mini role-plays on manners and helping behaviours over these first days and weeks (Rogers and McPherson 2014).

These early discussions about behaviour and learning can be developed into a *student behaviour agreement* that can form the basis for the teacher's behaviour management and discipline on the one hand, and student–teacher cooperation on the other (see later, p. 93f).

John Dewey has made an essential point about schools as "communities" (what we often – these days – speak of as "learning communities").

> All education proceeds by participation of the individual in the social consciousness.

The most formal and technical education in the world cannot safely depart from this general process. It can only organise it; or differentiate it in some particular direction. I believe that the only true education comes through the stimulation of the child's powers by the demands of the social situations in which he finds himself. Through these demands he is stimulated to act as a member of a unity, to emerge from his original narrowness of action and feeling and to conceive of himself from the standpoint of the welfare of the group to which he belongs. (Dewey 1897: 77; as cited in Nash (1968).

Developing a student behaviour agreement with the class: rights, responsibilities and rules

Many schools now develop *classroom behaviour agreements* in the first week or two of the school year. Building on the natural readiness and expectation of students (about

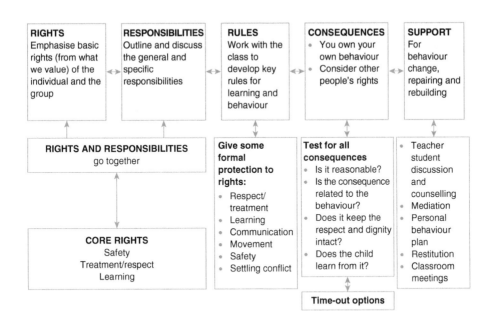

Figure 2.2   Class agreement – behaviour plan (adapted from Rogers 2006b: 51)

teachers developing rules and routines), grade teachers (at primary level) set aside some classroom time to develop a more collaborative model of classroom behaviour through the establishment of shared rights and responsibilities. Students participate, with their teachers, in an age-related discussion to develop "an agreement" addressing common rights, responsibilities and rules for behaviour and learning, core conse-quences for unacceptable behaviour and a framework of support to assist students when they are struggling with their behaviour and learning (Figure 2.2).

At secondary-age level such an agreement is best developed by tutor (or form) teachers who set aside one full timetabled period early, in the first week, to discuss – with their form groups – the key understandings about behaviour and learning. A common framework for such discussions is conducted across all form groups (noted in Figure 2.2). Once established, such an agreement forms the basis on which all teachers can fine-tune rules and routines pertinent to particular needs and contexts.

This agreement is published within the first fortnight of Term One and a copy is sent home to each family. At the primary level this classroom agreement (some-times called a behaviour plan) has a cover page with a photograph of the grade teacher and the students (Figure 2.3).

Any behaviour agreement needs to reflect the values and aims of the whole-school policy on behaviour. The advantage of a *classroom-based policy or agreement*,

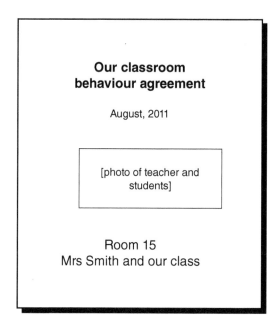

**Our classroom
behaviour agreement**

August, 2011

[photo of teacher and
students]

Room 15
Mrs Smith and our class

Figure 2.3

notably at primary and middle-school level, is that it raises a school-wide aware-ness and consciousness about behaviour, learning and relationships, and does so in a class-by-class, age-related and developmental way. This gives reasonable school-wide consistency on the common, and essential, aspects of behaviour expectations and assurances about *rights, responsibilities and accountability.*

Each teacher, from early years to junior, junior to senior, follows the same frame-work; modifying the language and concepts to age and comprehension so that all students across the school share the same understandings (Figure 2.2).

The process is as important as the outcome. On the first day the class teacher (at primary level) sets aside time to raise whole-class awareness about behaviour and learning, inviting student participation, understanding and cooperation for a plan or agreement about fair and cooperative/respectful behaviour that enhances positive working relationships, a safe place and space ... and how we cooperate and support one another in our learning. Some teachers will take a more discursive approach, perhaps through a classroom meeting; other teachers (at secondary level) are more comfortable with a more "formal" approach that outlines the key areas of the "behaviour agreement" and then inviting student discussion.

The policy, plan or agreement begins with a general statement, for example:

> Our behaviour plan has been discussed and developed by the children (or students) and the teacher in Year [X]. It is a record of how we seek to behave towards each other, and support each other here. It applies to all the people who come into our class and will be used through-out the school year.

Our common rights

The key elements of a student behaviour agreement

Non-negotiable rights are the basis of any classroom agreement about behaviour and learning: the **right to feel safe** at school; the **right to learn** (without undue, unfair, distraction/disruption); and the **right to be treated with respect**. Rights such as the right to equality, the right to have my say, the right to be an individual (without discrimination) and the right to teach are all subsumed within these core rights. These core rights are based in the **values of mutual regard and respect and equality**, without which no group or community could effectively, and respect-fully, relate and work together for mutual benefit. A right, in this sense, is that which we believe is fair, *right* and proper about the way we should relate to, and work, together.

Even very young children have an emerging concept of fundamental "right-ness". Obviously they behave in contradistinction to that rightness (as do we all, this is but human nature), but they hold to it strongly. It is the "natural law".

Simply stating that we have "a *right* to something" , however, is not the same as enjoying that right. We might include in our policy, for example:

> The right to safety doesn't just mean being safe – it is about feeling safe too. Put-downs, cheap shots at others, excluding others on purpose, harassment and swearing are all ways that take away someone's right to feel safe here.
>
> (From a Year 6 classroom agreement)

In this sense, rights imply – and necessitate – responsibilities. If we have a right to learn it implies that the teacher enables the best, most effective,learning and learning environment that is *reasonably* possible. (This further implies that when we're tired, and it's cold and wet, and we're stuck in the "excuse for a classroom" that looks like a shed, then we still do our best ... I actually had to teach in a bike shed 30 years ago!).

In discussing these rights with our students we provide a common focus for the way that we look at, understand and address our relational behaviour.

Responsibilities flow from our rights

Individual and group responsibilities overlap:

> Shared responsibilities mean that we care for ourselves and others here. Responsibilities and respect go together; when we respect others we are thinking about **how our behaviour affects others**.
>
> (From a Year 7 classroom agreement)

Whole-class "brainwaving" ("surfing the collective brain space" sounds less violent than brain*storming*) will quickly elicit shared norms, with our students, about their responsibilities to, for example: get to class on time; have the relevant materials; share (ideas, resources and even our time); do one's best; help out; listen to others; manage our whole-class noise level. A discussion on responsibilities will also need to address respect in terms of basic manners. Basics such as saying please and thank you; asking when we borrow, and returning when you've finished; saying "excuse me" when moving around others; being aware and respectful of others; allowing – and considering – others' personal space; using first names (rather than "he", "she" or "them"); taking turns; lining up considerate of others (without pushing); and so on, are all aspects of self-awareness as we interact with others day after day.

The *core* responsibilities can be summed up in "cooperative and respectful behaviour: the consideration of others as well as oneself" (see Appendix A).

Rules: protecting rights and encouraging responsibility

The primary purpose of a rule is to give a stated, formal, recognised and public protection to one's rights. Fair rules also highlight and encourage one's responsibility.

In the first few weeks teachers can be heard, across all classes, using rule-reminders: "Remember *our* rule for asking questions". "*We've* got a rule about respectful language". In the playground teachers will be heard going up to students inviting some behavioural awareness, by asking questions such as, "What's *our* rule about playing ball games?", "What's *our* rule for safe play on the climbing frame?" I've italicised the plural pronouns to highlight inclusive language when we give rule reminders. Not "*my*" rule but *our* rule, it emphasises the social/relational dimension of behaviour responsibility.

In framing rules it is important to remember some basics:

1. Develop rules that focus on the core rights (p. 41): a safe place and safe behaviour; a respectful place and respectful behaviour through the way we treat others; a learning place where we give our best and cooperate to learn.
2. Rules should be few in number but address the necessary behaviours that enable those core rights. I have seen classrooms where teachers have posted 20 or more rules on the wall, rules often stated negatively: "You must not …", "You shall not …", "You can't …" or "Don't call out …", "Don't interrupt others ...", "Don't talk while the teacher is talking". Simply telling a child what he should *not* do is hardly helpful; a helpful rule should at least contain the negative *within* a positive. For example, "In whole-class learning time we put our hand up to ask questions and to contribute (the positive and expected behaviour) *without calling out* (the "qualifier").

> **NB**   I have usually found it helpful to have several rules covering (see also appendix A):
>
> * treatment (courtesy, manners, respect)
> * communication (hands up, "partner-voices" – in on-task learning time – also positive language, active listening)
> * learning (cooperation and support, use of resources, how to fairly utilise teacher assistance)
>
> *(Continued)*

(Continued)

- movement (walking not running, considerate entry/exit to classroom, consideration of others' personal space, sensible movement)
- problem solving (settling problems peacefully, using teacher assistance, using classroom meetings for resolving common concerns).

3. Express the rules behaviourally where possible:

> To show respect in our classroom we are courteous, and we use our manners. We use positive language with each other. This means no teasing or put-downs. Bullying will *never* be tolerated here. When we solve problems in our classroom we talk it over or ask the teacher to help. We do not fight with words or fists or feet. If we fight we will have to go to time-out.

It can help highlight the key behaviour focus of the rule by having a rule heading such as: Our *Communication* Rule; Our *Respect* Rule; Our *Learning* Rule; Our *Safety* Rule. At secondary level my colleagues and I often have a few key posters that express the rule *within* the core rights. For example: **WE ALL HAVE A RIGHT TO LEARN – we learn well when we ...** (what follows are the several key, positive, behaviour expectations that *enable* the right ...). See Appendix A. It is annoying when we "call" on a student – even an aside call – and their response is "What?" (or in some "What?!"). Even when we cue students who are chatting in whole-class teaching time (p. 70f) you may get a "What?" Is it reasonable to expect "Pardon?" (explain first, of course).

I don't think that is unreasonable – again, it is basic manners. It needs to be done briefly, respectfully; a reminder (at any age).

4. Publish the rules in both the *classroom agreement* (see p. 39f) and on bright classroom posters (even at secondary level). This can also help with a teacher's verbal reminders about appropriate behaviour; the posters act as *visual aide-memoires* to the verbal reminder. Cartoon motifs can help the visual effect of the posters. At early years level teachers can further illustrate the relevant behaviour through photographs attached to the rule poster (these photos illustrate students working/relating cooperatively).

Co-operation

A critical goal of establishing a positive, and workable, learning-relational culture (in that small classroom space) is to enable social cooperation. Such cooperation is based on:

- shared *rights* and responsibilities ... (p. 38f)
- shared needs and feelings in day-to-day relationships
- a shared purpose for the daily round of formal learning (as well as the many informal learnings in a school community)

It is in everyone's interests, then, teacher and students alike, that we enable a cooperative climate. Again, the leadership skills, the discipline skills, the way we affirm and encourage our students, even the way we conduct behaviour consequences (Chapter 5) and restitution/reparation, *all enable* a student's cooperation.

Students will soon know how supportive their teacher is in *enabling* in supporting and encouraging students within their developing understandings and ability. *Building trust* is based on our students seeing we are worthy of their trust through the way we lead, behave, relate to them (as individuals and as a group).

Trust takes time to develop; it is always earned through *the respectful way in which we lead*, yes – and discipline.

Consequences

Students need to know that consequences follow inappropriate, irresponsible and wrong behaviour. Consequences are directly related to rules and rights. Students will need to understand that when a rule is broken, in effect a right is affected or even abused.

These consequences may involve (for example) a student directed to work separately if they continue to work noisily and affect others' learning time. It may involve a student having to stay back and clean up a mess they refused to clean up in class time. It might involve a deferred consequence where a teacher works with a student one-to-one to address a behaviour concern (in class time) ... (see p. 190f). If a student is *repeatedly* disruptive by calling out, butting-in, talking really loudly, interfering with others' workspace or materials, or acting unsafely or aggressively, then they are affecting others' rights to learn or even feel safe, and – of course – they are also directly affecting the teacher's right to teach. The necessary, fair, and appropriate consequence in such a case will need to be "time-out" (in-class or even out-of-class time-out). Students, therefore, can (temporarily) lose their right to be a part of their learning community through a consequence such as time-out (see p. 180f). Where this consequence is used it must be used respectfully within *whole-school protocols*. The initiating teacher should always follow-up and follow-through with the student later in the day to repair and rebuild (p. 126–132).

All consequences operate on a least-to-most intrusive basis. Students need to know they will always have an appropriate right of reply as part of the consequence process. Behaviour consequences are discussed at length in Chapter 5.

Support for our students

It is important to balance the *corrective* and *consequential* aspects of the classroom agreement with the offer of teacher support (Figure 2.2). Here is an example of how support is expressed within a Year 5/6 classroom behaviour agreement.

Supporting each other in our classroom

There are many ways we can support each other here. Most of all we support others when we take time to think about others – to help, encourage and cooperate. Of course, there are days when things don't go right; we recognise this. It is important, though, to explain to your teacher, or classmate, when you're having a "bad day". If we don't let others know they might get confused as to why we look (or sound) annoyed, upset, or angry. Sometimes we have concerns, worries or problems outside and inside our school. It can help to talk about this. Your teacher or school counsellor are always willing to help in any way they can.

If we are making poor choices, or wrong choices, about our behaviour, our teacher will help us with:

- discussing our behaviour with us
- helping us with personal behaviour plans

- giving us the opportunity to put things right (restitution) – sometimes we may need to put things right by talking things through with a fellow student (mediation).
- working with the student counsellor.

On some occasions our parents may need to be involved in helping us with our behaviour at school. Your teacher(s) will always be willing to work with your parents/carers to help us in our behaviour and learning and school.

Classroom meetings

Many teachers also include an extended note (in the classroom agreement) on classroom meetings. Some parents may not be aware of the concept of whole-class discussions that enable even very young children to share common concerns, problem-solve, work on common solutions to common concerns and issues. So a note about the positive and educational features of classroom meetings will assist in the understanding of basic classroom democracy. The example below is from a grade five/six Classroom Behaviour Agreement:

NB We have regular classroom meetings in our class. These meetings give all students an opportunity to explore common concerns, needs and problems. These meetings allow shared understandings, active problem solving and student-assisted solutions to common issues of concern.

Classroom meetings are also (obviously) utilised for planning time with students. The last page of a *classroom agreement* outlines the whole-class commitment to the process.

We have discussed, drafted and edited our behaviour agreement with our teacher. We agree to use it and support it.

The classroom behaviour agreement is also a document for parents as well as students and teachers; it enables *shared understandings about behaviour and learning* between home and school. A copy will be sent to all parents/caregivers of all children in each grade or class group. A covering letter from the head-teacher goes home with the classroom agreement/plan.

The letter discusses the elements of rights, rules and responsibilities (and consequences) and the support and encouragement we give to our students. The letter finishes with an appeal to shared understanding and support, for example:

> This behaviour agreement has been discussed, and developed, by the teacher and the children in Year 6 … It outlines the way we address behaviour and learning in our school. We ask you to read through this agreement/plan with your son/daughter. We look forward to your understanding and support this year …
>
> (See particularly Rogers and McPherson 2014.)

As the year plods on, all behaviour issues and those core rights and responsibilities are, one way or another, referred back to this behaviour agreement. Whenever a parent (or school) has concerns about a child's behaviour *the behaviour agreement* is the anchor focus for discussion and support.

Non-negotiable rules and consequences

There are rules, in a school, that are non-negotiable across all ages – all classes. These relate to issues such as health and safety, bullying, drugs, aggression and violent behaviour. These rules and consequences need to be made known in the first meetings with all students, in the school diary, and noted in classroom agreements and school policies.

For example, in Australian primary schools there is a "no hat, no outside play" rule in the hot summer months (that is, no direct sunlight play). It is a rule *directly related to health and safety.*

When schools have a common framework for classroom behaviour agreements, each successive year group becomes increasingly conscious of "the way we do things here and why". This enables some sense of common understandings and expectations about appropriate and fair behaviour, and also some reasonable consistency in behaviour management by adults across the school community.

As noted earlier, there are several phases in the ongoing life of a class group (Figure 2.1). If the teacher has thoughtfully established "the way we need to work here" (and why) and has developed positive routines and rules for classroom learning and social interaction, and if the teacher has communicated respectful teacher leadership within these norms, the class, as a group, becomes habituated into workably cohesive and just and fair "norms" of behaviour.

Cohesive phase (see Figure 2.1)

During the "cohesive" phase of a classroom community, the routines and rules become accepted, encouraged and *normal* regarding "the way we do things here". At the beginning of each successive term we might need to revisit the student behaviour agreement and some of the routines (such as noise monitoring) that we have established in those first few weeks with a new class. Students "forget" during term breaks, or are "resocialised" in non-school settings. A brief and positive re-establishment can help start each term with a positive, shared focus.

In this phase of the year, most of our behaviour management occurs within a *relational dynamic*. Hopefully, as teacher-leaders, we have built a positive working relationship with the individuals as well as the group. We rely less on the rules and routines now; the students are more self-aware and self-directed in their behaviour and learning. Students are taking appropriate "ownership" of classroom life.

During this "phase", teachers often utilise regular classroom meetings to discuss issues relevant to individual and group needs and concerns.

Communicating the rules to students

In communicating the necessary rules to students it is important to emphasise the *purpose of rules*: protection of rights and expectation of basic responsibilities.

In communicating the rules to a new class group (or year group) some teachers are more directive – outlining the expected rules, their reasons, and the normal consequences when rules are broken. Other teachers are more discursive in their approach, emphasising *shared dialogue* and engaging a *process* of agreement. Some teachers begin the year with a classroom meeting ("sharing circles" at early years) and use such a meeting to address the need for rules, responsibilities, consequences *and* support.

The approach taken will depend, in part, on the individual teacher's comfort about class dialogue and classroom discussion (particularly at secondary level). I have been in secondary schools where the rules are read out almost perfunctorily by tutor teachers or (more pedestrian) the students are directed to read the rules in the school diary – full stop.

If your preference is for a more directive approach to communicating the rules, it will be beneficial (at the very least) to give the reasons for the rules and invite student questions.

Visual reminding of routines and rules

In the establishment phase of the year the process of rule encouragement and maintenance can be assisted by basic visual posting of key rules and routines. At early years levels these could include:

- A photograph and name card for coat hooks.
- The key classroom rules can be illustrated as a visual *aide-mémoire* posted in a prominent place at the front of the classroom. Routines such as: "partner-voice" (working noise); what to do when the set work is completed; how to set out a piece of writing; use of wet areas ...

NB A class works well, learns well, when *each* class member makes an effort to CO-OPERATE with others.

IN ORDER TO CO-OPERATE WE HAVE TO LEARN TO GET ON WITH EACH OTHER HERE. IT'S OUR PLACE.

-   WE *ALL* HAVE RIGHTS (to feel safe here, to learn without distraction from others, and to show and give respect and fairness).
-   WE HAVE RESPONSIBILITIES SO WE CAN ENJOY THOSE RIGHTS.

(WE) TAKE TURNS IN CLASS DISCUSSION.

(WE) ARE WILLING TO HAVE OUR VIEWS AND OPINIONS CHALLENGED.

(WE) DISAGREE RESPECTFULLY AND GIVE *REASONS* FOR WHY WE DISAGREE.

(WE) ARE WILLING TO HELP/SUPPORT AND ENCOURAGE EACH OTHER IN OUR LEARNING HERE.

Figure 2.4 Example of a published rule (secondary phase)

- At early years level, teachers often take photographs of the children working cooperatively, tidying the room, communicating respectfully (sitting on the carpet with hands raised and waiting for the teacher to cue-them-in-so-we-all-get-a-fair-go …), sharing cooperatively … These photographs are displayed with the relevant rules the teacher has established. Many primary schools include such photographs within the classroom behaviour agreement.
- Simple signs for cupboards, quiet areas and the library corner all enable association of place, space and purpose, and shared responsibilities.
- I have used simple posters to remind students at *secondary* level about tidying work space: chairs under table; straightening furniture; chairs *on* tables at the end of the day; cleaning up any residual litter; and leaving the room in an orderly way (p. 86f).
- Baskets can be used for "finished work here" and there can be an "early finishers" box with worksheets or activities.
- A "noise-meter" (at primary level) can be used to establish and monitor working voice levels (p. 79–81).
- I have seen rule reminder posters (again with photos) on the inside of the glass window of primary classrooms reminding students of the distinction between "social time" (*outside* our classroom) and teaching/learning time (*inside* our classroom). (NB: It is worth changing any photos 2 or 3 times a year to illustrate growth (literally) and development …)

Discussing rules within the wider social context

When discussing rules with students (even up to Year 10) it can help to discuss them within the students' experience of rules in different places and contexts: the Highway Code; clubs they belong to; road rules (and road signs); their families; the swimming pool; and even board games. The purpose of, and reasons for, fair rules can be helpfully explored within these familiar contexts and a natural transition of understanding can be made to the classroom and playground.

Students have already learned that rules *help* guide, focus, govern behaviour, *help* protect people (at least potentially) and even *encourage* shared responsibility (thinking of others). They have also learned that rules – when broken – occasion consequences. They have seen the yellow card used with adult footballers and they have also seen adult footballers and other sports "heroes" throw tantrums and worse! (Shouldn't it be "champion" rather than "hero"? Of course it should, as I've frequently pointed out to my students. A footballer paid an obscenely high wage is hardly a "hero" for helping win a game!)

Maintenance and consolidation

It is crucial to *maintain and consolidate* the rules and routines that are established on Day One, Week One (Figure 2.1). Effective teaching and management in the establishment phase of the year includes planning for the typical distractions and disruptions in student behaviour in day-to-day teaching and learning, and developing a workable "system" for the smooth running of the classroom in terms of behaviour and learning. (This is discussed at length in Chapters 3 and 4.) Simply stating, or even publishing, fair rules and routines is not enough. We need to encourage and discipline *within the fair rights and rules*. Teachers need to consciously address issues and behaviours such as frequent lateness; unacceptable noise levels; calling out; intentional talking over others in class discussions; talking while the teacher is teaching; time off-task and task avoidance and inappropriate language ... on a day-to-day basis until there are "norms" of expected behaviour present in the classroom life and learning. The kind, and degree, of distracting behaviour in any classroom (and school) can vary with a number of factors, of course. However, even in very challenging schools, behaviour can vary considerably according to how an individual teacher establishes and leads, encourages and supports the members of that class group. Ideally, of course, these practices (in this and subsequent chapters) are best developed within a whole-school approach (see Rogers 2006a).

A teacher's "discipline plan" and their behaviour leadership form the central feature of a workable "system" that thinks through typical (or likely) disruptions and plans the sorts of discipline responses (especially one's language) that are more likely to invite student cooperation – not as a formulaic system but rather as an *enabling framework* (see Chapters 3 and 4). None of us would ever teach a lesson or activity without some kind of lesson plan, but I'm still surprised by how many teachers (even beginning teachers) continue to teach without *planning* for typical distracting and disruptive behaviours that can significantly affect the quality of teaching and learning social relationships.

As noted earlier, students expect the teacher to clarify rules, routines and cues in terms of "how things are expected to be here – and why …". It is also important to thoughtfully plan how we will communicate, establish and monitor these rules, routines and cues; not as an end in themselves (teacher control), *but as a means to an end (teacher–student cooperation in a shared learning community)*.

Seating plans and student grouping

When planning room organisation we will need to ask what the purpose of any physical seating layout serves ("U" shaped, "split rows", pairs, table groups) and also student placement (who sits where and with whom).

In some classes, allowing friendship groups on Day One may create unhelpful power cliques and habituated patterns of behaviour that are difficult to refocus later in the term. While it is important that teachers allow some student involvement in seating arrangements, this "freedom" is better given later in Term One.

On Day One it will assist in general classroom management to have students seated in alphabetic allocation (with a name sticker on each table or table group). This allows easy learning of students' names by the teacher and allows some early classroom socialisation outside the natural friendship groupings. It can also help (even for older primary/middle school age) to have a large, visual, seating plan (on a poster) at the front of the classroom to indicate who-sits-with-whom. "Random allocation", over the beginning weeks, may also need to include gender mix and – possibly – ability mix. Also if we know that some students do not work or relate well together, that knowledge will need to be translated into student seating arrangements.

In a Year 7 class I worked with two students who had robust and motoric expressions of ADSD (attention deficit spectrum disorder). They had promised their teacher that they would work well if they sat together. "Really Miss! We'll be good if we sit together. Please Miss, please!!" It was a time-wasting mistake. After several frustrating promises we relocated their seating arrangements and moved the whole class into "split" rows. They eventually settled down and actually became more focused in their learning behaviour.

While socialisation is an important feature of classroom life and learning, it is also important that the students understand, from Day One, that the classroom is not merely an extension of playground socialisation; *this* place is set aside for teaching and learning. Some children are very easily distracted, for example, when sitting in table groups, so in the establishment phase of the year it may be wiser to use a more "formal" seating plan ("split rows", or paired seating, facing the front of the classroom) to minimise unnecessary distraction.

Simply saying to students (Day One) "OK guys, sit where you want ..." (the "cools" sit with the "cools" and the "non-cools" get marginalised), or placing the students in table groups does not facilitate (of itself) cooperative learning behaviour. It can help to use small-group seating for more focused cooperative activities and retain seating in "split" rows for the core teaching and learning activities. In this way we can build up cooperative learning skills over smaller time allocations.

I have seen many teachers give up the positive benefits of cooperative learning by early helpful expectations that table group seating will – of itself – engage cooperative learning; it won't. Cooperative learning needs to be structured, and taught, over time and is normally more effective when the class is more relationally cohesive.

Welfare of our students (establishment phase)

Students new to a school can often be anxious about settling in, particularly at early years and reception level, and transition to the first year at high school. It is important for teachers to be aware of, and considerate of, a student's natural concerns about how they will fit in; whether other students will accept and befriend them; whether they will be able to cope with the demands of the work; the timetable; the different teachers. In short, whether – and how – they will "belong" in *this* class group, "*this* year group". The need to belong – to feel accepted and part of a group – is an important aspect of day-to-day existence at school; it is, indeed, a primary social need (Dreikurs, Grunwald and Pepper 1982).

Even basic considerations, such as who they will be asked to sit next to and for how long (will it be every lesson?), can concern some students. It can be helpful to rotate seating pairs, or groups, over the first few weeks (but not every day!) to enable basic group befriending and socialisation. It is also important to keep an eye on students who appear to be loners or students who have difficulty befriending others, particularly at playtimes and in sports sessions. Many primary schools (and some secondary schools) now have "buddy" programmes for reception-aged children and for students in Year 7 (transitional year) and for students new to a school. Older students take on a peer support role that enables the younger (or new) student to settle into the classroom group and negotiate the social climate of a playground (play areas, recreation options, the canteen/"tuckshop", even the toilets ...). The "peer-buddy" receives basic training beyond their natural skills and personality that equip them for such a role. (See Rogers and McPherson 2014.)

Group activities that involve games, activities and discussions can all assist in the settling-in process, in terms of getting to know each other. Name games can sometimes lose their novelty at upper primary level but a basic seat-rotation and getting-to-know-you time can enable a *basic* sense of group bonding at any age level.

One's welfare obligations to one's students is not confined to primary teachers. As part of a secondary year level team, the House Heads and Year Advisers (Home-room Tutors) have a particular responsibility to liaise with subject colleagues to keep the lines of communication open about how their students are coping with settling in their classes.

When seating plans don't work

I've worked with teachers who have allowed the friendship-seating option (from Day One) only to find it creates little coteries or cliques; the row of students down the back whose *esprit de corps* creates contestable, time-wasting, behaviours; the little group of girls (or boys) who won't let anyone else sit with them (the "cools"). At upper primary and secondary level I've found it helpful in such situations to change the seating plan by guided cooperation with the students. The teacher's concern about noise level and time off-task (as it relates to learning) is briefly set out in a pro forma with an invitation to the students to assist in a seat change plan:

> As your teacher I am concerned about the level of noise, and distracting behaviour, during class work-time. I believe a change of seating plan will help. I would appreciate your cooperation. Write down the names of two students you know who will make it easier for you to get on with your classwork and gain the best benefit of your time in this class/subject.
>
> While all fair suggestions will be taken on board, I will be the final umpire. I will let you know next class period. Choose thoughtfully. Thanks for your cooperation.
>
> Mr Rogers

When handing out the pro forma I remind students to "Choose wisely, choose thoughtfully – thanks." It is said in a spirit of goodwill. With a particularly difficult class it can help to have a supportive colleague come in and conduct the exercise with the regular class teacher (see also p. 274f).

The first meeting with the students

The first meeting with a new class at secondary level can sometimes "start" in the corridor (outside the classroom). I've had some students in more challenging classes immediately start hassling me: "Who're you?", "What's yer name?", "You going to be our teacher today?", "Eh … where's Mr Smith …? He was our teacher last time – he's a donk!" (guffaws). Several students are talking over each other and there's some pushing, shoving or playful "testosteronic bonding" by a few boys …. Some of this may well be intentional (if poorly expressed), some is clearly attentional posturing and "testing" behaviours …

I did this drawing of a Year 9 class arriving outside their classroom. The girl on the right, Donna, is letting the group know who the new teacher is: "Yooooo, Mr Rogers. I seen you before in another class. Yooooo, Mr Rogers!" She had a "notice me" kind of voice. I smiled at her but chose not to engage her in conversation outside the classroom.

I've seen teachers enter into long time-wasting responses to such group banter; answering their questions; over-engaging the "attentional" students no doubt hoping they are building an early friendly relationship. The students' perception is often different; they are seeking to define how they will "work" the teacher–student relationship.

It is wiser to *tactically* ignore most of the multi-student banter and questions with a brief greeting followed by a polite and clear statement: "settling down everyone (…) I'm not answering personal questions – now. We need to be ready to go into our classroom. Thanks." Our tone is pleasant, but businesslike; enabling some group "attentional focus" by a relaxed, non-verbal, "blocking hand", indicating such questioning is not on the agenda *now*. We direct their attention and focus, briefly, respectfully and expectantly – even to groups "lining up" ... to go into the classroom – so that the teaching and learning becomes the immediate focus.(not all schools, of course, have a line-up policy ...)

Once the students are in the classroom, and in their seats, it is important that the teacher consciously, and calmly, cues for *whole-class attention* (p. 58f, 70f).

As Robertson (1997) reminds us, it is important to *define* the first meeting(s) in our own terms as teacher; to be confidently secure; pleasantly firm, without any overtones of "force", perception of threat or overly perceptible anxiety.

The *brief* "corridor-settling" by the teacher (above) conveys the change in pace and setting: between *outside* the classroom (play, high motoric, naturally noisy, behaviour, which is natural and OK for the playground) to *inside* (quieter, sitting – mostly focused thinking, cooperating in our learning and social interaction). It will be important to create (even here) *an expectant tone* – quickly but calmly – before going into the classroom.

Scanning the group outside the classroom the teacher will often have some expectation of "lining up" – at least – or "considerate one-at-a-time entry" to the classroom. A respectful *reminder* to this effect can calm and focus natural student restlessness:

"Settling down everyone (...). [We'll need to repeat this whole-class cue-ing at least once!]. Good morning (...) Before we go into our classroom I notice a few hats on; if you have an iPod or music from phones on remember we're going into a classroom learning environment. Chewy *in* the bin, on the way *in*. Thank you." The teacher smiles and nods as he gives brief, positive, feedback to the individuals as they settle. "When we go in I want you to remember ..." Here the teacher *briefly* outlines the protocol about where students will sit, where their bags go, and so on (see also p. 52f).

Teacher confidence and authority

Robertson (1997) notes that "relaxed behaviour" in teachers is consistent with high role "status" and also implies that one is not threatened. Of course we may have natural anxiety but we need to project an approach, a manner, that in effect says, "I expect your cooperation, and compliance, in terms of reasonable behaviour". Of course such a leadership style needs to convey respect, good will and humanity.

When a teacher's manner, body language, posture and communication appear confident and authoritative, and when such confidence is further maintained in both teaching and management, students are likely to cooperate with the teacher's leadership. There is a reciprocity at work here:

> If the teacher feels confident the pupils are noticeably more responsive and this in turn reinforces his own assurance; if the teacher lacks confidence, the process can begin in reverse and he can quickly become thoroughly demoralised. (Robertson 1997: 66)

Confidence (not cockiness or arrogant self-assurance) is a crucial feature in the teacher's overall communication with a group of students.

Confidence comes in part from our wanting to *be* a teacher-leader and, then, from our confidence in core practices and skills of leadership (see Chapters 3 and 4); our ability to define our role in terms of practice and skill not merely personality. Such confidence is expressed within: *Our role*, as teacher-leader. Our "role" is never merely acquired from our qualifications. We have to be able to confidently and respectfully *be* a teacher-leader. This derives from one's characteristic – and genuine – "presentation of self": open, relaxed body language; not appearing easily flustered (yet willing to accept fallibility without "going to pieces"); the ability to regain composure quickly when one has made a mistake; a confident, pleasant, engaging voice; yet also being able to assert where necessary (pp. 11); effective use of eye-scanning, eye contact (p. 59f); *being aware of one's body language* when engaging students' personal space; and, most of all, our characteristic communication (particularly when we have to discipline) (Chapter 3). These are basic but significant features of a confident teacher's behaviour and our 'social, emotional intelligence' (Rogers 2006b).

○ This is not about "acting" The line I sometimes hear about a good teacher is a good actor is not appropriate to our profession.
○ Daily preparation, even in a subject, topic, unit of work – even in individual "lessons" (taught many times), is crucial to the confidence we carry into our classrooms every day.
○ So too with core routines we establish for the smooth running of a busy place/space like a classroom (Chapter 3).
○ Confidence is not merely a feeling, or emotive state; it is, effectively, centred in a *reasonable assuredness* we know what we're doing as teacher-leaders. This is why I've emphasised the crucial nature of skills

in this text. It is not *merely* our personality that will carry good teaching
to our students.

○ Confidence should never be confused with "bossiness"; that petty belief
that says "I'm right; *my* way is the only way; *I've* got it sorted (!)". The word
"cocky" is apposite to describe such teacher attitude and behaviour. (Cocky
teachers deserve everything they get!)

Can confidence be developed?

Yes – of course. I stress again, respectful confidence is based in *practices and skills*
and a leadership based in the core values of rights and responsibilities (p. 38f, 41f).
We can *learn* to be more confident.

Establishing whole-class attention within a classroom context

It is important to establish at our first group meeting with any new class the
importance of whole-class attention and focus. Developing the habit of whole-
class attention is crucial to an effective beginning to *any* whole-class teaching and
learning, on *any* day.

Verbally focusing attention

Once students are sitting in their seats the teacher needs to cue for whole-class
attention and focus. This can be initiated through a combination of non-verbal
cues and verbal direction(s).

• When using verbal cues it will always help to use a positive, directional tone:
"Settling down everyone (…)". Allow some, brief, tactical, pausing (...) (p. xxi)
to give the students *brief* take-up time to process the teacher's cueing (p. 118f).
"Looking this way and listening (…). Thanks." "Thanks" at the end of an imperative form of words conveys expectation. "Eyes and ears this way (...).
Thanks." We may need to repeat this calmly, positively, expectantly. We use
language cues that focus on the behaviour we expect: "*Settling ... looking ...
listening.*" We avoid easy use of negatives: "Don't talk while I'm talking ...",
"Don't call out ...".

• Avoid "questioning", i.e. those interrogative phrases: "*Would you* please look
this way everyone?", "*Can you* settle down please?", "*Would you* stop talking?",
"*Why* are you talking?", "You're not supposed to be talking now *are you?*", "*Do
you* have to talk now!"

- It can help to reflect on the language we use for addressing a *group*: "Class ..."; "Folks ..."; "Everyone ..."; "Guys ..."; "6D ...". "Guys ..." seems to be favoured as an inclusive, unisex, generic by younger teachers. It's not one of my favourites. (Must be my age! Guys meant male only in "my day".)

- Some teachers find a non-verbal cue helpful *before* they give a verbal direction. With new classes I often "ting" a small drinking glass with the tip of my pen; wait (some tactical pausing) then follow with the whole-class direction "Settling down ...". Some early years teachers use clapping rhythms or musical cues, some simply raise their right hand, scan the class and wait for students *correspondingly* to raise their hand, without talking, and eyes/ears facing the front. Of course any such non-verbal cue needs to be associated with (initially) a verbal cue such as noted above.

- Be aware of posture. An "open" expectant, confident posture and a positive, expectant tone in one's voice will convey our meaning ("settle", "look", "listen") as much as anything else will. We do not lounge back onto the teacher's table or lean against the whiteboard, or sit down (at upper primary or secondary level).

- Step the voice down with the *part* direction as we give the initial verbal cue. The initial words (for example, "Settling down everyone ...") may need to be said a little louder to gain initial attention; it may be necessary to repeat the first part of the direction.

"*Settling* down everyone (...)" a little louder (repeat if necessary),
　　"Looking this way thanks (...) softer,
　　　　and listening (...)" softer (in concert with increasing attention and focus by the students).

This verbal form ("Settling down ...") is a variation of "*Stop* (what you're doing), *look* this way, and *listen*".

- Scan the eyes and faces of your class *as you speak*, it can communicate one's positive manner as well as giving the teacher transitory feedback about student attention and focus. Allow time for the residual noise to settle (...), then proceed with the rest of what you want (or need) to say when the class are attending, for example, a class welcome and then proceeding with the whole-class teaching phase of the lesson.

- It may be necessary to address the distracting students *while* cueing for whole-class attention. For example, a few students are chatting, a couple of boys are fiddling with the window blinds ... We cue these students with a brief *descriptive reminder or direction.* "Bilal (...) Dean (...). You're fiddling with the blinds. Leave the blinds and face this way. Thanks." "Chelsea and Bec (...). You're chatting (...) it's whole-class teaching time. Facing this way and listening.

Thanks." We then give these students take-up time *as we refocus to the whole class* and the "flow" of whole-class settling and focus.

- Before we briefly cue any distracting students we also briefly cue the 70 per cent of students who have responded to our initial direction to "settle … look … and listen". "Excuse me everyone (or class) …" *Then* focus our brief discipline to the distracting students to raise their behaviour awareness (and responsibility) and then resume the *whole-class* settling and focus.

Some teachers will use a raised voice to initiate group attention and, when only half the class are listening, *continue* to talk to the group *while* the rest of the class are still whispering or chatting. All this does (of course) is emphasise that such talking or "chatting" or calling out, or fiddling with objects on the table, is OK during whole-class teaching time. It is important to scan, verbally cue, *and wait* for whole-class attention. While scanning the group, it will be important to non-verbally (or verbally) *briefly* affirm students who do settle, face the front and listen with readiness. We smile, give a nod, and a brief affirming comment: "Thank you, John, Damien, Tran, Bilal … you're ready"; "Nuyen, Lucien, Susan … thanks."

At early years level teachers will often give several such encouragers to emphasise the fact the students *are* listening, *are* sitting, *are* facing the front, *are* ready …

I often add a thank you *when* a class is settled and attentive. "Thanks. You're looking relaxed and ready. Good morning everyone." I will not say good morning or good afternoon (to the whole class) *until* I see (and sense) their returned settling and focus.

Always say "good morning"/"good afternoon". I have worked with some teachers who either forget, or don't bother, or even don't see the civil necessity of whole-class greetings (!).

Communicating "calmness"

What we say when we cue a class for whole-class attention and focus (particularly a more restless class) is very important. Equally important, though, is our ability to convey and communicate a calmness in our manner and voice tone. As we scan the class (and cue), our calmness enables a corresponding calmness in the group. I've put "calmness" (in the heading) in inverted commas. By calmness I do not mean that we are "unemotional" or "holding in" our emotions. Neither do we convey a kind of bland, anodyne, calmness. Our calmness is more to do with how we convey, and communicate, our self-control – under natural pressure – particularly when we need to convey assertion (see later, p. 90f, 25, 7f).

"Calmness" is not something that is easily claimed when under pressure. When working with particularly challenging classes it's natural to experience some stressful arousal. Our *self-calming* is aided by knowing we've planned as well as we reasonably can and we've been "here" before and that we have a behaviour intervention "plan" that will help (Chapter 3). The *natural excitation* and stress can actually motivate and self-cue our overall sense of our calmness and *enable us to communicate our calmness to our students*.

"I am as prepared as I can be". As a younger or beginning teacher we may tend to over-prepare for even a single lesson/activity; that's normal. As we continue on our teaching journey we may not plan as assiduously as "back then"; that, too, is normal. But we should also have reasonable-to-task (and to-group) preparation – even as an experienced teacher. We can "wing it" sometimes but good teachers *never* make "winging it" a habit.

Also, knowing what we can say/do in tense and distracting situations when we have to discipline will enable *our* calmness (see Chapters 3 and 4).

NB Self-cueing for "calmness"

- *Calm breathing* is not the same as deep breathing. Our calm breathing (breathe in to a count of 2; hold to a count of 2, exhale to a count of 2 ...). A simple habit, calm breathing will enable a *sense* of self-calming as we approach our class ...
- *Quickly tuning into any bodily tenseness*: untensing brow (frown) neck and shoulders. This "cueing" for body calming will enable us to *physically* feel less tense and, again, convey our calmness to others.
- *Voice and scan*: using a calm/clear voice – not fast or "kinaesthetically edgy" and eye-scanning (crucial with whole-class settling and focus) will enable our sense of self-control (p. 59).
- *Self-cueing:* what we say to ourselves (when under pressure – often very quickly) will also help our self-calming. "I can do this ...", "what do I have to do now ...?", rather than "I can't cope", "I won't be able to do this", "It's too hard". We can acknowledge the natural difficulties and stress in a given situation and still reframe to the positive possibilities.

Cueing calmness to the class group

It doesn't help student attention and focus if the teacher telegraphs too much motoric restlessness by pacing up and down at the front of the classroom while cueing for whole-class attention. The more "naturally restless" students (not to mention those with diagnosed behaviour disorders like Attention Deficit or

Autism Spectrum) will tend to over-focus on the teacher's movement, only half listening (if at all) to what the teacher is actually saying. I've watched teachers bouncing up and down on their toes while reading to the class, unaware that their overly motoric movement triggers "unconscious" corresponding restlessness in the students whose eyes involuntarily track the bouncing up and down movement.

It will also help to stand at the front of the room when initiating and sustaining *any* whole-class attention. A centre-front position, facing the class group, standing relaxed and scanning the faces of the students while cueing for attention will normally (and positively) signal the teacher's readiness and expectation.

Non-verbal cues to gain group attention

One of the common non-verbal cues to initiate or signal for group attention (at primary age) is the raised hand. When the students are in their seats (or on the "carpet area" in early years), the teacher faces the class (from the centre-front of the classroom) and visually scans the room with one hand raised. At this point the teacher does not speak; the raised hand is a *cue* to which the students respond by, likewise, raising their hand in a kind of "domino effect" across the room. Students look around and – in effect – copy the teacher cue. It is a cue to focus and refocus attention (as is necessary during the lesson) and can be quite effective at primary-age level and even lower secondary level. When the class has responded (5–10 seconds or so) the teacher lowers their hand, thanks the class for their cooperation and continues with a class greeting and the session's activity. One of my postgraduate students had been told this was a helpful signal for settling a class and proceeded to try it with a new Year 6 class. She had her hand up for a few minutes when a student finally said, "Yes, Miss … how can we help you?" When using non-verbal cues for the first time it will be important to verbally associate the expectation carried by the non-verbal cue. In the case above, the teacher could have raised her hand *and* at the same time verbally directed the group, "Settling down everyone (…), looking this way (…) and listening (…)…". When they were quiet and listening she could have then explained that the next time she puts her hand up *like that* at the beginning of the lesson (or at any time) … So much for hindsight!

Typical non-verbal cues used by teachers include ringing a small hand-bell; a sound from an instrument (many years ago I used my guitar – strumming a chord to signal to my, then, primary class to come and sit on the mat); a hand-clap rhythm copied by all early years students, the teacher then reducing the clap to a two-finger clap and, finally, a single finger "quiet clap" and hands resting in the lap.

Even standing still – relaxed – scanning the class and waiting can, *itself*, be a non-verbal cue. *Lengthy* waiting, though, will confuse students or (with older children) trigger possible inattention and restlessness.

Re-establishing group attention

There are occasions when a teacher needs to re-establish whole-class attention beyond the initial lesson establishment. There may be an occasion when the noise level of unnecessary off-task behaviour occurs, or the teacher may need to refocus an aspect of the lesson task/activity. The most obvious re-establishing needs to occur before lesson closure. It is important to allow appropriate time for packing up, lesson summary (if necessary) and an orderly and calm exit (see pp. 86f).

A primary teacher stops her class 3 or 4 minutes before the closing bell. The students are still busily colouring in or writing on their worksheet. She gives several instructions about materials and where to put finished work, adding, "Stand behind your chairs when you've finished". The problem is that the teacher is speaking over significant residual noise and activity. She is also moving around the room *while* she is giving the instruction. A third of the class is still working with pencils in hand while she is talking. She "allows" this behaviour to continue, where it would have been more effective had she gone to the front of the classroom and briefly refocused the class, and individuals, for whole-class attention and *then* given those instructions.

Whenever we give *group* instructions, directions or reminders it is important to wait for whole-class attention to enable attention, focus and processing of even routine directions. And, as noted earlier, it will also help to go to the front of the classroom to anchor and consolidate the whole-class teacher directions.

A further problem can occur if the teacher frequently talks *over* students when they are talking – and talking "through" their kinaesthetic noise – the students get used to it, developing a group habituation.

* Have a positive signal or cue for group attention (verbal or non-verbal, see pp. 58f, 62). Preferably not hands on heads (!)
* A brief tactical pause (...), so students can tune-in to the direction/instruction. Repeat the group instruction if necessary: "Everyone (…) eyes and ears this way now. Thank you (…). Paul (…), Rashida (…), Simone (…), Donna (…), Bilal (…), Patrick (…) – pens down." This to the several who are still not attending. "(…) Eyes and ears this way (…) Thank you." Firm, confident and pleasant; it sets the norm, the routine.

- Visual cue reminders can help at primary level (see p. 79f).
- A word of acknowledgement and appreciation will encourage : "I appreciated the way in which you all packed up at your tables and put the lids on felt-tip pens – that'll help them to live longer"; "Thank you for listening, and concentrating, when I asked you all to ...".

Sustaining group attention

The ability to *sustain* group attention depends on the teacher's ability to engage the students in the teaching and learning focus – at that point – and in the flow of the lesson from then on. The ability and skills necessary to teach effectively and to manage distracting and disruptive behaviours is crucial to the effectiveness of any group learning. This is discussed in some detail in Chapters 3 and 4.

The seemingly non-responsive, non-attentive class (first meeting)

This phenomenon can sometimes occur with more challenging classes and is more common at secondary than primary level. The teacher enters the class with a group of restless and noisy students. It seems that they are in a world of their own (and they probably are). The teacher stands at the front of the room waiting, waiting ... students are having private conversations, fiddling with *objets d'art*, even rearranging class furniture, wandering, walkabout ... Does the teacher "exist"? What should they do? This "phenomenon" can also occur in cover classes.

It will be counter-productive (if tempting) to shout, though we've all done it at some stage. It might, temporarily, stop the noise and the motoric restlessness, but it will probably restart or, worse, the key "catalytic" students will react in a hostile way, "stirring" the rest of the class. And, if we keep using an *overly* raised (or shouting) voice we, in effect, train our students to get used to this as the norm! It is also unhelpful to stand there *just* waiting.

Ideally, if such a class is believed to likely behave like this (even from Day One), the establishment phase (first few lessons) should involve a team-teaching approach with one of the teachers well known to the students in that group as a teacher with credibility and respect (incidental mentoring support, p. 288f). The new (ongoing) teacher plans the first few lessons (establishment) with this support colleague; this allows a kind of "credibility by proxy" (Rogers 2006b). It has to be genuine teaming and well planned. This collegial teaming could also include some ongoing monitoring of students' behaviour in (and out of) class (particularly the "catalytic" students). What is to be avoided is any *known* "difficult class" being given to a beginning teacher or a teacher new to the school without initial and ongoing colleague support.

When faced with a seemingly unresponsive class, rather than stand at the front of the room waiting, or even cueing for group attention, I've found it helpful to leave the centre-front of the room (where students expect the teacher to try to establish some class attention and "control") and move around the room initiating conversations with individuals and pairs. This is a kind of mini-establishment – in "their" space. It initially "unsettles" *some* of the students. They don't expect *this*. No doubt *some* of the students are thinking, "You should be up the front where we can make life difficult for you …". As I walk up to students and initiate conversations (beginning with a mutual name introduction) I sometimes get cocky, smart-alec responses. I find *tactical ignoring* of such behaviour (wherever appropriate, p. 97f) avoids *over*-engaging or over-servicing insecure, attentional behaviours. I seek to indicate *I'm* no threat, *nor am I threatened* by their behaviour, but at the same time I am initiating and establishing my leadership relationship with them in these brief engagements (moving around the classroom …). I ask a few questions about the sorts of things they might expect in *this* class and assure them that our time together will be worthwhile: the process is brief, conveying respectful confidence and the expectation of cooperation. Walking back to the front of the classroom I try to hold some key student names in my short-term memory and *then* go to the centre-front of the classroom. Using the remembered names I can now normatively cue for whole-class attention (p. 58f), "Settling down, thanks (…), Paul …, Dean …, Halid …, Kosta …". Most students are *now* settling, calming down and facing the front. They are affirmed (briefly), "Thanks, Crystal (…), David, Donna …". Having had some brief – relational – introductions, and chats (in the initial excursive roam), I can now use students' names with some early, relational, confidence. After a few minutes – and several tactical pauses – the class is substantially settled. It isn't easy, but it is an approach I have found helpful to initiate group calming and focus with such classes.

If a pattern of non-attentiveness by the class is typical (and increasingly disruptive) over the first few lessons with a new class, it will be important to seek immediate, senior, colleague support:

- It may help to see if the problem is wider than your own class.
- It can help to work with the key catalysts/ringleaders; those students who trigger non-attentive, distracting or provocative behaviour in their classmates. Follow-up (with such students) will need to emphasise the effect of their behaviour on the class and on the shared rights of all, and then work with them on their responsibility and commitment to change. Any such follow-up will also be helped by senior colleague support, but it is crucial that the class teacher engages in *any* one-to-one follow-up with these students to affirm their leadership relationship (p. 122f).
- It can help to conduct a classroom meeting with the whole class, outlining to the students the major concerns the teacher and the students have about behaviours such as general noise level, inattention and students talking while the teacher is talking, and then invite student responses about the need for change. Students then work with their teacher in developing a class plan – a

fresh start – to address these concerns about behaviour and learning. Such a meeting, though, will benefit from colleague support in planning, developing and follow through (see p. 274f).

It can happen – in some schools, the class where there are frequent behavioural disruptions – where there are several (or more) distracting/disruptive students and it's "all happening" at one and the same time.

Where several distracting/disruptive behaviours are occurring at "one and the same time" it is pointless trying to address any one behaviour (unless it's a major incident). It will help to walk to the centre-front of the classroom and decisively *re-cue and re-focus the whole class.*

Ideally we ought to have established our behaviour leadership in those critical first meetings (p. 37f): those essential core routines (p. 57f); our own behaviour leadership cueing to address the natural distractions and disruptions in more challenging class groups; the essential ability (and skill) of the teacher/leader in enabling restless class groups to settle and focus (particularly during whole class teaching time (p. 58f) ... Hopefully you are in a supportive school where genuine, initial and ongoing mentorship support is given to newly qualified teachers (NQTs).

I encountered a class like this when I was mentoring a NQT colleague in a school in the UK – a few years back. The school had been directed to special measures (by Ofsted). My role in the school was to set up an ongoing mentoring support approach (the opposite of Ofsted) to enable colleagues to reflect on – and gain colleague support – regarding their behaviour leadership (see Chapter 8).

The drawing on p. 66 is one I made after my three-day visit to set up the programme and also mentor colleagues over several classes (as with my NQT colleague in the far right-hand corner).

Have another look at the picture. This is a Year 7 (Form 1) class. It was my first of four sessions (over three days) with my NQT colleague in this school. It is the on-task phase of the lesson. It had taken a little while to calm and focus them in whole-class teaching time but we had a reasonable lesson; now, they seemed to be "returning" to their "habituated" patterns of behaviour ...

Several students were calling out to get our attention ("Miss!! Don't know what to do ...", "Ay ... Sir, Sir ...what do we have to do again?!" Several students are wandering (for no good reason) – and I'd previously spoken to one of them already about "walkabout" ... One of the boys (Rory) has thrown a pen at

Andrew so he has an "excuse" to pick it up and playfully hit him ... There is a lot of task avoidance/socialising going on among a third (or so) of the class. Terry (very far right in the picture) has just demolished a fat, liquorice, straw full of sherbet and with his spit is making a sticky slurry ... "just having a bit of fun (?)" ...

I glanced at my colleague and saw again her weariness, her "resignation" – I sensed she was saying "It's not just me, is it!"

Going to the centre-front of the classroom, I tapped my glass with my pen to re-cue (...). Lifting the voice – "Everyone (...) stop what you're doing (...) *Now* (...). Everyone – pens down, eyes and ears this way (...) Now ...". The students looked, listened (the wanderers hadn't gone back to their seat).

It's important to stress, again, 60 per cent (or more) of the class will cooperate when teachers lead confidently and respectfully. I always bank on this. The class were already "quieter" now ...

I cued the "walkabouts" – "Jacqui (...) Kirsty (...) Callum (...). Back in your seats (...) now." Kirsty whinged, "I was just getting a pen!!" I tactically ignored this and beckoned her to her table ... "Rory (...)", this to the lad who had thrown the pen ... "leave it there ... Andrew (...) you too ... Leave it there." They sighed, rolled their eyes ... all *tactically* ignored *at this point* ... (I spoke to them later, after class ... p. 116f).

"Terry (...) I'll be over with some Wipes soon ..." (the lad with the sherbet "slurry" ...).

This *re-cueing of the whole class* did not take long. Our tone and manner need to be firm, calm, confident and decisive. No ranting, "I'm sick and tired of your stupid behaviour!! What's wrong with you!! Can't you just ...!?" (mind you, it's tempting ...).

"Alright everyone (...)". This – again – to the whole class; front of room. "I'm not saying it's all of you [this is a crucial point], however a number of you are calling out to get teacher help, several of you were wandering around the class – it is our learning time. And we do not throw anything in our class, *even in fun*. It was also very noisy; remember out partner-voices (p. 75f)". Brief, clear, addressing the *behaviours* of *concern*. "If you need pens, rulers, pencils, paper ..." (I reminded them of the class supply, p. 74f).

I also reminded them of the core routine for getting teacher assistance, adding "Well (...) we've got about 20 minutes to go before the end of this class time." I reminded them of the learning task, adding "Let's get back to it. Thank you." Never underestimate here the brief and expectant "thank you".

The class was calmer now – refocused. Still residual sulking on the faces of several students. I went across to Terry with the wipes for the slurry ...

We were starting that (at times) slow journey of re-habituation; a "fresh-start" to what a teaching/learning community can be like. While this "circuit breaking"/ re-cueing is the important short-term intervention, we also need to communicate a belief to *all our students that we can be better than this*. Again, that 60–70 per cent of (normally) cooperative students will respond to this re-cueing quickly.

I also directed several students to stay back to work through early behaviour concerns (as the "new" teacher). See p. 122f.

The issue of hard classes and "fresh-start" approaches are addressed in Chapter 8 (see also Rogers, 2012).

Learning and using students' names

This may sound like a mundane point, but it is crucial – from Day One. I have worked with some secondary teachers who still haven't learned the names of some of their students by Term Two! I know it takes effort but it is significant in relational and management terms. It is also basic civility. More than that, it is essential in building positive relationships.

At primary level the students' names can be assigned and tagged to the desk itself for Day One; seating plans can be organised and name-games utilised (even at lower secondary level).

As a mentor/teacher in every new class I work with, I ask a student to draw me a basic classroom plan of the furniture and note down the first name of the student in relation to their desk (not all teachers are consistent with seating arrangements). I then use that "name plan" during the on-task phase of the lesson. I also find it helpful to double-check the *sound* of students' names so I don't cause unthinking offence (or embarrassment) to a student. I use these hand-drawn plans *at every* lesson until I've learned the names. This is important when we're covering an unfamiliar class; so too for supply teachers.

Most schools now utilise class lists with a small photograph of each student – this assists the teacher's short-term memory in each lesson as we seek to build those workable relationships. It is also important to use the students' names in non-classroom settings (corridor and playground), even in brief, transitional, exchanges.

NB   It isn't easy learning students' names as a secondary teacher (or if you are a "specialist" teacher at primary level). I've found that when I do forget a name I'm trying to remember it sounds a bit nicer on the ear to say to the student, "I'm trying to *remember* your name" (the truth), rather than, "I've *forgotten* your name" or even "I don't know your name".

Addressing distracting and disruptive behaviour during whole-class teaching time

Like any aspect of classroom management we need to initially establish and discuss with our students:

- expected behaviours within the "class agreement" (p. 39f)
- an age-related, established routine; at primary and middle school it might be "hands up without calling out", whereas at senior high level it might be "one at a time in class discussions".
- and be able to confidently address and "manage" the calling out or talking while the teacher is talking …, or distracting motoric restlessness … when it occurs and then *refocus the whole class* to the whole-class teaching phase of the lesson.

In the first few lessons (with a new class) the teacher will also need to define, establish and maintain the fairness of one person speaking at a time and others consciously making an effort to listen. Before any group discussion we can *preface* question time, or class discussion, by reminding our students: "Remember our rule (or agreement) for …". We might add, "I know some of you will be really keen to contribute; however, if you just call out, or talk over someone, that is unfair to the other person. If you are waiting to make a point or contribute and others call out, you, too, would feel their behaviour is unfair." If students do forget, or call out to gain some attentional advantage, then a brief reminder of the rule will be important to the several or the individual (see below).

It is also important to remember to remind our students that if a student asks a question *of* the teacher, or shares a contribution *with* the class, then that contribution is for everyone. Some students imagine a question *to* the teacher is merely between the teacher and that student. "I want you to remember that when you share in class discussion, and questions, that contribution is for all of us here – not just me as your teacher …."

When giving directions or reminders to any distracting student behaviours it is important to be brief, giving a few seconds of take-up time (…), and then *re-engage* whole-group attention to and focus on the *whole-class* aspect of the lesson or discussion. If we accept calling out and easily validate such behaviour in the first few meetings we will find it difficult to re-establish those expected, fair, behaviours later in the term.

It is important not to ignore such behaviour in the hope that it will go away or that the students will "naturally" settle and listen. I have seen teachers teach *through* such noisy, disparate, kinaesthetic calling out behaviour *as if* they are teaching when, in fact, several or more students are actively ignoring the teacher through their private chatting, or "cross-talking". If we accept students' butting in, calling out, talking *over* others or talking across the room to other students we effectively ratify that such behaviour is "acceptable", "normal".

A "hands up" reminder is a necessary and fair routine in most classes – even in some Year 11 and 12 classes – particularly in the establishment phase of the year. The following are some basic cues to remind *or* to correct and refocus calling out, or chatting while the teacher is talking.

- *A non-verbal reminder* (at infant or middle primary level). The teacher raises his or her hand (to simulate hands up) and, briefly, covers his or her mouth (to indicate hands up *without* calling out). She then acknowledges and affirms students with their hands up .
- *Incidental direction* (for older children). The teacher describes briefly what the student is doing: "Jason (…), you're calling out and clicking your fingers". This "describes the behaviour reality" and raises some behaviour awareness. The teacher *then* acknowledges the students with their hands up, naming them – "Jason …, Dean …, Carla …, I see your hands up 1, 2, 3" – and responds in turn to their questions or contributions. If a student does not "pick-up"/respond to an incidental direction we can give a brief rule reminder: "Jason (…) remember our rule for …" or a simple direction: "Hands up (...) without calling out. Thanks."

If several students are calling out it will be important to "stop" the class. The teacher cues with a blocking hand – and scans the room, waiting for quiet: "(…), several students are calling out (…) [a brief *descriptive* recognition]. We have a class rule (the brief rule reminder). Thank you." This to the several distracting students … It is important to differentiate "… *several* students are calling out …" It is not *all* the class. The 70 per cent or so who were waiting – without calling out – will pick this up. The teacher – then – in a positive, expectant manner, resumes the flow of the discussion. "I don't mind *which* hand, as long as you have a hand up [teacher smiles]. Alright … let's go for it …". As noted earlier, this is in preference to "*Don't* call out …"; "You *shouldn't* be calling out – *should you?*"; "*Why* are you calling out?"

These pointless interrogative questions frequently come from frustration and habit:

"Will you just stop doing that please …?"
"Can you please not do that …?"
"Do you have to do that?"
"What did I just say …?" "Weren't you listening …?"

If a child is doing something distracting, a desist is better expressed as a *clear direction* about what the student needs to do. If we need to use a firm desist we need to give a simple, brief specific direction to stop …; the request focus "will you …?" and "please …" is unnecessary and unhelpful.

Other examples of verbal cues to a group or individual:

- "Hands up without calling out, thanks …"
- "Remember our class rule for asking questions."
- "Hands up so I can see your voice."
- "I can hear questions; I can hear calling out. I need to see hands up, so we all get a fair go."
- "I get concerned when several of you call out (…) *we* end up not able to hear anyone." (This is a brief, *whole-class* reminder.)

Students chatting while the teacher is teaching …

If students are chatting we can also use brief descriptive cues/rule reminders, for example: "Melissa (…), Chantelle (…) you're chatting. This is whole-class teaching time (…)." Sometimes the "descriptive cue" is enough. With some students we will need to add a brief simple direction, "… Eyes and ears this way (…). Thanks." We may also need to add a *brief* "… without chatting."

> **NB**   Whenever we remind, or correct, to distracting or disruptive behaviour – in one (or a few) students during *whole-class teaching time* – it is important to briefly cue the 60 per cent who are behaving considerately and cooperatively. A brief, "Excuse me class", as we *then* focus on the student(s) who are distracting. This cue acknowledges their cooperation *while* we briefly address the distracting students …

The use of corrective language is discussed in some detail in Chapter 3.

If a student, has persistently called out during Day One it will be worth following up with them after class time one-to-one, perhaps even making some form of verbal agreement (one-to-one) about hands up – without calling out – behaviour (p. 122f).

Like any discipline, we need to have the preventative focus in place (the rule/expectation), and will need to have thought through simple, brief, *positive* forms of corrective language to remind students of their responsibility and to direct students back to the expected (fair) behaviour.

Transitions

When a teacher moves from the whole-class teaching phase of the lesson to the on-task phase of the lesson it is natural for the noise level of the class to rise; some students who were not listening earlier now tend to be unfocused and want teacher assistance ("Miss – what do we have to do?!", "I don't know what to do …!", "I forgot …", "Can you help me …?"); many students will start talking to their classmate (which is obviously acceptable providing such talking is not loud or significantly non-task in focus); there will also be some students who do not have the appropriate equipment; some may go "class walkabout" for no apparently helpful reason.

More than anything, teachers need to make the transition between whole-class teaching time and on-task time clear and definite. I've worked with teachers who have a fuzzy, inchoate transition, where the students are unclear about what they are supposed to be doing *now*. The teacher may just rattle off a series of task instructions, or even start answering individuals' questions, leaving the rest of the class uncertain as to where the focus of the lesson is *at this point*.

Task clarity

Basic – but crucial – points, like having the work task/activity written up as a question, or series of points/steps and having monitors for distribution of materials (particularly with group work), need to be established from Day One. Students also need to be aware of reasonable time-to-learning-activity and the progress of time-to-task. We need to think about the visual learners in our classes and those with learning needs. The visual cues, on a board, or task sheet, will always help with learning clarity and focus. For students with specific learning needs we will need to differentiate the task. This may be as basic as a personal task sheet that attenuates the activity *for that student*.

Behaviour clarity

Because of natural noise levels rising (during on-task learning time), some students may be unfocused or engaging in task-avoidance. It will be important to remind students of expected (and fair) behaviours at this point in the "on-task" phase of the lesson. Students need to know what reasonable "working voices" are and why such voices (partner-voices/inside voices …) are important in such a small place/ space and how such "voices" affect our learning time. It will also be important to discuss reasonable and acceptable movement *around* the classroom (this will, naturally, vary according to subject area and context). If students need teacher assistance they will need to know how they can – fairly and reasonably – get teacher help in a classroom of 25–30 students (p. 84f).

It will also help to have some spare pens (blue and red), some spare rulers, pencils and erasers, and some lined (and plain) A4 paper, just in case. Initially the teacher will not know if a student without a pen (workbook or paper) is being difficult, lazy, indifferent or genuinely forgetful. A box of "necessities" is essential in the first few lessons at upper primary level onwards. It is always worth checking if the pens work (!) before we go into class.

In developing such routines, cues and procedures with their students, teachers will find it helpful to plan ahead with colleagues who teach similar ages of students and in similar teaching/subject areas. This is crucial when working with students with diagnosed special needs for learning and behaviour.

Cater for the visual learners in the group

Some teachers over-rely on an auditory approach to teaching. We might (sometimes) be critical of the so-called "chalk and talk" days but, then, many teachers did understand the importance of visual cueing: writing key points on the board; building up concepts from main concept to subsidiary points; or using the "well-known to less-known" principle. Long before the modern emphasis on "multiple intelligences", visual, auditory and kinaesthetic learning, and the so called left-brain/right-brain learning, effective teachers were using "mind-map" concepts and catering for visual and kinaesthetic learners.[1]

I was team-teaching with a senior teacher in an English class some years ago. She was discussing (with a Year 10 class) aspects of positive communication. As she developed some quite complex ideas I noticed (10 ten minutes into the session) that at least a third of the class were restless and unfocused. I asked my colleague (casually) if I could "write a few of these points on the board". She replied (pleasantly), "… of course, Mr Rogers". As I wrote her key points up I noticed the students re-engage, some almost straight away. It was as if the "physicality" and organisation of the words on the board had given them a visual framework for the concepts and how key and subsidiary features were linked. This clearly aided both their thinking and discussion. This *fundamental* axiom (visual cueing) is relevant in any subject and any age.

If, for example, I'm conducting a classroom meeting I like to have a student write up key points on the whiteboard so the class can have a visual focus (it also validates a student's contribution). I also like to have another student record the points (as a class scribe) so I'm free (as the teacher) to manage and "chair" the class dialogue and discussion.

Noise levels

In an old *Punch*[2] magazine I noted an unusual word: "charivari". I couldn't figure out its meaning from the context so I looked it up. It's French in origin: "A serenade of rough music made with kettles, pans, tea-trays, etc. Used in France in derision of incongruous marriages … hence a babel of music …" (*Oxford Shorter English Dictionary*). I've had quite a few Year 7–10 classes exhibit charivari! Some students are not (seemingly) aware of how loudly their voices carry (along with 25–30 others) in such a small space. They may be unaware of the chair scrapes; the kinaesthetic movements of fiddling with pens, rulers, pencil cases, water bottles … (*while* the teacher is addressing the class). It can all contribute to a "charivari".

Teachers have differing levels of tolerance regarding noise levels. Some can tolerate very high levels of noise whereas the teacher next door may (rightly) find their next door's classroom noise inhibiting their own classroom teaching and learning. To ask a colleague if they are aware of how loud their "normal" classroom is can be a sensitive and touchy issue.

When 25–30 students are grouped several times a day in small rooms, with tightly orchestrated furniture and space, and are then expected to cohabit, think, concentrate, "process", discuss, cooperate, work and move, there is bound to be noise. How do we manage the environment, and student behaviour, so that we have reasonable and fair levels of noise proper to the place and activities we set?

We could try Cardinal Hume's risible approach when he was a school master: "I don't mind you making noise if you don't mind me stopping you" (Mortimer 1984).

It is important that the students understand and appreciate the difference (the relative noise *levels*) between "outside the classroom space and inside the classroom space" and the purposes of *each* "space" and "place". Some children bring all their kinaesthetic energy and louder (outside) voices into the classroom context and do not adjust and monitor their movement and voices accordingly (p. 79). It is also important that students are taught the difference between social time (outside class) and the appropriate limitations of "social time" inside a classroom space (p. 55).

A calm, quieter atmosphere inside a classroom will enable attention, focus and effective teacher–student communication. It also helps teacher stress levels!

- Explain why we – as a class group – need to have "inside" or "partner-voices" as distinct from louder, "outside voices". The classroom is, principally, a teaching and learning place: "we (therefore) use our voices, and the level of our voice, differently in here".
- Teach the difference between the *volume levels* of voices to emphasise whispering and appropriate "partner-voice" during on-task learning time. One of the ways I've found helpful in teaching this "difference" is to point out to the class that at any time during the on-task phase of the lesson, "I should be able to speak in a normal voice from the front of the room to the back of the room – without *significantly* raising my voice – and still be heard". Teaching this point by modelling can help. I have always modelled partner-voice to a class by, say, asking a student for a pen in different levels of voice to clarify, to the whole class, the meaning and extent of partner-voice. When I ask students (even at secondary level) to describe partner-voice they invariably use qualifiers such as "soft", "close", "using eye contact", "first name", "using manners – please, thanks, and so on"; *they know*.
- Monitor and encourage conscious habits of appropriate and reasonable working voices. There are a number of simple, visual ways to give students feedback about "working-voice" *levels* (see later).
- Review noise levels with the class during the first few weeks to maintain positive, and conscious, habits of monitoring, and moderation in, voice levels.
- Encourage the class when they utilise partner-voices.

I prefer, and use, the terms "partner-voice", "working voices" our "inside voices" or "classroom voices" rather than "working *noise*": I try to avoid easy use of the "noise" motif where possible.

The teacher's voice

Sometimes a teacher's normal – characteristic – voice level and volume are UNNECESSARILY HIGH AND LOUD ...(!). This contributes to the raising of the residual noise level of the students' voices, creating a kind of *normatively* louder classroom. Often the teacher is unaware that this is a feature of their NOR-MAL VOICE LEVEL. The problem is that when they need to project a firmer, or slightly louder voice (for emphasis) it is not *effectively* heard. If a teacher's normal voice is particularly loud or high (in tone), or it sounds as if he or she is frequently (and easily) annoyed or irritated (in their tone of voice), the classroom will be an unnecessarily tense place that will inhibit effective teaching and learning, even if the teacher falsely believes he or she has "good control" through the overly loud voice.

If the teacher has an overly *controlling voice*, and "peppers" their classroom communication with negative language (overusing language cueing such as "don't", "mustn't", "shouldn't", "why?" and "are you?", p. 58f), the classroom can become an unpleasant place to be for children. I've seen older students, eventually, react against such teachers by overt or covert "sabotage" of classroom dynamics.

Keeping our tone and volume of voice *normally* pleasant, confident and respectful will aid group calmness and enable student attention; it will also aid positive relational tone.[3] Then when we need to raise our voice for *particular* attention, or to communicate our frustration, or even anger, (Chapter 7), it will carry the appropriate effect and impact; and convey the intended "moral weight". When we do need to raise our voice to *emphasise*, or to gain *attention*, it helps to – then – drop the voice (de-escalate) to a calmer or more controlled (firmer) voice. This reduces residual tension within the dynamics of the classroom.

Caveat: I'm talking, here, about our *characteristic* "voice"; not bad-day syndrome (p. 22f).

Reflective teachers are well aware of the exponential axiom that "loud teachers have loud classes". A high level of cognitive processing is necessary – in children – for the learning experience. Noisy and distracting classroom environments (25 children in a small space for long periods) will have a detrimental effect on attention, focus and comprehension (Rogers and McPherson 2014). Add to that, those children raised in very noisy homes: televisions blaring during meal times (even breakfast) and, in some homes, overly raised voices or frequent shouting (even yelling). This necessitates – even more – that we enable calmer, more relaxing, classroom environments for our students.

Obviously in subjects like drama, music and PE there will be a louder volume of "social noise", at times, but not when *whole-class* focus and attention is necessary to discuss, share, explore, plan and develop the shared learning experiences.

Teaching partner-voice(s) to early years

Like many social experiences that involve self-control, we cannot assume that all the children in our classes understand what we mean by "working noise", "partner-voice", "taking turns", "lining up", "hands up without calling out" and "moving *carefully* and thoughtfully around the room" ...; even basic manners can't *simply* be assumed.

In the establishment phase of the year (Day One, Week, One) it will be important to explain why we need to use our "partner-voice" inside our classroom, and to teach and monitor "working voice" levels. Then, having explained, discussed – even taught – reasonable "working voice" volume we need to maintain, consolidate, "habituate" that as a classroom expectation (see Figure 2.5). A classroom is a physically small environment in which to creatively house and engage 20–30 young children. If poor habits of working noise volume develop it can be stressful for the teacher (and many students).

OUR CLASSROOM (LEARNING COMMUNITY)

6B Ms P. Davies

WELCOME

BEFORE WE GO IN, WE REMEMBER :-

- Playtime is over / calm, relaxed and considerate entry.
- Hats off / chewing gum binned / w. bottles and coats and bags away.
- REMEMBER, this is our learning space/place time together.
- Partner-voice / co-operative talk / movement around our classroom.
- We look after / care for each other and our learning community.

Figure 2.5

The grade one children are sitting on the carpet area at the front of the classroom – Day One. Before the first on-task session for the day the teacher talks about the large room and 25 (plus) voices, sometimes all talking at the same time. She hypothesises with them about what could happen if we talked loudly during work time at our desk. She models with her hands apart as far as she can stretch, to indicate a loud voice. She speaks, about places in the school where we would use loud(er) voices (such as the playground), and why. She asks why we need quieter (*much* quieter) voices inside our classroom. She discusses what a partner is and introduces the concept of "partner-voice" or "inside" or "working voice" (Robertson 1997; Rogers and McPherson2014). Here she indicates a "smaller", *quieter* voice with a non-verbal cue of hands close together.

She invites a few students to role play "partner-voice" with her in front of the class. A table has been set aside and she sits at the table with a couple of students, asks to borrow a coloured pencil, modelling "partner-voice" and asks the children what they noticed. She soon has class feedback on observed behaviours such as "soft voice" and "manners" as well as observed eye contact. She models "whisper voices", and "quiet-work talk" as features of "partner-voice". She invites modelling from the other children in the role play. As a contrast she models "playground-voice" and the children laugh. "Imagine if I used that kind of voice if I was asking to borrow a pencil or scissors or even if I was talking *that loudly* to someone about the work we were doing ... What would happen ...? How would we feel if we were trying to concentrate ... and work ...?"

The "noise meter" (Rogers 1998)

The teacher introduces some large drawings (at least A3 size) depicting children in classroom situations. The first picture illustrates the key expected student behaviours during "carpet-time", depicting children sitting facing the teacher and listening. Some of the children in this picture have their hands up (they are not calling out). The children look relaxed and are smiling (see over page). "When we sit together on the carpet we face the front and listen ('listening with eyes and ears') and we sit comfortably."

It will help to explain sitting options that do not annoy others during sitting together time … The teacher also discusses other behaviours such as "taking turns", "listening when others speak", "hands up without calling out if you want to ask a question or share", and waiting for your teacher to call on you.

By having the picture – as a visual cue – the teacher can refer to it during whole-class teaching time, or class discussion time, and can simply say, "Remember our rule about hands-up …" and physically point back to the rule reminder poster.

The second picture illustrates a table group during work time. In the background are a few faces and in the foreground the table group are portrayed using partner-voices.

The third picture is similar to the second picture but the children at the table group are clearly using loud voices. The children in the background are frowning, indicating social disapproval.

As with all teaching concerning social behaviours, we seek to emphasise the effect of individual behaviour on others and that we don't just live to/for ourselves.

The fourth picture is the same as the third picture but has a circle encompassing the loud-talkers and a diagonal line through the circle, indicating that we stop, remember and refocus.

The teacher explains what each picture represents; what it means in terms of *how we use our voices here*.

These pictures are displayed together with a coloured meter (a circle of cardboard about 10–15 cm in diameter) in the centre. Each quadrant is coloured: white (carpet-time voices), green (partner-voices), orange (partner-voices getting too loud – this signals a reminder/warning) and red for stop and we all remember, we all refocus. The meter has an arrow (with split pin) that can rotate to any of the four pictures. The teacher explains what the arrow and colours represent. The teacher rotates the arrow to white during carpet-time and green for partner-voice time.

If children become too loud during on-task learning time the teacher can put the arrow on orange as a non-verbal and visual *aide-mémoire*. The teacher will wait to see if students pick up on this visual cue. If necessary the teacher will verbally cue for class attention (wait) and point to the warning reminder picture and either non-verbal cue for partner-voice or will give a brief, positive, verbal reminder, "Remember our partner-voices. Thank you", before putting the arrow back to green.

If the teacher puts it on red it signals to the class to stop and everyone has to refocus back to partner-voices. This involves a *brief* – whole-class – reminder about partner-voices. Like any routine, it takes time to develop general, reasonable, habituation about noise *levels* inside a classroom.

At Year 1 to 3 level it can help to appoint "noise monitors" on each table group. Their role is to keep an eye on the noise meter from time to time. The teacher can assist their role by cueing the noise monitor with a brief reminder. It can also help to rotate this role in the first few weeks.

As the teacher roves the room they will also encourage students when they are using their partner-voices.

"You're using your partner voices, and I noticed you're looking at each other when you speak and you're remembering your manners … That all helps us to get our classwork done. Thank you." In this way the teacher describes what students do that helps cooperation at their table group (brief, descriptive feedback) and encourages group members.

The noise meter and picture cues are a means to an end; they are props and prompts. They have their acute focus in the establishment phase of the year and can be shelved as the desired behaviour generalises. My colleagues have even used variations of this with upper primary classes. The noise meter is both an establishment teaching device and a monitoring *aide-mémoire*. In time it can be replaced by a simple table card reminder: "At our table group we use our partner-voices". There's an "app" that can be downloaded to a "tablet" for this kind of visual cue … Google away! (Who would have thought we'd be using the verb "Google" in this way? – or "tablet" as a noun, in this way?) When I first began teaching we didn't even have photocopiers.

Partner-voice feedback

Primary level

If an individual student is still struggling with their voice *level*, and *use* of voice, it can help to develop an individual behaviour plan with them. This plan attempts to teach the child (one-to-one) the "why" and "how" of a quiet working voice (in effect, it teaches him *individually* what most students have adapted to normatively – and thankfully – as a group). In teaching a child *one-to-one* (in non-contact time) the teacher can:

- use simple picture cues to illustrate how individual – *noisy* – voices affect other students
- "mirror" the child's typical noisy voice (ask permission, "Do you mind if I show you how it sounds when you …?" Keep any such mirroring brief (5 seconds or so) (p. 128f, 235f)).

> **NB**   We would not use brief 'behaviour mirroring', like this, with children diagnosed within the autistic spectrum. With any *brief* behaviour mirroring it is important to ask permission : "Do you mind if I show you what it looks/sounds like when …?"

- *model* appropriate partner-voice
- *practise* partner-voice with the child (one-to-one)
- give the child a reminder plan (a small card illustrating the student using his partner-voice). The bottom picture becomes his *aide-mémoire* (see picture).

As with any individual plan for behaviour or learning it needs to be developed away from other children, one-to-one, (in non-classroom time), with an emphasis on support and encouragement (p. 152f). (see also Rogers 2003a; Rogers and McPherson, 2014).

Upper primary and Secondary level

It can also be helpful with upper primary and middle-school (aged) students to give some non-verbal feedback on how the students are using their partner-voice

during the lesson. A simple way to do this is through a graph on the board. The vertical axis of the graph runs from 0 (silence), through 2 (whisper zone) and 5 (the upper limit of partner-voice) to 10. Any noise in the 5 to 10 region is too loud (10 being House of Commons on a normal day!). The horizontal axis is divided into three to five minute sections. Every three to five minutes during the *on-task phase of the lesson* the teacher goes to the board and draws in the vertical line denoting the *level* of partner-voice at that point in the lesson (see illustration). Students are often unaware of how loud they sound when conversing and working during on-task time. This simple graph gives the students visual feedback every five minutes (or more often if necessary). I've heard, and seen, students (many times) nudging each other as I go to the board and give the "histogrammatic" feedback on the chart.

If the noise level – of students – creeps above the 5 mark (vertical scale) it can help to see if the class picks up the visual feedback cue and brings the level down by themselves. If they do, a visual scan of the room, with a non-verbal OK sign, indicates our encouragement. If the "working noise" is becoming too loud we go to the front of the classroom, cue the class to stop, and have a *brief* reminder about our partner-voices ... then ..., "Back to work class ... Thanks." This approach is an "establishment routine"; it is a means to an end, like the noise meter, the end being reasonable working voice levels and the enabling of a cooperative learning environment.

- Explain and discuss "partner-voices" with the class on the first day, or session.
- Explain visual cues (such as the graph) and the feedback cues.
- At the end of each class period give the class some descriptive feedback on how "we worked as a class group" across the on-task time period: " ... you kept your partner-voices well below 5 for most of the lesson (...) a couple of times you crept over 5, however you remembered when reminded. Thank you ... I appreciate your efforts. It helps everyone."
- As with any establishment routine it can be phased out as positive group behaviour generalises and "habituates".
- With particularly loud and kinaesthetically robust classes I've used a points system whereby the teacher grants points for students (as a group) when they have made the effort to keep their partner-voices below 5 (and awards more points if the level is below 4 or 3). If the class has "achieved" 20 points, five minutes or so before the bell, the teacher directs the class to "pack" up early, and students chat quietly until "bell time". A kind of group "celebration" (not a *reward*).

Giving assistance to students during the on-task phase of the lesson

The main point behind any cue, or routine, for giving students assistance *during on-task learning time* is the reasonable fairness, and distribution, of teacher assistance and support for many students over a short period of time. Teachers, of course, should be moving around the classroom during on-task learning time to offer support, feedback, micro-teach and give advice and encouragement.

- The teacher should explain – even discuss – how they can equitably support students requesting assistance during work/task time. The explanation will include the obvious point (humorously made) that a teacher is not an octopus.
- The teacher should discuss the importance of "checking set work yourself first – read through, ask yourself: 'What am I actually asked or required to do here and now with this learning activity?; where should I start?; how do I set the work out?'" These self-monitoring questions can be taught as part of a class discussion on positive learning habits.
- For set work procedures it can help to have a class poster with the basic reminders about drafting a piece of writing, page layout, and the writing process to check for punctuation and spelling (put a circle, in pencil, around the words you're not sure of ... ask a classmate ... use a dictionary – we still have dictionaries!), re-read *'in your head'* for *sense and meaning*.
- The teacher should also remind students that they can quietly check and discuss the work with their immediate classmate (not a classmate on the other side of the classroom, or a student in a row in front, or behind them). Table groups operate differently ("Check with three before you check with me ...").
- When the class group is working cohesively (several weeks into Term One) it can help to appoint classroom mentors (peer-mentors) who can assist their fellow students with conferencing about their classwork. Such students need to be held in positive regard by their class peers and possess natural social skills such as effective listening, communication and relational empathy (high "social intelligence").
- At primary-age level (even secondary level ...) it can help to have the key learning tasks for the day set out on a separate board, as a visual focus, so that students can rotate between tasks as they complete each appropriate phase or stage of a learning activity.

- At upper primary onwards it will help if students go on with other work *while they wait for teacher assistance or conferencing*. One way of visually focusing the teacher assistance process is to have a ***teacher help board*** where the students note down their name if they need to conference with the teacher. Of course before they note down their name they will need to have:

  ○ checked the set work requirement/task/activity themselves
  ○ checked with their classmate or working partner. If they note down their name they can – then – go on with other set work (or other options) *while* they wait for their teacher. This avoids having children just waiting with their hands up until the teacher gets around to them. Other options can include user-friendly worksheets; an ongoing project; read the class novel …

- Some teachers utilise a small coloured disc on each students' desk/table – one side green (I'm OK – don't need any direct help …) one side red (I need help please …).

The important point *in any routine* is that we have thought through why we are using *this particular* routine: how does it enable students and teachers to work more cooperatively? As always, it is worth discussing the use, viability and utility of one's classroom routines with faculty (or grade team) colleagues prior to our first meetings with our classes.

Lesson closure

It is important to plan ahead for lesson closure, particularly in the first few weeks with a new class. The teacher will need to discuss with the students basic routines, such as:

- packing up and straightening the furniture; chairs under the table (or *on* the table at the end of the last class period of the day)
- picking up any residual litter and putting it in the litter bin on the way out
- leaving the classroom in a considerate/orderly fashion (this may need to involve dismissing the class, row by row, or table group by table group).

It is also important to finish the lesson, or activity, positively (even if it has not been the best lesson in the world). Aim for a calm, positive closure. At secondary level we add the reminder that, "Another class is coming in after us, *let's do them a basic favour*. Chairs under …; litter in the bin …; we leave quietly, row by row (teacher nominates the rows. We can change the row nomination each lesson …). Thanks …". At the end of the day we say something like, "Let's do the cleaner a favour, thanks … Chairs on tables … Check for any litter …."

Homework cues are best written up on the board or printed reminders handed out. Auditory reminders about important topics are miscued by many students in the last few minutes of a lesson as most students are just "waiting for the bell". In fact some students will already have packed up well before the bell! It will be important to speak to such students (one-to-one) and encourage them to recheck their work, or read the class novel, or go on with a related activity.

It may be important to remind the class – respectfully – that the bell is a reminder to both the class and the teacher that *this* lesson has ended; it is the teacher's responsibility to dismiss the class.

> **NB**   Don Campbell (2000) notes two contrasting teachers engaging in pack-up routines in their early years classrooms. One teacher – a few minutes before lunch – sings some lines to his class, "Let's put away our pencils", the class sings back the words as they pack up. "Let's put away our work", the students musically echo back the lines … "Let's line up at the door." It does not take long. The children enjoy the game. The teacher next door is heard – shouting – "I told you 15 minutes ago to pack up … – Why has it taken so long?"
>
>   "Such teachers are", says Campbell, "using rhythm and tone to connect with their children …" (2000: 148). That rhythm, tone, kinaesthetic "musicality" affect motivation and emotion in a positive way and they make "routine" a more enjoyable activity.

Caveat: There are some occasions when a *brief* "stay-back" of the class may be warranted.

A quarter or more of the class make a bee-line for the door on Day One (Lesson One) as soon as the bell goes. The other 70 per cent or so (of the class) hold back. The teacher calls the several students who had raced to the door back inside (she does this quickly, firmly, confidently, "hopefully").

"Stop (…). Back inside, fellas (…), back inside."

If she knows their names she will use them (a small but crucial point).

"Craig, Bilal, Nazim, Dean (…) back inside (…) now (…), thanks."

They whinge; naturally. "Gees – it's recess, come on!"

"I know it's recess," she partially agrees. She redirects: "Back inside fellas (…), won't keep you long."

Most students come back (certainly Day One, Session One, the students are generally more likely to "comply" if the teacher is confident, decisive, respectful … They come back in (grumbling and muttering). I've been in classes where some students (at this point) flop in their seats sulking and muttering some − residually − swearing ("Sh−t what kind of class is this!") − yes, I know it's pathetic, but it does happen with *some* students ... even where we've been positive and respectful.

She stands at the front of the class, scans the group, tactically ignores the whispering whingers who are sulking, and says, "When you're all settled, I'll explain (...)"

They quieten − they want to go, obviously. She is brief and clear:

"This is not a detention folks. *It's not even a minute past the bell.* In a minute you're out of here." She smiles. "This is a class reminder. In *our* class we leave the place tidy, straighten the tables, chairs under the tables, litter off the floor. As I said earlier (...), let's do the next class a favour. Let's try it again. Thanks to all those who did make the effort when the bell went ... So; let's all try it again. Row by row ... Thanks."

This time when the class leaves they are more subdued, more focused. This approach is preferable to saying, "Right!! If you're all going to waste my time, I'll waste your time!!" (and making the *whole* class suffer a lunchtime detention).

She stands at the door saying a brief goodbye as the students leave. It has only taken a couple of minutes but she has re-established the class routine she had discussed earlier about a "thoughtful class exit".

If something very valuable has gone missing (lost, mislaid or stolen) the teacher will (where possible) finish the lesson earlier and have a class discussion about the missing item.

"I don't know if someone has taken item X by mistake, or accidentally put it in their bag, but item X has gone missing. It is very important to _____ [the person concerned], as I'm sure you can understand. I'll stand outside this classroom for three minutes and I expect the item to be back on my desk, no questions asked. I'll *then* dismiss the class."

Prior to this mini "class meeting" the teacher might send for a senior colleague to give some immediate assistance in supporting the teacher in addressing the class and finding the item. Situations like these are always tricky, especially when time is of the essence. Senior colleague support should always be involved if the item is important and is not returned.

Before you leave your working area

1. Put all materials away (lids on felt-tip pens, pencils in containers, work away).
2. Tidy your own work space; help others out too.
3. Chairs under tables. (ON tables at end of day.)
4. Litter in bin. Check.

THANKS! Mr Rogers

Reflection

The establishment phase of the year is crucial to the positive, working, relationship of teacher and students alike. It is important to remember that we are working with a natural student readiness; students expect us to clarify routines, rules, procedures. We need to positively engage and focus that readiness and expectation (p. 36f).

- How did you communicate the rights, rules, responsibilities, routines to your class(es)? Are they published? How? Are they positively construed?
- How did you establish your class(es): individually or within a shared, team, approach?

- Do the rules reflect core rights? How? (p. 41f)
- If you're a secondary teacher, what role does the tutor/form teacher play in communicating shared expectations across year groups? (See Figure 2.2.)
- As a primary colleague, how does the concept of a common, published, classroom agreement fit with school-wide school practice (p. 39f, 46f)?
- How did you plan for your first meetings with your students, particularly being aware of typical distracting behaviours in more attentionally demanding students (pp. 37f, 55f)?
- How aware are you of how you cue a whole class for focus, attention and engagement? Are you aware of communicating calmness? How?
- How have you engaged behaviour clarity (for example, levels of volume in on-task time; how to get teacher assistance) with your students? Are the essential routines for behaviour and learning expressed across a grade/year level? How? How are such expectations fine-tuned across faculties at secondary level (or grade teams)?
- Do you have a *least-to-most intrusive framework* for intervening in distracting/disruptive behaviour? How was the framework developed? Are there any – whole-school – common practices/skills that inform your "personal discipline plan"? How do the skills (in this chapter) inform/contrast with your daily practice? These skills are more fully developed in Chapters 3 and 4.

Notes

1   A "mind-map" is a visual representation of a core idea, issue, question or concept with its supporting and subsidiary ideas, concepts or questions. It can give focus and direction and help to hold several ideas or concepts "'together".

2   *Punch* was a popular English satirical magazine. In fact the earliest editions were called the magazine the London Charivari (in the mid-19th century).

3   Some early years teachers affect a babyish voice when working with small children. ("Oh!! You're sitting SO NICELY!!" "Are we all going to be *good* boys and girls today?") This is unnecessary. Obviously we need to modify concepts in our language use, but we don't need to adopt the kind of tone or manner that the actress Joyce Grenfell portrayed so skilfully in some of her comic monologues about teachers.

 Visit **https://study.sagepub.com/rogers4e** for additional resources to help you better manage classroom behaviour. You'll also be able to hear from Bill himself as he talks you through common behaviour management scenarios.

3

The language of behaviour management and discipline

No formulas!

This chapter will address the way we communicate, within our behaviour leadership, across a range of distracting and disruptive behaviours, from calling out and talking while the teacher is talking through to confronting argumentative and challenging behaviours.

The language of management, and of discipline, operates in a dynamic relationship. Developing skill in this area does not simply involve our choice of words, phrases or sentences. If it is our *intention* to discipline with respect and confidence, that intention needs to come *through* the language. Only then will our language be relationally dynamic in a respectful and positive way.

Being assertive (for example), when it is called for, requires some skill in communication and control over one's non-verbal behaviour, but it is the *intention to assert* one's needs or rights, or to protect someone else's needs, feelings and rights, that really signals assertive behaviour. Assertive behaviour also needs to be context-appropriate. Assertion often means we communicate with a firm, resolute, unambiguous tone of voice, and manner, matched by confident (non-aggressive) body language. In this sense the *skill* of assertion is "conscious" and not simply the outcome of reactive feelings; respect and assertion are not mutually exclusive concepts (see p. 57f, 257f).

Two students were rearranging the furniture as I was seeking to establish whole-class attention and focus in a Year 9 English class. It was my first meeting with this class. They already had a "reputation". I walked across to the students and asked them their names.

"What?" was the sulky reply. "What is your name please?" I asked again, pleasantly and indicating no threat. I was just initiating a "name check". One of the girls leaned back in her chair – sighed – and said, "Crystal!" (a sharp, very sulky tone in her voice) and tut-tutted loudly as if I'd asked her to do some great, onerous, task.

I said in a relaxed, but decisive, tone, "Crystal (...) I'm not speaking to you in a disrespectful tone of voice and I don't expect you to speak disrespectfully to me either." I then added, "You're moving the furniture and I'm ready to start the class. I want you to leave the furniture as it was and be ready for teaching time. Thank you."

She sighed (less demonstrably now) and I walked to the front of the classroom to cue for whole-class attention and focus (and to give them take-up time, p. 98). If she had refused to cooperate with the direction about the furniture (it happens), I would have made the deferred consequences clear and left the "consequential choice" with the student.

Although this class had a "reputation" there were many cooperative and support-ive students (a good 70 per cent). In working with this class (as mentor-teacher) I believed the whole class could – and would – regain that shared sense of purpose, even enjoyment, in working together. We revisited core routines – together – and my colleague and I sought to balance positive behaviour leadership and encour-agement in each session. We followed up one-to-one with the more attentionally demanding students (like Crystal) (p. 122f).

The students started to regain that sense of purpose in their learning behaviour; we particularly focused on the need for cooperative behaviours (p. 302).

Assertion is not about winning: it's about establishing and affirming fair rights and needs.

I was discussing the issue of corrective language (discipline) with a group of teachers. We explored the issue of positive language and someone raised the ques-tion "But that language isn't *me*". We were discussing reflective rephrasing of, for example, negatives: "When … then …" rather than "*No* you *can't* … because …," or "Hands up for questions …" rather than "*Don't* call out …." I think what my colleague meant (when she said "that language isn't *me*") was, "Should we have to *think* about what we say when we discipline?" Does "being *me*" simply mean I say the first thing that comes into my head? And should it really matter what I say when I use discipline language?

I believe we have a responsibility, as professionals, to think about the way we typically, *characteristically*, communicate in management and discipline contexts *and why*. It can even help to plan a basic repertoire of language that can enable us to discipline and manage more effectively, respectfully, and (hopefully) less stressfully.

The language framework developed in this section is not formulaic; it is meant to give some conscious focus, and some utility, about management and discipline language when developing a personal discipline framework. It is pointless (for example) to use a potentially positive sentence – "Michael (...), Dean (...), you're talking; you need to be facing this way and listening, thanks" – if we say these *words* in a mean-spirited, sharp, petty, pleading or whining tone of voice.

Language is obviously dynamic and context-related. It is, however, the essential basis for positive, workable, relationships. Language is what makes us *uniquely* human. When we use language in a corrective context (discipline) we need to be ever more acutely aware of why we choose certain forms of language expression over others. The *skills* of corrective language that are developed in this chapter arise from, and operate within, essential aims and principles of behaviour leadership.

The aims of discipline and behaviour management: within our behaviour leadership

Every time we speak to a student (or several students or a group) in *any* context where their behaviour is distracting or disrupting others, where such behaviour is infringing on others' rights, we aim to:

- engage *behaviour awareness*
- to engage the students towards *behaviour ownership*
- emphasise (even in discipline transactions in a busy lesson) awareness of *others' rights to feel safe* here; *to learn without undue distraction or disruption; to give and expect respect and fairness* in our relationships with others
- seek to build *workable relationships* and a *cooperative teaching/learning environment*.

Discipline – behaviour management – is never an end in itself. Its broad aim is to enable the student to be aware of and own their behaviour with respect to others' rights. Overall, we discipline to enable our meta-goal of a cooperative teaching and learning environment. These *aims* (above) sound laudable – are they achievable? Well, without fundamental aims (in any significant role or enterprise) we lose *focus and direction*.

Rashid and Adil (in one of my Year 8 classes recently) were playing with a "minion" toy (from the film *Despicable Me*) and a loud water bottle. It was whole-class teaching time – the first few minutes (I was "settling" the class ... (p. 58f, 70f)). A *brief cue* to the rest of the class, who are basically beginning to settle (in those first critical minutes of class entry) – after all they too have to put up with this distraction to whole-class teaching and learning time.

We briefly cue the class, "Excuse me class ...". We – then – address the two distracting students (from the front of the classroom): "Rashid (...) Adil (...) you're fiddling with that toy and water bottle; it's really distracting." This *descriptive* cue seeks to raise their *behaviour awareness* (our aim). They grinned. Sometimes (for "low-level" distraction) raising awareness – by briefly "describing" the student's distracting behaviour – is enough. Sometimes we need to add a brief, *simple direction* or rule reminder. Such a direction focuses on the behaviour we – fairly – expect to see, that is: "Leave the water bottle and toy and eyes and ears this way. Thanks." We *direct to the behaviour we expect to see* rather than the negative direction, "Don't be silly with that toy ...". Our tone is positive, expectant; decisive but respectful.

I took my eyes off them – as it were – to give them take-up time and *refocused back to the whole class* and resumed the flow of whole-class teaching and learning time.

When – in the same class – Nathan called out several times (during our class discussion) I said, "Nathan (...) you're calling out." The brief *descriptive* "part" followed by a rule reminder, "Remember our class rule ... fair go for all" or, "Hands up, thanks, without calling out (or clicking fingers) – fair go for all". This directing/reminding focus is – briefly – drawing attention to "respect for others' rights" (our aim) (see poster Appendix A).

When Renee made a smart alec comment during discussion, while another student was trying to make a point, I turned to the student and said, "Renee (...) if you want to disagree – disagree respectfully", then turned my attention back to Elise's contribution to the class discussion. Renee sat back in her seat and sulked (behaviour I *tactically* ignored). Here, our aim is to emphasise the *right to learn* without put-downs or cheap shots, and to emphasise – to all – the cooperation we need to exercise here (see Appendix A).

We seek, then, to utilise language that will seek to realise those aims (p. 93). All the core skills noted later – particularly the language skills – seek to engage students within those aims.

A discipline "transaction" is a social transaction

Whenever we discipline a student in the busy ebb and flow of a classroom we are not merely addressing *that* student; it is also a *social transaction*. All students hear – and see us – address the distracting/disruptive student(s). Within that peer audience all students make an assessment about our behaviour leadership; how fair, reasonable we are in our discipline and whether we can keep "control" (p. 29f, 73f).

Key principles of the language of management and discipline

1. Keep the corrective interaction "*least-intrusive*" wherever possible. For example, we can manage such behaviours and issues as calling out; lateness; students overly leaning back on their chairs; uniform "misdemeanours" and students without equipment, with "low" intrusion discipline (a brief non-verbal cue, an incidental *descriptive* direction, a rule reminder). By keeping most correction "low" in degree of "intrusion" we can often enable a positive tone to classroom life so that when we need to be *more* intrusive (as context may demand) the degree of intervention will be seen to be significant in relative terms of moral/behavioural "weight". These are times, of course, when our first response to a student's behaviour needs to be assertively intrusive, but that is the exception (reserved for harassing language, unsafe, dangerous, hostile or aggressive student behaviour).

2. Avoid *unnecessary* confrontation. This includes embarrassment, *any* sarcasm (tempting as that may be), any sense of intentional hostility or threatening communication. A core aspect of our leadership includes *the ability to communicate calmness* when addressing the group or an individual student. Such "calmness" is not inconsistent with the need to be firm – even assertive – at times. Our "calmness" lies in our ability to manage our own behaviour as we – in turn – seek to lead others. That calmness also includes a conscious sense of creating a calm *presence*: our body language, how we move around the classroom space and how we characteristically communicate (p. 60f). Humour: repartee, the *bon mot*, the witty Pythonesque turn of phrase (as distinct from sarcasm, "cheap shots", so-called humorous put-downs) can defuse and reframe tension and lift the spirits of teacher and student alike. Sarcasm *invokes* hostility and resentment – why wouldn't it?

3. Keep a respectful, positive tone of voice wherever possible.

4. Keep the corrective language itself positive where possible:

   - "*when – then*" is more invitational than "no, you can't, *because* …"
   - avoid *overuse* of "shouldn't", "mustn't", "can't", "won't" and interrogatives such as "why?" or "are you?" (see, p. 58f, 72).
   - avoid pointing fingers, or gesticulating, when making a corrective or assertive point – use an "open hand" when emphasising or asserting.
   - be brief, where possible (avoid *long* directions or reminders about behaviour).

5. Re-establish working relationships with the student as quickly and reasonably as possible. Even a brief return to a student's desk to ask how their work is

going is often enough (if we have had to discipline them earlier in the lesson). A pleasant manner and a brief encouraging word will *always* help.

6. If we need to communicate appropriate frustration – even anger – we do so assertively rather than aggressively (see particularly Chapter 7):

    *   keep the assertive statement brief. "I" statements can help here. "I don't make comments about your body (or clothing ... or ...). I don't expect you to make comments about mine." This to an adolescent who had made a so-called "jokey" comment to a young female teacher about her body ... We should never pretend such comments are OK, acceptable ever.
    *   If the students protests "C'mon! I was *just* joking. OK?!" (as he leans back – big man – in his chair, seeking to play to the "theatre of his peers"), the teacher replies, "It's not a joke to me. I expect it to stop now." She then refocuses to whole-class teaching/learning.
    *   If a student continues to pester she will stop the flow of teaching and decisively, calmly, make the consequences clear to him either to stay and work by our fair rules or to leave for time-out.
    *   focus on the "primary behaviour or issue" avoid over-servicing "secondary behaviours" (p. 12f).
    *   de-escalate any residual tension and enable the student(s), wherever possible, to regain composure and focus.

I have worked with teachers who create unnecessary tension and confrontation by their overly vigilant tone, manner and language.

A teacher has just explained the rule for asking questions and a little later a student calls out. The teacher "says", "is that using the rule, *is it?!*" Does the teacher really want an answer? "Didn't I just say to you *all* to put you're hands up *without* calling out? Didn't I?!" Pointless questions. Some teachers add innuendo or sarcasm: "Are you deaf or what…?"; "Don't they teach you manners at home?" Such *characteristic* teacher behaviour only creates palpable tension in a room; it creates (in some students) anxious *and resentful* learners. It is unprofessional, disrespectful and unnecessary. In other students it creates antagonism – breeding uncooperative, even rebellious, attitudes and behaviours even in those students who are – normally – responsible and cooperative. If we need to communicate annoyance, or even anger (where necessary and appropriate), we can do so in a professional manner, consistent with our feelings and focused on the behaviour (without "attacking" the student(s) (Chapter 7).

7. Follow up with student(s) one-to-one on issues that matter *beyond* the classroom context. This emphasises that the teacher cares enough to make clear the issue of concern with the student and to offer support to improve things.

A framework for management and discipline language skills

These skills are detailed in case examples used throughout this book. They are set out here – in *summary* form – to highlight the "least-to-most intrusive ..." nature of management and discipline language. These skills are illustrated, developed, explored within each case example and case study throughout the text.

Tactical ignoring

The teacher selectively attends to the student when on task, *tactically* ignoring particular aspects of "secondary behaviour" – the indulgent sigh, whine or moan, the tut-tutting, the raised eyes, the averted eyes, the overly drawn frown ... (p. 12f). *Tactical* ignoring is a context-dependent skill. We should *never* ignore any repeatedly disruptive behaviour, safety issues or harassment behaviours. It is combined with *selective* attention as (for example) when we acknowledge a student *when* they have got their hand up – without calling out.

Tactical pausing (...)

The teacher briefly pauses in a spoken direction or reminder (...) to emphasise – and convey – attention, and focus to the students they are addressing (p. xxi).

Non-verbal cueing

The teacher communicates with a non-verbal cue that carries a clear (unspoken) message, reminder, or direction. If a student is leaning back – heavily – in their chair, the teacher uses a non-verbal cue where they extend thumb and three fingers in a downward motion, as if to say, "... four on the floor thanks." A beckoning hand, cupped, ... this to a student who needs to bring their seat in to their table ... To a primary student "aimlessly" wandering the classroom during on-task learning time ... the teacher calls his name (...) and non-verbally cups her right hand into the left indicating "back in your seat". The relaxed teacher smile helps. As the student gives a returned frown and a compressed pout (as he slowly goes back to his seat) the teacher tactically ignores this "secondary behaviour" and "gives" him take-up time.

   Even the slight shake of the head, as we give a direct – and brief – eye contact to a student can cue a student's behaviour awareness. This kind of non-verbal cue, though, depends on the teacher having a good working relationship with their class.

Again – the positive tone and manner will carry the teacher's *intent*.

Incidental language (descriptive cueing)

The teacher directs or reminds the student (or group) without directly *telling* them: for example, "There's some litter on the floor and the bell is going to go soon …" (that is, "you know that I know that I'm encouraging you to pick it up" by *describing* what I've just seen). In this approach the teacher describes behaviour reality and allows the student to process the "obvious" expectation: for example, "This is quiet reading time" to students who are whispering to each other. Sometimes it will be appropriate to combine the "descriptive cue" with a *behavioural direction*. For example: "This is quiet reading time now [the incidental *descriptive* comment]. Read quietly inside your heads. Thanks" (the *behavioural direction*: teacher taps own head). This approach is very effective from middle primary level onwards.

Take-up time

This refers to the teacher refocusing eye contact and proximity *after* having given a non-verbal cue, a direction or reminder. It most commonly involves the teacher "moving away" after having given a direction or rule reminder. During whole-class teaching time it means the teacher briefly cueing the class, "Excuse me everyone …", and then focusing on the student(s) who are distracting/disruptive with a descriptive cue, direction on rule reminder. *Then* the teacher turns her attention back to the whole class to convey to the distracting students that she *believes* and *expects* they will comply. It invites and encourages (even "allows") the student to cooperate without the teacher standing "over them" as it were.

Behavioural direction

The teacher directs a group – or individual – by referring directly to the expected or required behaviour: for example, "Jason (…), Dean (…), facing this way, thanks". Behavioural directions are appropriate for communicating the *required/expected* behaviour, as when students are talking while the teacher is talking and the students need to be facing the front and listening. When giving any behavioural direction we:

- focus on the expected, required, necessary behaviour.
- use verbs/participles (rather than negative clauses): for example, "*Facing* this way and *listening* …" rather than "Don't talk while I'm talking please", which only tells the student what we *don't* want them to do. "Please" here is unnecessary; it's not a *request*, but a direction. Bilal, Nazim and Shayne were being silly and distracting, playing with the cords on the window blinds in one of my recent Year 8 classes (it was whole-class teaching and learning time). A brief cue to the class, as a whole, "Excuse me class …", cueing a brief pause to address the distracting behaviour of the students: … "Bilal (…) Nazim (…) and Shayne (…). You're fiddling with the blinds, it's really distracting." The *descriptive* cue *raising behaviour awareness*. "Leave the blinds, thanks, and facing this way." The behavioural direction. They grinned, raised their eyes; a big sigh from Bilal … I – then – focused back to the class – as a whole – "Thanks …" and then resumed the lesson.
- In the direction "*leave* (the blinds) and *face* … (the front of the classroom …)" we're focusing on the behaviour we fairly, reasonably, expect to see, rather than "Don't fiddle with the blinds …," which only tells them what we don't want them to do. By de-engaging eye contact and refocusing to the class we are also giving *expectant* take-up time to the three boys.
- Finish with "thanks", or "now" if the student(s) vacillates and prompt attention is necessary.
- Keep the direction, or instruction, brief (where possible): "Michael (…), Troy (…), sitting up and hands in laps and facing this way. Thank you – now." This to two grade one boys half rolling on the mat …). In this example, "now" is said firmly and respectfully, not sharply.

Rule reminder

The teacher briefly reminds the class group, or individual(s), of what the rule is: "We have a rule for asking questions" (a *descriptive* reminder); "Remember our rule for safe scissors …". The teacher does not need to "spell out" the rule *each time*. Rule reminders can also be expressed as a question: "What's our rule for …?" This raises the student's awareness and responsibility. If they do not answer we will remind – clearly and briefly. "Remember to …" is a more positive verbal focus than "Don't forget …". We would not – normally – use this question "form" in discipline interventions in whole-class teaching time (we would during on-task learning time or in non-class settings …).

Prefacing

The teacher gives a positive greeting and focuses on a positive issue *before* engaging discipline (wherever possible). For example, the teacher sees students being a bit silly at their table. He has a chat about the painting they are working on. As he turns to leave he adds, quietly, yet firmly (as he scans the table group), "Remember to use the paints thoughtfully". This approach is effective when one has a positive working relationship with the class. It sets the discipline within a *relational focus*.

Two students (Year 9) were texting – surreptitiously – during on-task learning time. I was mentoring in this class recently. I walked over and checked I'd got their names right, "Maddie?"

(...) Taylor? (...)." It was my first lesson with this class. They looked up, frowned, muttered a sulky, "Yes." They knew, I knew, they knew ...

I asked them how their work was going. They muttered – again sulkily – "It's OK ..." They wanted me (as the second teacher in the room) to go away, effectively saying, "Leave us to enjoy our social time and we'll be no trouble ...." It looked as if they had done no work. I had a brief chat about the work; I wanted to be task-focused *first* (prefacing) before addressing the phones (the "discipline" issue). I did a little bit of micro-teaching to task and added – quietly – "The phones; the school rule is clear, they need to be off and in your bag or on your teacher's table until the end of the lesson" (a directed choice, within the known school rule). Maddie looked up, "Paula (her teacher) doesn't mind sometimes!" I refuse to argue, "negotiate", or "reason", or cajole about a fair, sensible, school-wide rule. I made no reference to Paula (her current teacher); I repeated the directed choice " ... off and in your bags Thanks," and walked away (take-up time). I heard them whingingly mutter something. I tactically ignored this. I went back later to check and encourage them in their work. They had "learned" which teacher to "manipulate"; it happens in many classes in many schools.

If they had refused to put their phones off and away, I would have made the *deferred* consequences clear (p. 102f, 190f). The important key here is to communicate the *directed* choice calmly, respectfully, and quietly (it's on-task learning time – we don't need to "megaphone" it, or use unnecessary confrontation).

Such "prefacing" is obviously more effective in the *on-task phase of the lesson* (and in non-class settings). I have also found it helpful, sometimes, to direct a student aside (from his immediate peers) to then have a *brief* disciplinary chat. The distraction, early enough, may stop a subsequent disruptive pattern of behaviour. Prefacing should also be normative in managing behaviour in non-classroom settings (corridor, lunch supervision, playground ...). The most basic "prefacing" is to greet and ask a student's name and "How's the work going?", "Need a hand?", "Where are you up to ... making sense?"

Distraction/diversion

The example in "Prefacing" (above) is a typical "distraction"/"diversion" (as well as a social courtesy).

The teacher notices that a student is folding a worksheet during the whole-class teaching phase of the lesson, and says, "Damien (…), the worksheet will be easier to read unfolded. You'll need it later". Calm, *not* sarcastic (even a touch of humour). The teacher then gives take-up time.

One of my colleagues notes some typical distractions/diversions she uses in her early years classes. They can prevent a scenario from getting out of hand by not over-focusing on the negative behaviour, but rather redirecting to the positive.

"I can see that most of you want to help in getting the plasticine. You remember I did say that we need one helper. What do you think we should do?" Then I thank the children for waiting and being patient. Or before saying that, I could say, "Tom has his hand up and he is also sitting quietly with his legs crossed. Tom would you like to get the plasticine?"

Ryan is playing with a pencil. "Ryan, can I see your picture please? What would you like to tell me about your picture?"

Mary is crying for her mother. "Mary, I have a picture for you to colour in and take home to show your mother. What colour are you going to use for the bow?"

Joshua is wandering around the room. "Joshua when you finish counting with the blocks would you like to paint the big picture of Humpty Dumpty?" (*When* is a useful word; it carries an element of "choice".)

Joshua throws the tambourine into the box after the teacher explains to put it away carefully.

"Joshua what did you do?" (We don't ask why the student did what they did …)

"I threw the tambourine in the box."

"What were you supposed to do? Show me the way you were meant to do it. Why do you think we need to be more careful?" If the student doesn't say what they did, then I'll remind them how to do the fair/right thing.

Direct questions

The teacher uses a direct form of question rather than an "open" form: for example, "what", "when", "how" or "where" rather than "why" or "are you".

"What are you doing?" rather than, "Are you being silly with the paints …?" or, "Why are you being silly …?"

"What should you be doing?" or "What is our rule for …?"

"How are you supposed to …?"

These sorts of questions direct students' behaviour awareness (p. 93) and to to their responsibility rather than asking for reasons. Direct questions focus on a student responding to their *present* responsibility rather than looking for reasons *why* they are not behaving considerately or responsibly at this point.

"We need you to do your work in a way that doesn't create a problem for … How are you going to do that …?" to a Year 10 student engaged in time wasting and noisy off-task behaviour.

I asked a Year 8 student what she was doing. I had noticed her doing some maths homework instead of the set classwork. She had tried to "hide" the Maths work as I came over to her table …

"Jacinta (…), hello (…) what are you doing …?" I looked at the half-hidden Maths work.

She said, "Nothing …" and covered her work.

I gave some brief, quiet, feedback, "Actually it looks like you're doing … Is it your maths homework? What are you supposed to be doing at the moment?" (the direct question).

She answered quickly, "This shit … I mean, sorry, this sheet …". We both grinned. "Sounds like you know what to do …". I walked off (take-up time). I came back later to check, and encourage her, now she was back on task.

Directed "choices"

A "choice" is given by the teacher within the known rules or routine: "Yes you can work on the drawing when you've finished the diary writing" ("when … then"; "after … then"). In this sense, the "choice" is expressed as a *conditional* direction: "We'll organise a toilet break when I've finished this part of the lesson". All "choices" given to a student are, in a sense, conditional. They refer back (one way or another) to the rights and rules and responsibilities. See the example of phones (in class) earlier … (p. 100; see also p.16f).

"Choice"/deferred consequences

I have put the word choice in inverted commas to indicate that no choices are *free* choices as such; they are choices *directed within the rights, rules, responsibility* dynamic. In this case the teacher makes the consequences of *continued* distracting/ disruptive behaviour clear within a consequential "choice": "If you cannot work quietly here … I'll have to ask you to work separately …" (to two repeatedly noisy students).

"If you choose not to put the iPod (or phone, or nail varnish, or comic) away I'll have to ask you to stay back after class [or …] to discuss your behaviour" (p. 122f).

This assumes that, earlier, the teacher would have reminded the student about the rule and (if necessary) given the student a directed choice to "… put the iPod in his bag or on the teacher's desk".

The language of "choice" is not conveyed in any sense of threat or win/lose. We clarify the *deferred* consequence and give take-up time. This is in preference to forcing the student to hand the phone over or snatching a toy, iPod or phone … Witness the ludicrous situation of a teacher walking over to a student to simply hand it over. "Right, give me that phone!" The student says, "I'll put it away alright?!" "I *said* give it to me!" "No way," says the student, "It's *my* phone." "Right, if you're not going to obey school rules you can get out of my classroom." (It's *our* class not merely *my* class.) The student storms out – making a scene. The teacher believes he has to be tough; he's "won" … Even if the school has a confiscation policy we do not simply *snatch* the "object" – we extend the hand as we clarify the rule. If the student refuses to cooperate we leave the *deferred* consequences to their "choice", responsibility and accountability. It is not about "winning"; it is about *leading* and (later) carrying through the "certainty" of the consequence away from peer audience (p. 179f).

"Blocking", partial agreement, refocusing

"Blocking" is a communication approach whereby a teacher "blocks out" a student's procrastinating argument by not entering into the student's prevarication or attempt to argue …

A teacher directs two students to face the front and listen (during whole-class teaching time). They whinge, "We're not the only ones talking …". The teacher blocks their avoidance whinging by gesturing with an open hand, palm towards the student(s) (this gesture is not forcefully overdone; it is a relaxed – but obvious – cue …). She then *repeats* the direction. *In effect* she is saying, "I'm not interested in *why* you were talking, or who else was talking. Hear the direction and face the front and listen." In this, she is *redirecting* the students to the main issue (at *this* point in the lesson) and she also avoids over-servicing their "secondary behaviour" (the grumpy frown, the sigh …). It is normally helpful, having "blocked" the procrastination, to give the students take-up time and reclaim whole-class attention (p. 98).

There are occasions when students whine and whinge, for example when infants try to explain "who took whose toy". The teacher firmly – kindly but firmly – blocks: "Michael (…), Troy (…). Stop" (hand gesture). "I'll listen when you use reasonable voices." It can help to then tune in to how they are feeling ("I know you're feeling a bit upset …") and then *refocus*: "What is our rule for …?," or "How can we sort this out so that …?," "What should you be doing now …?"

Partial agreement

The teacher deals with the student's procrastination or avoidance by *partially* agreeing with the student (where appropriate) and refocusing back to the rule or required task. This is particularly helpful with adolescents.

A teacher reminds a student (who is chewing gum) of the rule. The student challenges by saying, "But Mr Scroggin lets us chew gum in his class" (a very common whinge …), "Other teachers let us dance on the tables …!.

Instead of arguing, the teacher *partially* agrees, "Even if he does". The teacher *then* redirects, "In our class the rule is clear. (There should be no sarcastic reference to what other teachers do or don't do.) The bin is over there; thanks" (the incidental direction). At this point it is often helpful to give the student some take-up time.

> **NB**   "I don't care if …" is not the same as "*Even if …*".

Assertive comment/direction/command

There are degrees of assertion in one's language and voice. Fundamentally, however, whenever we *assert* we are making our rights (or others' rights) clear, in a decisive, firm, non-aggressive way: "That language is *unacceptable* here. We have a rule for respect. I expect you to use it". (This to a student who has been stridently disrespectful in tone/manner …) *Firm* – non-aggressive – eye contact, a *clear, calm voice* and *directed, focused, language* are at the heart of assertion. Our confident "calmness" will often affect the other person's calmness – *and the peer audience* – who naturally feel the ambient tension (p. 60f).

Sexist or racist comments or put-downs should be dealt with assertively, unambiguously, and then followed up one-to-one with the student (later after class time) away from the peer audience. It may be helpful to ask a senior colleague to sit in during such follow-up (p. 122f).

Disrespect and discourteousness

Overt – and overly – disrespectful and discourteous behaviour should be addressed briefly, clearly, decisively and calmly. It is our calm assertion that will carry intent and just concern, not just to the student but the audience of peers (they need to hear our values expressed).

To younger children: "Shae (always use the student's name where possible) I'm not speaking in a mean, or nasty voice … We don't use nasty voices here." Use adjectives that are likely to connect. With older students – again – a brief, clear "I" statement: "I don't speak disrespectfully to you, I do not expect you to speak disrespectfully to me" (this, of course, presumes truthfulness about *how* we do *normally* speak to our students …) or "That's disrespectful; we do not expect that here." Then redirect the student to the appropriate behaviour *now*. The redirection is often a positive rule reminder.

We will need to be behaviour-specific at times: "I don't make comments about your body (clothing, sexuality, race …) I don't expect you to …" (see also, p. 11).

- It is not a discussion, it is an assertive statement.
- Remember there's always the peer audience; our *calm* assertion will garner their support.
- Make the assertive point – briefly – and redirect the student to the appropriate behaviour/task *at this point*.
- Allow take-up time.
- If they continue to evidence overt disrespect, make the consequences clear, if necessary time-out … .

This isn't easy. But we are professionals. Assertion enables our professional skill to *decisively* emphasise rights and expectations, without getting into a heated argument or slanging match. If the student argues, we will need to block and refocus. In effect *reassert*, and – if necessary – cue time-out provision if the student persists (p. 103f).

Commands

When giving commands, it is advisable to keep them short. Establish direct eye contact: "Michael (…)!" The first word should be said firmly, even "sharply", at times, and contextually louder – to gain *attention*. "*Michael* (…)," bring the level of the voice *down* as eye contact is established, and cue the command in a firm, decisive, assertive voice: "get down off the table – *now*." "Jayden (…) put those scissors down *now*." This to an infant student who had been stabbing his work with his scissors (causing anxiety in his table group). We do not use the word "please"; it's not a request. In a fight situation (most typically in corridors or playgrounds), if the names of children aren't known, use the loud – generic attentional – command, "Oi (…)!, Oi (…)!" – then (when there's some attentional eye contact) a firm assertive voice, "Move away (…) *now*." Use non-verbal cues to indicate that the students should separate. Direct the audience of peers away and *immediately* send for adult assistance. It is preferable to give commands in those situations where unambiguous – *immediate* – stopping of disruptive behaviour is warranted. In some command situations (where there is danger of harm ...) we would not use a "sharp" voice but we will always use a decisive, clear and calm voice (p. 66f). We also need to be able to back up our commands if a student refuses to obey. Our back-up should consist of a school-wide time-out plan, involving adult support, that can be invoked as quickly as possible in a crisis anywhere in the school.

Obviously, we cannot plan for every contingency. These key language skills are suggestions of the sorts of things one can say in typical management and discipline contexts. The language "forms" can serve as *aides-mémoires* to give some prepared focus. These key principles and skills are the underlying framework for the way we communicate and relate to students in our teaching and management to enable that *least-to-most* principle (p. 95f).

> **NB**   Finding one's "own voice" in behaviour leadership is important. Being more conscious of how we express ourselves, how we communicate, is essential to our leadership role. The language cues here, are based in well-established psychological theory and practice as applied to discipline/behaviour management and social-learning settings. By utilising these skills as a "working template" they can enable, inform and strengthen your "own voice" as teacher-leader. I know I've mentioned this several times in this text: our tone, manner, intent is as powerful – perhaps more powerful – in communication than the words *we* use. We seek to discipline *relationally*; our students soon pick up the difference.

Settling the class outside the classroom (see also p. 37f, 55f)

As I approach 8D, in the corridor, I scan the students arriving. Some have US-style "baseball" caps on; some wear sunglasses; a few are still eating; a couple of students towards the back have mobile phones in their hands; a couple of students are listening to iPods; a couple of boys are "testosteronically bonding" (a mild punch, a push in the rear, a "friendly" strangle ...) ...

I've worked with colleagues who make no *conscious* management of this kind of corridor restlessness. Opening the classroom door they let the students in with no focused distinction made between the outside (playground) culture and the inside (teaching/learning) culture (p. 79). Some teachers don't even greet the students as they form or line up outside a classroom. There are sensible reasons for corridor settling and *age-appropriate* lining up. The brief settling (outside the classroom) signals (by the teacher) *a change of pace, place, space and purpose* in terms of group behaviour.

I find it helpful to comment briefly on hats, phones, iPods, chewing gum and any testosteronic bonding or pushing ... *before* directing the class group inside.

First a brief, group-settling direction as we scan the group or line.
   "Settling down everyone ... (...). Wait until they face you ... "Sean (...) Halid (...) playtime's over." This to the two "playfighters". "We're just mucking around!" They try to drag the teacher into a "discussion" (and gain peer attention). "We don't muck around like that in our class." Brief, clear, firm ... The teacher then *refocuses* to the group and repeats the direction (they are quite a restless class), "Settling down (...). That's better. Thanks. Morning everyone – just before we go in (...) ... I notice several students with hats on ..., Ben (...), Lucas (...), Marcus (...)."

 The brief *description of reality* is often enough to make the issue of "hats off" clear, without directly *telling* the students. Sometimes it is enough just to give a non-verbal cue (hand to head) for caps off.

"Down the back, I can see mobile phones (...). Remember we're going into a learning environment ...." Giving a non-verbal cue to the lads listening with ear phones "plugged in", we add, "We're going into the classroom. Remember the rule about iPods and phones. Thanks." Re-scanning the whole group, "Looks like we're ready folks. When you go in, remember to take your seats in the seating plan. It's the second lesson with the class; this "corridor settling" did not take long and it made a difference on the other side of the classroom door ...

This is very important in the establishment phase with any new class (p. 36f).

It can help Day One, Session One (and the next few sessions), to emphasise our expectations about seating and settling *once inside the room*. With early years I find it helpful to ask them, "What do we need to do when we go *inside* our class?" and then briefly fill the gaps in their forgetfulness as necessary (about hats, water bottles, bags ... and so on). It's important not to lecture this student in this "corridor settling".

This corridor settling *prefaces* the teacher/student expectation about purposeful behaviour on the other side of the classroom door. In time, the outside settling should become a habit so that all that is necessary is a *brief* line-up, or grouping, before moving into the classroom.

If a school has a line-up practice then it is always worth discussing with colleagues, in one's grade-team or faculty, how they normally settle a group prior to classroom entry: what sorts of things they do and say, *and why*.

The first three minutes (once inside the classroom)

The first two or three minutes are important in any lesson. The teacher has to *initiate*, *sustain* and *focus* group attention (p. 58f, 70f).

Obviously the teacher needs to allow a little time for the students to take their seats (or sit on the carpet area in early years) during which time the teacher needs to convey that he or she is purposefully – and expectantly – waiting for the class to be seated ("eyes and ears this way …") and ready to begin.

It will help to have a brief discussion with each new class – in the establishment phase – concerning the basic expectations about classroom entry and settling at their work area or desk. Such "settling" varies with age and subject area, of course. In drama classes it may involve having shoes off, against the wall and sitting in a semi-circle; in an information technology (IT) room it may mean finding a seat, turning it around (away from the computer or lids down on lap tops) to face the front and sitting, relaxed, waiting. What is important is to have a workable routine that will enable 25–30 students to settle smoothly, relaxedly and consciously and to attend to *whole-class* teaching and learning time (even where there is no "line-up" policy). Students also need to know that their attention (in the first three minutes) is expected ("eyes and ears facing the front, thanks", "hands in lap" at infant level – explain what "lap" means). It is worth thinking about *what* to say (as a verbal cue) to the class – particularly more restless class groups during those first three to four minutes as we seek to initiate and *sustain* whole-class attention and focus. It can even help to consider basic aspects such as making sure the class door stays open (as students enter). Avoid talking *at any length* with students *as they enter*. A brief, positive greeting is appropriate as students walk in – past the teacher – to their seats. If any student wants to chat or "raise an issue" (in the first minute or so) it is enough to assure them – briefly – you will chat later. It is then important to go to the front, centre, of the classroom to visually – then verbally – cue for whole-class settling. As noted earlier, it is worth considering what we say and do in those first few minutes. Our ability to convey, and communicate, a sense of calmness (at that point in the lesson) is crucial to how positively students settle and focus (p. 60f).

- Avoid using questioning cues to the class group. "*Would you please* be quiet and listen?", "*Can you please* stop talking and …?", "Excuse me! *Are you* still talking?" (It is not a *request*.) (p. 72).
- Use direct behaviour-focused language, for example, "*Settling … looking … listening … thanks …*" or "Eyes and ears looking this way and listening (…). Thanks."

- Briefly address distractions such as overly restless seat leaning, "private chatting", loud fiddling with objects (for example, pencil cases/water bottles) *while* still cueing for "settling ...". Brief, descriptive, directional or reminder cueing is enough (see p. 97f). Having dealt with any distractions – briefly – we then refocus the class to, "Settling ... listening ...."
- Greet the class and then begin the whole-class teaching/learning time. Give a whole-class greeting *when* the class has settled.

It can help (at upper primary and middle school) to establish and maintain a reasonable "target time" for group entry, settling, having relevant materials (where appropriate) and being ready to engage in whole-class teaching and learning time. A reasonable target could be, say, 1–2 minutes (it *seems* longer). This target time is consciously set as a *class target*, and encouraged and reviewed over the first half dozen lessons or so (Pearce 1997).

Cueing for attention in some classes may mean students go straight to an activity, as in English, where students file in, take their seats, quietly get out the class novel and read for – say – five minutes or begin with a "starter worksheet", with degrees of difficulty so all students can achieve something (on the sheet) in the first two to three minutes of settling and *quiet* activity. Some schools still direct students to stand behind their seats quietly at the beginning and close of each lesson. Carried through positively, even this can be a useful cue. There are a range of non-verbal cues to establish group attention in the instructional phase of the lesson (see p. 59). They should always be *verbally explained* when used for the first time.

Managing distracting and disruptive behaviour during whole-class teaching time

The typical distractions and disruptions that can occur during this phase of class time can range from rolling on the mat and hiding under tables (hopefully only at infant level – although I did have a lad hide in a low cupboard once in Year 7!), through to those annoying pockets of private chatting while the teacher is seeking to engage and teach the class.

The most common disruptions in this phase of the lesson tend to be: talking while the teacher is talking; talking *across* the classroom; calling out to the teacher; lateness; leaning back on chairs and motoric restlessness; fiddling with stationery (or other secreted *objets d'art*) ... Most of these behaviours (at least in the challenging schools I mostly work in) tend to be exhibited in the establishment phase of the year as students test out their relationship with each other and with their teacher.

When exercising discipline in *any whole-class, whole-group, context* it is important to be aware of what we do and say such that we avoid alienating the cooperative students. In this part of the lesson or activity, anything we do or say, in discipline terms, has an immediate audience effect beyond the individual (or small group) that we address. For example, if we are overly confrontational when we discipline the few individual students, we create a tone – an emotionally palpable tone – that can hinder the motivation and cooperation of *all* students. As noted earlier, each discipline transaction is a social transaction (p. 94). While there are some occasions when a brief, unambiguous communication of frustration and anger is appropriate, most of the time, when we are dealing with the sort of disruptive behaviours noted earlier, it is important to be respectfully positive and "low intrusive" where possible (p. 95). Being positive, confident and *appropriately firm* are not antithetical concepts.

Several students are engaged in private conversations as the teacher is establishing initial class attention and focus. The teacher visually scans the room, standing relaxed (not slouching), and cues for group attention (p. 70f, 59f). She briefly describes the behaviour of several distracting students.

"A number of students across the room are talking while I'm trying to teach explain/share ... (...)." Sometimes this "description of reality" is enough; it acts as an incidental direction (p. 97f). Sometimes we will need to add a behavioural direction. "Facing this way and listening, thanks." The teacher then gives take-up time (p. 98) and refocuses the flow of the lesson. If it is several students chatting, or calling out, or ..., we say, "A *number of students* are ..." For example: "A number of students are calling out (the descriptive cue ...). Remember our rule for ..." or "Hands up without calling out so we all get a fair go ..." (The rule reminder or directional cue ...). We do not say, "*All*". The distinction is important in group awareness.

As noted, "Thanks" is to be preferred (in this context) rather than "please". "Thanks" carries an expectation of compliance.

Sometimes this private natter – or talking while the teacher is talking – is *unfocused* student behaviour rather than *disruptive* student behaviour. Either way the approach noted above keeps the discipline least intrusive.

Students coming late into class

A student comes into class late. The teacher has been teaching for five minutes or so. The teacher quickly walks over to the door and says to the student, "Are you late?" (It is surprising that the student doesn't answer, "Course I'm late!"). If the teacher asks, "*Why* are you late?" it can sound (particularly if the teacher is frustrated) as if the teacher is "interrogating" the student, when in fact the teacher may only want a reason. Does it matter (however) – at that point in the lesson – *why* a student is late? Trying to get answers, and reasons, at the classroom door only feeds (in some students) incipient attention-seeking or even power provocation. We are also being drawn away from *whole-class* teaching/learning time.

Teacher: "Why are you late?"
Student: "People are late sometimes you know." If the student's tone is sulky, petulant, or hostile (the "secondary" behaviours) the lateness issue can quickly become a scene where the student believes he must play to the "gallery" of his peers.
Teacher: "Don't you speak to me like that!"
Student: "Yeah – well I'm only late, you don't have to hassle me. The girls are late sometimes – you don't hassle them, do you?"
Teacher: [The teacher's extended index finger appears, in the air, in the space between them. The teacher's voice is now rising.] "Who do you think you are talking to?!"
Student: "Yeah well you're hassling me about being a few minutes late – What's the big deal?" (Did he just grin!?)
Teacher: "Right! Go and sit over there. Now!" [The teacher points to the few spare seats. The student doesn't want to sit there. He wants to sit in his "normal" seat with his mates. That seat is already occupied.]
Student: "I'm not sitting there. I sit down the back with Nathan and Travis …"
Teacher: "Look, I don't care where you sit. I said sit there!"
Student: "Why should I?" [He sulkily folds his arms and looks away. The student, and audience of his peers, are having a "field day" on this one.]
Teacher: "Right! Get out – go on, get out! If you're not prepared to come to my class on time you can get out. Go on, see Mr Brown!" (the head of year).
Student: "Yeah, I'm going anyway, this is a sh-t class …!" [He turns and storms off.]

Of course we need to address the issue of the student's lateness, but it is unnecessary to dwell on the lateness *in front of the class like this* and *at this point* in the lesson. Some teachers get drawn in easily by the student's "secondary behaviour" (the tone of voice, the "slouch", the folded arms, the frowning face, the reactive tone of voice, the "grin" …).

  When students are late it is *always* helpful to welcome them – briefly and positively – especially in the first few lessons. We don't overdo "the positive" either. For example: "Oh Hi!" "It's great you're here. Jayson's here everyone! Isn't that wonderful?" In our first meeting with a new class/establishment we won't know if a student is late because he or she is lazy, disorganised or time-wasting, or if there are home-related issues (relevant to late arrival for form class or Period One, for example).

In the following example the student is five minutes late; a different class and a different teacher.

Teacher: Briefly cues the class he had been teaching until the arrival of the late student] "Excuse me for a moment class …." [Welcomes student at the classroom door] "Welcome (…). It's Tony, isn't it?" [Teacher is still learning names. He puts his hand out to shake hands with the student. Tony frowns, looks a little tentative – he was not quite expecting this approach. The teacher briefly, quietly – and respectfully – acknowledges Tony's lateness. "You're late. There's a spare seat over there – next to Carlos." [The teacher doesn't tell Tony to sit there: he "describes the obvious reality". He focuses on the important issue *at this point* in the lesson: direct the student to be seated and get on with the flow of the lesson.]

Student: "I don't sit there … I sit down the back with …" [He's less defensive with this teacher, but still procrastinates.]

Teacher: "Those seats are taken, Tony …" [The teacher could add, "And if you"d been here on time you would have had "your" seat!"… He resists the temptation.] "We can organise a seat change later Thanks." [This adds a – future –"choice", defusing any residual tension. At this point the teacher redirects his eye contact away from Tony, turning to readdress the class; he scans his eyes across them giving Terry take-up time (p. 98).] "As I was saying everyone …"

The teacher resumes his lesson flow, as if Tony will (naturally) sit down where the teacher has incidentally directed. He does – he walks across to the seat in a slightly exaggerated, posturing, way and flops down. The teacher *tactically* ignores this … keeping his focus – and the class's attention – on the lesson at hand.

If the student blatantly refuses to sit where the teacher nominates, we need to make the consequences clear – calmly, briefly. "If you choose not to sit there, I'll have to ask you to leave our class and go to …." It is pointless "pleading" or "bargaining" with a student if there are only one or two spare seats left and they refuse to sit there; it happens. This sort of possibility needs to have been discussed within the school's time-out policy and practice.

He follows up with Tony later, at the end of the lesson, for a brief chat about the student's lateness. If the student is persistently late (say three times over several consecutive days, or lessons) the teacher will take the lateness issue further with the year adviser to see if there is a pattern across other classes.

When students are late

- Welcome the student and *briefly* acknowledge their lateness.
- Direct the student to a seat or a nominated seat (if there is a whole-class seating plan, p. 52f) and give them take-up time (p.98).
- Resume the flow of the lesson or activity.

Discipline in the establishment phase of the lesson

- Scan – focus – scan (avoid maintaining eye contact for too long with any one individual or small group).
- Keep corrective language brief.
- Use positive language where possible.
- Focus on specific behaviour (when disciplining) or focus on the relevant rule.
- Avoid arguing with students – verbally block or partially agree, and refocus back to the rule or the required behaviour.
- Give take-up time where appropriate (p.98).
- Tactically ignore non-verbal secondary behaviours wherever possible and wherever appropriate. If a student's secondary behaviour is also inappropriate, or disruptive, *address it briefly and refocus* the student(s) back to the expected rule or behaviour (p.97).

Description of reality (directing incidentally) in a civic setting

Have you ever had someone push in on you in a supermarket queue or bus queue or taxi queue ...? It surprises me how many people let others, in effect, have more "right" to the front of the queue. On these occasions I often incidentally, politely and briefly describe our little bit of shared reality: "Excuse me (...), the queue starts there." An open hand rather than a pointing finger indicates the back of the queue. A pleasant smile – no hint of sarcasm or "I'm threatened by you" or "I'm better, more important, than you". We then look away, *as if* ... (take-up time). On some occasions I've had people say, "But I'm in a hurry". I find it helpful to briefly add (before turning away and giving some take-up time), "We're in a hurry too (referring to self and to the others in the queue), the queue starts there. Thanks." I've often seen other queue members give a grateful, shared, smile. Of course if the pushing-in person is 20 stone and has emblems of the Wehrmacht tattooed on his head, let him pass (or move to another queue)!

I was in the crowded underground station at London's Victoria Station on one occasion – a frantically busy place ... The many scores of commuters were going through the ticket barriers at a rapid pace. There was a New Zealand couple (I could tell by the accent from a few yards away) trying, vainly, to get their crumpled ticket into the automatic barrier. (This was Oyster cards). They don't have underground railways in New Zealand. I was annoyed by the several pinstripe-suited gentlemen huffing and puffing because this couple (replete with the fruits of their London shopping) were holding them up for 30–60 seconds of their life.

I walked over and said, in a firm voice, scanning the 20 or so in the queue who were whining, complaining ... "Excuse me folks (…). These people are clearly struggling with the machine (…). There are several more machines over there. Thanks." I beckoned with my hand. They moved away, frowning and huffing, a few sighing – several (though) looked sympathetic. I think they thought I worked for London Underground. I don't – I'm a teacher and I wanted to support my "Kiwi cousins".

I said to the older couple, "G'day – these machines aren't easy, are they?" They looked relieved, more relaxed.

"You're Australian?"

"Yes …"

We had a brief chat, sorted the ticket, and they went gratefully on their way.

Kyriacou has noted, "if one behaves as if one has authority, it is surprising how far this attitude exerts a momentum of its own leading pupils to behave accordingly" (1986: 132).

I would add that even in *some* civic settings adults can similarly pick up the subtle cues and signals (through our language) and behave more considerately. Obviously we need to "read" these situations (emotional/social intelligence).

Non-verbal cueing

As noted earlier, some distracting behaviours can be addressed – even nipped in the bud – by a non-verbal cue.

Non-verbal cues minimise the need for the teacher to verbalise the required behaviour *every time*. This is particularly helpful in early years classes. Typical cues are:

- The teacher crosses his index fingers then beckons with the right hand to indicate facing the front to cue for "cross your legs and face the front".
- The teacher raises one hand and covers his mouth with the other to indicate "hands up without calling out" (to early years students who call out in class discussion time). Some calling out can be *tactically* ignored if the teacher is

confident with such an approach, but a non-verbal cue can act as a *brief* reminder without disturbing the flow of the lesson or activity too much.

- The teacher puts one hand over the other and pulls it into the chest to indicate "keep hands and feet to yourself". This is an important cue for restless, touchy, early years children.
- The teacher touches one eye with a forefinger, then an ear, and uses a beckoning hand to the front of the room to indicate "eyes and ears this way now".
- The teacher holds up a thumb and forefinger a little distance apart to indicate "use your partner-voice, thanks". This is an effective reminder/direction during on-task learning time as the teacher is moving around the room. He or she may be working at one table and can remind a table group nearby by cueing across the room. I have used this reminder cue countless times in secondary classrooms.
- A similar cue I have used for years is the thumb and two fingers turning down, rotating an imaginary volume control (old-fashioned technology that one – it still works even in my year 8–9 classes at secondary level).

The first few times we use any non-verbal cue we also add the verbal cue as well. After several uses, we drop the verbal cue and allow the non-verbal cue to carry the normative reminder. As with any management strategy it is important to avoid any unnecessary tension. If any of the cues noted above were given with a jerky, thrusting, hand and a glare and a big sigh from the teacher it would hardly be seen as a *simple* respectful reminder!

Eye contact

Eye contact can engage attention, cue for social engagement show interest and indicate intent. A fixed *stare*, however, can create ambiguity if unaccompanied by verbal direction. Too long a stare may reciprocate, in some males, a perception of hostility or threat particularly if it mutates into a *fixed* glare. Dodge (1981, 1985) has researched attributional bias in aggressive children, observing that aggressive boys *selectively* attend to the available cues in their environment. Overly aggressive males tend to have a *perceptual and attributional bias* towards aggressive intent in the other party.

As teachers, we can avoid unnecessary hostile attributions with such pupils by considering proximity, and following eye contact with a brief direction or reminder; avoiding unnecessarily *extended* eye contact; giving take-up time; and avoiding unnecessary win–lose perception by how we frame language – such as, using appropriate choices (p. 105). It is important to be aware that in some cultures (notably South East Asian countries and Aboriginal communities) extended eye contact cues do not operate in the same way we may be used to in European culture. "Forcing" eye contact can cause significant embarrassment – even shame. Most importantly, however, we seek to communicate calmness, in tone of voice, body language *and eye contact* (p. 60f). While a teacher's frown is not inappropriate, particularly when giving commands or assertive directions, we do not normally need to sustain an *extended* frown unless giving an assertive statement or command. Even here, though, we will seek to avoid a threatening posture (too close, pointing and gesticulating finger...).

Tactical ignoring

Tactical ignoring is a difficult skill. It is a *conscious* decision not to attend to some student behaviours, such as sulking, sighing, eyes to ceiling, the rolling of eyes, the "hang-dog look", the over-extended frown when we direct students to do something really difficult like go back to their seats, or put their hands up without calling out, or put their pens down while we're talking to the class ... *Tactical* ignoring is also a form of non-verbal communication to *all* students (not just the student we are *tactically* ignoring). It demonstrates that the teacher is focused on the main behaviour issue – *at this point* – and it further avoids overly reinforcing attentional "secondary behaviours": for example, "Don't you raise your eyes to the ceiling like that ...!" "Why can't you do a simple thing *without sighing*? Is it *so* difficult? What's wrong with you?! Do you have to sulk like that?!" We obviously should not ignore behaviours that the students know should not be ignored: any *repeated* and loud calling out, or butting-in that affects a teacher's right to teach or puts down another student; *any* verbally rude or defiant language (p. 11, 90f, 116f); *any* hostile or aggressive behaviour; *any* unsafe behaviour. The cooperative 70 per cent of students know the difference; they know when a teacher is *tactically* ignoring.

In a class discussion, for example, it can be very effective to *tactically* ignore the few students who call out several times. It sends a message that the teacher will notice students *when* they have their hands up *without* calling out or finger clicking. Of course, the teacher needs to do this in a way that does not appear anxious, tense, uncertain or conveying superiority. Otherwise the ignoring can add confusion, or annoyance, to what is happening.

A common alternative approach is to *preface* any tactical ignoring. If a student calls out (in whole-class teaching time) we give a brief rule reminder, or direction, refocus to the lesson and – if the student calls out again – we then *tactically* ignore. The "prefacing" clarifies – and in effect cues to the class (and to the individual) – *why* we are tactically ignoring this student now.

Prefacing the tactical ignoring

The teacher is moving around the Year 3 classroom assisting, encouraging and clarifying. Bilal calls out across the classroom for "Miss" to help him. He has his hand up – he thinks as long as he has his hand up, *even if he is calling out* or *clicking his fingers*, he's "within the rule" and will always get his teacher's attention. From a distance, across the room, the teacher gives a conditional direction and *then* tactically ignores Bilal's subsequent calling out: "Bilal (…), when you have your hand up without calling out then I'll come over to help." The *subsequent* tactical ignoring now has a frame of understanding ("*when … then*").

A common example at nursery age occurs when an overly concerned, or anxious, mother drops off her 4-year-old on Day One, Week One. The child cries, holds on to its mother and pleads. The mother assures the child, over and over again, "Yes I love you … my precious. I'll be back … I will. I promise … be a good boy … yes, I do love you." The child is really crying and may be anxious (although some children do learn to manufacture tears for attention). The mother naturally wants to reassure the child, but ends up reinforcing the child's attentional behaviour: "the 45-minute goodbye". Most early years teachers quietly reassure the mother that if she goes – leaving the child with a confident, smiling assurance (once or twice) – the child *will* settle down. ("Please ring later, in half an hour, Mrs Smith ….") The teacher (after initial, warm assurance) will then *tactically* ignore the child's crying and firmly – pleasantly and kindly – redirect the child without over-servicing the child's attention-seeking behaviour. She will also (obviously) distract the child by pairing them off with a more socially confident child. In this example, tactical ignoring involves *selective* attention; reassuring, and refocusing *as the child settles*.

Behaviour overdwelling

Some teachers address and correct the distracting behaviour and then add the "nag tag" – what Kounin (1971) called "Behaviour Overdwelling". "Jayson!, Jayson! Stop being silly with the playdough – *now*! Can you see anyone else being silly; I can't. Every time we have an activity like this you have to muck around instead of making something productive. Is that so hard? Is it? You know what you are supposed to do, why can't you just …"

It is as if speaking *longer* (and louder) the teacher can "drive the point home …"

Take-up time

I was teaching a Year 10 Maths class as a mentor-teacher (a few years back) and as I scanned the room during on-task learning time I noticed that a student had what looked like a novel on top of his exercise book. I walked over.

"It"s Damon, isn't it?" It was my first session with the class and I was still learning names. I added, "Good morning."

He looked up (not attempting to close the book). "Yeah – it's Damon."

"I notice you've got a book there, a novel? What's it about?"

"It's about a serial killer," he said, looking up with a grin.

"Well, let's hope he's not after a teacher," I said (and meant it). This brief chat is a form of prefacing prior to some task refocusing. I thought it best to focus on the learning task.

"How's the work going?"

"It's boring," replied Damon.

"It may well be boring, Damon – for you – however, it is our work for today. Do you know what to do?" My tone was pleasant; expectant of cooperation. He sighed, leaning back.

"Yeah, sort of."

"How can I help?"

I gave a brief reminder of the task, pointing back to the whiteboard and adding, "By the way, the novel. I'd like you to put it in your bag or if you like you can leave it on my desk till the bell." (a *directed* choice ... (p. 102)). This was the "discipline" part of the brief engagement. He grinned back. I added, "I'll come back and check on your work a little later, Damon." The walking away, at that point, allowed some take-up time for the student and also gave a task refocus. With older children it only escalates unnecessary confrontation to take, or snatch, the distracting item. Similarly, if a directed choice is given to the student (as above) and the teacher continues to stand there, waiting, until the student puts the item away it also creates unnecessary tension and, in some students, contestability.

Take-up time can also convey trust in the student that they will respond appropriately. It allows some face saving in potentially tense situations. It is important to go back to the student – later in the lesson – to check if they are back on-task and also to briefly re-establish the working relationship and give some encouragement.

With younger children the teacher may need to repeat a direction or reminder a few times until the child responds, and *then* give the take-up time commensurate with their response.

> **NB**   As children get older our management and discipline language (Rogers 2011) should seek to engage the "emergent adult" within the young person by:
>
> - not "talking down" to a student, or merely talking *at* them
> - seeking to engage the student in thinking about their behaviour: hence incidental and "descriptive" language (p. 98) and thoughtful use of questions and directed choices (p. 93, 102); particularly so in front of a student's peers
> - not forcing students into a psychological corner (instead using deferred consequences, p.102f).

An aside on uniform "misdemeanours"

Some schools still retain pettifogging application to rules (and rule governance) about uniform and jewellery: only sleepers, but no pattern on the sleepers; studs, but only gold or silver, again – no pattern; socks must *always* be worn knee-high; no rings, or bangles, or friendship bands; hair must be a certain length; and so on (hence the word misdemeanours in inverted commas). There may well be good reasons for some of the rules but it is the application of the rules that ought to concern our *thoughtful* management.

A young girl is wearing a "non-regulation", large, finger ring in class. A present from her father. It has a sentimental, almost "Linus-like" psychological comfort for her. New to this school, she comes across a teacher who notices this major crime and asks her to hand it over. The girl is upset, confused and becomes anxiously frustrated.

"No. No way. I'll take it off if I have to."

The teacher repeats his command, "Give it to me." He puts his hand (palm out) to indicate he expects her unquestioning compliance.

"No!" the girl clenches her fist. She (quite naturally) doesn't know if she'll ever get it back. She mentions that the teachers in the other classes hadn't said anything. "I don't care what other teachers do. I said hand it over." If she doesn't (believe it or not) he'll put her on detention!

This may sound like a manufactured example, but – sadly – it isn't. True, the teacher concerned may not have known the girl's psychological attachment to the ring. True, the teacher may be seeking to be "managerially" vigilant (but here he is *overly* vigilant, perhaps *maniacally* vigilant) about the uniform/dress code. The problem is he has not tuned into the girl's feelings, or considered her welfare as part of the management/discipline process. He lacks any empathetic, perspective-taking in managing natural adolescent behaviour. He seems only concerned about the pettifogging application of the rule; about "winning", "proving", "controlling". He may also hold demanding, absolutist views about control and vigilant teacher discipline ("Children *must* obey their teachers", "Children *should not* answer back. They *should* do what I say." "Good teachers *must be in control* of students …"). (See p.20f.)

In another class at the same school a teacher comes up to a student wearing a similar ring during on-task time.

"Rachel, that's an attractive ring."

The girl has a brief chat with her teacher about the ring.

"You know the rule about large rings?" (The teacher's voice is quiet. She is keeping it low key.)

"But other teachers haven't said anything," the girl frowns.

"Maybe they haven't, Rachel, however the school rule is …" The teacher partially agrees and refocuses to the school rule. The teacher gives a non-verbal signal to the student's pocket indicating for the girl to put it away in her pocket. The girl owns her behaviour. Relaxed vigilance; even in a school with such pettifogging rules.

End of story. If the girl refuses a fair directed choice like this, the teacher will defer the matter to an out-of-class follow-up (p. 122f). If the teacher catches her with the ring on again *in a school like this* the issue *may* occasion a stay-back session to emphasise the rule.

If you ever happen to teach in a school that promotes a confiscation policy on "rule-breaking jewellery" (excuse my cynicism and sarcasm here), at least give the student the dignity of an assurance of returning it the same day. I've known "power-merchant" teachers to keep rings, jewellery and non-dangerous *objets d'art* until the end of the week, in some bizarre cases, the end of the term! That is simply psychological harassment. It always staggers me that some students will easily hand such items over and put up with rubbish like this. In schools where students do not evidence such unquestioning compliance to teacher control such an order to hand the ring over would be rightly laughed at.

More than personality

I have heard teachers observing some of their colleagues' behaviour management practices with the disclaimer, "Oh, it's just their personality. That's why they can get through to those students". While personality is important, if they observe more carefully, they will note that these colleagues are also aware of their own non-verbal communication and the impact of their "global set" of behaviours on others (Rogers 2006a). They will also note that these teachers are particularly conscious of their management and discipline language and the language they use to encourage their students (p. 152f).

There are skills that can enhance "the personality" we bring to our profession; these skills can aid positive communication increasing positive congruence between what we communicate (content); how we communicate (non-verbal tone); timing (when we intervene); and *why we choose to communicate this way at all* (our values and our aims, p. 93f).

While some people are naturally effective communicators, most of us have to learn that *our non-verbal behaviours and what we characteristically say* carry significant weight in our daily communication. These non-verbal behaviour cues can enable positive, workable, relationships with our students (and colleagues). Even when we are frustrated and angry, some non-verbal cues will make the communication process less stressful and easier to repair and rebuild when the heat has died down (Chapter 7).

As in all reflective teaching, we should, essentially, consider the *effect* of our behaviour on others and trust that they will do likewise (no new message this; just a difficult one). "Do unto others ..."

A common belief is that group management skills are simply a natural gift. You either have it or you don't. Our evidence does not support this belief. Its most damaging feature is that teachers who have difficulty controlling classes tend to put this down to personal inadequacy rather than to a lack of particular skills that can be acquired through training or advice from colleagues.

The most talented, "natural" teachers may need little training or advice because they learn so quickly from experience. At the other extreme, there are a few teachers for whom training and advice will not be properly effective because their personalities do not match the needs of the job. *It is clear, however, that the majority of teachers can become more effective classroom managers as a result of the right kinds of training, experience and support* (Elton Report 1989: 69, emphasis added by author).

Seen on a staff noticeboard

I will not yell in class and I will not throw things & I will not pinch or even hit and I will not have a temper tantrum & I must always be a good example to all the kids. ... because I am the teacher ... I am the teacher ... I am the teacher ... I am the teacher ... I am the teacher ...

I saw this A4 sheet in a prominent position on a school noticeboard. Some wag had added at the bottom:

To be read each morning in case it will be one of those days.

(When is it not?)

Following-up with students beyond the classroom setting: balancing "short-term" intervention with longer-term one-to-one intervention

There are behaviour concerns that cannot be adequately addressed in the "public arena" of the classroom – we have to spend some time (with the student) away from their classmates. This may be as basic as a five-minute "after class chat" or a more involved behaviour interview. It may involve a detention session where we can work through the concerns we have about, and for, the student's behaviour and learning.

In one of my mentor-teaching schools (recently) I was teaching in a Year 8 English class. It was the on-task phase of the lesson and we had about ten minutes to go before lesson closure. Moving around the front rows, I chatted with students about their work (encouraging, giving some last feedback ...) and I noticed, in a glance towards the back row, Tyson, looking down at the floor, concentrating on a long, slow, mucally substantive spit. It was stalagtitical (or is it stalagmite(ical?) in size and formation. I caught his eye as he looked across the room ... He knew I knew. Surprisingly, the girl sitting next to him hadn't noticed (he'd managed a "quiet" – if substantial – "spit drop").

Just before my colleague and I dismissed the class I let Tyson know I wanted to "see him after class". He frowned and asked , "What for?" I replied that I wouldn't keep him long (it was morning recess). I said goodbye to the class and dismissed them ...

Tyson stayed near the classroom door, leaning back against the wall, arms folded and frowning …

I briefly tuned into how I thought he might be feeling – "Tyson, I know you want to be outside with your mates … I know I'm not your regular teacher. You may be feeling annoyed."

He quickly replied, "Well what did I do?"

I said I'd seen him drop a long, slow, spit; direction – floorwise.

"Eh?! – I just spat on my shoe not on the floor," he corrected me; it seemed important to him that he'd landed the spit on his runners. "Truly," he elaborated, "I spitted on my trainers. I can show you!" I'd intended to go back to where he'd been sitting in the back row to direct him to clean up what I imagined had been a floor spit … (My colleagues and I always have a box of tissues *and* "Wet Ones" in class time …).

"Tyson, I thought you'd spat on the floor."

"No" – his reply was swift – "It was my shoe!"

I asked him what he normally did when he felt a big spit coming.

"What?"

"Tyson, when you feel a big one coming what do you *normally* do?" (Most children don't carry handkerchiefs).

He frowned – musingly – "I don't know …"

"Do you normally *just* drop it?" I wasn't annoyed. He raised his eyes adding "I just – sometimes, just cough it back … But it's on my shoe you can look if you want." It was important to him he hadn't messed the floor(!) I said I believed him about the shoe and didn't need to actually check …

"Am I going on detention?"

I replied, "Would detention teach you to walk up to the front desk and take a few tissues and skilfully, quickly, deposit … and bin it …?"

He grinned. "So I'm not on detention then?"

"It's your break time Tyson, I just wanted a quick reminder about tissues. Enjoy your playtime – see you next time."

He looked relieved and waltzed off down the corridor.

(By the way, it's stalactitic – I think …).

Sometimes the "after class chat" (if we don't have back-to-back classes) can be as brief as this (about five minutes …). Other times (if it's not a recess break) I make an appointment with the student to meet me at lunchtime to "follow up with them …". I give them a short reminder note. Students almost always register annoyance – or sometimes anger – that I've directed them to "stay back". This is normal. It's what we do *then* that can enable some constructive, consequential, outcome.

In another Year 8 class (same school) I'd reminded Jake several times (during whole-class teaching time) to put his feet down and sit – chair on floor; "sitting in …" He'd had his foot up on the table, leaning back "balancing" … while calling out … I – briefly – directed him "Jake (…) feet down, chair in; remember our rule for class discussions." As I took my eyes off him to give him take-up time (p. 118f) he sighed loudly. I *tactically* ignored the sigh, the loud foot drop to the floor and chair ever so slowly moved in …

The second and third time he went through this "attentional" seat-lean I gave a brief non-verbal cue as I proceeded with the whole-class discussion … He gave a sulky, loud, groan … eyes to the ceiling and more loud sighing each time. During the on-task learning time there was more heavy seat leaning and significant task avoidance.

Just before lesson closure I directed the class to "pack-up" … We had a brief chat about what we'd covered that lesson … and I reminded them to "do the next class a favour" (with straightening furniture, etc. row by row, p. 86f). I looked at Jake (as I held up my yellow notebook) "Jake (…) I need to see you briefly after class."

He said – with annoyance – "What for …?! I didn't do anything. C'mon it's lunchtime!"

"Won't keep you long Jake …." I turned my eyes back to the class group. Jake pushed his seat back, folded his arms sulkily frowning and grunting …

I dismissed the class. Jake went for the door. I called him back.

"C'mon! What did I do?! I didn't do nothing!" He leaned heavily against the wall, near the door (ready for a prison break …?)

"Jake (…) look I know you're feeling annoyed."

"Too right – why am I in trouble?"

"Jake, I won't keep you too long. I need to speak to you about the way you were leaning back … foot up on your desk and calling out during whole-class teaching time."

"What?!" – again the sulky indignance.

"Do you mind if I give you a brief demo – show you what I mean?"

Less indignant now but still frowning he said, "What do you mean …?"

"I just want to show you – *briefly* – what I saw …"

"I don't care – do what you want." He was less angry now – but watching me …

I went to "his" seat and showed Jake what I'd seen (several times) regarding his foot on desk … the lean … the calling out … the loud foot drop and chair in … I walked back to the door … He'd watched me closely. I'd mirrored him (as it were) for 15 seconds at most. "That's what I mean Jake …"

He laughed, adding, "That's stupid …"

"Well it's stupid when I do it … I'm ten times older than you, but that's what I saw you do over half a dozen times. Can you see, and feel, how loud that is with just you, me and your regular teacher … Several times Jake … imagine what that's like when I'm trying to teach, and we're *all* trying to have a class discussion and you call out like *that* …" This *brief* "mirroring" (p. 128, 235f) re-addresses the "kinaesthetic memory" (as it were – "like *that* …").

Before I could give Jake a right-of-reply he said, "Anyway do you know what my problem is? I got ADD [sic] – you know what that is?"

"Yes," I replied – "What does it mean for you?"

"Well sometimes I go on a rampage [sic] – the other day, right, I chucked my books down and kicked my chair …"

"Well (I replied) you didn't go on a rampage today."

[Always focus on the behaviour we saw *that* class session … We don't drag up what the student did last week – we work on the "today" …]

He told me he was on medication. I asked him if the medication taught him *how to* sit relaxed (without foot up – leaning 45° or more back ...)

"Eh?"

"Does the medication teach you to sit relaxed and put your hand up without calling out loudly (like I just showed you)?"

"No ... what do you mean?"

"Well Jake (...) taking tablets can't *teach you how to do anything. You* have to decide how you'll behave. My job is to help you get the best out of your time as a member of our class, your 'job' is to decide how you'll cooperate with us all here ..." (p. 50).

I briefly reminded him of our class agreement about learning and respect (see Appendix A). We'd been chatting for less than ten minutes.

"Anything else you want to say, Jake?"

"Other kids call out too – what about Roscoe and Bilal ..."

"True (I said) you saw me keep Bilal back last week – remember? And Roscoe settled when I reminded him about our class rule for discussion. I asked you to stay back because you called out several times ... well like I just showed you before."

"Jake ... thanks for staying back."

"I didn't have any choice, did I? If I didn't stay back you'd dob on me ..."

"Dobbing" is "telling" on someone – he meant I'd tell on him to the head of year or the deputy. I briefly added, "I don't do dobbing, Jake. I"ll see you next Thursday."

He gave the faintest of frowning smiles as he left – adding – "Shit, I thought you were just coming for today."

"No Jake I'll be back – enjoy lunch time."

He sighed and wandered off down the corridor ...

In Jake's case there were, over the next weeks, a number of disruptive incidents, across several classes. We then, as a year-level team, decided on a year-level response (see Chapter 6).

Where we have had several "chats", or several detentions (with a student), or more formal behaviour interviews over a few weeks, this will, naturally, raise questions such as:

- How *frequently* does this student distract/disrupt others *across different subjects with different teachers?*
- Are such behaviours *durable – more than "bad-day syndrome"?*
- How have the colleagues who teach this student addressed such behaviour *so far*, both in the public forum of the classroom and in any one-to-one settings?

It is unreasonable, untenable and unfair to expect any teacher to have to come up with a behaviour plan for students who are *repeatedly* disruptive and who do not respond to normal (and respectful) teacher follow-up. This issue is addressed later in Chapter 6.

There are a number of reasons why we will need to follow-up with students (one-to-one) beyond the classroom:

- To clarify an issue relating to class learning (misunderstanding about class work, or a student getting behind with their work, or homework). In this case the follow-up is normally to emphasise empathetic teacher support. There should not be any emphasis on punishment for students who are currently struggling with classroom learning, or work/task assignments or homework.
- To initiate a discussion about a concern regarding the student's behaviour (this may – at times – occasion a brief 5–10 minute stay-back session, as in the case examples above).
- To follow through with any *deferred* consequences (p. 102f). A typical example is when a student has left a mess and has made no effort to clean up. At primary level, teachers sometimes use *deferred* consequences for students who have made no effort to complete classwork (this would assume the student was able to do the set work).
- To initiate a process of mediation with students who have exhibited conflict behaviour in class time.
- To initiate detention or more formal stay-back procedures (p. 198–201).

At secondary level it is often difficult to follow-up issues between classes (especially during a six-period day!) unless it's break (recess) time. Sometimes one can manage a *brief* word of follow-up after class and sometimes that may be enough. If the issue is important enough, though, it is worth directing the student to come to a later meeting (for example, during the lunch break). In that brief moment after class we won't be able to go into the details; it will be enough to make the appointment to meet with the student later that day, or (if it's an issue that occurred after lunch) we make an appointment to meet with them the next day. Obviously we will only engage such follow-up on issues that matter.

Ethical probity

When conducting *any* one-to-one teacher–student stay-back session, it is crucial to be sensitive to ethical probity, particularly with a male teacher and female student. It will help in any *extended* one-to-one sessions to have a colleague of the opposite sex present in the room (abstractedly working on her work programme) while conducting the follow-up.

- Whether the follow-up is a brief chat, a task-based consequence (that is, cleaning up mess left), an interview with a student or even a detention it is important that the teacher emphasises the fair *certainty* rather than the severity of the consequence.

  I have seen teachers confront students after class with their pointed index finger a few inches from the student's face, extracting their "pound of (psychological) flesh" (emotional, psychological, pay-back). "Yes. You're inside now, eh? Missing playtime. Well it serves you right. If you had done what I said you could be outside now, couldn't you?! You've been wasting time all morning and I said if you didn't stop mucking around you would have to stay back after class. And what did you say? Hmm? You said you didn't care. You're caring now aren't you? You had to play the big man didn't you?! ..." I can understand how some teachers *feel* at this point. I can understand that they may even be tempted to make the child *feel* bad, and even "suffer", through this process. But it is counter-productive, and unnecessary. It is also unprofessional and unacceptable. The student, in this case, will hardly learn anything constructive about the consequential nature of his or her behaviour through such teacher behaviour and is hardly likely to engage in *any* cooperation with the teacher. What it will do is breed resentment, even retaliation in some students.
- Tune in briefly to how the student may be feeling at this point – they obviously want to be outside with their mates and may be really annoyed, even angry. Some students may even be feeling anxious. By *briefly* tuning into how we think they are feeling we humanise the follow-up *while retaining consequential certainty*. "You're probably feeling annoyed that I've asked you to stay back after class [or to have this meeting at lunchtime, or …]." Our tone and manner here (as so often in discipline transactions) is really important. If we sound as if this follow-up session (however short in terms of time) is some kind of "win" for the teacher, the student will probably perceive and define the issue in those terms as well. Our respectful calmness is important. We also do not need to apologise for keeping them back. "I'm so sorry I had to keep you in at playtime ...". We're not sorry; this consequential time is fair, necessary, appropriate.
- Focus *specifically* on the student's behaviour, or the issue of concern you have as their teacher: "I'm concerned about *what happened* in class *when* ...". If it is a task-related consequence it is enough to direct the student(s) to the task-requirement: "Bradley when the work area is tidy [be brief and specific] then you'll be ready for recess ...." With task-focused consequences it can help to refer to the class routine/rule: "In our class we leave our work areas tidy ...".

In helping to *specifically* focus on a student's disruptive behaviour it may be appropriate to "mirror" the student's behaviour to them (Rogers 2003a). "Behaviour mirroring" involves the teacher *briefly* "acting out" the typical, characteristic, disruptive behaviour of the student (for example, the calling out, frequent seat leaning, loudness or talking while the teacher is talking) and even their "secondary" behaviours (that is, *frequent* sighing, eyes raising, loud muttering, and so on (p. 12f).

When "mirroring" a student's behaviour in this one-to-one context (and only in a one-to-one in non-class time context) we should always:

○ Ask permission of the student: "I'd like to show you what I mean when I'm referring to you calling out …"; "Do you mind if I give you a brief demo of how loud you often speak in class …?"; "Let me show you what I see you do when you push and pinch others when you're sitting on the mat in carpet time [this to an early years student]." We do not touch the child obviously. We pinch, push, hit an "imaginary" child … We briefly simulate the behaviour. "Maybe you weren't aware of how you spoke to me when … I'd like to briefly show you …"

○ Keep the actual mirroring (of the student's behaviour) *brief* (10–15 seconds).

○ Avoid the impression you're getting some satisfaction out of showing the student how annoying, silly, disrespectful, or stupid they are; we illustrate their behavior, we don't "score"(!)

○ Having mirrored the student's typical classroom behaviour, we physically step back (as it were) from the "kinaesthetic re-creation" and refer back to the mirrored behaviour to further clarify the issue of concern: "So; *that's* what it looks/or sounds like when you …"

○ With older students it can help to invite a response to the specific behaviour we have "mirrored": "So how many times do you think you call out like *that?*"

Mirroring is an attempt to *illustrate* and *clarify* a student's characteristic distracting or disruptive behaviour and to enable a teacher–student dialogue. It is used in the context of teacher *support*, to help the student to be behaviourally "aware" and assist them in owning their behaviour.

NB   When talking one-to-one with children diagnosed with autism spectrum disorder we would not – normally – use a mirroring approach. We would – instead – specifically focus the student's understanding about the necessary/appropriate behaviour(s). We do this specifically, with direct/clear language and model the behaviour to enhance clarity and then practise the required/appropriate necessary behaviour (see p. 211f).

> We often use picture cues and brief behaviour specific cues to give a framework within which we talk about, discuss and clarify expected behaviour.

- Where appropriate, invite the student's right of reply. This can be verbal or written. Ask questions that will enable the student to focus on their behaviour in the light of what happened (that occassioned them staying back). We also refer back to the basic rights and responsibilities in the student behaviour agreement (p. 39f). In this, the teacher is making the important point that, in some way, the student's behaviour has affected someone else's rights – a crucial aim in any behaviour transaction (p. 93f).

The basic questions we can ask are: "What happened …?" (regarding your behaviour); "What rule or right was affected by your behaviour …?"; "How do you see what happened, and how do you feel about it?" (their "right-of-reply"); "What can you do to change things … fix things up … sort things out … make things better …?" These can even be presented as a written pro forma. We call this pro forma the "4W" form, after the four questions prefaced by "What …?".

Some supplementary questions when involving a student in a longer follow-up session can include:

- "What do you want to happen – for you?"
- "What do you think will happen if you … (keep behaving in class like …)?" Be specific.
- "What can you do so that others can get on with their work without [make reference, briefly, to the student's current disruptive behaviour]?" "What can you do so that others can feel safe or learn here?"
- And – most importantly – "What can I (and your other teachers) do to help you to …" Above all be clear and specific about the key behaviours that need to change for the student to get some success back into his classroom learning and social engagement.

The spirit and tone in which these questions are asked are crucial. If they are asked in a provocative, confrontational way they will (obviously) create the very resentment and resistance the teacher is seeking to refocus with the student. If the student is calm enough (in the one-to-one setting) we can direct them to write their responses … If the student struggles at all with their writing the teacher can ask the questions and record the student's responses.

- We normally use the pro forma questions in a time-out session (when the student has calmed down), in a detention or as preliminary focus before in a mediation session.
- When I'm working with children on restitution (between student–student, or student–teacher) they will often say things like, "I won't ever (or never) do that again ..." We then talk about "never" and "ever" being very big words and how adults find it hard to *keep* to "never" or "ever". These words are easy to *say*. We then focus on what they (with our help) can *do* now – today – to show they are sorry; to demonstrate some care, some restitution. We also distinguish the difference between "sorry words" and sorry *behaviour*. What happens from *now on*, in the way you treat others, speak to them, work alongside them ... your *actions* will show your "sorryness"..
- As George Eliot said, "I am not imposed upon by fine words; I can see what actions mean" (*Mill on the Floss*).
- The emphasis with all *extended* follow-up on issues of behaviour is to enable the student to become more self-aware (with regard to their behaviour).
- The outcome of these questions should be to enable some understanding, even some "plan", that will increase the student's sense of self-monitoring and regulating of their behaviour (see Chapter 6).
- If the student does not respond to *supportive* questioning, or even refuses to cooperate, the teacher can still make the following points clear so the student is as aware as possible of what needs to change:
  - "This is what I see, and note, about your behaviour ..."; be specific.
  - "It isn't helping you when you ..."; be specific.
  - "This is what you'll need to do if you want to change your behaviour so that you can ..."; be specific.
  - "I'm *always* ready to help." Allow take-up time for the student to respond to *each* issue raised (above), and assure the student of your willingness to support them in making a behaviour plan.
  - Another approach when working with students who present with resistant patterns of behaviour is to explore, with them, their likely goals behind their behaviour in terms of attention and power (see Chapter 6, p. 218f).
- Some students will frequently use the line (even whine) that "I can't ...": "I can't do the work ...", "I can't control my temper ...". A firm, *supportive*, focusing can often help: "Perhaps you can't do the work:
  - *because* you're not facing the front and listening during the class teaching time ...
  - *because* you haven't got your pen, ruler and pencil ready to start ... (I can help you with a plan ..., Chapter 6.)

     ○   *because* you haven't read through the task [assuming their reading skills are proficient – if they're not we should always find creative, supportive, ways to adjust the task as well as extend their thinking] or provide "reading-partners" (in class time).

     ○   *because* you're easily distracted by sitting near Dean … So let's make a plan [to … address the *can'ts*]."

A plan can then be developed that will incrementally build the student's "academic survival skills" and behaviours, and enhance the student's learning and relationships with others at school (Chapter 6).

- When we direct students to stay back for task-based consequences it is enough to direct the student to the task, give them some take-up time and check for task completion (that is, to clean up the mess, finish the piece of work …).

- Always separate as amicably as possible after working through behaviour consequence with the student (even with a brief five-minute chat after class). I've heard teachers raise the strained-relationship stakes by having the unnecessary last word: "… and if you pull that stunt again you won't just be speaking to me, or your form teacher, or the year head, or your mother! Or I'll, I'll, I'll … what? ring the Minister for Education as well!"

- Track the student in terms of ongoing disruptive behaviour. If the follow-up session sees no discernible (subsequent) change in the student's behaviour or attitude it will be worth checking with other colleagues (through the team leader/year adviser) to see if this behaviour is *typical, frequent* or *characteristic across the year level and across classes*. If there is typical, frequent and durably disruptive behaviour in such cases it is wiser to have a year-level, whole-staff, approach to working with the student in question (see Chapter 6).

A colleague recently shared with me: "I followed up all my rude/disrespectful students, all the difficult ones, and also the students with learning problems. I even sometimes withdrew students from colleagues' classes where necessary, to follow up. I used the 4W form (p. 129f) (they didn't like that; they said "Why don't you gives us lines like the other teachers? We have to think with these questions!"). Well, by the end of first term I was buggered! But second term was a breeze."

   He wasn't being smart, clever or arrogant when he said "it was a breeze". This colleague is a good, kind and patient teacher. What he was saying was that early and consistent follow-up and follow-through in the establishment phase of the year had paid off in establishing a fair, respectful certainty in consequential follow-up, and rebuilding of positive relationships – with his more challenging students.

   As with all communication with students in situations where there is natural, ambient tension. We, therefore, seek to:

- calm ourselves before seeking to calm the student
- avoid rushing the dialogue (allow some time for student response)
- allow the student a right-of-reply (and responsive dialogue) even in a brief after class stay-back. It will help to ask the student, "Is there anything you want to say?" If they say (I've had this many times) "I don't do that (the calling out) all the time." "I'm glad – Troy. You called out lots of times today, though, that's why we're having this chat ..." If the student says "Others call out too! (or whatever)." We'll add, "Yes – and I'll be speaking to them too. At the moment – Troy – I'm speaking with you about *your* calling out." If they deny what we are addressing in their behaviour, we will need to decisively – and patiently – point out what we saw/heard.
- be aware of our open, non-confrontational, body language; avoid crowding the student's personal space
- keep the focus directed to the "primary behaviour" or primary issue of concern (avoid pointless arguing)
- refer to the student behaviour agreement as it is affected by the student's behaviour
- keep a supportive, invitational, tone wherever possible.

Reflection

- How aware are you of the fundamental *aims of* discipline within your behaviour leadership? (p. 93f)
- How aware are you of the language you characteristically use in behaviour leadership? (p. 15, 97f) Have you ever *consciously* reflected on what you do and *actually say*, when you have to address "typical" distracting/disruptive behaviours?
- How do the key practices noted earlier (p. 97–106) inform your own discipline practice? Do you have any school-wide expectations about daily behaviour leadership and discipline? Should we have some common school-wide discipline practices (beyond one"s natural personality factors)?
- There are some quite challenging skills noted here. How aware are you of using (for example) *tactical* ignoring? (Within a framework of selective attention and positive feedback?) Take-up time? Assertive language; in high-risk situations?
- How do you engage students in follow-up beyond the classroom (even the five-minute behaviour chat)? (p.122f). How do the protocols noted (on p. 95/96) inform your practice?

 Visit https://study.sagepub.com/rogers4e for additional resources to help you better manage classroom behaviour. You'll also be able to hear from Bill himself as he talks you through common behaviour management scenarios.

4

Effective teaching: fundamental understandings and skills

"Reflect for a moment: imagine what it would be like to be a student in a class where you were the teacher…"

(Bill)

Effective teaching: some fundamental considerations

The term "effective" needs a little reflective thought. Effective at what? For whom? At what cost? In what way?

If "effective" is pursued merely, or only, in utilitarian terms, then intentional humiliation, manipulation, sarcasm, public shaming and embarrassment can all be utilised (as they obviously have by some teachers) as long as such behaviour "effectively" shuts a student up, quietens down a class, creates anxious compliance or "gets the work done". Hopefully none of us would want that. Many of the children of my generation (1950s–1960s) grew up with teachers who made us stand when we got less than five marks out of ten in a spelling test (or whatever), or made us do a maths problem on the board (and we couldn't) or said we were "stupid" or "thick" because we didn't understand something the first time. Thankfully, there are few teachers like that in schools now. "Effective …" also does not merely mean to teaching-to-test outcomes or to "SATS-based" study. "Effective" teaching also means enabling students to more consciously be aware of themselves as learners – with *skills for learning* – able to integrate what they learn within – and across – the curriculum. *Effective teaching enables more effective learning* in our students as we enable them to identify and develop their skills as learners. "Effective", in any meaningful sense, also needs to include the *values* that underlie what we aspire to in "effective teaching". Core values such as respecting all students (even basic civic respect) and equality of treatment (fairness) are universally accepted by students of any age as redolent of "effective" teaching.

We seek to enable in our students a sense of "belonging" as a member of a learning community, not merely as a "student". The need *to belong* is a primary social need and children spend a third of their day with us. A positive sense of belonging will always enable more effective learning. Even a positive greeting to the whole class (as well as to individuals as they enter) can assist in engaging a sense of basic *belonging* here in *this* place – our classroom.

There are a number of characteristics of effective teaching that are present across every age of student and teaching situation:[1]

- The teacher expresses – in their leadership – a self-confidence, patience and general calmness (see pp. 60f) (bad days notwithstanding, p. 22f). The teacher also displays a genuine interest in the subjects/topics/skills they teach and makes a genuine attempt to be actively involved in and concerned with each student's progress. Even a basic commitment to acknowledge and affirm a student's effort in their work, in their progress, will affect student motivation in a positive way. Of course, our acknowledgment, affirmation, feedback and encouragement need to be genuine if they are going to be accepted and valued by students (pp. 164–168). And they will know the difference. The teacher's explanations and instructions are clear and pitched at a level likely to "connect" in terms of student understanding, needs and comprehension. One of the most basic aspects of effective (and competent) teaching is that the teacher explains the purpose and relevance of what they are teaching and the particular learning expectations and outcomes that flow from them. They do this every lesson; every activity. When we set up learning tasks and experiences (that flow from shared dialogue in the whole-class teaching/instructional phase) we need to make the aims of the task and activities clear to our students and outline the basic expectations (even steps) about how the learning can progress. *Task clarity* is basic – but crucial – in every lesson (p. 74f).

NB   Whenever we teach, and whatever we teach, we enable that creative interplay between the:

-   oral   ...   to the written,
-   known   ...   to the less known, and to the unknown,
-   shorter   ...   to longer,

- simple   ...   to the more complex,
- whole   ...   to the more detailed.

For example, whenever we seek to develop a student's writing we encourage them to ask questions about what they want to transfer from their creative thought and imagination to the page ... *What? When? Where? How?*

Knowledge of the fact(s) differs from knowledge of the reason for the fact(s).

Aristotle, *Posterior Analytics*

The natural way of doing this [seeking scientific knowledge of the fact(s)] is to start from the things which are more knowable and obvious to us and proceed towards those which are clearer and more knowable by nature ...

Aristotle, (The) *Physics*

- It is also essential that teachers make an effort to *engage* students and sustain reasonable attention to the teaching and learning process each teaching period. Such engagement also involves conveying some enthusiasm for the topic at hand.

  I have heard teachers say things like, "Well ... what we're doing today is pretty boring ... but we have to do it ... so ..." (followed by a heaving sigh). If it is "boring" our students will find out quickly enough – why tell them? If it is a routine/"boring" activity we just *do our best with it*; even a familiar, "tired" topic. How many times have I taught aspects of grammar (in English) ... Yet each time we try to find those "connections" (visual, even kinaesthetic) that will engage our students and enable integrative learnings. We do not need to telegraph "boringness" in advance!

Teaching is an affective process as well as a cognitive one. It is essential therefore that one conveys positive attitudes not only towards one's subject but also towards pupils ... it is never advisable to devalue what one is about to teach ... better to present the subject to the best of one's ability and let the pupils decide whether it has any intrinsic merit. (Robertson 1997: 70)

Mr Smith sees his Year 8 class lining up haphazardly, in the corridor outside Room 15. As he walks towards them he doesn't greet them: not even a basic "Hi". He opens the door and walks in, and the students file in noisily.

He doesn't welcome them, or consciously seek to calm the class down. He really hasn't made an effort to learn their names yet (it's Week Three). He does not introduce the topic or integrate it into any

prior learning. He starts to write algorithms on the board (Year 8 mathematics) with little or no
enthusiasm. There is no apparent consideration that some students struggle significantly with some of
the more abstract aspects of mathematics and could benefit from some visual connectedness, or
"connectedness" to other areas of knowledge or experience. There is a lack of basic commitment to
the fact that children learn in different ways and that this will affect student learning; not all students
are auditory learners. Yes, he may be tired today. He may be bored. But if he characteristically teaches
like this is there any wonder that there is a correlation between:

- student inattention and his approach to the topic that day?
- his lack of enthusiasm, or even basic engagement, and student indifference and lack of
  motivation in his students?
- student learning outcomes and his teaching style?
- behaviour distractions? (And such distractions will often arise from lack of teacher
  engagement.)
- his approach and his self-talk about this class ("*They* don't listen …", "I wonder why I bother …",
  "*They* should be making more effort …"). They …?

As Robertson notes:

Perhaps with the exception of the first few meetings with a class, a warm and
relaxed greeting before the lesson begins will often make all concerned feel
better and no matter how many times a lesson has to be repeated, nor how
tired one feels, one's interest with the material must be kept alive or the class
will soon share the lack of interest (1997: 69).

- The teacher is aware that his or her *characteristic* voice and actions can significantly facilitate students' attention, interest, motivation and cooperation.
  Although we are *not* actors, we do have to project a visible, confident and
  enthusiastic presence, and pay some conscious attention to voice usage, manner, attitude and approach so as to *engage* students in our teaching presentation and communication (see Welch in Thody et al. 2000). Such enthusiasm
  does not mean a "hyped-up" state where it's all "fun, fun, fun!" or "great" and
  "brilliant …" It does mean, however, we make a conscious effort to convey
  interest in what we are teaching; to utilise the reciprocity of class discussion to
  keep the topic "alive", "related" and "*connected*" to the students' prior experience and learnings. This clearly means much more than the ability to talk,
  "tell", and "direct".
- The teacher makes both a positive and *varied* use of questioning to motivate
  and monitor students' understanding and raise the level *and* quality of students' thinking. This issue is discussed at some length later (p. 150f).

- The teacher monitors the progress of a given lesson *and* monitors general and individual behaviour as it affects teaching and learning. Such monitoring enables the teacher to make appropriate adjustments to the flow and development of a given lesson as well as addressing any inattentive or disruptive behaviour with a focus back to the central business of teaching and learning. This monitoring is conducted as unobtrusively as possible (see case study later, p. 164f).
- The teacher makes a conscious and willing effort to encourage students in *their* effort and progress and gives thoughtful praise and encouragement and – particularly – feedback (see later, p. 152f):

  - keep the encouragement, and feedback, *descriptive* rather than global, for example: "You've described the box in several ways so you can get a clear picture of what it looks like ..." The teacher discusses how the student has utilised several adjectives of colour, shape, size, etc. "A *large, red* box sits on the table. The box is *empty* ..." "That was a moving and thoughtful description of ... in your poem about ...", rather than simply noting "good work", "brilliant work" or "nine out of ten, *great* work ..."
  - use "private" rather than public praise (which can create unnecessary embarrassment with older students), that is, the quiet private encouraging asides we give during on-task learning time
  - focus on the students' effort and progress as well as errors and mistake; use errors and mistakes as opportunities for the student to learn and gain. The topic of encouragement is discussed later in this chapter (p. 152f).

> **NB** In John Hattie's research (2009), he notes that a teacher's effectiveness is related to their "credibility". Children know which teachers make a difference to their learning; to *their development as a learner,* not just their knowledge within a given subject (we all remember those teachers. Good teachers build trust from their competence as a teacher, expressed in: their clarity of communication – the way they communicate the intention and purpose of the activity with some enthusiasm; how "knowledge about" a given topic integrates with the overall goals they seek to establish with their students; and the feedback we give to individuals within a lesson as well as longer term feedback. (See J. Hattie, *Visible Learning,* 2009, London: Routledge.)

A colleague outlines how he encouraged a reluctant learner in a Year 10 mathematics class.

It is Thursday afternoon, last period, in Year 10 mathematics. Students are tired and it has been a hot week. Just around the corner looms the end-of-year mathematics exam. The kids have started revision lessons with me but they are still a bit unsure about exactly which topics are in the exam and which are not.

Michelle listens as I list the topics and chapter reference and exclaims, "No, not lighthouses. I hate lighthouses!" when I mention that Chapter 7 (trigonometry) is on the list. I continued the session with my students, building them up and encouraging them in the strange "language other than English" subject called mathematics, and genuinely looked forward to teaching the group again first period on Friday.

Michelle's comments triggered in me an automatic response to stop the standard "how high above sea-level is the lighthouse" problem, being a stumbling block to her mathematical progression, and make it a springboard into a whole ocean of mathematical wonder (or at least give her the chance to pass this type of question in the exam!).

I created a hand-out sheet with three or four revision questions for the Friday morning class. The most important question on the sheet, of course, had a stick figure diagram of Michelle firing a shot from a cannon towards a lighthouse with the appropriate trigonometric detail on the diagram to help the students find out how far the shot travels to destroy the lighthouse (an old lighthouse under demolition).

The result the next day was very satisfying and fruitful. The class saw the stick figure named Michelle and the class tom-toms soon got the message around the room to check out question three on the sheet. Michelle read the question and asked me, "Did you make up this question because of what I said *yesterday*?" I acknowledged it and was pleased to read on her face a look of "I'm important. My teacher has gone to all this trouble just for me. I better have a red hot go at these lighthouse questions". Michelle now owns that trigonometry question and, through her efforts to do her best to learn mathematics skills, has overcome the fear of the "lighthouse question".

It is my joy to be teaching in a lighthouse to shine out light to students to guide them away, around and past the dangerous rocks of doubt and "I can't do it" attitudes and "I hate maths because I don't understand it".

- Any management of distracting and disruptive behaviour is minimised by keeping attention on the core business: teaching and learning.
- "Relaxed vigilance" is a useful descriptor when addressing typical disruptions such as lateness; calling-out; butting-in; talking while the teacher is talking; inattentive motoric restlessness …
- "Relaxed vigilance" describes the teacher's confident, assured, firm expectations about cooperation with their students when engaged in behaviour management. Group monitoring, through periodic scanning and eye contact (of the class as a whole as well as individuals), is a way of saying "I know that you know that I know …".
- Circulating (during the on-task phase of the lesson) and proximity can even divert some potentially off-task and poor attentional behaviour. Circulating also allows teachers to monitor task engagement, engage in micro-teaching, and to give feedback and encouragement. I've seen teachers (particularly at secondary level) characteristically sit at their desk for the whole lesson, rarely circulating among their students during the on-task phase of the lesson.

When addressing distracting and disruptive behaviour we:

- keep the level and degree of intrusiveness low. Recall the principle of *least-to-most intrusive* (p. 95f).
- keep the engagement of disruptive behaviour brief and keep the language positive (where possible) (Chapter 3).
- remember that tone of voice and manner are as important as the words themselves when communicating respectful discipline.
- focus on the "primary" behaviour, or "primary" issue, wherever possible – avoid getting easily distracted by "secondary" issues and "secondary" behaviours (p. 12f).
- give take-up time (where possible) following corrective discipline (p. 98f).
- use directed "choices" instead of threats (p. 102f).
- Refer the student back to the class agreement on core rights, responsibilities and rules (p. 39f, 46).
- *where possible*, conduct any "criticism" of a student's behaviour privately, or if it has to be given publicly do so in a least-intrusive, *brief* and respectful manner.
- have a well-planned time-out policy at the classroom and exit-from-the classroom levels. No teacher should have to cope with a situation where a student effectively holds a class to ransom. Collegial back-up and follow-through is essential in any time-out process. The issue and use of time-out is addressed at length in Chapter 5.
- always follow-up and follow-through with a student one-to-one on issues that matter. Avoid easily passing-on discipline/behaviour/management concerns to other colleagues. Utilise their skills, however, and their relational goodwill and their expertise to *help with* the follow-up or follow-through (p. 122f, 126f).

- There are many (and varied) *potential* disruptions to a lesson from lateness, calling out, noise levels, not having equipment and seat-rocking through to play-punching, testosteronic bonding and (rarely, one hopes) hostile or aggressive behaviours. Effective teachers, and effective teaching, addresses potential (and likely) disruptions to learning by thinking through classroom management issues *preventatively*. Issues to consider are:
  - organisational issues (from lining up and seating plans through to students who "haven't got a pen …") (Chapter 2).
  - lesson materials and their distribution and use at *appropriate* times (so the students don't distract particularly during whole-class teaching time) – materials monitors can help so we don't have many students "up and about …"

I noticed this young lad (Year 8 class) not doing his work. I also noticed that he was engaging his hormonal bridge-building-possibility eyes on his amour. I asked him (quietly – an aside), "What are you doing?" He replied, wistfully, "I'm thinking love thoughts."

- ○ thinking through how we'll *engage* students' interest within a given lesson or topic and how we'll stimulate some marginal motivation through examples, current issues, use of questioning, concrete examples or illustrations, and so on (see later, p. 164f).
- ○ thinking through *how time will be managed in a lesson* and telegraphing that (in an age-related way) to our students.
- ○ planning how we will deal with typical distractions or disruptions in the *establishment phase of the lesson* itself, such as lateness; noise level; settling a class; initiating and sustaining class or group attention; dealing with students who call out, butt in or seek to derail a lesson. Such planning has to include what sorts of things we'll say to address these typical, or likely, distractions or disruptions (p. 97–106).
- ○ how we will deal with typical disruptions during the *on-task phase* of the lesson.

The key question we need to ask is: "How can I *prevent*, or *minimise*, unnecessary hassles or problems …?"

Most of this preventative aspect of teaching and management occurs in the establishment phase of the year. This is where we develop, then *teach* and monitor the rules, responsibilities and routines to students about lining up, hats off, phones off (and away), and iPods away; rules about toilet provision, going for a drink (even chewing gum); routines for noise level; seating and how to get reasonable teacher assistance; through to how to pack up; leaving the room tidy and how we leave and exit the classroom (Chapter 2) (see also, Appendix A).

In establishing these fundamental routines and rules it is essential to discuss *with* students *why* we have such routines (basically, a fair go for all), and also to try to increase some commonality of *core* routines across classes and year levels.

- *Colleague planning for core routines.* Most of all, the preventative issues are best explored within the context of colleague support. Colleague support can give assurance that we're basically on the right track (or the best track at the moment!). It can also enable some reasonable consistency about core routines and behaviour leadership and enable that "relaxed vigilance". Colleague support can give the moral back-up that we're all in the same boat, facing common issues, concerns and problems and have common responsibilities and – mostly – we're doing *our* best. Colleague support can also give us the long-term professional support we need to reflect, evaluate, assess and even appraise our day-to-day teaching. Such appraisal, of course, needs to be based in professional trust and professional goodwill. Teaching can, at times, be a "lonely" profession. We spend a significant portion of our day with children; a lot is asked of us as we seek to lead, guide, enable, encourage and teach 5–6 periods day after day, week in week out. Those outside our profession have little idea of how naturally stressful that is. Even those in the academic world of education sometimes forget what it is really like. Colleague support has the potential to meet the basic need we have to belong and work as a team of professionals (see Rogers 2002a).

Some years back now I was sitting in a very large lecture theatre listening to an international lecturer. I was at the back – in tiered seating – and could see the few hundred fellow participants below. The lecturer was introduced. He had an hour; presenting a keynote address. Within ten minutes he had "lost" the attention of a significant group of adults. He was hesitant and looked flustered, and his visual displays – on the large screen – were complex and – at times – unreadable. They were displayed too quickly to register, connect, let alone engage. I was appraising all this (even "critical") – as a teacher and as a "student". His examples seemed abstruse and unrelated. His voice was often vocally monotonic and he rarely smiled or scanned the eyes of the group (scanning, of course, would have given him some feedback from sections of his audience). He frequently looked down at his notes. There were no lifting moments, or defusing moments of light humour (I'm not talking about jokes either). In effect, he didn't connect with us. We never really heard what he felt, as well as what he knew about the topic in question or what impact his subject and topic had on him and his world. I'm sure his research was more than adequate. He just wasn't communicating; he wasn't making his world more common to, and with, us. I felt his struggle, his anxiety; I sensed something of his emotional pain.

In front of me sat two colleagues (psychologists) who had started to write notes to each other, and giggle and whisper (quite loudly – as if they were back at school!). They were completely ignoring this lecturer.

I leaned over and whispered, "He's trying to communicate to us." They replied, in a governed whisper, "But he's so bloody boring!" I thought (yet again) how fragile one's hold is on others' attention *as a teacher*.

I felt for this man – he was clearly nervous and anxious – yet I also understood why my colleagues behaved as they did.

We teach within a relational dynamic.

Effective teaching *behaviours* are not mere technique; it is not a matter of "a bundle of skills equals an effective teacher". The skills of effective teaching can be learned, but those skills need to be engaged within a desire to teach and a willingness to engage and relate to children and young people. The behaviours of effective teaching are not inconsistent with the appropriate sharing of our humanity and feelings.

Effective teaching is our normative, *professional* responsibility.

Humour, warmth and rapport

William Glasser has said that one of our basic needs is the need for "fun" (1992). By this he means that the classroom teacher needs to recognise the importance of feeling both emotionally and intellectually positive. It also means we seek to communicate such within the working relationship with our students.

Children of all ages value and enjoy working with teachers who have a sense of humour, which can range from the funny turn of phrase to facial expressions, Pythonesque irony, appropriate farce and self-humour (as with *faux pas*). One doesn't have to tell jokes (my memory for jokes is weak). The *bon mot*, repartee, and an apt turn of phrase can all defuse tension, refocus jaded students and lift their spirits (even transitionally).

I have seen classrooms where there is no laughter, warmth or basic *joi de vivre*. They are depressing places to work and learn in. Of course learning cannot always be fun. It is a bit of a grind, actually, on some days. That's the point, in the "gristle" of it all, the humour gives the enabling sense that "we're all in the same boat, going in roughly the same direction". Shared humour affirms something basic about our humanity.

I was mentoring in an English high school a few years back, a maths class – decimal fractions. As I "roved" around the class I noticed a girl surreptitiously reading the *Sun* newspaper inadequately concealed under the worksheet. I approached and asked her how the work was going, "Making sense?" She sighed and said, "It's so boring – all we do is the worksheets ..." I said how I'd struggled with maths at school, adding "It can be annoying doing subjects you don't like or that are boring."

I asked if I could take a look at her progress. She had done little work. I concentrated on what she had done and, before leaving, noted – casually – the *Sun* newspaper ... "Ah *the Sun* ..."

She said, quickly, "I wasn't reading it ..."

Raising the eyebrows and affecting a relaxed frown, I whispered, "I wouldn't mind if it was *The Guardian* or *The Independent!*" I then gave a directed choice about the newspaper and moved on. She looked visibly relaxed. I left with a smile and assurance I'd drop in later "on my rounds".

Speaking with a Year 11 student recently she said how much she enjoyed maths, yr adding, "It's surprising really because I never really *enjoyed* maths ..." Talking further it was clear that the difference was the *teacher* of maths she had this year ... It's the teacher who makes the difference.

Recently, in a Year 10 History class, I noted Jack had put on his music from his iPhone. As I did the rounds (on-task learning time) I came over and beckoned him to take the ear buds out, "It'll help if you turn it off." I then asked how the work was going. He looked up with a mischievous grin and said, "I put them on deliberately ..." I added, with a wink, "As long as you don't mind me deliberately reminding you to take them off and away." Was that a glimmer of a smile? Did I sense he knew, I knew that he knew "the game"? "See you later Jack."

It takes time, of course, to build rapport and trust with the very wide range of personalities that make up a classroom group. From the way we greet the class and individuals; from the way we communicate our enjoyment – even passion – (at times) in our teaching; the way we always seek to keep fundamental respect intact with our students (even we discipline); the way we always seek to repair/rebuild beyond necessary discipline – not holding grudges – starting each day afresh, will all convey that rapport and extend that relational trust.

A note on teacher status and authority

When teachers seek to establish both appropriate moral authority, and role authority, it is important to realise that such authority is established, and earned, within the context of relationships built by the teacher. The fundamental nature of such relationships is dependent on conveying respect, knowledge and enthusiasm for what one teaches. Authority is also communicated through a relaxed confidence in one's management and teaching, and a healthy acceptance of fallibility in self (and others). As Robertson notes:

> Teachers who wish to establish their authority should behave as if they are already *in* authority. This is not as simple as it sounds. A teacher by virtue of (a certain) "status" has certain rights to behave in ways denied to pupils, and in exercising those rights he reinforces his authority. This does not mean that he should be repressive or authoritarian but rather that his behaviour should be consistent with his "status".
>
> Pupils are less likely to question a teacher's authority if, by his behaviour, he defines the situation as one in which his authority is legitimate. It is particularly important for a teacher to do this in the first meeting with a new class. (1997: 10, 11)[2]

Some key aspects in conveying appropriate authority and "relational power"

- Moral authority superintends role authority. The power associated with one's authority always needs to be understood as more than power "over" others. We use our "power" (as adults-in-role) *for* and *with* our students; not merely using power *over* our students. There is a conscious use of the preposition here (over). Many teachers (of my generation) grew up believing they had power *over* children; their leadership behaviour was often reflected in their views, particularly concerning punitive discipline. In time – of course – we have reflected more vigorously on how we understand and engage our "power" and that our relational/moral power is "earned" within our leadership and our ability to engage workable – and positive – relationships with our students.

  Do we use our leadership, experience and legitimate role authority to lead and guide young people towards increasing self-discipline and respect for others' rights? Our leadership, management, teaching and discipline are not aimed merely at controlling others but at helping them to control themselves and manage themselves, their learning and their social relationships at school (p. 29f).

  "Relational power", rather than the mere utility of "controlling power", is a crucial factor when establishing and maintaining one's moral authority with students. This is also not inconsistent with the need to be assertive and to bring control *to situations and contexts* where there is distraction, disruption, disorder – even danger in student behaviour.

Relational power is in part established in the first meetings with our students and developed, and sustained, through demonstration of mutual respect and mutual regard.

- When establishing and maintaining such authority the teacher:
  - always leads from and to the core rights and responsibilities (p. 38f, 41f).
  - creates a positive tone of purposefulness about "why we are here together in school …" and "why we are here today in *this* lesson and doing *this* activity …".
  - sustains students' attention and motivation; this is a crucial factor in effective teaching. Without the ability to initiate, engage and sustain attention and show some enthusiasm for one's subject or lesson, students are unlikely to either involve themselves in any workable (or meaningful) learning let alone behave in ways that consider classmates and teacher alike (see also p. 58f, 70f, 108f).
  - ensures the appropriateness of the learning activity and task. This (obviously) ranges from catering for students' ability range and differentiation, through consciously considering visual (as well as auditory) learning styles and how resources can be best utilised with individual or group learning experiences.

Fundamentally, a teacher's authority needs to be based in effective teaching and behaviour leadership rather than a status position based on coercion or displays of authoritarian management (which ultimately fail in the longer term).

Well-prepared lessons, the ability to present and communicate clearly and to communicate knowledge, information and skills with some energy and clarity, together with the ability to engage student attention and interest, are fundamental to any concept of *effective* teaching. Such teaching also includes the ability to develop shared dialogue with our students, and to clarify learning tasks and activities so that students can engage meaningfully with what we seek to teach (see case study on p. 164–169).

- A teacher's authority is quickly assessed by students through how they perceive his or her *overall* leadership behaviour. The *characteristic* tone of voice, facial expressions, eye contact, scanning and posture can all signal one's emotional state, and can convey how confident, assured or anxious the teacher is. The teacher's characteristic "global set of behaviours" (verbal and non-verbal) are typically assessed by students in the early stages of their relationship with a class (Rogers 2006a, 2011).

Pupils are typically reported as liking teachers who can keep order (without being too strict); are fair (i.e. are consistent and have no favourites); can explain clearly and give help; give interesting lessons, and "are friendly and patient" (Kyriacou 1986: 139).[3]

- When exercising *our rights* of leadership and authority we need to recognise that such rights depend on cognate responsibilities. There is a sense in which a teacher's authority is acknowledged and accepted by the *reciprocity* occurring in their leadership role. That "reciprocity" can be seen in how students typically respond to our leadership. For example, when a teacher walks across to a student's desk and comments about a toy on their desk and then gives a directed choice (p. 100f), "David, I want you to put that toy in your bag or on my desk, thanks …", and the student puts the toy in his bag, the student, in effect, gives the teacher *the authority that the teacher confidently exercises at that point*. This is the nature of the "reciprocity" occurring within relational authority. For one teacher the words used in the "choice" about the toy could sound like a directed choice; in the mouth of another teacher they could well sound like a challenge or threat; yet another teacher may make such a choice appear as a plea.

  When a teacher says to a class group, "Eyes and ears this way now, thanks" (or variations on how we cue for whole-class attention/focus), the fact that most students do face the front – and actually listen – indicates a notable feature about this relational reciprocity. The authority to lead, guide, remind, direct, create (and give) "choices", give consequences (and so on), depends on students acknowledging such authority *by their reciprocal action(s)* and responses. This is the natural – even creative – tension in teacher authority. Our leadership behaviour does not merely *cause* students to act in accordance with our direction. How they *already perceive* their relationship to us, particularly in regard to relational status, will always affect their responses to us.

Authority exists in a relationship and is to a large extent granted by the students. It is in everyone's interest that there should be a context in which teaching and learning can take place and teachers must be granted the authority required to perform this role. For their part they will have to earn this authority by the quality of their teaching but it is also helpful from the outset to behave as if they already have it, in a more formal manner consistent with their "rank".

When a person behaves in a confident and efficient manner we are inclined to believe that such behaviour reflects knowledge and experience. In the school situation the reality is that teachers *are in* positions of authority in relation to students but their behaviour must be consistent with this and hence imply knowledge and experience; thus the teacher can "claim" authority (Robertson 1997: 75).

- Always be prepared to follow up and follow through with a student (one-to-one) on issues that count, such as concerns about a student's learning or work, concerns about behaviour or the need to carry through with appropriate consequences (p. 122f). As with all follow-up beyond the classroom setting, a teacher needs to communicate care and concern as well as the authority to address behaviour issues or apply consequences. Alongside any such follow-up one should also be willing to repair and rebuild the relationship if there is any anxiety, tension or animosity.

  As noted earlier, in any one school, there can be significant differences in the authority granted to teachers by the students. Those differences transcend age and gender. According to Robertson (1997), Kyriacou (1986) and Rogers (2006b, 2011), it is one's personal qualities, demonstrated in effective teaching and management, rather than mere *role*, that determines one's relational, and moral, authority.

  While this may sound obvious in print, I've seen many teachers – in practice – merely expect, even demand, to have their authority accepted when they clearly are ill-prepared; do not find workable engagement, interest and entry points into student understanding; teach in a boring uninteresting way with little enthusiasm; and give infrequent encouragement and feedback to their students.

It should also be expected of teachers that they are of such a personality and character that they are able to command the respect of their pupils, not only by their knowledge of what they teach and their ability to make it interesting but by the respect which they show for their pupils, their genuine interest and curiosity about what pupils say and think and the quality of their professional concern for individuals. It is only where this two-way passage of liking and respect between good teachers and pupils exists, that the educational development of pupils can genuinely flourish (Kyriacou 1986: 139).

Dialects and accents – an issue to be considered

There are some quite distinct dialects across the UK. I still struggle, sometimes, to understand *every* word in some UK accents. No offence – I'm sure it's the same with understanding some Aussies; although *Neighbours* has been on your television screens for a long time now! There are teachers whose dialect (or language other than English) or even their *English accent* sometimes becomes an occasion for children to tease them, or have a bit of fun. I've worked with teachers who have sometimes been demoralised by calculatingly snide comments, where several students collude by laughing loudly at the teacher's turn of phrase, use of words or accent, or fast/rapid speech pattern. Communicating clearly, and speaking clearly, are crucial aspects of day-to-day teaching. Where teachers are aware that their accent, typical voice usage or English pronunciation may – potentially – affect their teaching and classroom management, the following will help.

- Plan ahead by discussing with colleagues what they might, or could, do – should the issue arise. This could include thinking through (ahead of time) responses to typical student comments and how they can confidently broach the issue with their class(es).
- It can help to explain, briefly – and confidently – to students at the beginning of each of their first classes, that "you will, quickly, notice that my accent, in English, is a bit different. Sometimes I might mispronounce words from time to time. I work hard on my English. Thanks in advance for your understanding and support." *Prepare* a brief "explanation" beforehand, think through how best to *briefly* explain it; even the words used. I've seen colleagues from Vietnam, Italy, Greece, India, Lebanon ... communicate this initial shared understanding skilfully, with tact and even humour. It may be helpful to invite questions from the students. My own view is that the explanation should suffice. If our subsequent teaching is effective, the *accent* shouldn't matter too much.
- It can help, on occasion, to repeat a word (or phrase) if we think some in the class are genuinely unclear about our pronunciation.
- If a student is derogatory about one's accent or use of English, it will be enough to briefly, firmly – without any hostility – make the brief assertive point, "I don't make unfair disrespectful (or put-down) comments about your speech; I don't expect you to make unfair, disrespectful, put-down ... comments about mine." The tone of such a statement needs to be confidently firm and calm. It is not a threat, it is an assertion – avoid any argument. In such cases it is enough to assert and then to move on with the lesson or activity. *Sometimes* even brief repartee may be appropriate. Though one should be careful not to reinforce mean-spirited, or nasty, comments with repartee.
- If some students *persist* in being disruptive by snide comments (in tone and manner), "I can't understand you, Miss! You're not saying it clear. What do yer mean?" (or worse) then use the time-out provision in the short term. We do

not want to make students' assumed misunderstanding (of one's accent) an easy affront or a "game" or lead to *any* harassment.

- *Always* follow-up *any* abusive comments made by students (p. 122f). If necessary ask a senior colleague (early in the first week) to call a meeting with the students concerned and conduct an "accountability conference" (p. 280f).

Inviting and sustaining engagement

Students need to know that their *participation* in the lesson will be expected by the teacher. At the beginning of each lesson students will need to be reminded that their contribution to their learning process will be monitored, and their involvement expected. For example, in an English lesson on Shakespeare's *Hamlet*, students know that later in the class time they will be asked to think about the main character in terms of "his relationship with his dead father" or his so-called "step-father", or "his mother", or "Ophelia" or "his moods" ("… though this be madness, yet there is method in't."). Having been given a set time, students are then asked to share: "We should be ready now to hear what you think about how Hamlet coped with …". In sharing, publicly, students will need to be given time to develop and construct their public contribution:

- "relate this topic (issue or question) to your own experiences"
- "give an example of, or analogy of …"
- "explain 'this' (a given concept) in *your own words*"
- "give a summary of …"
- "explain this … as if to someone who had never seen, or heard, of …".

Students then discuss this in pairs, ready to share with the class later.

Teachers will often preface their teaching time with a statement: "You will need to be listening carefully – you might be asked to contribute to someone else's answer …"; "Listen up, here folks – you'll need to know this …"; "I wonder if anyone will have heard of this?"; "This is going to be a little tricky so …".

When inviting student engagement teachers can use a wide variety of approaches beyond simple "public" questions and answers:

- Ask all students to write their answers on a card (or mini whiteboard) and hold it up (this "old-fashioned" approach can work well for simple "scan checking" by a teacher at primary level or middle school). Not all students have interactive lap-tops or iPads (at least in the schools where I teach).

- Students can answer questions in an answer notebook; they then share their answers in a paired discussion or be ready to contribute to class discussion.
- The questions asked can be answered in a daily journal.
- Students can be directed to write a brief summary in response to a teacher's questions to a whole class. This increases task focus and avoids easy distractibility.

Questions and effective teaching

The purpose of questioning is to *engage* thinking; *confirm* thinking; *share* thinking; or *clarify* and *extend* thinking. There are many ways questioning can be used in whole-class and small-group teaching. Questions also allow the teacher to check for understanding and clarify meaning. They also provide an obvious form of feedback for the teacher. Even rhetorical questions can be used in this way.

- It is important the teacher does not do most of the talking in class dialogue. We need to avoid, too, piling topic upon topic with several multiple questions that can often sidetrack and even confuse student understanding of the key issue, topic or focus. I've seen teachers talk for up to 20 minutes without any genuine student involvement. Enabling students to be task-directed (through whole-class discussion) is a crucial feature of effective teaching and learning. We need to pace and focus our questions to both the *immediate* learning focus as well as the integration to prior understandings and *then* extend the topic to the current learning.

  Making the task(s) explicit (and visible) and stating the desired and positive outcomes of a lesson are basic – but crucial – in most learning tasks. It is then important (generally speaking) to stick to the aims, and the task focus, through any spoken, or written, questions.
- Some key questions are best written up on the board, or in a worksheet, to *keep the focus* for the learning activity.
- Short extending and refocusing questions can also keep the students focused. During a vigorous class discussion, a teacher, in responding to an individual student, can extend their thinking through short refocusing and reframing questions: "So, you're saying … Is that right?" Even a brief, and *positive*, "So? Extend that a bit more …" or even a simple "And …?" "That's clearer" can cue the student to more fully form and express their answer and ideas.
- Questions by the teacher (and by fellow students too …) should (where possible) also link back to what students already know to develop and extend their natural curiosity.
- After a general cue to the class, "I want you to think about the main (issue, character, point). The teacher, then, directs the class to share, or in pairs, then

invites students' responses: "Alright (…), *we* should be ready to hear what you think about … Hands up, folks, so I can see who is ready to share …".

- Avoid discussing any *one* student's answer at length.
- If the teacher *invites* students to illustrate/develop work on the board, in front of the class, at least direct other students to work on the solution at the same time. Answers can then be compared. Any such approach requires a cohesive class environment and no student should ever be forced to display knowledge in front of the class.
- Avoid embarrassing a student by picking on them (as a 'discipline device'): "What do you think, Mark? Eh?!" "Were you listening …?" "So – do *you* know what we're *actually* talking about?"

At primary-age level many teachers now include a teaching unit on active listening skills to enhance student attention in shared class discussion time (see McGrath and Francey 1993).

Thoughtful questioning can also increase the active *cognitive* participation of all students. When using directed questions the teacher is also directing student effort into sharing their *thinking*; not always in merely a right or wrong way, but rather supporting the process of learning.

Overuse of questions that require only one – right – answer or require a single-word response can limit useful development in student thinking and expression: for example, "Who can …?"; "What is …?"; "Who is your favourite character in *Harry Potter* …?"; "Who can read *this* word?". Such questioning – alone – tends to limit extension to a student's thinking.

Contrast these questions:

- "Share with the person next to you about who was your favourite character and *why* …". The "why" extends the sharing and allows the student to develop their thinking.
- "Think of your own example of hope or courage in … Write the key points down … When you have several points recorded down, look up, here, to the front, so I know you're ready and we'll share as a group … *Thinking hats on everyone* …".

"Wait-time" when asking questions

Rowe (1978, in Cummings 1989) develops an interesting case for what he calls "wait-time", where teachers allow some time ("wait-time") after asking a general question to the class or an individual. Rather than a simple "What is the …?" (expecting a right or wrong answer and these questions do have a place at times …), the teacher frames the question more thoughtfully: "Think about the *difference* between … Raise your hand when you are ready with the answer. Take a moment to imagine *how*, or *what*, or *where*, or *if* …". The teacher then scans the group allowing some "wait-time" *after* asking the question and *after* the student's response.

According to Rowe, creative use of "wait-time" can:

- increase the length of a student's response
- elicit a wider response rate among students
- increase confidence in answering
- increase the contributions of "slower" students
- have a generally more positive effect on class behaviour.

> **NB** According to Cummings (1989), teachers smile more often and nod their heads more if they perceive a student to be "bright", giving the student more encouraging non-verbal feedback and more opportunity to respond. Obversely, when teachers respond to "low-achieving" students their perception of low-achieving affects the way they interact with those students.
>
> This is a pattern of behaviour linked to what is often termed the "expectancy effect" (see Rosenthal and Jacobsen 1968). See also Robertson (1997), McInerney and McInerney (1998) and Rogers (2011).

Using encouragement

In a Year 9 graphics class a few years ago my colleague and I were teaching calligraphy using large Gothic script with flourishes, and miniature illustrations and motifs within and around the large capital letters. Using an ink wash, fine felt-tipped pens and gold and silver pens the students were in the final stages of some demanding, well-developed and very attractive work.

I was talking with one of the lads about the shape and colours of his letters. "So, how did you get that neat scroll effect there, with the bronze and pale blue background?" I was genuinely interested. He shared – with some enthusiasm – the drafting and planning process that had led to this final product. I hadn't once said his work was "great", "wonderful" or "brilliant", but we did talk about his penmanship, the design, the final effect. In short, I was letting him know that I had noticed his effort, his journey (here) as a learner; an artist. What my colleagues and I call "conversational encouragement".

As I walked away, one of the lads (who must have been listening) beckoned me over and said, "Hey, Mr Rogers, can you look at my work too?"

Students value encouragement and feedback. They benefit from the assurance that we have acknowledged their work; the effort and the direction of their work. Feedback can also clarify students' thinking and direction of their work. It can help fill in gaps, extend ideas or even just make the students aware of *their own* work.

It is important that children experience some success in their ongoing learning. Encouragement is a major way that we, as teachers, can let the students know how they are doing and where their strengths and areas of further development lie.

Encouragement works on both our feelings and our thinking; because we *feel* better with encouragement and feedback, we often – consequently – think we can do better. This is particularly important when we are struggling with challenging topics, developing new skills, trying to integrate knowledge into meaning ...

Encouragement enables self-confidence.

Conversely, when teachers criticise and negate a child's effort it breeds discouragement (we can all, no doubt, remember our own schooldays ...).

Take the common example of a teacher commenting on a child's writing ...

"Yes you have used some interesting examples of adjectives of comparison here *but* your writing is very messy. Why can't you write more neatly ...?" When we give encouragement we don't need to add negative caveats. "OK you've marked the line where to cut the wood, but you're not holding the saw properly. How many times have I told you? No wonder you've cut the wood crookedly ...", "No, that's not the way to do it! Come on (big sigh) this is the proper way to ..." (how many times have I heard teachers say that?).

"No, that's *not* how you say deuxième ..."

It is likely that it is only the last bit that is heard – and remembered – by the student, particularly with a child who feels inferior in their writing ability, or using a saw (in a woodwork or technology class) or learning to come to terms with the French language ...

I recall, in a woodwork class (as a student), my teacher saying, "If you put your index finger on the handle of the saw it'll help stabilise it; it won't jar as much. Do you want me to show you?" He was *always* encouraging; never, "No you don't do it like that!" or "What did I say, weren't you listening?" He never patronised me, judged me; he patiently enabled me to focus on *where I was* in my current level of skill. He helped me to refocus through questions, "*Do you notice* how you're holding the saw ..." If I was using a particular tool incorrectly or unhelpfully he'd also add, "Do you mind if I show you ...?" then add, "What do you notice now ...?" He sharpened my focus and directed it. This gave me confidence in *my ability* and developing skill. I owe much of my confidence in using woodwork tools to this teacher.

While we need to help students with errors, we can do this constructively without overfocusing on a child's struggle, or failure, or past.

- "You've really got that idea, now, of how to multiply decimal fractions. The last few questions were a bit tricky though; I can see how it might have been more difficult to do this. Let's go back and have another look and see ..."
- "By using that sharp pencil, Michael, you're able to get an accurate reading with the protractor on those angles."
- "The way you've set your chart out, Shaun, makes it easier for me to read what the steps are ... particularly for someone who's not a science teacher ..." (I said this to a student when I was mentoring a colleague in a science class recently – and I meant it).
- "The way you've carefully labelled your diagram makes each part of the process really clear ..."
- "There's been some difficult words to remember this week, Elise; you've made an effort to use them (and their meaning) in your writing on this topic ..."
- "Those are interesting adjectives, Ahmed; see how many ways you've been able to describe that box ..." (this to a student where we were discussing adjectives of size, comparisons, shape, colour, etc).

When students reject our encouragement

If a student rejects (or seems to reject, our feedback/encouragement – for example, the student says something like, "Anyway I think it's rubbish (my work)" – it will not help to over-service what may be a form of attentional behaviour. "Oh it *is* good; your work *is* good. I *really* meant it. Please don't say your work is rubbish ..." It's enough to say, "I meant it" and walk away (at that point) to work with another student. I've had students put their hands over their work and say, "No you can't see my work, it's not good." I give the same answer as above without over-serving their (often) attentional behaviour. I'll see their work eventually.

I still hear some teachers say things like "You are the best student I've ever had ...", "You're the best at ...", "That's a great drawing ..." Praise like this focuses on the child in terms of "how good *they* are ..." or "how good they are *at* something". When such comments are said in other children's hearing it can breed natural resentment and unnecessary comparisons (as when the *best* essay is read, and when the *best* art work is shown ...). Praise, in this sense, can actually be manipulative of the student's feelings and sense of self. "*You* are a good boy/girl for ... (or because) ...". As Ginott

(1972) noted in his writings on praise and encouragement, *supportive* praise recognises and affirms a student's effort, allowing a student to begin to understand and *fairly* evaluate *their* work/behaviour. This kind of "praise" *encourages* and motivates rather than judges; the teacher is not the sole *validating* person in the student's sense of work.

Positive teaching style

The most basic expression or form of encouragement is the teacher's positive body language: the encouraging and approachable manner, tone of voice and smile that says: "You can do it"; "Hang in there"; "You're trying hard"; "You handled that well"; "That's hard work, however you're trying; I can see …"; "Give it your best shot"; "I'm sure you'll make a responsible decision".

Even 'basics' like how we enter a student's personal space and ask to see their work; remembering to use their first name; specifically noting what they are doing and giving short-term feedback on their work and effort applied; empathising when they struggle with difficult concepts; re-explaining (several times if necessary) are all expressions of encouragement.

I have worked with teachers who will come into a student's working space (also their *personal* space), pick up a student's workbook (without asking permission) and start making comments about the work: "Is *that* what I asked you to do … is it?" I have seen teachers walk over to a student's work and tap (with an overly motoric index finger) on their book: "… and *where's* the margin, hmm?" I have actually heard some teachers say, "Well, am I supposed to *ask permission* to see a student's work?" The answer is – of course – "Yes". It is *their* work. When we come alongside a student to chat, "micro-teach", give feedback, or offer help (during on-task learning time) we ask: "Do you mind if I have a look at your work? How's it going …?" When a teacher says this (in a positive tone) she is modelling basic courtesy; it is not a matter of asking "permission".

A positive, encouraging, manner engages a more positive learning atmosphere and can help in the maintenance of long-term positive behaviour with our students.

When students frequently hear "You *never* …". "You *always* …". "*Can't* you get it by now?" and the appalling "Are you thick or what …?" one can understand that they would probably experience low motivation and feel discouraged. While it seems unbelievable that teachers would ever talk like this to students, some do. One hopes it is *never* intentional. Contrast this with teachers who will explain a difficult mathematical process many times (if necessary), assuring students that,

"Yes, it can take time to come to terms with this concept. It isn't easy, but we'll get there. I struggled with positive and negative integers and algebra too …!"

As Dreikurs et al. (1982) have noted, both encouragement and discouragement contain the word *courage*. Giving a child some fundamental "courage" – as a learner – is in part how we relate to the student, and in part the language we use. Even as an ongoing, adult learner, I've noticed it was always the way I was treated, *along with* non-judgemental feedback, that enabled my learning, my motivation and even my assurance that mistakes and misunderstandings did not mean that I was a failure; that I could do it ….

When I was a full-time teacher, I started (and finished) some postgraduate study. It was long and arduous and I wondered (at times) if it was all worth it. During the course of the research I was undertaking I was required to do some statistics units. My first university teacher was somewhat offhand in his manner. He seemed unaware that we (his mature-aged students) had all had busy days of teaching and had trudged off, in the evening traffic, to the university to further our knowledge, understanding and our careers. His teaching style was high on expectation (that we all knew quadratic equations, orthogonal contrasts, and so on) and low on tolerance of struggle, confusion and "where the hell does all this fit in our postgrad studies?!" His non-verbal sighs, eyes to the ceiling and tut-tutting frustration at our "obvious" and "simplistic" questions contributed to us feeling like inadequate learners. It all came back to me; I was a student again, at high school, with a teacher I didn't like who was seemingly unconcerned, unconnected, seemingly uncaring about us and how we felt …

My second "teacher" (another statistics unit) was a professor. The first day we entered the university classroom (as adult learners) Brian welcomed us personally and when we were sitting down as a group said, "Hello and welcome, everyone. Look, I know you're probably all feeling bushed after a long day with your Grade 5s or Year 8s … You can see I've got some tea/coffee, hot water and cups over there. I'd like you to grab a cuppa, regroup, settle down and I'll explain the course, the way in which we can work together in this unit and the sorts of projects we'll tackle together". We, all, immediately felt better (the cuppa helped). We felt we could probably do this none-too-easy subject.

Brian never failed to explain the statistics concepts carefully; in several different ways where necessary. He used visual examples and examples that would relate to our work. He encouraged us to engage in small-group work to support one other. He never failed to address and answer what we thought (at times) were simplistic or "stupid" questions. He was always willing to chat after class, to fine-tune or qualify misunderstandings. He always gave *descriptive* feedback on our work (rather than merely "18 out of 20. Well done", "5 out of 10 – have to do better"). I enjoyed going to Brian's classes (although maths has never been my high-comfort-zone forte). I even passed – quite well. He wrote a personal note to me (to everyone) on the completion of the exam.

I learned a lot more than statistics from Brian. I was reminded about how to be an effective and supportive teacher.

It is easy, as teachers, to become conditioned to negative behaviour; to easily notice and over-attend to the range of distracting behaviours that occur from shuffling and whispering while the teacher is talking, to addressing lateness and calling out and task avoidance and more ... While we have to manage – and correct – distracting and disruptive behaviour, we also need to balance our correction with encouragement: *this should be normative in our teaching practice*. I've heard some teachers come out with the ludicrous comment (about encouraging positive behaviour and effort in work): "Well, they *are supposed* to be doing that anyway!"

It is very important to balance any correction with encouragement. This can be as basic as moving around the room and acknowledging the students' presence (smile, nod, OK sign) when they *are* working, *are* on-task; or encouragement can be as focused as specific attention to task and giving descriptive feedback and praise.

Sometimes all that is required are just a few apposite words, as when a student, answering a question in front of his or her peers, hears the teacher say, "That was a thoughtful question and an interesting way of looking at ..." rather than saying, "No, that's not the right answer". If the student is wrong in his or her work or in answer to a question, a brief noting that, "... was incorrect ... however you tried ..." is enough. We do not need to communicate that the student is inept, stupid or can't learn.

Here are some key features of encouragement:

- Be conscious of even the small – as well as more involved – expressions of encouragement: the affirming smile that basically humanises and reassures; brief task-checks such as "How's it going?"; "Where are you up to?"; "How's it coming together here?"; "Have you considered?"; "Can I suggest?"; "It might help if ..."

The teacher notices a student's page without the margin and date. Instead of asking why there's no margin, the teacher asks if she can have a look at the work, gives some feedback and as she turns the book around to face the student she runs her finger non-verbally down the left-hand side of the page to indicate to the student to remember the margin, and points to the top right of the page as if to say remember the date. She winks. He smiles back. Done. Small acts – but important small acts.

- As noted earlier, when giving verbal or written encouragement and feedback it helps if we focus on *descriptive* comment rather than merely global praise or negation from a child's work to their behaviour (p 163f). "That desk looks tidy and well organised, Stephen … books on one side, writing materials on the other. It'll be easier to find things now, eh?" Here the teacher focuses on the child's effort (his behaviour). The teacher describes what the student has done. "That was a kind thing to do … [or a *thoughtful* act, or was *cooperative*, or was *considerate*]". Descriptive feedback takes a little longer but it *acknowledges* and it *affirms* the student's effort and the direction of that effort. It also engages the students' self-respect as we show appreciation for their thought and effort.

  This approach can be applied to the student's academic work as well. To write "Well done", "Great work", "Marvellous" or "Excellent work (9/10)" on a student's work can, of course, encourage a child but it doesn't say *what* is "great" or "marvellous" or "excellent" (or why). Compare those remarks with comments like "The words you've used to describe the loneliness and isolation of the moors … I could feel how the main character must have felt when …". Here the teacher is adding a few words to *describe* what was "good work"; more importantly, the teacher is also affirming the student's effort. The student can also see where their strengths are acknowledged by their teacher.

  Errors and deficiencies can also be acknowledged: "remember to check your work for spelling and layout …". It can help to use prearranged symbols to highlight (on their workbook) where margin, paragraphs, spelling and even grammar need to be checked. This avoids too much red marking, which can sometimes make a visible mess of a student's work. Avoid judgemental reminders: "*Don't* forget the date … [the margin, the paras]" or "You *should* know how to spell 'because' by now". "Remember to …" is a more cooperative reminder to read on one's work.

NB   John Hattie and Helen Timperley (2007: 81) note that teaching feedback "is a consequence of performance". To be effective, "feedback needs to provide information specifically relating to the task or process of learning that fills a gap between what is understood and what is aimed to be understood" (p. 82).

Hattie also has noted a negative correlation between extrinsic, tangible rewards and task performance (p. 84).

Key questions that relate to feedback are: Where am I going? (What are the goals?) How am I going? (What progress is being made towards the goal?) Where to next? (What activities need to be undertaken to make better progress?)

> It is also crucial that the teacher's feedback is "targeted at students at the appropriate level" (p. 86). In this sense, goals can be more effective "when students share a commitment to attaining them" (p. 89).

- When encouraging a student it can also help to acknowledge the effort and struggle and improvement in their progress (particularly when the student whinges that "It's too hard …"): "Yes, it can be difficult to roll clay into a flat shape …"; "It took me a while to understand the accent on some of these French words … Some?! Phew!", "I remember how you used to struggle with this … look how far you've come …" Encouragement, in this sense, gives children the emotional safety to "fail", to get things "wrong" and learn from (and within) their natural struggle. Conversely, it doesn't help if we easily, and frequently, do for the student that which he can do for himself: "Here, give me the scissors … I'll show you". It would be more helpful to say, "That's a difficult shape to cut. Can I show you how to make it easier?", "If you're not happy with it the way it is … what do you think you could do so you'd be pleased/happier/more settled with it?" Yes, there will be students who seemingly reject even the most supportive and well-intentioned encouragement. As noted, if a child appears to reject our feedback it is enough to meet such rejection with a brief assurance that it was well meant and leave it at that (p. 154f).

When using feedback to assist a student with frequent errors or unhelpful patterns of behaviour it can help to begin a one-to-one feedback session with comments like: "Have you noticed …?"; "Are you aware that …?"; "Do you hear yourself say …?"; "Are you conscious of …?"; and "How do you feel when …?" These openers can lead to specific, supportive, feedback comments about students' work or behaviour. Primary colleagues often use the student home–school diary to give encouragement:

Congratulations on your spelling, David. This word list was not easy and I can see you are really trying; 7 out of 10 shows improvement and application; you're really trying. (Do you know I found spelling a bit hard when I was your age!) All the best Mr Smith.

Karl, I noticed you shared your colouring pencils with Taylor during art time. That was a considerate thing to do. Taylor felt you cared about him (and it saved me trying to find some spare pencils) – thanks for the cooperation. Ms Joyce.

This brief comment shows that the teacher identifies with the student as well as giving some descriptive feedback and encouragement. What often happens is that these comments are also read by the parent who (often) gives "secondary encouragement".

As with any comments home to parents (diary, notes, letter, certificates), their value, as encouragement, depends on the quality of the relationship between the giver (as teacher) and the receiver (the student).

- Avoid easily qualifying – even discounting – the encouragement or feedback. If we notice a student putting litter in the bin thoughtfully, without a reminder, it is enough to say, "That's thoughtful, David – makes the cleaner's job easier". We don't need to add, "and if you did that more often we'd have a much tidier classroom, wouldn't we?" If a student demonstrates neat writing (uncharacteristically? – who knows he may be on the cusp of a change), what he doesn't need to hear is, "Now – *why* can't you do that *all* the time?" Comments that begin – or include – "never", "but …", "why", "if", or "always", as in "You *never* finish your work" and "You *always* call out in class", "…if only you would or could …" are also very discouraging.

  Also, when marking a student's work we need to be sensitive to the fact it is *their* work (and avoid scribbling comments or feedback all over the pages). Unobtrusive marking can demonstrate that you care about the student's finished product. Careful, thoughtful, marking (brief side/end notes rather than big crosses/ticks) still gives feedback to the work where errors/miscues/erroneous conclusions exist … but can still give dignity to the student's effort. It is their effort, too, we need to affirm and build on.

  "You've *finally* finished nearly all your maths work today. Now why *can't you work like that all the time?*" Or the teacher had put an immediate cross against the wrong maths work, then adds, "You weren't concentrating were you?" or, "You haven't made any real effort here have you, look how many you have got wrong." "If *only* you would concentrate …". Even if that is true (and well intentioned by the teacher) it doesn't help if a child frequently hears it … When a teacher immediately, and frequently, adds the qualifying caveat it negates the actual "praise" comment.

  What encouragement seeks to do is to initiate and engage a student's self-awareness about and meaningful understandings, even "assessment", of *their* work (or behaviour). Children know when our feedback and encouragement are genuine. As Dreikurs et al. note, "Children are keen observers and they know who is sincere and who is not. When anyone tries to put up a front, most children will sense this and resent or ridicule it" (1982: 93).

My friend and colleague John Robertson distinguishes between qualified and *unqualified appreciation*. He gives the example of making a special meal for, say, a spouse or partner which they enjoy "with relish". Imagine if the response was along the lines of … "… delicious; so tasty … See what you can do when you *really* try. Now if you can also keep the kitchen a little tidier…" (in Rogers 2002b: 35).

I would add to John's example … how would we feel if our partner/spouse added the supercilious "Hmmm?" question at the end of the qualifying remarks.

- With older students (upper primary onwards) there is a tendency to feel uncomfortable about the more public expressions of praise particularly for "academic effort". A brief, positive, word to a student aside from his or her peers is often well received.

Working with a Year 8 student in a school for students with emotional and behavioural disorders (a few years ago) I was trying to encourage one young lad to use a quieter voice in class time. I made an individual behaviour plan with him to focus on "partner-voice" in class. I drew a cartoon picture of him using a quiet voice while working at his desk. I gave him a copy of this postcard-sized reminder of our plan and I had a copy for myself, and his regular teacher.

On a number of occasions during class time I noticed him making an effort to remember to use his partner-voice. I quietly beckoned him to come over to the front desk area. Here – away from his classmates – I gave him some quiet feedback. "Ahmed, I noticed you were consciously using your partner-voice. It makes it so much easier for everyone … your teacher and me. You're remembering your plan, old chum."

I put a tick on my copy of the plan (and, later, on his copy). Sometimes I just caught his eye and gave a small OK sign. When he forgot his plan I gave a private cue to remind him of partner-voice: thumb and forefinger a little apart to show a small distance (as it were); the distance of "partner-voice".

Many teachers also use incentives such as stickers, stamps, charts, "freetime" activities, certificates and even vouchers such as those used in primary playgrounds where naturally observed thoughtful, cooperative, behaviour is "caught" and a voucher given that can be traded for an ice-cream, and so on.

Whatever incentives teachers use, it is essential that our *characteristic teaching practice includes the principles of supportive and descriptive feedback and encouragemen*t to our students regarding their effort, their goodwill, their contribution, and their thoughtful and cooperative behaviour; even if they are supposed to be doing that anyway! Like us, students benefit from – and even look for – acknowledgement and affirmation.

Rewards

"What do I get if I do this plan?"

I was working with a 9 year-old student (diagnosed with ADHD) on a personal behaviour plan. He had been very distracting to other students in class time as well as significantly off-task during learning times. We discussed how he could stop calling-out behaviours, rocking in his seat, wandering behaviours, task avoidance ... Much more importantly, we went through specific skills of *what he could do to start behaving in a way that could help in his learning and relationships* (many students were getting fed up with his distracting behaviour in class time ...).

He seemed interested as we progressed the plan together; it made "sense". I'd drawn some little "cartoon type" drawings to enhance the "start" behaviours headed by "To help me with class learning my plan is to: ... (with the specific skills we'd discussed and would practise in one-to-one behaviour support sessions ... p. 228f).

He then looked at me and said, "So what do I get if I do this?"

"What do you mean?," I asked. He quickly made it clear he expected some kind of reward ("special time" on computer games / iPad games, etc. ...).

The issue of "rewards" has vexed many teachers. Should we give special "treats", "rewards", "bribes" (it can sound like it sometimes ...)? If you do this – the "good behaviour" – then you'll get this ... At least that's how some children will perceive it. Other children who see a child who behaves distractingly and who frequently gets student of the week (easily it seems), or special privileges from the principal (being sent to get an edible treat etc. ...), naturally gets annoyed.

I said to the young lad, "What you *get* is the feeling in here (I pointed to my head and heart) that you're doing your best in your learning time, you're trying hard, you are remembering how *we* work together (cooperate) in our class. This plan shows you, us (your classmates, your teachers and your mum) ... that you care."

The class teacher worked with him on the plan day by day. There was a place for "ticks" (on his reminder sheet) to acknowledge where he'd remembered his plan. There were stickers, too, to highlight cumulative ticks and, *most of all*, his class teacher used descriptive encouragement and feedback to enable the student's self-esteem and confidence (p. 158f).

At the very least (primary or secondary) we should discuss not only *how* but *why* and *if* we should use "rewards" (especially tangible/food *rewards*). Some schools have quite elaborate reward or affirmation/acknowledgment schemes. One I've seen (at secondary level) is "rewards" for attendance/effort/participation/coopera-tion ... involving a graduated card system: bronze/silver/gold that students can utilise in local shops, businesses, even gyms. Sounds elaborate but it – at least – has the advantage of being open and available to all and is valued by the students.

Some teachers will utilise *whole-class celebration* (rather than individual rewards) to acknowledge effort and commitment. Everything from a special afternoon tea, board games, DVD ... In one early years class a grade one boy (on a personal behaviour plan) would come up to the front of the room (on Friday) to prick one of three coloured balloons to reveal (on a small card) the *whole-class celebration* contained in that balloon.

Motivation

Children (like adults) are motivated by a range of factors: the approval of parents, peers and teachers most commonly, although sometimes by unreasonable parental demands .... Sometimes motivation is linked to "rewards", public acknowledgment and achieving "success at" some skill, activity, sport ... We also want our students to be self-motivated, in that "balance" between extrinsic and intrinsic motivation. It is *how* we seek to enable a student's self-concept so they are not dependent on extrinsic approval or "rewards for"...

Human nature – being what it is – will often act from self-interest and self-gain. This is not necessarily the same as *selfishness*. Our students need to learn to balance self-interest with cooperation and even altruism.

Students can learn that selfless acts are – in a sense – their own "reward" and that there is a wider social good where our cooperation and altruism can speak to the best in us.

Under-praising, over-praising

Understandably teachers will say "why should we reward a student with praise when they do – only now and then – what other students do 'normally' in work/behaviour?"

The issue is – again – what we mean by "reward with praise". Some teachers over-praise, with the loud gesture, "That's great!", as if what the student did in writing a sentence ... was "amazing!" or "brilliant!"

We wouldn't (hopefully) speak that way to students who do make a consistent effort to do their best work and to cooperate with others. Why, then, do we "need" to speak that way to children who do struggle?

Some students will be naturally resentful when a teacher over-praises and *then* gives added rewards (special "free-time" on computer games ...) to the student who has special needs, or who has made little effort in the past ...

Hopefully our encouragement is normatively given – to all.

Case study

He had been told that it was a very difficult class; a Year 8 "low-stream" English class (predominantly boys). The teacher's personal preference was for mixed-ability teaching but ability streaming was the school's current policy. He was determined to help these students go beyond their "label" and not let his personal views on mixed-ability teaching affect his desire to positively engage this new class.

It had taken him several lessons to establish the beginnings of a positive working relationship with the group and – particularly – several students with learning needs and challenging behaviours.

Most of the disruptions to class learning were minor – annoying and frustrating at times, but minor. For example, as the students entered the classroom there was some general chatter and restlessness. Having greeted them in the corridor, he detected a sense of group calmness and settling. He now stands by the door to greet them as they come in. He doesn't, however, engage in chit-chat, or have mini discussions about homework or issues that can be addressed later (if necessary) during the on-task phase of the lesson. He smiles as he briefly greets and acknowledges the students and beckons them to their seats.

He stands at the front of the classroom – purposefully waiting – scanning the room. As they settle he cues for class attention (p. 58f, 70f, 108f). Sometimes he needs to raise his voice a little; he then steps the voice down as the group settles. He thanks them, greets them – as a group – and begins a fresh lesson. He never shouts at them to be quiet. They like that (I know, a number of students told me).

Today he is developing a unit on punctuation – a revision unit. He is aware that the students may think this is "old hat" or even "kindergarten stuff", but it is part of the revision requirement. He begins by engaging in a class discussion about bicycles, punctures and repair kits.

He uses the analogy of a puncture repair kit to associate "puncture" and "punctuation".

"How many of you still ride bikes?" Hands go up. "What sort of bikes do you ride?" Some students excitedly call out; some attentionally call out; he reminds them of the rule, "Remember our rule for class discussion (see Appendix A) ... Thanks."

As the sharing proceeds, one of the students comments that, "Gavin's bike is a shit bike."

It's just audible. The snigger goes around the room. The teacher looks in the direction of the comment (he's not exactly sure who said it) and says, "That's not a helpful comment (even if it's true)." His tone is pleasant, matter of fact and he moves on.

> **NB** If a student makes an inappropriate comment or, say, asks an inappropriate question, we need to be brief, clear and directly focus on the expected behaviour:
> "That's not an appropriate question ..."
> "That's a distasteful comment ..."
> "When you say things like (be briefly specific) it *shows* eg: discourtesy, disrespect, ... (be briefly specific) ..."
> "That's an unnecessary comment ...".

When we have a good working relationship with our students a comment like "Jason (...) come on – you can be better than that." This for a "mild" thoughtless, discourteous or showing-off comment. We also do not need to add discursive qualifiers, for example: " ... is it?" This invited unnecessary attentional engagement.

"We've got a rule for respect – use it."

See also p. 99.

"How many of you have ever got a puncture?" Several hands go up. They're interested; they still like their bikes. A few students call out. The teacher reminds them again (briefly) of the rule. Scanning the faces he adds, "Fair go for all ..." He keeps the discussion going on; he refocuses ...

"Jacinta (...)," he nods and smiles toward her, "tell us about the worst puncture you remember." Several students laugh. She recounts her story. As others contribute he is aware of not over-engaging on any one answer or contribution, and he continues to periodically scan the class group (making brief eye contact) even as he listens to each individual contribution. A student walks in late, posturing a little. The teacher welcomes him quietly, acknowledges that he's late and directs him to a seat (p. 30f, 110f). He continues with the lesson.

He develops the analogy from a puncture (a hole, or several holes, like Jacinta's punctured tyre) to punctuation in a mass of words: commas, full stops, question marks, "talking marks" to show where direct speech is being used, exclamation marks and even capital letters. He puts up a large poster with a dozen sentences. The written vignette is an account about "my first bike", written in the first person without punctuation, so it is quite confusing to read; a mass of words. He invites a few students to read it. They find it, naturally, difficult. The teacher reads some as well, acknowledging the difficulty of reading a "mass of words ..." *without punctuation*. There's good humoured laughter as one idea runs into another, giving confusing messages from the text. He is clearly enjoying himself, although (as I have) he must have taught punctuation many, many times. He is aware that each lesson is a fresh lesson. He does his best (bad day notwithstanding). He doesn't over-dramatise; he is not overly ebullient, but he has a relaxed, positive, good humoured rapport that is able to engage interest and sustain motivation – he can even enthuse his students on most days.

He notices Jason leaning back a bit heavily and noisily on his seat. He's aware that this is probably just unconscious restlessness.

He beckons with a non-verbal cue (p. 114). He moves on with the flow of the lesson. He notices a few students chewing gum. He tactically ignores this *now*; the chewing isn't affecting the flow of teaching and learning. He'll address it later; in the on-task phase of the lesson.

Krista has her hand up. He acknowledges her question, and she asks to go to the toilet. He suspects she might be wanting just to get out for a few minutes. He says, "When I've finished this part of the lesson, Krista, we'll organise a toilet break." She frowns and leans back, "satisfied". (If she had appeared desperate he would have given her the benefit of the doubt and addressed the issue later if repeated requests were made in subsequent lessons.) He moves on.

"So, folks," he scans the group, "what can we do to this mass of print to make it *meaningful* and *sensible*?" He discusses the role of punctuation; these marks (punctuation) help us to clarify meaning in written expression. "How? We 'puncture' the text – all these words. We need to make sense of it all." He taps the text on the board (with his finger), "We use capital letters to begin every sentence *why*?; we use commas for ... *why*?; we use speech marks for ... *why*? What difference does it make *now* when we read the text?"

As the answers come he sometimes extends or develops them. "So, what you're saying, Matt, is ... is that right?" If a student is on a helpful track with their answer or contribution he extends by simply adding "So ...?", or "and ...?", or "keep going ...?" with a smile and eye contact that says: "Keep going, you're on the right track".

"So, what does punctuation do then ...?" "What purpose does punctuation serve?", "How will this knowledge – today – help you in your writing?" "Think about the tyre on the bike that's punctured. Remember when Jacinta and Rob shared how they learned to fix punctures themselves using a puncture kit?"

"I have a punctuation kit here, which is a kind of 'reverse' of what a bike repair kit does." He holds up a poster of an open tin. "Right, what do we need in this kit? This little kit will help us repair our writing; put it in some ordered form so it makes reasonable sense, eh?" He puts up a poster that illustrates the tin and its contents each card in the tin denotes: capitals, full stops, commas, speech marks, question marks. He then takes suggestions from the class on how to repair the text on the board using the "punctuation kit".

The rest of the lesson (and the next lesson) is involved with focused activities to apply the "punctuation repair kit" to differing texts (on worksheets). They are now developing the skills of punctuation. If students talk at any time when he is engaged in group teaching or discussion he will not talk over them. He knows how easy it is to reinforce the tacit acceptance (in students) that it is OK to chat and natter quietly while the teacher is talking. Sometimes he just tactically pauses, sometimes he just gives an incidental reminder to the group (or individuals): "A number of students are talking ..."; or "You're talking and I'm trying to teach." His primary focus is not the disruptive behaviour itself; it is always the teaching and learning process for that class session. Any discipline is a means to enable the protection of fundamental rights and the engagement of focused learning in a cooperative environment (p. 93f) (see also Appendix A).

Before they move on to the on-task phase of the lesson he reminds them of the task requirement: the need for "partner-voice, thanks"; "and you know what to do if you need my assistance – check the set task, read through, check with your immediate classmate first, ask for my help, go on with the class novel while you're waiting for me to assist ...". (He has a poster at the front of the classroom with those positive reminders noted ...). As he moves around the room later, in the on-task phase of the lesson, chatting, encouraging, refocusing and clarifying, he asks questions that assist, probe and encourage: "Anything still unclear?"; "What questions do you have about ...?"; "Is it easy or difficult – why?"; "What do you need to know to help it connect?"

When he notices a student off-task for any length of time he walks over and quietly says, "I notice you're not working …, do you know what you need to be doing now …? how can I help?" He doesn't ask the student *why* he isn't working. He is also conscious of how he comes into a student's personal space, as it were. He asks to see their work, "Do you mind if I …?". He doesn't merely pick it up and peruse, nor does he write on the student's work without a respectful cue, "Do you mind if I …?"

NB   "This work is boring!"

Foreign languages (in Australia, we call this subject LOTE: Languages Other Than English); I've worked as a mentor-teacher with LOTE teachers (at secondary level) many times. In the more challenging schools I work in, I often come up against student comments like "I really don't like LOTE!" and "I hate LOTE!" Some of this (no doubt) comes from parental attitudes: what do we need to learn Indonesian, or Italian, or German for?! (or whatever is "on offer"). "Waste of time!"

When a student says that to me either in the "public forum" of whole-class teaching time or when I'm "micro-teaching" alongside them (at their desk/table group) I'll always acknowledge, "It must be difficult doing work – at times – you dislike or hate …" Not patronising, not cloying – just an acknowledgment, sometimes with a knowing smile. I won't *defend* any subject, *per se*, or *pretend* they can't live without Maths or poetry (or French, German, Italian, Indonesian). Just *briefly* tune-in to their feelings and refocus … "However, it's the work we're doing today; how can I help?" The student will often reply, "I said I didn't like it!" "You did – and you don't have to *like* it. My job is to help you get some workable mileage out of LOTE (or …). Come on let's look at this together. What are you asked to do …?" And we refocus and encourage the student to the learning activity at hand.

Towards the close of the lesson (a double period), he makes time for a "round-Robin" of class questions, calling on students at random to invite responses about the lesson topic and asking questions such as: "What do you think the purpose of today's activity was?"; "Is there anything that still isn't clear …?"; "Does anyone have any questions …?"; "Would you be able to use what you've learned today in any other classes? How?"; "How can you recall, remember, the key ideas from today?"; "Would anybody like to share how they could punctuate more easily, clearly, now?"; "What's made the difference?" (He has a "summary session" – like this – every 3–4 lessons.)

He finishes the lesson early enough to briefly summarise, collect work, cue homework and remind the students to leave the room tidy and leave the room in a considered way … (p. 86f). Most of all, he tries to end each lesson in a positive way (even if it has not been the best lesson).

Those students who do not really apply themselves, or are "calculatedly lazy", he speaks to away from their peers (one-to-one; p. 122f). He doesn't berate them, or make them feel guilty or punish them for poorly developed and poorly applied work. He does point out (privately) that he knows they can do better, that the choices we make about learning *now* affect what we do later and that he'll always be available to help.

He knows that building a cohesive class group takes time, but he plans thoughtfully towards that end, not leaving such cohesion to mere chance. The lessons do not always go this well. There are some difficult days (from time to time) but he has built up the general confidence, and cohesion, of the students in this class to believe they can communicate more thoughtfully, more effectively and more interestingly in their written expression – an area these students have really struggled with.

When he's had a particularly good session – a lesson that has gone well – he spends some time (personally) reflecting on what happened to contribute to the relative success. Was it the lesson content? Was it the engagement and the way he taught that day? Could it have been the timetable slot at that point in the week? Was he feeling particularly well?

When he's had a particularly difficult session with the class he similarly reflects. How did he deal with the students who were distracting, lazy, off-task? Was the learning task clear? Was he trying to cover too much? Did he give enough feedback? He discusses these issues with his colleagues from time to time as well. He is a reflective practitioner. I know; I've worked with him.

Skill development takes time

I recently mentored a colleague in an English class, Year 8. They were getting ready for the national SATS test. They were "swotting" up on grammar. I asked them what they had been looking at … nouns, adjectives, verbs.

One lad earnestly had his hand up (a boy diagnosed with Asperger's Syndrome) "Mr Rogers, do we have to do prepositions?" Several students laughed; I beckoned it down. Most students had no idea what a preposition was…

"Well, we use prepositions every day, scores of times." I decided to utilise an approach I've used many times in teaching basic grammar: "The job of a word in a sentence."

I asked several students if they would be willing to come to the front of the class to help me (including Andrew, the lad who had asked the question).

I took a whiteboard marker and noticed an empty cardboard box on the teacher's desk. "Right … whiteboard marker – what's this? We *name* it, yes Shannon?" "Noun". "The box – Ahmet?" "Yep – noun." "So – the 'primary' noun *the pen*, 'secondary' noun the box. Andrew I want you to put the pen *in* the box. Ta." I gave the pen to Shannon, I want you to put the pen *near*, or *beside*, or *behind*, or *before* … *the* box. Ta." So it went on: *in/on/over* the box, gently flick the pen *off* the box. We decided it wasn't worth trying to push the marker *through* the box … We then had a class discussion about *placing* (verb) *carefully* (adverb) *beside* (preposition) the *box* (noun); talking about each word's "job" within a sentence.

As noted earlier, no matter how many times we've taught a topic, idea, understanding, concept, skill … we make an effort to:

- engage the visual (and, as here,) even kinaesthetic learning awareness. The visual (as here) can help clarify and focus a concept (pre) *position* of object to object (as in grammar).
- enthuse and engage interest and motivation and *understanding*.
- enable the movement from known, familiar, comfortable to ... (p. 134f).

Working as a mentor-teacher I have noticed colleagues struggle with new skills (as we all do ...); notably new ways of communicating when managing, disciplining or even encouraging students. As with any new skill it is important to remember that it takes time to develop any skills within the "comfort zone" wherein the language comes easily and naturally, without too much conscious thought.

I've played golf only several times (by invitation – it's not my game). As I watch others play, as I watch their fluidity of stroke and eye, and follow through, it *looks* easy. When I try to play I *feel* wooden. My legs (on those occasions) did not seem to connect with my arms and head. I hit the ground several times with the club, then I hit the ball too hard. I can't even see where it is going. It skews off a long way from the green I aimed at. I *over*-concentrate.

But I can still swim quite well; and dive; ride a bike (although infrequently); draw reasonable pictures (there are some in this book); and juggle three balls in the air (well, for two or three goes!). Why? Because I *practised* these skills many times; I had felt a need; I was motivated and I kept at it until there was a kind of "second nature" about the skills I chose, wanted and needed to learn and develop (like driving a car ...).

To get to that habituation level one has to go through the discomfort zone, as it were. That is normal. Knowing about skills (through reading or in-service education and training) and being able to use them in an integrated way – as a teacher – are two different things. Initially the new skill *feels* uncomfortable; the words, the tone, the manner, may not seem "to be me". As P.G. Wodehouse once put it, "My tongue seems to get entangled with my brain". However, if we see a need and value in the skills, and if we see how those skills can be integrated into our *overall* teaching and management, we will succeed (with effort, time, normative failure and some colleague encouragement). With all the skills noted so far in this text regarding our leadership and teaching, it is our willingness to reflect on our *characteristic* behaviour, to make time for professional (and collegial) review and even appraisal at times, and learn – still – and "practise" the skills we know that will enable effective teaching and behaviour leadership. And in time we won't need to think, "Am I avoiding unnecessary focus on the secondary behaviour by *tactically* ignoring the residual secondary behaviour; and refocusing the procrastinating and reframing to the core issue?" "Am I using the encouragement descriptively?" "Am I using positive corrective language where possible ...?" We'll just do it.

Home truths

Our daughter once said to me, "Dad, why do some teachers bother to get into teaching when they hate kids?" By "hate" she meant dislike expressed (at its worst) in mean-spirited, churlish, petty, unthinking (well – we hope it is unthinking) behaviour; a lack of fundamental humanity expressed in a sense of caring, positive support and mutual regard. Having worked with some teachers who seem to present a *characteristically* "miserable-soddish attitude" to teaching and to their students, I knew what she meant.

Whenever I've discussed the issue of "good teachers" with students they always emphasise several key aspects of teacher behaviour. The comments below in brackets are directly drawn from high school students I have taught. (Some of the positive behaviours are expressed in negative terms.)
Effective teachers:

- Teach clearly and with interest in the subject and the students' needs: "the work is interesting"; "they try to help you connect to what they're talking about"; "they help us with the work"; "they don't moan if you ask them to re-explain things"; "they give us a chance to talk and explain too".
- Build a sense of class cohesion as it relates to learning together and being together here in "this place" – the classroom: "they let you all know why we're doing this subject or lesson"; "they give choices"; "they have manners"; "they trust you"; "they have a sense of humour" [this is a very frequent descriptor]; "they're not chauvinistic or sexist"; as one student said with a wry smile, "If we're stuck here together ... and *we're all human beings* ... (that is often emphasised) we have to do it with less pain!" I knew what he meant.
- Discipline fairly: "they discuss/explain the rules"; "they don't take sides"; "they don't shame you in front of the class"; "you get a fair chance"; "they give you fair warning even non-verbal [*sic*]"; "you make mistakes but they don't hold it against you"; "because they have a good relationship with the class the correction is accepted better"; "they're fair"; "there's give and take"; "they hear your side of the story ...".

The kind of relationship a teacher builds, and sustains, is central to effective teaching and learning. It also increases the likelihood that the students will cooperate with us when we exercise necessary discipline.

Our own children have said – about their teachers – that they often enjoyed a *particular* subject because of the *particular* teacher who taught it that semester or that year.

One of the most powerful and influential aspects of a teacher's relationship with individuals and groups of students is the teacher's willingness to empathise and encourage (p. 152f). Perspective-taking means the ability to see a student's struggle with work or behaviour or their relationships in a school; to tune-in to a student's frustration or anxiety; to give feedback on learning and behaviour, and always to give a right of reply. As Branwhite (1988) reported, a teacher's capacity to empathise was the most valued teacher quality cited by pupils (cited in Kyriacou 1991: 57).

Teaching is not for everyone

Teaching in schools is clearly not for everyone. It is a profession that is naturally, inherently, even normatively, stressful. Its daily demands are multiple and various and simultaneously require one to not only have planned well on the one hand, but also to be flexible and able to think on one's feet. The ability to relate well to others and to communicate clearly and effectively, the ability, and skill, to enthuse and motivate, and the ability to cope with multi-task, group-oriented activities, as well as individual activities, are not merely desirable; they are essential attributes and skills.

There are teachers who present with poor – or ineffective – teaching and management practice. Supporting teachers who struggle because they, themselves, are a key factor in a hard-to-manage class setting is not easy; in part because we need to see, and support, the colleague's failure and struggle without seeing them *as* a failure (Chapter 8).

If such teacher behaviour can be addressed within a school-wide perspective of shared values, aims and practices about managing classroom behaviour the task is made somewhat clearer, although not necessarily easier.

If a struggling teacher does not request or invite colleague support it will be important to approach that colleague to informally share – at the very least – our concerns about their welfare. If we have walked past a really loud class on enough occasions to know that the behaviour in that class (even briefly observed) is more than bad-day syndrome, it is professionally irresponsible not to meet with the colleague in question and offer support. In providing such support we will need to consider the following:

- Wherever possible any offered support should be "early-intervention"; before a spiral of discouragement, or defeat, sets in.
- Senior teacher involvement can often set up further colleague networking (even mentoring) and address more serious concerns, such as harassment by students (p. 280f).

- The offer of support should be made discreetly and confidentially.
- The emphasis in the first meeting allows the colleague to share their concerns, needs and problems with honesty and balance. Emphasise the positive areas of their teaching and management as well as the areas of concern.
- Set up a plan of support, developed with other colleagues (perhaps even a mentor; p. 288) to enable ongoing support. Early features of any support options may need to include thoughtful, careful, time-out plans, and working with any "catalytic" students who are overly disruptive or harassing (see Chapter 6).

Where there is *characteristic* laziness; indifference; lack of commitment; poor teaching; inappropriate management and discipline; insensitivity and even active dissent in some teachers' behaviour, this will need to be supportively and professionally addressed, within the school's shared values and practices as they relate to a teacher's professional rights and responsibilities.

Teachers who *characteristically* present as ineffective in their teaching practice (global descriptors such as "ineffective" and "poor" need careful and thoughtful delineation) are best advised and counselled to reconsider if the profession of teaching is really for them.

The drawing shows an early years class (5 year olds). The teacher on the right, Joy (my colleague, the grade teacher), is comforting a young boy who is upset. I am supervising play-lunch. (In Australian schools, children eat packed lunches in the classroom with their class teacher.) Infants have morning play at 10.30 am, but play-lunch needs to start aeons before then. They take a long, long time!

A cooperative and supportive school-based appraisal system working with a more consciously supportive Office for Standards in Education (Ofsted) could help such teachers to reassess their professional choices, obligations and responsibilities earlier in their teaching journey. (We do not have an equivalent of Ofsted in Australia.)

I'm also singing to the group. "I can see some sandwiches, some sandwiches … I can see yummy sandwiches in your play-lunch today." As I sing a student comes to my chair with a pencil and starts to comb my hair. I hadn't asked her. I am thinking of a cup of tea (meagre pleasure!). I ask myself, "Why does it seem so really long 'til morning tea time?"

Teaching infants is different. On top of the whiteboard is Boris the mouse. I'd made him out of Blu-Tack.

Reflection

The issue of what we mean by "effective teacher" needs values and utility to enable any purposeful, and appropriate, sense of effectiveness:

- What indicators does your school note/suggest for "effective" teaching? (beyond Ofsted!)
- How do the noted understandings of effective teaching in this chapter reflect your normative practice? The research on effective teaching has a clear – anchor – variable: that of personal and collegial reflection. Do you take time to personally/collegially reflect on your teaching practice? How?
- If you sought to consciously address change in your teaching practice, what would motivate or occasion such consciousness Where would you start?
- How do you respond to the distinctions made between encouragement and praise? How aware are you of your characteristic use of encouragement and supportive feedback to your students (verbally and in writing)?
- Have you reflected on your use of questions – and questioning – within your teaching practice (p. 150f)? How do the suggestions of use of questioning inform your practice?
- Research distinguishes between authority (earned/developed in relation-ships) and "control". More crucially, our authority is directed related to our ability to engage a positive teaching and learning culture. How do you sense and perceive your "authority" in relationship to your students? How do you think they perceive your authority? (Bad days notwithstanding of course!) (p.22f.)

Notes

1 These are drawn principally from Kyriacou (1986), Robertson (1997) and Rogers (1998, 2002b and 2011).
2 One of the best texts I have read in this tricky area is John Robertson's *Effective Classroom Control* (3rd edition, 1997).
3 While this sounds like a tall order, it is not inconsistent at all with the bad-day syndrome. Children fully understand and respect bad-day syndrome in adults, and if the teacher communicates, briefly and respectfully, why they are having a bad day, children are normally quite forgiving. Of course, if our frustration or anger has been thoughtless, tactless or disrespectful, we should always apologise.

Visit https://study.sagepub.com/rogers4e for additional resources to help you better manage classroom behaviour. You'll also be able to hear from Bill himself as he talks you through common behaviour management scenarios.

5

Management beyond the classroom: behaviour consequences

"We are what we repeatedly do ..."

Aristotle, *Nichomachean Ethics*

"Tell me – I may listen. Teach me – I may remember. Involve me – I will do it."

Chinese proverb

Behaviour consequences (punishment?)

During most of my teaching career teachers tended to use the word "punishment" to describe what happened when a student had to face the consequences of inappropriate or wrong behaviour. The verb "to punish" was often used – uncritically – to mean anything we did *to* a child, such as detention; "giving lines"; withdrawing a privilege (such as missing out on a valued activity); wearing the dreaded dunce's cap (a conical hat with "D" for dunce[1] written on it and worn by the student while standing in the corner of the classroom) or, of course, the cane (whoosh! ouch!). I had that a number of times (even as an infant child in a bleak London school). We even had "public caning" (on school stage) for the worst offenders (late 1950s early 1960s). This after a hymn, a bible-reading, perhaps some poetry ...

In his *Childhood, Boyhood, Youth*, Tolstoy recounts the experiences of some of his tutors and teachers: physical pain (kneeling in the corner, face to the wall ...) and humiliation, "the despair, the shame, the fear ..." (Tolstoy 1964: 153). As a 14-year-old (1960) I was made to stand in a cold – open – shower on two occasions by a particularly barbarous Phys. Ed. teacher for "forgetting my kit". As Tolstoy said, "the punishment lay in the humiliation" (ibid.). I put the word *punishment* in parenthesis in the heading of this section (adding a question mark) because I wanted to question the easy facility with which we use the word. Whether we use the word "punishment" or "consequences" may mean little to the child. It is what *happens* to the child through the process of any consequential outcome that matters.

The degree to which a child will see the teacher's action as fair "punishment" depends on several factors:

- Do we set out to *punish*? Engage accountability? Teach? That is, teach the child to *own* their behaviour *and* its consequences?
- The *intent* we convey through the "consequential process".
- Whether we use the "consequential process" as an end in itself (mere punishment) or as a means to an end – the end being some understanding, some meaningful learning (in the student), about their behaviour.

For example, a fair consequence can easily be applied punitively by a teacher whose intent is to make the child *feel* punished by the way he or she speaks to, and treats, the child through the consequential process (p. 122f, 179).

Behaviour consequences, as a feature of thoughtful discipline, are an attempt by the teacher to link the disruptive or wrong behaviour of the student to an outcome that, hopefully, will emphasise fairness and justice, and may even teach the child something about accountability and responsibility. When we apply a consequence, even a simple consequence of directing students to stay back after class and "clean up their mess", we are organising outcomes so the students experience the consequences of their own behaviour. Through *behaviour consequences* teachers seek to emphasise that as students "choose" to be disruptive, they also "choose" to face the consequences of their behaviour; they are not *simply* pawns or mere victims when they do the wrong thing. We treat the students as if they are responsible for what they do, say and how they treat others.

One of my colleagues has introduced her Year 5 class to the term "reparation":

> Sometimes we let classmates and teachers down by choosing not to be responsible towards people or property. Sometimes we're irresponsible because we do not care enough.
>
> Sometimes we do the wrong thing by mistake; we don't mean to.
>
> When that happens we work to fix things, or sort things out through an apology or paying back that person in a helpful, positive way.
>
> We call this "making reparation". When we do the unfair and wrong thing our reparations help earn our class's and our school community's trust back again.
>
> All our behaviour has consequences and we are responsible for the consequences of our behaviour.

In this sense the teacher is emphasising a consequence as something the child is involved in as well as something organised by the teacher.

In working through consequences with children we need to make clear that all behaviour (one way or another) has consequences. Some consequences are naturally occurring: when we stay out too long in the sun without a hat, sunglasses and sun-cream, we risk sunburn; unbrushed teeth, in time, will need dental work and may lead to halitosis (phew!); if you don't plan the progress of a long assignment the due date comes quickly (help!). Children can see the reality of situational consequences like these and – hopefully – learn from them. *Behavioural* consequences are also an attempt to teach responsibility and accountability. The teacher links a consequential outcome to a student's rights infringing/rights assaulting behaviour: "If you choose to leave the mess like that you'll need to stay back at play-time and …"; "If the work is not completed now … *then*"; "If the assignment is not in on a due date … *then* …"; "If you *continue* to make it difficult for others to work *then* you'll have to work away from others …".

Managing consequences

- *All* behaviour consequences are referred back to the student behaviour agreement, which outlines the rights, responsibilities, rules and consequences (p. 39). It is within the emphases of the classroom agreement that the student needs to see his or her inappropriate behaviour, while also being encouraged to accept the support offered to face the consequences of thoughtless, irresponsible and wrong behaviour.

- Consequences are both "non-negotiable" and "negotiable":
  - *Non-negotiable consequences* should be known in advance, clearly stated in the school policy and applied decisively. Non-negotiable consequences are applied for such behaviours as: repeated, and *very frequent*, *disruptive* behaviour in the classroom (this would occasion time-out, see p. 180f); swearing *at* a teacher; any possession (or use) of drugs or weapons; violent behaviours; harassment and bullying. Non-"negotiable" consequences normally occasion some form of time-out, detention, or formal temporary suspension procedures. They may also include withdrawal of privileges, as when a repeatedly aggressive student is denied (excluded) from a school camp after due process.
  - *Negotiable consequences* normally refer to consequences worked through with the teacher who is witness to the inappropriate or disruptive behaviour. Teachers often use a stay-back session (or even a detention) to discuss with the student questions such as: "What happened?"; "What rule (or right) was affected by your behaviour?"; "What's your side of the story?"; "How do you see what happened …?"; "What can you do to fix things up (sort things out, make things right) …?" Teachers will also often ask "How can I help …?" The "negotiable" features of any such consequences are directly related to the non-negotiable rights and responsibilities (p. 41f).

Most students actually come up with a tougher consequential outcome – through such negotiation – than their teacher. We often have to help them trim their consequential suggestions back to workable reality.

- A consequence is more than mere punishment; we seek to address the reality of the inappropriate or disruptive behaviour by applying a consequence that seeks to gain some *relationship* between the behaviour and its consequential outcome. For example, when a student is caught smoking at school, the rule, and consequence, is clear: a detention. In this case, though, the "smoker's detention" occasions a "Quit" video (a positive educational video addressing the habit of smoking and how to seek support to break the habit).

If a student has damaged school property, or another individual's property, he is required to make "reparation". This normally occurs after some "cool-off time" and subsequent discussion or mediation with a teacher who has some skill in this area.

An infant child uses the class waste-paper bin as a urinal (he knows the difference). It was attention-seeking behaviour. In his own time, later, he washes the bin out with detergent. Another infant washes out a boy's jumper that he has thrown mud on. Many reparative, and "task-related", consequences can be applied in this way.

The emphasis is one where students experience the consequences of their own behaviour and (hopefully) see some relevance in the applied consequence; they are encouraged to be more responsible next time in similar situations.

- Concentrate on the *present* and the future change flowing from the consequence. Avoid over-focusing on the child's past misdemeanours.
- *Keep the respect intact* when working through a consequence with a student. I have seen (too many times) a teacher keep a student back after class for a "talk", or a detention, only to berate the student and harp on at the student about why he or she is a rotten, unthinking, uncaring, nasty "piece of work" (or words to that effect!).
- As Nelsen (1987) has noted, it is important to emphasise the *certainty* of the consequence rather than severity. At the very least this ought to mean keeping the fundamental respect intact.

Keeping the respect intact means that even when we have to apply significantly serious consequences we do so without the easy temptation to engage in some kind of psychological payback. "You could be outside playing now, couldn't you?! But you're not, you're in here with me! What did I say to you before in class? Didn't I say that if you kept wasting my time, and your time, you would have to stay back at recess? Didn't I – um?! Well? You've lost your playtime now – serves you right doesn't it? You don't listen do you? That's your trouble!"

- Consequences should also be applied within a school-wide framework that has "degrees of seriousness". We wouldn't, for example, give detention for not completing homework, whereas we might give detention for *continued* refusal to cooperate with reasonable teacher requests in class time. We would, then, probably use the detention process to sort out the problem behaviour with the student (p. 198–201).

The "punishment fitting the crime"

Sometimes I hear teachers (and politicians, and – on the BBC recently – some interviewers) talking about school behaviour and how "the punishment" needs to "fit the crime". A manifestly inadequate "metaphor", most of our students are not criminals (thankfully) – some will become criminals (even in their school life). However, we do not predict who will become criminals; we work with the students where they are, *now; while they are with us*. We don't build a behaviour consequence policy on such a premise. Where there is crime associated with any of our students, we work with community police, due process and – wherever possible – restitutional, and restorative, opportunities.

> **NB**   The key questions to ask when framing and applying any behaviour consequence include:
>
> - Is the consequence related, in some way, to the disruptive/wrong behaviour?
> - Is the consequence reasonable in terms of "degrees of seriousness"?
> - Do we keep the respect intact?
> - What does the student learn from the consequence? Can the student understand the *reason* for this consequence?
> - Can we build in reparation/restitution where appropriate?

The messages of *consequential* discipline – whether an after-class chat or a detention – emphasise:

- Our school has fair rights and rules expressed in the behaviour agreement (p. 39f)
- "Your behaviour is effectively your choice" (even if others were involved)
- When teachers apply consequences to irresponsible and wrong behaviour they do so because people's rights are affected and individuals ought to be fairly held accountable for their behaviour and to face their responsibilities.

We also need to balance consequential aspects of discipline with appropriate *support*, such as mediation, restitution, counselling and (when appropriate) individual behaviour plans (see Chapter 6).

Time-out: a necessary consequence

I can recall my primary school years at Harlesden in London in the 1950s, where I did my early stretch ... It was a drab, brick school, asphalt playgrounds and narrow stairs to the head-teacher's office (a place of fear!). The pointed iron railings gave a prison-like appearance to the enclosed asphalt, concrete and brick. I recall standing in the corner of the classroom with a dunce's cap on: it was that school's version of time-out (in effect a public shaming)!

   Time-out, thoughtfully – and respectfully – utilised, is a consequential step or process that seeks to link separation from the classroom group with serious infringement, or abuse, of others' rights. Time-out is a necessary consequence in a school's behaviour policy and practice.

Reading a story to a Year 1 class (all the children in a semi-circle in front of me), I saw a boy at the back of the group (sitting on the carpet) pinch the lad in front of him a few times. I gave Patrick the rule reminder: "Patrick (...), hands and feet to yourself." I had already directed him to sit away from another student he had been annoying on the carpet area. He stopped. A little later he started again – pushing the boy this time hard in the small of his back – and the other lad fell forward. This time I directed him to take time-out (cool-off time). "Patrick (...), Patrick (...), cool-off time. Over there – now." I started to walk over to the cool-off-time area (to convey take-up time).

I beckoned to an area at the back of the room, with a chair, a small table, an egg-timer (5 minutes) and a sign on the wall simply saying "cool-off time" (the term in this early years classroom for time-out consequence). I cued the rest of the class, "Won't be a moment everyone ... thank you. Just taking Patrick to cool-off-time." I was well aware they were "tuned into" the calmness and brief escorting of Patrick away from the group. "Whisper voices everyone ..."

He whined back at me, "No, I'll be alright, Mr Rogers, I will!" I repeated, "Patrick (...), cool-off time. Over there – now." He came, sulking and stamping his feet.

On such occasions our voice needs to be calm but firm – decisive. There should be no plea-bargaining ("Are you sure you'll be good now, Patrick, will you promise me?"). Once we have decided on a consequence like time-out it is the *certainty* of the consequence that will carry the message that "If you *keep* annoying others, or hurt them or make it *repeatedly* difficult for them to learn you will have to sit away in cool-off-time to think about your behaviour and remember ..." Patrick slumped into the chair. I left him, went back to the group to continue the story and class discussion. We could hear occasional sulky grunts from the cool-off-time

area. I tactically ignored this, keeping the class focus on our story. When I directed the children to their table groups (for their activity …) I went over to speak – briefly – with Patrick before escorting him back to his table group.

This form of time-out (in-class) is normally reserved for early years and middle years at primary level.

There are some important considerations when using any approach to time-out.

- Time-out is a short-term behaviour consequence; it is never an end in itself. As a means to an end, it can help and support disruptive students by giving them a chance to calm themselves (away from their immediate peer audience) and give them a chance to think about their behaviour. It is also fair for the other students in that they, too, have a chance to refocus (to class learning and activities) beyond the disruption to their basic rights; it is *balancing the rights* of the individually distracting (or dangerous) student with that of those students directly affected by such behaviours.
- Time-out, as a school-wide consequence, needs to be utilised as a least- to most-intrusive consequential option in managing disruptive and unsafe behaviour. At the least intrusive level, *in-class* time-out (as in Patrick's case) may be an option; at the most intrusive level of application students may need to be escorted from the classroom to a time-out place where they can calm down and, if necessary (in more extreme cases), parents (or caregivers) may need to be notified (see later).

When applying time-out as a consequence it is important that the teacher exhibits calmness *and* firmness *and* respect. If the teacher starts using a loud voice, or shouting and grabbing the student, not only will many students become uncooperative and resistant (or even violent), but the students watching will become unnecessarily anxious or give unhelpful attention to the disruptive student. There are some (rare) occasions when a teacher will need to physically restrain a student. The school should have a policy on this sensitive aspect of behaviour management.

My colleagues and I have a small poster in the time-out area to enable some calming focus. It has a few questions to calm, reflect and focus the student. A drawing of a student showing a calming face can visually cue the goal of self-calming.

There may be occasions when a student's behaviour is too disruptive for in-class time-out. On these occasions the teacher will:

- Direct the student to leave the classroom and go to a nominated teacher or place in the school. That nominated place could be a colleague's classroom next door, or nearby. That teacher will supervise the cool-off time of the student "sent".

They will also decide if and when to send the student back to the host classroom. Some schools have "time-out rooms" set aside where students can be directed for time-out. Here they are supervised for the rest of that class period during which the disruptive behaviour has occurred. Early years children will need to be escorted from their classroom, by an adult, to any such a time-out place.

- In directing students to take time-out it is important that the initiating teacher *briefly* makes it *clear* to the student what is happening. The teacher needs to communicate that it is the student's behaviour that is being addressed; we are not rejecting the student: "Troy, I've asked you several times to work in your seat and not wander and annoy the other students. If you're not willing to settle down here you'll have to leave our classroom and take time-out. You know the class rules. I will get together with you later to help you sort things out." – No discussion *now*. Direct them to leave. At primary level onwards we would send a responsible student with them to make sure they get there.

- If a student refuses to leave the classroom to take time-out, or we suspect that in directing the student to leave he will become even more disruptive, the initiating teacher should have the back-up of *colleague-assisted time-out*. All teachers have a cue card in their classroom – a poster-sized card with a symbolic colour (for example, red) and the classroom number on it. This cue card can be sent – with a trusted student – to a colleague teaching nearby (maybe even next door). In a more disturbing (or dangerous) discipline situation the card will be sent to a senior colleague (team leader, year head, deputy) who will come, speedily, to escort the student away from the classroom (and their peer audience) to a *supervised* "time-out place". Schools also use internal phone cues to call a senior colleague to the classroom for such assisted time-out support.

  There are occasions when even senior teachers (yes, even senior teachers) cannot "make", or get, a very disruptive student to leave a classroom or playground setting where they are engaged in *repeatedly* disruptive, or dangerous, behaviour. In these rare situations it is wiser for the senior support colleague to stay *in* the classroom with the disrupting student while the class teacher calmly escorts the rest of the class away from the classroom (in effect, escorts the peer "audience" away). The supervising teacher then stays with the student until they have calmed down and are ready to leave the classroom (see later, p. 184f).

- With early years children any *directed* exit from the room for time-out should be accompanied by an adult. In many schools, teachers utilise the support of a teaching colleague next door. The cue-card (mentioned earlier) is sent to the support colleague, who briefly leaves her class (door open for line of sight) and escorts the disruptive student to the next door classroom to calm down and refocus.

- Teachers should *always* follow up with any student later that day (or later that week at secondary level) to work through the concerns or issues that occasioned time-out. This is especially important at secondary level where a teacher may not see a student for a day or two. If there is no follow-up of behaviour concerns by the teacher initiating the time-out consequence, the old animosities may still be there and brought back in the classroom (unresolved) later that week.

- During the time-out period it is important that the student is not unhelpfully reinforced, or over-attended to, by counselling or special activities or "jobs for the teacher". Time-out is not primarily a punishment – it is however, a decisive consequence where we send the clear message that "if you *continue* to make it difficult for others in our class to work, feel safe or be treated with respect *then* you will have to take time-out away from your classmates until you have calmed down, thought about your behaviour (hopefully constructively) and are prepared to work by the fair rights and rules here". Counselling, and reparation, should of course occur at a later stage. If students associate time-out with counselling, or special jobs (or activities), some students may use disruptive patterns of behaviour to gain what they perceive to be "special privileges", or "special time" away from class work, during time-out.

Case study

Working with a very challenging Year 7 class, some years ago, one of our students was repeatedly showing off (during whole-class teaching time), calling out, talking over others in whole-class teaching time and making silly comments. I reminded him of our class rule. He called out again, I briefly repeated the rule reminder, "Scott, you're calling out. Remember our rule so we all get a fair go". *I resumed the flow of the lesson*, he then called out loudly, "You can't say nothing here!" His "last word". He folded his arms, leaned back noisily in his chair and sulked for the rest of the whole-class teaching time (his "secondary" attentional behaviours).

During the on-task phase of the lesson – when the students were settling to their learning activity – Scott dragged his chair into the centre of the U-shaped seating arrangement and started rocking on it, head back looking in my direction (I was working with a student at the back of the classroom). He then started "singing" "I'm not f___ing doing it! I'm not f___ing doing it!"

Of course every student stopped any work and watched (to see what would happen – the "theatre"). Some students looked anxious, some (obviously) grinning – more "theatre". It was the second week of the first term. I looked across at Rosie (the teacher I was mentoring) and her returned – pained – expression seemed to say "Now you know what I have to put up with!" The look was not of reproach (it's a very supportive school), it was the feeling that *now* – in this shared existentiality as it were – another teacher (mentor colleague) was seeing the sort of behaviour she (and other colleagues) had been struggling with.

The student's "singing" was intermittent, "goading". He kept rocking noisily on the chair, in the centre of the room. I went over, and as calmly as I could (not too close) said, "Scott (...) Scott (...)" (he wouldn't return any eye contact) and before I could say anything he started to sing again, "I'm not f___ing doing it ...". Trying to find a "break in the traffic" (as it were) – in this intermittent "singing" – I said, "You know you need to be back in your seat. When you're back in your seat I'll come and help ..." I walked off back to the student I'd been working with. Before I reached the back of the class (to resume the support I'd been giving to students there) Scott started "singing" again ...

He was "forcing" events; this was much more than attentional behaviour (notice me) – this was arrant power-seeking, "Come on *make* me – you can't, can you!!?" He was (effectively) "holding the class to ransom". I refused to engage in a power struggle to try to get him to go back to his work table or even to direct him to leave the room for time-out.

My other Year 7 colleagues and I had already discussed behaviours of some of our students (like Scott) and agreed that if we couldn't use calm, firm directions to direct a student to *out-of-class time-out* (with senior teacher support) we could utilise a form of time-out where we would take "the audience" (the rest of the class) away from a student who is *repeatedly* disruptive or aggressive. In this form of time-out, a senior colleague is sent for (though in this case I was already in the room). The senior colleague stays with the challenging student and the class teacher "calmly" directs the rest of the class to leave the classroom (with their class teacher). The key, here, is the assertive calmness of both teachers.

It is not the most "elegant" strategy but it can send a decisively clear message to the student in question; "you will not force us into a major power-struggle in front of your peer audience" and "you will not be allowed to hold our class to ransom".

Scott continued to "sing" (his swearing "song ...") as the students were leaving the class (some still looking at him, some still grinning as they walked out, adding to the last minutes of "theatre") ... Most students – thankfully – ignored him.

I'd been standing by the class door as Rosie calmly directed the class out – in case he made a run for the door.

Within a minute of the last student leaving, Scott went under the computer table, huddled up and still f___ing and cursing. When there was a break-in-the-verbal-traffic, and I sensed some "self-calming" I said, "Scott, when you've settled down, I'm over here, we can talk." He continued to swear for a while, I tactically ignored his posturing and swearing. Then he started crying bitter and angry tears. He eventually "settled", and I walked with him, away from the now vacated classroom to the "interview room" (near the principal's office) and we began one of many conversations about his behaviour and how we could support him to understand why he was behaving this way and how we could support him in meaningful behaviour change. It is very important to stress again, even when a student has complex needs and a very disturbing home life (like Scott), It does not help when we "re-victimise" the student by effectively saying, "Well he can't help his behaviour because of his oppositional defiance disorder, his attention deficit hyperactive disorder [Scott was on medication for both disorders ...]. We also can't help him because of his terrible home life, or ...". Of course we need to be empathetic and supportive to at-risk students but we must balance that with the rights of *all* members of the school community.

We were well aware of Scott's ADHD and ODD (and his medications). Medication, while it can often be helpful, cannot *teach behaviour*. We set up a personal behaviour support plan for Scott first to support behaviour awareness and behaviour change for Scott but also to gain some supportive consistency of approach across all Year 7 staff.

"You can't make me!" "You can't make me!" I've heard this many times from highly attentional or power-seeking students in class time. For example, when I remind a student about work requirements and time progress. When they make the "You can't make me" statement I "partially agree" with them. "Of course I can't make you. However, if you continue to choose not to do the work then I'll have to follow this up at recess time. If you need any help, though, let me know." Then "leave them" – as it were – to their choice/responsibility and appropriate consequences. It is very important not to make this sound like a threat; it is a form of consequential "choice".

It is also important to give some 'take-up time' (the walking away to convey our confidence and expectation that the student will make some effort to cooperate).

I've had students respond to consequential "choices" (like that above, or those on pp. 190f) with a sulky, " I don't care ...". It's enough to say (if anything) "I care", then walk away, giving take-up time.

Of course if they then start hassling other students we may need to make the time-out consequence clear. "If you continue to (be specific) then you will have to leave our class for time-out (be specific) ..." .

As with any student who is seeking power, the more we meet such behaviours with counter-power ("*I will win* here!") the more it reinforces that student's behavioural goal. This does not mean we are excusing their task avoidance/ refusal; it means we are aware of their goal and are *adjusting our leadership behaviour to avoid unnecessary power struggles in front of their 'peer audience'*. We cannot (in reality) decide what the student will do; we can, however, decide what we will do ...

What about other students copying such students?

Remember, most students (70 per cent or so) in the class do not seek to behave in highly attentional or power-seeking ways (thankfully). It is our confidence in the awareness of group dynamics, and the compensatory behaviours of *those few challenging students*, that informs and enables the stance we take in our behaviour leadership.

Where our teacher leadership is confident, respectful and based on a well-established (and maintained) rights/responsibility dynamic, the 70–80 per cent of students will not easily "side" with the "catalytic few".

It is also crucial to remember that it is what we do in our one-to-one follow-up with such students that is likely to support a change in the student's perception and understanding of their behaviour in relation to others (including their teachers). Such one-to-one sessions also demonstrate that we do care and do want to (and will) support our students.

The emotional struggle with power-seeking behaviour

A student (like Scott) who is seeking power, directs his behaviour towards controlling, even "defeating" those who try to suppress or stop him. This creates significant tension and stress for teachers. This is understandable, particularly when some teachers believe that "a good teacher *must be in control* at all times...", "A teacher with authority *must show they can win* ...", "*No child should get away with it* ..." (meaningful authority is – of course – always earned and not merely based on controlling power (see p. 29f).

Dreikurs et al. (1982: 23) make a salient point that has helped my colleagues and me many times when children seek to engage us in power struggles:

The first obstacle towards conflict solving ... is the widespread assumption that the adult has to subdue the defiant child – to show him who is boss and make him respect law and order. The second stumbling block is the adult's personal involvement in a power conflict. The teacher cannot avoid the conflict unless (they) are free from feelings of inadequacy and concern with their own prestige. No conflict can be resolved as long as (the teacher) is afraid of being humiliated, taken advantage of and personally defeated.

Hard words? Yes. This does not mean we *ever* put up with derogatory or abusive comments, or highly distracting and confronting behaviours; they will always occasion our appropriate assertive response. What it does mean is that we don't *pursue* and *extend* power exchanges by verbal battles, or sarcasm, or pointless threats (tempting as that may be). With power-seeking students it is tempting (but counter-productive) to simply force the student to simply *obey*.

When we act assertively – in situations like this – *our decisive intervention is crucial*. This is clearly not a time to "invite", "discuss", "negotiate". This student has – temporarily – lost his right to stay in class and be a part of the group. This student's behaviour has denied the others in the class their right to feel safe, to continue (in *any* meaningful way) their learning (let alone the teacher's right to teach). Time-out, in this context, is a totally appropriate – and necessary – consequence.

No student should be allowed to hold a classroom to ransom by *repeatedly* disruptive behaviour in the course of a lesson or activity. Nor should we ever convey the message to students that we will ever tolerate *repeatedly* disruptive, unsafe, threatening, aggressive or dangerous behaviours (p. 184f). Students should be made aware of what time out is, and what it means. This awareness-raising can be occasioned when teachers are developing their student behaviour agreements in the first week of Term One (p. 39f, 46).

If a student has been in time-out on several occasions, in close succession, they will probably benefit from an individual behaviour plan to help them with the behaviours or learning issues that have necessitated time out (p. 180f).

Extreme situations – "restraint"

There are sometimes very extreme situations in schools where forms of restraint procedure may be necessary; where there is likelihood of serious injury to a student (or teacher).

This issue is not addressed in this text. The overriding message of this book is that teachers should seek to use *their* leadership and support behaviour in a calm and positive way (wherever possible) to remind, direct, assert, defuse, de-escalate potential conflict and hostility. Such "calmness" is not inconsistent with appropriate assertion.

The successive Children's Acts (in the past 20 years) have rightly stressed the nature and purposes of professional, supportive, care for the child. The actual, specific, guidance regarding appropriate and strategic use of restraint (in situations of danger) is less clear. Teachers and care workers in special schools, care settings, pupil-referral centres and young offenders institutions do receive particular – and focused – training; teachers in "regular schools" do not normally receive such training.

Whenever an adult uses *any* physical means to address extreme and dangerous behaviour – in a controlled, restraining, way – they are in a vulnerable position, physically and legally. Terms like "positive handling"; "minimal/reasonable restraint"; "proportionate restraint"; "safe restraint …"; "restrictive intervention" are widely used in the literature addressing this issue. These terms are rarely explained *practically* in the Department of Education documents. All schools are required to have a Behaviour and Management and Discipline policy. Such policies, however, rarely mention *restraint* (for obvious reasons); they will speak about *staged intervention* (including time-out) or *levels of intervention*. On the rare situations where a teacher might restrain a child (in some way – even minimally with a holding hand/arm) risk assessment is always a challenge in the immediate emotional moment. Many teachers have taken the risk and intervened in very serious fights (where a child is at risk of serious hurt and they've been physically hurt, kicked at, spat at, bitten, punched …). I have done it myself a number of times over the years. We, hopefully, do so with protective goodwill, and using calm verbal cueing to de-escalate emotional arousal in the child. It is never easy or simple. We often have to act in "the heat of the emotional moment" – risk assessment often has to be swift.

Using common sense – professional common sense – informed by our experience and shared practice is our starting point. "How dangerous is *this* behaviour, *this* situation, in terms of what I know about these 'types' from my experience?"

Knowing those students who are most at risk at school will help us fine-tune our policy and practice so we are as clear as we can be in this difficult area. Any practice, and "form" of restraint – even holding a student's arm, or placing an arm, or one's body, between students engaged in a potential fight (or engaged in a "full-on" fight) – should always be conducted within the least-to-most principle. This is not the book to address "techniques" and practices in this area. There are a number of training providers who address this area of management in the UK.

Any teacher who decides to use any form of restraint should always *carefully* report what they *actually* did; the predisposing factors, the participant children, any adult witnesses (hopefully there were!) how the incident progressed and its outcome (Rogers and McPherson 2014).

The teacher, too, should debrief with senior colleagues and be given support after any restraint episode. Obviously parents, too, should be notified of *any* restraint procedures involved in a critical incident – no second guessing.

Key education department Acts and Directives regarding this topic are noted in the Further Reading section under "Extreme situations".

After any first occasion of using any safe restraint procedure it will be important to discuss "restraint" with the parent of the student; to clarify what we actually mean and to engage their understanding and support. This is essential with students diagnosed within the autistic spectrum. Parents also need to know that our *primary* support is to enable their child within a *personal behaviour support plan*.

Deferred consequences

While consequences for repeatedly and unremitting disruptive behaviour need to be applied immediately, or close to the occurrence of disruptive behaviour, there are occasions when behavioural consequences need to be deferred to a later stage (see also p. 102f).

It is pointless to force a behaviour consequence in the immediate emotional moment if a student is too upset or angry. The student (and sometimes the teacher) needs time to calm and settle before the consequences of their disruptive behaviour can be worked through.

Nathan (Year 2) had left his work area messy (pencils on the floor, bits of screwed up paper). I had reminded him, prior to lunch play, that he needed to clean up. He didn't; he groaned and moaned and complained that other students hadn't cleaned up yet, although they were actually doing it.

He prevaricated. I gave him a directed choice, with a deferred consequence: "If the workspace is not tidied before big play (I beckoned him non-verbally to the mess) you will need to stay back to clean up at playtime."

He moaned. "I don't care!"

I replied, "I care, Nathan. We always clean up our work area." It can help, with reminders about classroom routines, to use inclusive language: "our", "us" "we". This can help remind the student of what *we all are responsible for here*. He sat and sulked, doing nothing in the last five minutes before playtime.

When I directed him to stay back, at the close of the lesson, he did so, but sulkily. I reminded him briefly of our class agreement (about having our work areas tidy) and directed him to clean up (the deferred consequence). The message that I was trying to convey – through the consequence – was that if the mess is left it will need to be cleaned up later and that an individual's responsibility will be called in, "eventually".

We only used deferred consequences for less serious behaviour issues, say when we direct two noisy, chatting students to work separately, or the *objet d'art* ... Say a try, make-up, phone that the student has on their desk ... we give a clear directed choice ("in your bag or on my table?") If, (after brief take-up time) they are still playing with/using their phone ... we will make the deferred consequence clear. "If you choose not to put it away ... I'll have to follow this up with you after class time." We then leave the student to own the consequential chain-of-events, as it were. If they say 'I don't care:', it's enough to say, 'I care.'

Sometimes (during on-task learning time) I'll drop a short note on to a student's desk to raise their awareness about their behaviour. I always carry a small, bright yellow notebook (like the yellow card in soccer!). The first note briefly "describes" their behaviour.

For example.

> *Fazil and Mohammed, you're talking quite loudly. Maybe you weren't aware. Remember our partner-voices. Mr Rogers.*

I'll then, quietly, place it on their table and walk away, giving take-up time (p. 118f).

If after reasonable take-up time, they continue to talk noisily I'll pass them another note, something like:

> *Fazil, Mohammed (always use names) I've reminded you about our class rule for partner-voices. If you can't work quietly, here, I'll have to ask you to work separately. I know you can be responsible. Mr Rogers.*

If they – then – continue to work noisily I'll direct them to work separately (the consequence). If they argue I'll make the *after class* deferred consequence clear.

Giving choices within behaviour contexts

Directed choices are appropriate in a discipline context to the extent that they are able to direct the responsibility and accountability back to the student. With older primary and secondary-aged students a *directed* choice can facilitate and enable cooperation.

I say *directed* choice because we do not simply give "free" choices between alternatives. The choice we give is given within the rights, rules, responsibilities (held and valued) within the school community.

A student was texting on her phone in class time (Year 11); it was on-task learning time (my colleague and I had finished whole-class teaching/discussion ...). I walked over to her table group and reminded her of our school rule, "Harmony, we've got a school rule for phones ..." Before I could finish the student said, "C'mon, Lindsay [the teacher I was mentoring in that class] doesn't care, anyway it's a job placement call". Her tone of voice was sulky, she frowned (oh so deeply), raised her eyes to the ceiling and sighed again. I didn't demand she hand the iPhone over – a pointless power-struggle. Nor did I argue with her; that – too – would accede to an unnecessary power-struggle. I gave her a *directed* choice.

"Your phone needs to be off and in your bag, or you can leave it on the teacher's table until the end of class time. Thanks." I walked away to give Harmony some "take-up time". Behind my back she sighed, huffed, and muttered loudly, "I'll put it away then if it makes you happy!" Again – more seeking attention; "I'm going to try to get you, and the class, to notice me ... to *extend* this ...".

I chose to *tactically* ignore these "secondary" aspects of her behaviour. She reluctantly began to do her classwork project. A little later I went back to her table group see how the students were working. When I asked her how her work was going she said, "Alright ..." Her tone was still very sulky, eyes raised a few times, and the sibilant sigh. It was as if through the sighs, and the sulky demeanour, she was still saying, "C'mon *notice me*, say something about the way I'm behaving ...". Again I chose to tactically ignore these "secondary behaviours", seeking to focus on her work *at this point*.

This is not easy because we may well *feel* frustrated, even very annoyed by these "secondary behaviours" (p. 12f). "She *shouldn't* speak like that!" [she did!] "She *should* show me respect!" [she didn't, at least not in that context as she played to her peer audience]. With regard to the tone/manner of the student, if we say anything about their disrespect it's enough to calmly (and firmly) say, "I'm not speaking to you disrespectfully, I don't expect you to speak disrespectfully to me." A brief, firm, "I" statement. Then – at this point – remind the student of the expected behaviour *now* and give take-up time. The key here (and there is no perfect key!) is to avoid unnecessary confrontation or pointless argumentation.

Our feelings of frustration (even anger, at times) are understandable, however our feelings obviously do not tell us what to actually do in the natural tension of working with challenging behaviour in group settings.

Going back to the Year 11 student with the phone, imagine if the teacher had said, "Look I don't give a damn why you were using that phone. I said put it away – now!!" While a display of this kind of "power"/"authority" may seem resolute (I *will* win ...) all it does is reinforce that latent attentional or power-seeking goal in the student.

Imagine, then, the teacher forcing a student to hand over their "third hand" (their phone). "Right give it to me. I *said* give it to me *now*!" You can easily imagine an adolescent (an emergent adult, Year 11) whose goal may well be power, matching (easily matching) the teacher's demand (p. 187f, 219f). Some students might say, "I'll put it away if I have to!" The teacher "must" still win here, "I said give it to *me*." "No way, it's my phone!!"

Some teachers (having now backed themselves and the student into a tense confrontational corner) will then *demand* the student leave their classroom. "Right, get out! Go on, get out. I'm sick of your pathetic arguing. You can get out!"

The student marches off, head raised, with their last word, "I'm going, it's a shit class anyway!" (or worse). Who won? The problem here (and I've seen this many times) is how the teacher defines their behaviour leadership – as one of "winning".

Our power, as a teacher-leader (see also pp. 29f)

Our "power", as a teacher-leader, is derived not from how bossy or controlling we seek to be, but from *our ability to control ourselves* (as teacher-leaders) within the day-to-day group contexts of classrooms. As noted earlier, we use our power *for*, and *with* our students rather than defining power as merely power as control *over* our students, as a teacher-leader: "I must win here!" (win what?) "I must control this student ..." We can't really control others anyway; it's hard enough controlling ourselves! Within the role, and relationship we build with our students, it is our ability to use our power (in role) constructively to build, and enable, trust and enhance cooperation.

By giving *directed* choices (where appropriate) we're enabling cooperation (even when given grudgingly by students). Most students do put *objects d'art* away when given such "a choice" (with appropriate take-up time). We don't stand over the student demanding them to put the object away ... (see case example earlier p. 94).

If, after reasonable take-up time, the student still hasn't put the distracting object (such as the phone) away, we can *make the consequence clear*. In this case the consequence is *deferred* (not immediate); there is no safety issue at stake. When we give any *directed consequence*, the tone and manner is not one of threat, "If you don't do as I say you'll be on detention!" (or whatever). The element of "choice" is still there. "If you choose not to put the phone away – the school rule is clear – I'll have to ask you to stay back at ..." (either after class, if we have time, or a five minute lunchtime chat).

Again, we don't argue with the student or try to debate the veracity or fairness of the school rule about phones (or whatever the issue is ...). We "walk away" (giving take-up time) leaving the students to *own their behaviour and the consequences*. If they still choose/refuse to put the phone away, it is important we follow through with the behaviour consequence: in this example, the *deferred* consequence. It is important that we then (later) make sure we follow up with the *fair certainty* of the consequence, even if the consequence is a five to ten minute chat after the audience of peers has gone (p. 122f).

As noted earlier, when we apply *any* behaviour consequence, whether it's the five minute after-class chat, or subject teacher (or faculty) detention, it is important to emphasise the *fair certainty of the consequence*, not intentional severity. Some teachers will use the one-to-one consequential time to "get back" at a student (the one-to-one "lecture", even vilifying the student).

While it is understandable that student behaviours can create significant frustration for us, it is important to keep the fundamental respect intact even when we're following through with behaviour consequences (Rogers 2011).

If a student refuses to stay back for the after-class chat, or refuses to turn up for detention, we will still pursue the "certainty principle" by involving senior colleagues to support us in setting up one-to-one consequential time (for the student in question). Even here, though, it is not about *winning*; the emphasis is on the responsibility, accountability, and certainty aspects of the consequence.

Behaviour consequences can be used constructively by teachers to enable students to be aware of their behaviour (away, now, from their peer audience) and to take some accountability for such behaviours (although it is pointless *forcing* apologies or promises ...).

If we have had to follow up with behaviour consequence a number of times (in those first few weeks of Term One) we will need to pursue some kind of *year-level* individual behaviour plan with the student. This will involve the support of senior colleagues in the establishment and "maintenance" of such plans. This is particularly important at secondary level (see later, Chapter 6).

> **NB**   In the case of Harmony (p. 191f) I did, eventually, develop a reasonably positive working relationship. It was in that early establishment phase, with the class group, that she had "tested" her relationships with the group and the new teacher.

I had been teaching a social studies class and I was moving towards lesson closure. I noticed Anne get up out of her seat in the last few minutes, walk from the back of the room and stand with her bag in the doorway. I saw the class watch her as she moved towards the denouement of this potential *contretemps*. It was my first lesson with this Year 10 class and I had been warned that it was a difficult class. I looked across to Anne standing there (as did the class).

"Anne." She looked back at me from the door. "You're out of your seat – we haven't finished yet and the bell hasn't gone."

The class was watching. I could feel that ambient tension – the students were wondering what was going to happen and what I was going to do. It was my first lesson with this class (as a mentor-teacher). I'd already had to address a range of attentional behaviours and with this student in particular.

With hand on hip she said, "If the bell's about to go I might as well stay here then, mightn't I?" The voice carried (it was meant to) a clear tone of "What are you going to do then?" Anne's little attentional/power play with the new teacher. It's wearisome at times, isn't it? A few minutes to go and I'm thinking of a well-earned cuppa and also saying to myself (at nano-second speed), "Well, what do you do next, old chum?"

In the language of deferred consequence I said, "Anne, if you stay there and choose not to leave with the rest of us I'll have to ask you to stay back after class."

"I don't care!" How many times have I heard this? The hands on the hips said it all. I can understand teachers who, at this point, want to rush over, wag a finger, and say, "You will care!! I'll make you care!! I've got the power to ...!" The power to what? To yell? To threaten? To play the game of "I have more power than you have?" Who is the adult here? I cannot (in reality) make this young girl do anything. I cannot control her, or force her to go back to her seat. This will only, and *easily*, replace the attentional behaviour or power-seeking she is after.

When Anne said, "I don't care!" I replied that I did care.

"Do you?" was the sarcastic reply.

At that point, with the bell about to go, I turned my attention back to the class group. Some of the students no doubt had possibly been disappointed that I hadn't given Anne a chance to over-react and storm away.

"Alright, folks, time to pack up. I'll see you again on Thursday. Remember there's another class coming in next period. Let's do them a favour ..." (the cue for straightening the furniture, picking up any litter and leaving quietly in an orderly fashion). Anne was still standing there, arms crossed now. I imagined she was waiting for her friends. The bell went. As her friends met up with her at the door, she walked away. I called her back.

"Anne (...), Anne (...), I need to talk with you now thanks."

"Naa! –, it's recess. I'm going!" I could sense she was "winding herself up".

"I know it's recess. I still need to speak to you ... for a minute or so."

"Nope, I'm going ...," she whined. As she started to walk off I added, "If you leave now it will get messy. I'll have to involve the coordinator." Another deferred consequence – not a threat. I walked back into the classroom leaving the choice (in effect) with her. Less than a minute later she came into the classroom. "Well – what do you want?!" Her face had a practised scowl; her tone and manner sulky. I said that I knew she was annoyed and I knew she wanted to be with her friends who were a little way off in the corridor – waiting. I would not keep her long. We had a calmer chat, her audience having gone. I briefly recounted her behaviour and how I felt it affected the class, and also me as a teacher. I then asked her how she saw the whole thing. She complained that she didn't like social studies. I explained that she didn't have to like social studies; the issue I was wanting to focus on was "getting out of your seat, throwing your bag in the doorway and refusing to go back to your seat before the class was dismissed". We also briefly discussed her tone and manner. She grinned through this; a "knowing" grin. And I gave a wry smile back.

The chat was brief, by the open door (for ethical probity (p. 122f)). We parted as amicably as possible and I noticed that Anne was far less "abrasive" during the next lesson. We were on that road – that sometimes slow road – to a "workable relationship".

- Deferred consequences can often be linked to a "choice" statement or reminder: "If the work is not completed now, you will need to ...". This assumes, of course, that the student is able to do the work but has been task-avoiding. No student should ever be forced to do a set amount of work that he or she is unable to realistically manage.

- Deferred consequences can carry the message of certainty: "If ... then"; "When ... then". If (however) the language is framed as a threat, or carries a *tone* of threat, the deferred consequence loses the message of *reasonable and fair certainty*. It is not about winning; the process of deferring consequences is to create a management context of fairness, and justice, through reasonable certainty.

- Deferred consequences allow there to be a calmness between the initial distracting/disruptive event and the consequence applied, enabling the parties to more effectively address the behaviour and appropriate recovery or restitution. For example, it is unhelpful to force a student to apologise in the heat of the moment (to an adult or a child). I have seen some teachers make an already difficult situation significantly more difficult by forcing the student to "apologise *now* or else …". Even adults would find that difficult.

Students who don't/won't stay back after class

It was Period 6 and my colleague, Frank, and I had been team teaching a Year 7 English class. Matt and Craig had thrown pencil cases at each other. From a brief glance, as it happened, it looked as though Matt had started it. I quickly redirected them to work separately. Matt picked up his pencil case and walked over to another desk muttering "oaths and incantations". He sulked and did no work during the last 15 minutes of class.

Just before lesson closure (and the bell for freedom) I reminded the class about "doing the cleaner a favour" (chairs up, litter in the bin, and so on). Taking my yellow notebook from my top pocket I directed my gaze at Matt and Craig and said, "I'll need to see you both briefly after class."

I always carry a notebook with me in (and out) of class to record names of students I need to follow up with for a chat about either work-related issues or behaviour concerns. It acts as an *aide-mémoire* for me and acts as a "quasi-legal", and 'visible' reminder to the student that I'll need to follow through on issues of concern with them from time to time.

When I gave Craig and Matt the direction about the brief stay-back (to make a further appointment for some follow-up about pencil case throwing) Matt got really agitated.

"I'm not staying back for you!! I gotta get a bus!!" He nearly shouted the words.

I said, "It'll only be for a few minutes, Matt."

Craig's body language indicated he was ready (maybe not willing but reluctantly ready) to stay back. But Matt was adamant.

"Nahh!! I gotta get a bus!!"

He dropped a few, muttered, f—ings *en route*. I noticed my colleague, Frank, tense up as Matt started to badmouth me. I knew that Frank (a beginning teacher) had had a number of earlier run-ins with Matt. I tactically ignored the outburst and finalised the class dismissal (as positively as I could).

The bell went; as the class filed out Craig stood to the side of the room and leaned against the wall. In a flash the other student, Matt, raced for the door like a jack rabbit! I managed a quick last attempt …

"Matt, back inside … c'mon."

"I'm f—ing going – I gotta get a bus!!" were the last words as he raced away down the corridor.

My colleague started to chase after him into the now-busy corridor; students from all directions were all leaving classes near us. I called him back.

"Frank (…) Frank (…) Leave it." He came back into the room, very tense, fists clenched and forgetting Craig was there, and said, "Just once Bill, just once I'd like to get him!" I could see he was really tensed up so I said I'd go through the chat with Craig and suggested he get a coffee and I'd catch up with him a bit later.

Ten minutes later we were having a coffee in the Humanities staffroom. He was noticeably calmer.

I asked him, "Frank, if you had actually caught Matt, as he ran down the corridor, what would you have done and said? Presumably you would have had to restrain him. Just calling 'Halt' or 'Running is verboten!' would probably have had little effect."

He gave a weary, frustrated, laugh and said: "I don't know what I'd have done!"

And that's the real issue – he didn't know what he'd do.

"Neither of us are really fit enough to chase a student like Matt – no offence, Frank. If you had caught him in the mêlée of the Years 7 and 8 students in the corridor, and restrained him, can you imagine his mum within 24 hours, in the newspaper or on the television: 'Teacher maims boy on way to get bus!' Frank, it's not worth it. … The Pyrrhic victory is not worth it … Your career …" In the larger scheme of things whether we "win" in the immediate moment at 3.40 pm today is not important. Even the concept of "I must win", in this context, is inappropriate. We discussed the *certainty* of the consequence as distinct from the *severity* of the consequence (p. 179f).

"We can catch up with him tomorrow …" and we did – after the heat had died down. Matt was a lot more reasonable (next day); we used the lunch detention time to work through some of the issues about his disruptive classroom behaviour. The rest of the class also picked up the *certainty* that we had followed-up with Matt (the tribal tom-toms …).

I remember viewing a short BBC television series, a drama. It was a very challenging school that set out to show how a newly qualified teacher had coped in his first school. It was pretty black (and bleak) at times, illustrating the pressures of one's first year, and first school. The struggle for class management as it interfaced with the struggle for teaching and learning was the dominant theme. At one point in this bleak picture of modern schooling in a very challenging school, an older teacher (early fifties) is seen chasing a Year 8 lad down a busy corridor. The boy has refused to stay back after class and has bad-mouthed the teacher. The teacher finally grabs the boy, pulls him into a vacant room and knocks him over and is seen raining frustrated blows on him. The newly qualified teacher is half a minute behind his colleague. He pulls his older colleague off with some difficulty. Standing between the puffing, angry older colleague and the student on the floor he tries to calm his colleague. The older man says words to the effect that, "There [puff, puff!] wouldn't be a teacher here [puff!] who hasn't wanted [puff] to do that to him!"

I can understand how such a teacher in real life (convincingly played by this actor) would have felt. But it's just not worth it – ever.

Detention

Most schools utilise detentions of some kind, even if they do not use the term as such (other terms I've seen used are "stay-backs" and "time-in"). Essentially, the consequence of detention emphasises detaining a student (during the day or at the end of the day or even weekend detentions in fee-paying, private schools (!)) because of certain kinds of disruptive behaviour. Theoretically, the purpose of detention is to link the withdrawal of time privilege (or right of their time (playtime/lunchtime/hometime ...) with some attempt at helping the student to reflect on his or her behaviour.

Detention is a significant behaviour consequence. Its effective currency can be devalued, or even abused, when teachers:

- merely use detention as a *stand-alone* "punishment".
- use detentions for minor behaviour management issues such as homework not completed or "uniform misdemeanours" (hard to believe it, some teachers do). These issues can be addressed more thoughtfully by the teacher following up the issue with the student in a supportive discussion. In such cases it is important to assure the student that this "is not a detention but an opportunity to work through the issue or concern".
- keep whole classes back for (say) a lunchtime detention. This strategy is sometimes used by teachers in the mistaken belief that they can set in motion peer-pressure from the more responsible students. That does not work (of course); it does, however, lead to resentment from the more responsible, and cooperative, students.

I've worked with teachers who have used whole-class detentions as threats and pay-backs ("I'll make you suffer"). When I've explained to such teachers that they are – effectively – losing the goodwill and, potentially, the cooperation of the responsible members of their class, I've had some say, "I don't care – they've *got* to *learn*", as if this indefatigable exercise will eventually turn the tide on the disruptive element; it doesn't. *We have to care*. If there are several students who are disruptive we use detention for these students, and not for the whole class. If the disruptive behaviour is low level, but disparate *across* the class (talking/chatting while the teacher is talking, calling out, general noisiness), it will be more effective to have a classroom meeting to assess and refocus group behaviour (see p. 274f).

Some teachers will use detention merely to punish the student by making them sit and do nothing for half an hour or more. It is important to clarify what we are seeking to achieve through detention. Is it *just* a punishment or is it a means to assess *what* happened, seek some student reflection and further reparation? Many schools use the following general approach for detentions.

When a student enters a "detention room" (sounds a bit like a benign remand?) they are welcomed by the supervisory teacher. They are given a pro forma that has four or five questions on it:

- "What happened …?" (that is, "that caused you to be in detention")
- "What is your side of the story …?" (a right of reply question)
- "What rule or right was affected by your behaviour?"
- "What can you do to fix things up/make things better?"

A supplementary question can be added:

- "What can your teacher (the one who sent you …) do to help you fix things up, improve things, work things out … ?"

A copy of this completed pro forma goes back to the tutor/form teacher, a copy stays with the initiating teacher (who supervises the detention) and a copy may be sent to the administration (with date, name, form group, etc.). In some schools, students keep a copy. If it is a year-level/faculty detention – supervised by a senior colleague – a copy of that pro forma needs to go back to the teacher who initiated the detention, so that they can – later – engage in some restitution with the student.

It is pointless getting the student merely to "write lines" during detention ("I must not …", "I must …") or copy out the school rules (I have actually seen some schools who still use the practice of "writing lines"!). In a recent discussion on "traditional punishments" it was canvassed in the British media that we should "go back" to giving lines to students – this in 2014 (!) If we are going to use writing as a consequence, at least we should direct, and focus, the student to write *about their behaviour* (p. 129f). In some schools each detention session begins with a brief referral by the supervising teacher to the rights/responsibilities code (p. 38f, 41f) as a context for why the student's behaviour has occasioned this detention.

As with any consequence, we need to try to link the disruptive behaviour to the detaining (time) experience. Getting students to use detention time to clean up will be less effective if the reason for their detention was repeated calling out in class, or being rude to a teacher. In this last instance the student should use the detention time to work through an appropriate apology and reparation. The supervising teacher's role is to enable that process. In this sense detention is *part* of a more involved consequential chain of events.

Hopefully your school will have a thoughtful detention policy that addresses questions and issues such as:

- What sorts of behaviours or issues do we detain students for?
- What are we primarily seeking to teach the student through detention (time)?
- How should we conduct a detention session? What sorts of things do we typi-cally seek to do (and say) in managing the detention session? What should the student, normally, be directed to do *during* detention? What are the preferred options? What is the role of the supervising teacher?
- How do we utilise incident report sheets and the 4W pro forma noted earlier (p. 129f)?
- What is the link between detention as a "primary" consequence *and the* "secondary" consequences that may need to be developed *from* detentions, such as apologies, some restitutional process or some behaviour agreement for the future?

One of my colleagues was supervising the school buses at the end of the day (bus duty – a large primary school). One of the boys on the bus was teasing a grade 6 student walking by. His response to the teasing was to kick the bus and yell back at the student ... The bus duty teacher called the boy over but he ran away, shouting and swearing. Rather than chasing him (unwise) the teacher followed it up the next day with a lunchtime detention. During detention she discussed what happened, how the student had felt about being teased and the fact that he had run away, ignoring the teacher. She communicated her care and understanding but spoke about the "kicking-the-bus" incident. She asked how the bus driver might have felt. She further asked, "What can you do to help fix things up, or sort things out?" Through the teacher's mediation the student agreed that even if he was angry he shouldn't have kicked the bus and he should apologise to the driver.

He wrote a letter to the bus driver apologising that he had kicked the bus but he was angry because of the teasing from the boy in the bus. He assured the driver he wouldn't kick the bus again.

The teacher took the young lad to the bus driver – early (before the Period 6 bell) and the lad nervously gave his short written apology to the bus driver and said, "I'm sorry for ...". The bus driver read it and said, "It's not easy to apologise, is it?" Tuning into the lad's probable feelings, "Especially to an adult, but you did. I can see a little scuff mark on the bus. Next time you get angry with another student let your teacher know rather than the bus, eh?" and he shook the lad's hand.

The bus driver's goodwill and the teacher's mediation skill enabled a useful outcome from the detention. In this sense the detention was used as a primary consequence with the apology/restitution acting as a "secondary consequence".

In some schools, detentions are conducted by senior staff on referral from their colleagues. In other schools, each teacher conducts his or her own (subject- or class-based) detentions. Some schools use a combination of both approaches. If a teacher initiates a detention carried through by another colleague it will be important for the initiating teacher to effect some repairing and rebuilding with the student concerned rather than seeing the incident as handled, and somehow "finished", by the colleague conducting the detention. If the initiating colleague does not make an effort to be involved in some checking and re-establishing with the student, the detention process may adversely affect the ongoing teacher–student relationship. Detentions can also to be used to track which students, classes and teachers are experiencing difficulties. They are an "early warning", from which senior colleagues can (and should) offer moral and practical support.

Bullying

Bullying has always been a disturbing feature of school life; any large social mix will experience bullying behaviour as insecure individuals seek to exercise their distorted sense of social power. I saw bullying as a student at school. I saw disgusting – unchecked – bullying as a young army conscript "doing" my National Service (during the Vietnam conflict). I saw bullying when I worked on building sites as a young man. I always fought back verbally and, at times, physically – it always stopped but I saw many go under; hurt, damaged, even destroyed by this gutless human behaviour.

Anti-bullying policies have been a feature of schools for several decades now – they do have an effect if the emphasis is more than *anti-bullying* (it is easy to frame policy language in the anti-negative). In effect, any feature of a whole-school policy needs to focus on *pro*-rights – essentially the right to feel psychologically as well as physically safe in school. Our emphasis needs to be the building – and enabling – of a school culture where it is not "normal" or "OK" to ever hurtfully tease, harass and bully.

In supportive school cultures, key features are consistently noted – in the literature – that enable rights affirming and rights protection and confront bullying *at every level* (Lee 2004; Rogers 2003a, 2006a).

- The issue, and clarification, of *what constitutes bullying is made clear* to students in the establishment phase of the year. A clear understanding that bullying is more than *physical* behaviour is essential. *Most bullying is psychological/social*: teasing and name-calling; racist/sexist/homophobic language; threats, friendship/ play exclusion; "posting" message texts, photo/captions or "video links" on social media – "Facebook mobbing"(!)
- Many schools conduct educational programmes using discussion groups, drama and literature-based examples to raise a shared consciousness about:

  ○ Why does anyone bully others? What are they seeking to do when they ...? (give typical examples including social-media bullying).
  ○ What is the role/responsibility of onlookers? When we see someone bully-ing others, what should we do? What can we do? As Lee (2004) notes, the role of audience participants in school bullying can have a constructive – as well as a collusively accepting – role in dealing with bullying at source and in behaviour consciousness.
  ○ What to do when others seek to harass/bully you?
  ○ Why you need to report it when it *continues* (as bullying often does); *to whom and how?*
  ○ What should you expect to happen when you report? What/how can we support those who are bullied

- Students need to know that all staff are committed to confronting bullying (in all its expressions).
- Some schools conduct "bully-proofing" coaching: how to "ignore", "walk away" or speak assertively to a student when they seek to tease, harass or threaten. However, when any bullying is particularly provocative and frequent it is unfair to expect young children to "ignore" or "walk away". They have to report it and know that the perpetrator will be confronted with their bullying behav-iour, that it will not be tolerated-ever.
- Many schools have also found success in helping students understand the role of "spectator"; what happens when students "watch" bullying episodes and some collude and join in by "laughing along with" or goading the bully (even on social media). Bullies rarely exercise their bullying behaviour "in secret" (apart from secrecy from adults, of course). They need their sense of "social power and pres-tige". As Peter Fonagy suggests, bullying is often "performance art" of which only 10–20 per cent of the school population are involved, though it is supported by the bystander audience (Labi 2001: 45; see also Lee 2004).
- Many schools use surveys (among students and teachers and, even, parent groups) to ascertain attitude, kinds of bullying, and the extent of bullying in

the school (and even nomination of bullies) – "in-house surveying" (Rogers 2003a; Lee 2004).

- Any school approach to bullying must make clear that it is not "wrong" or "tale-telling" for students to let an adult know when they are being bullied. *We need to let an adult know so they can help make this stop* ... This is a crucially important message children need to hear. It is crucial that the students be reassured on this matter. I have seen far too many examples where it is the victim of bullying who ends up having to leave the school rather than the bullying student (see also Appendix B).

Accountability conferencing

A key feature of any approach to victim support is to encourage the victim to confront the bully in a planned, supported, one-to-one meeting. "Confront" sounds like a tough verb to use here; I mean the opportunity for the victim to sit and speak to the bully clearly, specifically, about what they have done, said, implied, written about them (in any form or forum, such as social media) and the effect such behaviour has had, and to have a clear assurance – from the bully – that such behaviours will stop. Any such meeting must have the consent of the victim and discussion *and planning* needs to occur prior to any one-to-one meeting with the bully. The meeting, conducted by a teacher with some training and skill in mediation, will give a clear voice to the victim (in the presence of a senior teacher). Bullies trade in "secrecy" from adults about their bullying behaviour – while exercising their social power among vulnerable peers. Such a meeting exposes that "secrecy" while calling the perpetrator to account in the presence of the victim and the protective support of a senior teacher. Most victims want (and rightfully deserve) clear assurance that the bullying behaviour will stop. They also want assurance that we (as their teachers) will enable a safe environment at school. *Review meetings* are conducted within a week/fortnight to see what has occurred regarding the bullying behaviour. It is also helpful to meet with the collusive bullies (one at a time). Collusive bullies are those students who will "egg on" the bully, giving social approval as it were. It will be important to speak with them as well to indicate, clearly, their part in bullying even if they suggest it was "a joke", "just mucking around" or they "didn't actually do anything".

There also needs to be a consequential framework for bullying behaviour in schools, including exclusion for repeated bullying. Where a student refuses to cooperate within a safe-school policy and is persistently refusing any and all support, exclusion is a just – and necessary – consequential necessity (see also Appendix B).

One of the best texts I've read for developing a whole-school approach to harassment and bullying is Chris Lee's *Preventing Bullying in Schools* (2004).

Restorative practices

Restorative practice is a concept (and practice) increasingly utilised in schools. It seeks to emphasise, *and enable*, the participation of victim and perpetrator in guided restorative mediation: teacher–student, student and student, extending, at times, to family conferences.

Many schools now receive training in this area, to train mediators and raise restorative and cultural awareness across a school. Such restorative practice can range from how we conduct an after-class chat, through to a family conference. Embracing restorative practice throughout the whole school challenges traditional views about discipline as punishment, control and power (p. 129f). In building a restorative culture, a school will focus its discipline and behaviour leadership around the following:

- The core rights and responsibilities of all members of the school community (p. 41f).
- See our "teacher power" as *power for*, not merely power *over* … (p. 129f).
- Consciously distinguish *authoritative* practice from authoritarian practice in our behaviour leadership (p. 144f).
- Focus on the *purpose* and aims of *behaviour ownership* in our students as it affects others' rights.
- A commitment to *whole-school behaviour leadership practices* based on skill rather than seeing discipline and behaviour leadership in "terms of temperament and personality", or (merely) utility. We acknowledge that discipline practices and skills need to match our values and aims and *that they can be learned. Preferred practices* delineate our best attempt to actually detail "good practice" (and why we believe it is "good"). (See Chapters 3 and 4 in particular.)
- To see *consequential* discipline as more than punishment but as an opportunity for repairing, rebuilding and reconciliation.

Reflection

- How do you distinguish between behaviour consequences and punishment?
- Is there a framework for use of behaviour consequences in your school? (That is, beyond non-negotiable consequences for serious behaviour.)

- Are there suggestions, or guidelines, for *typical* behaviour consequences as utilised by class teachers? How do they fit with the 3Rs framework (Related? Reasonable? Conveying Respect?)?
- Do you have any "staged model" for behaviour consequences in your school policy/practice?
- How does your school utilise time-out on a least-to-most intrusive continuum? Is this published? At what point(s) are senior teachers engaged in supporting class teachers with time-out?
- What are the protocols/practices for time-out usage in your school?

  - Are they published?
  - What is the moral responsibility – and professional role – of the teacher who *initiates* any time-out consequence regarding follow-up with that student later that day or the next day?

- What supports are available for teachers to follow up with students who have been in time-out? It is important for any teacher who initiates time-out to *also* follow up and follow through with that student (within 24–48 hours).

Note

1 "Dunce" was a word introduced into the English language by the disciples of (St) Thomas Aquinas (in the thirteenth century) to ridicule those who followed John Duns Scotus, a medieval philosopher and theologian. It has come to mean someone who is slow-witted, a dullard; in other words, stupid. Actually, John Dun Scotus was not stupid at all; he was a Franciscan who had studied, and lectured, at Oxford – his opposers did not like him; he did not fit the theological mould of the time.

 Visit https://study.sagepub.com/rogers4e for additional resources to help you better manage classroom behaviour. You'll also be able to hear from Bill himself as he talks you through common behaviour management scenarios.

CHAPTER 6

Challenging children and children with emotional and behavioural difficulties

"There is always one moment in childhood when the door opens and lets the future in."

Graham Greene 1940 (in Magnussun, 2004 p. 43)

Argumentative and challenging behaviour in students

Argumentative and challenging student behaviours – it seems – are far more common in classrooms these days. I've worked with a number of private (independent) schools and teachers there, too, have noted a perceptible increase in more challenging behaviours. It is difficult to garner reliable, and meaningful, statistics (or even measures) in this whole area. There are frequent newspaper articles on "increases in violence" in schools (including recently in Australia – several serious knife incidents). Surveying teachers themselves, however, indicates that while extreme violence is rare (thankfully) there is a noticeable increase in "attitude" by students – by this teachers mean disrespect, "rudeness", argumentativeness, resistance to reasonable teacher directions.[1] This was acknowledged in the Elton Report (back in 1989) and seems to be a common experience among teachers. However, the perception *does* vary according to how such perceptions correlate with teacher confidence, skill, whole-school emphasis regarding behaviour policy and practice and – crucially – the nature, kind and degree of colleague support in a given school (Rogers 2002a).

In one such school, where I had worked as a consultant, a beginning teacher (this was a fee-paying school) recounted how she had asked a Year 10 student

"Why" she was out of her seat during work time. The young girl turned, faced the teacher with a firm "I've-got-you-sorted look" and said, "Why? If you *must* know I was just talking to my friend about borrowing a pen [sigh]". Here she ticked off the first point on her finger. "Secondly, I really don't think it's any of your business, Miss, and thirdly we pay your wages here … and I was *just* going back to my seat, OK?" The student had said all this in a quietly confident, "street-lawyer" way. I asked my colleague what she did in response, she said, she was just lost for words! "I felt stymied!"

When I've shared this account with other colleagues, more than a few have said how they feel they'd like to really "have a go" at the student, to tell them in front of the class how arrogant … how dare they …?! etc. I can understand both the feeling of perceived loss of authority and control that some teachers might feel, and the possible temptation to want to score here!

How would you deal with this minor out-of-seat behaviour (for it is minor disruptive behaviour)? What is more annoying here is the "secondary behaviour"; the attitude, manner and words used by the student in response to the teacher's questions (p. 12f) rather than the out-of-seat behaviour.

It is worth pointing out, again, that an interrogative question about behaviour ("*Why* are you …?"), especially in front of the student's peers, is an invitation to a pointless discussion, or a possible "slanging match".

I've never had a student say to me "… we pay your wages here". If I ever did, my response would be an exclaimed and satisfying "Eureka!! So you're the one – You've been paying my wages, eh? I've been looking for you for a *long, long* time …!" However, a brief "I" statement with a redirection to the task at hand is, normally, more than enough to deal with this little piece of "cock-sparrow" behaviour. For example: "I'm not speaking to you rudely [or disrespectfully]. I don't expect you to speak to me disrespectfully". Then the teacher could *refocus* from the student's avoidance behaviour ("I was just getting a pen") to the task at hand. Sometimes a direct question can help: "What are you supposed to be doing now?" Of course, a pleasant, business-like and respectful tone is important.

In response to the question, "What are you doing?". I've had students say, "I don't know what I'm supposed to be doing, do I?" (sometimes genuinely, sometimes sarcastically). In this case it is enough to simply, briefly and firmly point out what they should be doing and give them some take-up time. It will be important to come back, later, to check for time on task and (also) to re-establish a working relationship with the student. It may also be helpful to have a "follow-up" session (in non-class time) to address any student disrespect. Such follow-up is important because what *we* perceive as disrespect (tone of voice, body language, sighing, eyes to ceiling, and so on) may not be seen so by the student. This does not excuse their behaviour, of course; they may even be unaware that they "come across" like this. A one-to-one meeting, with some "mirroring" (p. 122–132) can help make clear what we (as teacher) see, hear, feel when we perceive insouciance and disrespect.

Is there a "distribution" of challenging students in any one class?

In any classroom group, there is often a basic distribution of challenging students in proportion to those students who are more cooperative and considerate:

- 70–80 per cent of the students are probably reasonable, considerate, naturally respectful, cooperative and display basic civil, social, behaviours – *given the chance* and given respectful, positive, teacher leadership.
- 10–15 per cent of students are attentionally distracting, some are argumentative (at times), or can be challenging in their behaviour. Sometimes such students are exercising attention-seeking goals, in effect saying: "Hey (…) *notice me*. I'm being funny, stupid, 'cool' …"; "My calling-out, my seat-leaning, my late entrance with a body language flourish … is inviting you (the teacher and my classmates …) to *notice me, attend to me*!" And, of course, if a 5-year-old boy is rolling under a table and barking like a dog, it is difficult *not* to notice and attend simply in order to discipline him and protect the learning, and safety, rights of the other students.

  Sometimes students challenge others, particularly the teacher, through expressions of inappropriate power-arguing, defying, ignoring, walking away, yelling at, swearing at … – where the student, in effect, says, "I can do or say – basically – what I like and how I like and you can't stop me …"; "I'm the boss here …" (p. 217f).
- 1–5 per cent of students display *frequent*, and often intense, patterns of disruptive behaviour. In some schools this percentage may be as high as 10 per cent. They may also present with social, emotional or behavioural difficulties (SEBD), or behaviour disorders such as attention deficit or attention deficit hyperactive disorder (ADD/ADHD) or autism spectrum disorder (ASD) or oppositional defiance disorder.
- There are, too, those children whose home background has a significant effect on their behaviour at school: domestic violence, substance abuse (in parents or siblings); poor diet; disturbing values and attitudes (misogyny, homophobia, sexism).

Caveat

It is very important that in using terms like SEBD, ADD or ADHD, ASD or ODD we do not easily *label* the child as an *ADD child*, or as autistic – as if that label "defines" the child. The negative effect of labelling is well known in education literature. Children often conform to the expectations that adults have about them and may also view themselves as inadequate, ineffective, useless or a trouble maker *within* these labels and expectations. The term SEBD (social and emotional behaviour disorder(s)) generally, as used here, is descriptive of children's more typical distracting and disruptive behaviours in a given context.[2]

Attention deficit spectrum disorder (ADSD) is a frequently diagnosed disorder in children in the UK (as in Australia and the USA). Children diagnosed with ADSD are often prescribed Ritalin or Dexamphetamine, medications that can assist with aspects of concentration, focus and impulsivity. Like any behaviour disorder, however, the positive assistance offered by medication will always need support from behaviour support and therapy to give some direction and guidance to a child's increased concentration or decreased impulsivity that can be assisted by such medications.

Corey (aged 14) had been diagnosed as ADHD and was on a fairly high dose of Ritalin each day. In my early one-to-one discussions with him (as part of behaviour support) I asked him if his tablets had taught him to enter the classroom without "grandstanding". He returned my smile with a knowing grin.

I then asked if the tablets had taught him to "sit in his seat without serious rocking backwards", or had taught him "to put his hand up without calling out or clicking his fingers". I had also asked his permission if I could show him (briefly) what these behaviours looked like to me (I'd worked with him in a few classes). He grinned again – adding a "No".

"Well – do the tablets teach you to stay in your seat, focus on the learning task and give it your best shot for – say – ten minutes or so without getting up and wandering?"

"Course not – no." We discussed other aspects of behaviour such as a quieter voice in class time and supporting other students by not annoying them by hassling them while they were trying to concentrate …

I asked him who was "in charge of Corey". "Who really *drives* Corey along in the minutes and hours of a school day?" I used the analogy of a car and a driver (Corey was learning to drive …). It seemed to connect. We then discussed how a driver has to be focused, has to check rear vision mirror, seatbelt, position; he has to select his gears, speed, indicator, has to decide where to go, and why, and how. We then discussed how he, Corey, could better (more helpfully, more thoughtfully, more cooperatively) "drive his own behaviour". From this came a behaviour plan as both "map" and "guide"/reminder. This analogy of driver/car/behaviour is one that my colleagues and I have found quite helpful in developing behaviour plans with older secondary students.

Corey still kept on with the Ritalin (although the dosage was reduced) but the behaviour plan gave him added confidence and specific focus to work on aspects of his behaviour, and the special attention he received from key teachers assisted in building his self-esteem within his plan. It was "three steps

forward and one, even two, steps back" on some days, but the colleague support – across all the
teachers who taught Corey – helped to give some consistency and supportive encouragement to both
the teachers and Corey.

When working with, and supporting, children diagnosed with ADD (or ADHD)
it can help to:

- direct them to sit near a classmate who is both a supportive and a positive role
  model. If table group seating is used, be sure these children sit with the quieter,
  less distractable children (even if they promise they will be fine if they sit next
  to overly motoric classmates!). At primary level teachers will sometimes utilise
  the support of a responsible student to act as a "learning buddy" to sit with, and
  support, the student with special needs.
- use visual cueing to assist student focus and attention. Seating near the front
  of the room (near to where the teacher engages *whole-class* teaching, learning
  and class dialogue) can also help. Small picture cues for work tasks (on their
  table) can also act as an *aides-mémoires* (see p. 236). (See also Rogers, 2003a.)
- develop work schedules for key learning tasks, with set structure for work
  progress. It can help to have a daily progress sheet with goal-based targets
  (even small, incremental, targets – breaking up the total requirement into
  time-manageable tasks). This gives a sense of time sequencing. Structure is
  important for children diagnosed with ADD or autism spectrum disorder;
  avoid giving too many choices.
- check for understanding when giving task instructions by asking the student to
  repeat back (correspondence training); this can be conducted quietly in those
  one-to-one exchanges during on-task learning time. Make normal learning *routines* clear; even how to utilise workspace, set out workbook(s) and analyse
  tasks (read twice, check "do I understand?", "Do I *know what* is asked of me
  here?", "How do I get help?"). This is where a positive learning buddy can help
  (even at secondary level). A table pencil case instead of a huge pencil case (full
  of interesting distractions). An uncluttered desk will also help. *Specifically
  teaching* a child (one-to-one) *how* to organise desk space and work time as basic
  "academic survival *skills" is deceptively* basic. This is addressed later (p. 234f).
  Allow time for *reasonable* movement by the student in class time, if only to
  quietly leave their work area (desk/table group) to come and check their in*cre-
  mental* progress (every five minutes) with the teacher or teaching assistant. The
  teacher – then – gives a brief, positive feedback. This will give some "physical
  release", as it were, for sitting for long periods.

- Avoid keeping such children in for extended lengths of time at recess – they (particularly) *need physical* activity at playtime.

Autism spectrum disorder

When I first began teaching (thirty years back now) teachers knew little about "autism". We were aware that we had some children who seemed "uniquely" different from time to time, who seemed to "shut off" and "shut out" others, whose bodily mannerisms at times seemed very strange, quirky. We struggled to elicit language, social connections and social empathy from these students – but we persevered. No doubt we were working with children (in reflective hindsight) who would now be diagnosed within the autism spectrum. Back then we had no specific training in working with "autism", even ADHD (as a behaviour disorder) was just beginning to enter the educational consciousness. Teachers, of course, have always had to work with a wide range of behaviours in children within and beyond a "diagnosed label", as it were.

These days, with inclusion policy rightly allowing children with diagnosed ASD into mainstream schooling it is essential that teachers be aware how autistic behaviour can present in children. What are some of the salient behaviours we might commonly see? Although I have heard this statement from a number of parents with children diagnosed with ASD, "If you know one autistic child you know one autistic child ...", by this they neither equate the child with their "autistic behaviour" (the child *is* autistic), neither do we simply define the child as limited by a formal diagnosis. There can be a significant range of behaviours across the autistic spectrum – within "low" to "high" functioning.

Our awareness of "salient" aspects and features within the "autistic spectrum" will enable both our understanding and our support.

What is often noticed is a child's struggle with social communication and interaction. Children in the autistic spectrum struggle with *processing* and communication, particularly social communication. This, in turn, affects their social *imagination* and the way they interact socially. They often find difficulty empathising with others because they may fail to perceive/understand why others feel upset, or hurt or angry. There may well be confusion and uncertainty regarding "normal" social situations, social cues and social interactions. The child diagnosed with ASD may often display speech limitations in social situations and present with what appear to be insensitive and isolationist behaviours:

- their ability to cope with and encourage change (particularly unexpected change) may precipitate anxiety ("tantrums" in young children), withdrawal or unintended distressed, even "aggressive" behaviour. Children diagnosed with ASD like and will always benefit from predictability and structure in classroom routines and learning tasks/activities.
- They may well present with obsessive and inflexible patterns of speech/interest/behaviour.

Like all diagnosed disorders, the 'degrees' of such behaviour (as those above) present within a spectrum of frequency, intensity, generality and duration. Teachers should not merely assume or *predict* a child is "autistic" if there has been no *formal* diagnosis because of such behaviours.

If teachers do frequently observe such behaviours (as those noted above) they should – of course – alert (and discuss with) senior colleagues. A *formal* diagnosis is crucial.

In working with children diagnosed with ASD (or who present with symptomatic, undiagnosed, "ASD behaviours") it is important to:

- build, and sustain, a calm working – and relational – environment and use a calm voice (firm, not loud or raised or characteristically "fast" ...). Children diagnosed with ASD are often *very* sensitive to loud (and fast) voice levels.
- take care in not directly touching the child unless parent(s) have made clear how their child perceives and understands *any* touching.
- use clear, *context-specific*, language cueing when giving directions.
- have clear routines; always prepare (with the child) – in advance – for *any* significant changes in daily routine.
- the child may not fully appreciate encouragement in the same way as other children, however we still need to keep our focus on the effort and application in specific – supportive – ways (rather than "great", "well done", "marvellous" ...) (see also p. 152f). Again, it is worth checking with the child's parents in terms of the child's familiar language cueing and the child's perception/understanding. It will rarely help, for example, to appeal to children (diagnoed with ASD) with emotionally loaded cueing, such as trying to create a sense of "guilt", or simply displaying overt frustration at any inappropriate behaviour ("Come on – please be nice ...", "Be a good boy!", "Do the right thing ...!").
- have an *individual* behaviour plan, which can often be helpful with the more extreme aspects of inappropriate social behaviour in school. An individual plan can *significantly* teach and support key social and academic behaviours (see p. 228f; see also Rogers and McPherson, 2014).

I have included a section on "Autism" in the Further Reading at the end of this book. It lists helpful texts and websites.

Attention-seeking behaviours

Chris, a Year 8 student, was repeatedly calling out in one of my English classes; eight, ten or even 15 times a lesson (on occasion). His calling out was sometimes masqueraded as asking a question; sometimes it was a silly comment; mostly it was "attentional behaviour". When I believed his behaviour was affecting my right to teach *or* other students' rights to learn and participate I would firmly – and briefly – remind him of our classroom rule: "Chris, we've got a rule for asking questions and sharing. Use it thanks."

He would often use such a rule reminder as an occasion to further seek attention, "But I was *only* asking a question! Is it a crime to ask a question in this class?" He would then – often – sulk when his attentional behaviours were not reinforced.

I could easily see why other teachers found Chris's behaviour so frustrating at times. It also doesn't help when a head-teacher, who having interviewed and chatted with a child (presenting with significant attentional behaviours), then says to the teacher, "He's no problem with me – I get on with him very well". Of course! With an audience of one he's fine, but back in a classroom setting, the child's behaviour is always affected by how he believes he can "belong" in this social group of his peers. "I belong when I get my teacher and classmates to *notice me* a lot ..." (see later).

- *Some* attention-seeking behaviour can – in the short term – be *tactically* ignored. Early years teachers know that by not giving any verbal or non-verbal recognition we can sometimes avoid unnecessary reinforcement of the behaviour; I say *sometimes*. The teacher will – then – respond (briefly and positively) *when* the child is behaving appropriately; cooperatively. In this sense *tactical* ignoring and *selective* attention reinforce the same outcome (p. 97f). As with all teacher discipline and management, there is no guarantee – no simplistic formula in any management or discipline approach (Chapter 2 and 3).

  It can help to *preface* any such tactical ignoring when a student is calling out. Prefaced tactical ignoring involves the teacher giving the student a conditional direction, *then tactically ignoring* subsequent calling out behaviour: "Chris, *when* you've got your hand up without calling out [the prefacing, *conditional* direction] *then* I'll answer your question." It can help to briefly add,

"Remember our class rule for ..." The teacher then turns their eyes and attention away from the student to focus on students with their hands up ... tactically ignoring any subsequent calling out. As much as possible we are giving the student attention *on our terms*, rather than simply reacting/reinforcing the child's attentional pattern.

As noted earlier, the skill of *tactical* ignoring in teacher behaviour is a context-dependent skill (p. 97f). We should never ignore any behaviour that sees a child hurting others (even pinching, or so-called low-level "testosteronic bonding", the friendly punching ...) or *persistently* disrupting other students' right to learn (by *repeated*, loud calling out; frequently touching others' work; annoying them). The test of any efficacy regarding tactical ignoring is the degree to which the student reduces, or stops, his disruptive behaviour. Tactical ignoring is only effective if the rest of the class takes their lead from the teacher and also ignore the disrupting student.

- If the disruptive student gains any significant *kudos* from others in the class it will be important to briefly and firmly describe what the student is doing (in their attentional behaviour) and direct them to the appropriate behaviour: "Chris (...), you're calling out (...). Remember the class rule (...). Hands up without calling out." If the student challenges, argues or tries other diversionary tactics, the teacher will keep the focus on the primary issue or behaviour (necessary at that point).
Avoid the temptation to debate, argue or be sarcastic and score points. While repartee, and even a workable *bon mot*, can defuse and refocus some attentional behaviours (from upper primary age upwards), sarcasm only feeds attention-seeking and power-seeking behaviours. If the student makes silly, rude comments the teacher needs to make *that* point clear but without *discussion*. Being overly discursive will only feed the attention or power goal in front of the student's peer audience:

"That's not a helpful comment, Chris. You know that."
"That comment is disrespectful, hurtful, rude [or ...] and not acceptable here." (p. 104f)
"We have a rule for respect. I expect you to use it."
"We don't use put-downs in our class."

In such cases a brief, firm, assertive, tone will carry the meaning.

On some occasions an immediate in-class consequence will be appropriate. If a student continues to be disruptive by, say, talking to, or annoying, students next to (or near) them, we can often use a choice/consequence statement: "If you continue to ... I'll have to ask you to work somewhere else in our classroom". If they continue with the disruptive behaviour and we then direct them to move and work somewhere else (the consequence) some students prevaricate or argue: "But I'll be alright now! I will Miss, I'll be good …!!" If we have raised the consequential stakes it is important to carry the consequence through with certainty (p. 179f).

If the student refuses to move to another place in the classroom, when directed by his teacher, rather than end up in a win/lose situation it may be preferable to give a *deferred* consequence: "If you choose not to move now and work over there I'll have to follow this up with you at recess in your own time" (p. 122f). An alternative is to use the colleague-support exit/time-out plan (p. 180f).

- In some cases where the attention-seeking behaviour is significantly affecting the teacher's right to teach and the students' right to learn, or students and teacher feel unsafe-then we will need to exercise the time-out consequence immediately. When directing a student from the classroom to take time out, a *calm* exit is important. "Sean (…) I've asked you several times to … (be briefly specific). You know the fair rule. You will have to leave – now – and go to (be specific about the place/person for time-out in your school). A teacher has a right to expect time-out support for students who are repeatedly disruptive (in class time) or are behaving dangerously or aggressively. While they should expect time-out support from senior colleagues, the initiating teacher (the class teacher) also has a responsibility to follow up and follow through within 24–48 hours. Avoid any last-minute grandstanding by using a loud voice or threats ("and you're going to be in detention *as well!!*").
- If repeatedly attention-seeking behaviour has occurred several times, over a few lessons, some early and thoughtful follow-up will be imperative beyond the normal after-class follow-up noted earlier (p. 122f). It is often in these longer-term (one-to-one) sessions that teachers can (more consistently) make clear to the student what he or she is doing in class and even *why*, and engage the student's understanding and cooperation (p. 221f). Such a process needs to be seen as helping the student to understand and take responsibility for his or her behaviour rather than merely using such follow-up time for yet another punishment. In such one-to-one settings it is important that the teacher assures the student that their main concern is the student's *behaviour*, and the effect it is having on other students' learning, and (of course) the teacher's right to teach.

If we are uncertain or uncomfortable about pursuing a "semi-counselling" approach like this, invite another colleague to work with us. The key focus areas in such a follow-up will address the following:

- ○ Is the student aware of their typical distracting/disruptive behaviour? "Are you aware of what you do in class when you call out …?" It is important to be *specific* about the student's typical, characteristic behaviour. As noted earlier, it can sometimes help to briefly "mirror" the student's behaviour to clarify what we mean (pp. 128f). In response to such questions, students often shrug their shoulders, and some laugh (nervously, or because they think their behaviour *is* actually funny).

- ○ Describe the student's disruptive behaviour, specifically and briefly (some mirroring may be helpful; p. 120f). Ask the student *what* they need to do to change the way they currently (and characteristically) behave. Point out that this behaviour is affecting others in the class; describe *how* it affects others.

- ○ A simple, achievable agreement – or plan – may help the student have a *focus* for *personal* behaviour management. I have found that a simple, printed agreement can often help such a focus by concentrating on three things (behaviours) that the student needs to *stop* doing (so that others can get on with their work without having to put up with X, Y and Z behaviour), and three things (specific behaviours) they need to *start* doing to gain some success in their learning *and* so others can get on with their learning (without having to put up with the distracting/disruptive behaviours).

The three "things" are *specific*, achievable, *behaviours*. For early years children "the thing" (the behaviour) we discuss with them, may be one "overall" behaviour, such as "sitting on the mat" (this includes sitting without rolling around or touching others; and facing the front and listening with eyes and ears – and joining in with hands up …) (see also, later, p. 228f).

Teaching in a Year 8 class I noticed (how could I not) Liam making frequent hand gestures across the room, to a classmate, while I was teaching to the whole class. Several students laughed and giggled. I directed them to "face the front and listen, I directed my attention to Liam; … Liam (…), Liam (…)!" He turned and faced me, sighing.

   "You're making hand signals to your classmate." I briefly looked at his classmate. "You need to be facing this way and listening, thank you." He raised his eyes to the ceiling and folded his arms – and settled for a while. He repeated the same behaviour a little later.

   This time I called his name, "Liam (…) …", and non-verbally cued him to face the front.

   He was getting, if briefly, the attention he was after. I was doing my short-term best to keep attentional focus on teaching and learning while giving minimal attention to his "secondary behaviours".

Later, in the on-task phase of the lesson, I noticed he wasn't working; he was chatting to his classmate, but clearly not working. When I encouraged him back on-task he became resistant. "NO ... I don't want to do this. I hate this kind of work ...," he muttered.

I helped him refocus and gave him some take-up time, but he still refused to do the work. At times he refused to listen, or look at me when I spoke to him, or walked away while I was talking to him. This was more than attention-seeking. (See also the case study p. 184f.)

It is understandable that teachers feel threatened, even somewhat defeated (at times) by such behaviour. I can also understand why some teachers feel they need to "show the child who is boss here". The child's displays of power may be active and vocal, or expressed in passive displays of power through non-verbal resistance. The child's private logic here focuses on beliefs such as: "I can do what I want and others can't stop me..."; "I am going to be the boss here ..."; or "I count only when I can do what I want; when I call the shots ...".

The need to belong: "goal" and behaviour (Dreikurs et al. 1982)

When a student enters the "society" of a school, and a classroom, their primary *social need* is "to belong". A child has many needs, of course, but their primary *social* need revolves around how they will "fit in", "relate to ...", be "accepted/approved of" by others – particularly by their immediate age peers.

Many children (thankfully) learn to "belong" (socially) in reasonably cooperative ways. They learn the fundamental social norms and expectations. They also learn to "give" and "take", to work by the rules and routines ... good and bad days alike (again – thankfully!).

Some children, however, display highly distracting and (at times) destructive social behaviours, such as *frequent* attentional behaviours and confronting and power-seeking behaviours. Rudolf Dreikurs et al. (1982) has argued that such behaviours are the child's attempt at "belonging" to their peer group; they are not *only* (or merely) poor or "bad" behaviours. In this sense their maladaptive behaviour is "compensatory"; the student's goal (as behaviour – even maladaptive behaviour) is their mistaken way of "belonging". Alfred Adler (in his earliest writings) had earlier coined the term *"inferiority complex"* to denote and describe these behaviour patterns (in children and adults) that seek to over-compensate for one's sense of social inferiority.

"Private logic" and mistaken goals (of behaviour)

Adler and Dreikurs argued that human beings are biased in their perception of the world around them. As they seek to find their place – their "social belonging" – they make evaluations of situations and relationships from that primary need and utilising their developing "private logic" to come to terms with their social reality. *Private logic* is a term Dreikurs et al. used to focus on what they called biased perceptions of individuals (of how to belong ...).

> Private logic or private intelligence is a "mistaken reason" in [sic] which an individual solves his problems in a "private sense" ... An individual's private logic consists of what he *really* believes and intends ... [it] involves a process, beginning in childhood, by which a person explains his experience to himself with varying degrees of insight and by which he produces and justifies his behaviour. (Dreikurs et al. 1982: 27–28)

Dreikurs et al. note that the child is not always aware of his goals. "However the child recognises the purpose of his behaviour when we disclose his goals to him" (see later p. 221f).

A child's "mistaken goals" are *characteristically* expressed in patterns of attentional and power-seeking behaviours and arise from faulty self-evaluations where a child believes he can only really belong when he gains attention or power (even in maladaptive ways). In this sense the student is not *only*, or *merely*, behaving badly; his behaviour is *purposeful* – even though such behaviours are, at times, negative, extreme, disturbing and dysfunctional.

A child's mistaken goals (through their behaviour) obviously create significant social tension and frustration for teachers as they seek to work with such children.

Yet the awareness of these goals and reflection on how we can address such behaviour in the public forum of the classroom (as well as one-to-one with the student) can enable us to manage that normative stress more constructively.

Dreikurs et al. (1982) identified what they called "mistaken goals" in children's behaviours, expressed in the child seeking:

- to gain *undue* attention [emphasis mine]
- to seek power (negative and confronting power)
- to seek revenge or "get even"
- to display inadequacy (real or assumed).

It is not merely the gaining of attention or seeking of power (as such), it is the *frequent* and *characteristic* gaining of *negative* attention and *confronting and destructive power* that characterises the sorts behaviours that create significant concerns for teachers, and the student's peers, in the social context of the classroom.

There is, of course, nothing "wrong" in children wanting attention or social power; what Dreikurs et al. refer to as the *inappropriate and maladaptive* expressions of attention and power in a student's behaviour. It is these behaviours that significantly distract and disrupt workable and cooperative social behaviours and work against a positive learning environment for the individual student (in question) as well as their peers.

For example, when a child is *frequently* showing off in class, or clowning around, or is seemingly a "constant" nuisance, or *repeatedly* lazy (when we know he is able to do the work), we (naturally) feel annoyed or frustrated because of the time it takes to keep addressing such behaviours. When a child is *overly*, and *very frequently*, "eager to please", who displays *overly*, and repetitively, and uses attentively "sensitive" behaviours, teachers also get resentful – again because of the time it takes to address *frequent* attentional demands (be they active or "passive" in expression). When a child is very stubborn, argues frequently, wants to be "the boss", to win and frequently does the opposite of what is asked or directed, or is frequently deceptive and lying ... there is a "purpose" behind such behaviours; the student's goal of power.

A colleague of mine "forced" a Year 7 child to stay back after class to finish written classwork. He thought that the student needed this consequence because he had wasted time in class.

He "stood over" the student (as it were) saying, "You will not be going to lunch recess until you have finished the written work." (The "work" entailed about half a page.) The student stayed back after class, grumbled, muttered, sulked and rapidly finished the task in five minutes or so – a cursory scribble. The teacher was about to check the work when the student picked it up, tore it in two, then threw it on the floor and walked out. The teacher called him back, threatening him with a detention. "I don't give a shit!!" and he was gone.

I know I was there.

This is a not untypical example of power-seeking behaviour. The student is effectively saying, "You can't *really make me* do what you say", "I'll do what I want, I'm *really* the boss here ..."

Goal-directed behaviour

When Dreikurs et al. talk about "goal-directed" behaviour, such as negative attention or power, it doesn't mean the child is always aware of their "goal"; this is certainly so in very young children. The attentional or power-seeking behaviours are the "ways and means in which each child has discovered his expression to gain status and significance" (Dreikurs et al. 1982). Such behaviours (as those noted earlier) are "purposive"; the child is a "*social being* and (he) wants to find 'his place' at home, in school, in the world" (ibid.). "The child's interest in belonging exists from the outset" (ibid.: p 8). This understanding about how children seek and strive for their sense of "social place" and "belonging" is a crucial insight into understanding behaviour motivations in classrooms.

It is through this seeking, this natural developmental striving to belong, that children find their "ways of belonging". In the parental and school dynamic, children – naturally – seek approval, attention, security, esteem. Some children, however, through their family experiences miscue and "*over*estimate" the importance of (frequent) parent approval. Some children have learned that the only way to have "status" and "belonging" is to exhibit *frequent* attentional behaviours that force their parents to attend to them and *notice* them when they demand such attention/noticing through their behaviour (frequent tantrums [even in adolescents!], persistent sulking, forcing sibling arguments ...). Sometimes children seek to "belong" by exercising their power to control or manipulate others, or situations where they have to feel they must "win", or always have their own way.

As teachers we've all worked with children who "want to be right all the time ..."; "who *frequently* overreact to any sense of failure or mistake"; "who are *overly* sensitive and try to get others (particularly the teacher) to do things for them; to make decisions for them". Even this behaviour – when it is *characteristic* – can be a form of overcompensation for a feeling of inferiority ("I only *really* belong when I can get the teacher to service my need for attention").

A typical classroom example is the acting-out attentional student who frequently calls out (loudly), in whole-class teaching time or calls out over others;

says "Miss!!", "Miss c'mon!" – calling out 20 or more times until he gets what he wants. Or the student who frequently refuses to cooperate, who manipulates others (or the teacher) if they can't get their own way displaying their 'goal' of power.

Of course in these sorts of attentional and power-seeking behaviours there are personality factors as well as family modelling, parenting and discipline factors that affect the child's social perception. However, *when they are at school they still have to come to terms with how they believe they "belong"; how they perceive they "fit in" with others that daily social dynamic.*

Where we see very frequent attentionally distracting and disruptive patterns of behaviour in classrooms, and power-seeking patterns of behaviour, Dreikurs et al. argue that: "It is not the cause but the purpose of the goal that explains such behaviour. Behaviour makes sense only when we understand its purpose. The goal of behaviour itself, is the cause." Whether the child is aware of the "goal" or not, the *child's behaviour* is indicating the "ways and means by which (he) tries to be significant" (1982: 10).

A significant sense of "inferiority" (the inferiority complex – Adler) affects a child's sense of belonging, often leading to "compensatory behaviours". These *behaviours* are the child's "mistaken" means of trying to belong. While we obviously have to address such behaviours (when they affect the rights of others in the classroom), this insight – about social belonging – can enable us to discipline in a way that minimises unnecessary attention and power – conflict within group contexts.

These insights are particularly helpful when we are working with the student one-to-one.

Enabling a student to understand their behavioural goals

Dreikurs et al. (1982) propose an approach designed to supportively help the student understand "why" they are behaving the way they do. This approach involves a counselling approach that utilises particular questions being asked to raise the student's awareness about the possible goal of their behaviours. The tone of these questions needs to be supportive and non-judgemental if they are to help the student understand their "purposeful" behaviour. This approach needs to take place in a supportive, one-to-one, context (away from the audience of peers). The teacher – in question – needs to have a positive working relationship with the student to pursue this approach away from the classroom context.

The first question raises the child's awareness about their specific behaviour through an open question: "Do you know why you …?" We need to be specific about the student's actual, disruptive behaviour: "Do you know why you call out many times in class …?"; "Do you know why you make frequent comments like (here the teacher recounts typical clownish, and silly, comments)?" Most students respond to such a question with a non-verbal response (a shoulder shrug, a wry frown or smile); sometimes there is a muttered, "Nope". Allow some brief reflection, even if the silence is a little uncomfortable. It can also help to increase the specific shared awareness about the student's behaviour, some *brief* mirroring of their distracting/disruptive behaviour can help the student's behaviour awareness.

The teacher then *suggests* what they think about *why* the student typically behaves the way they do: "I'd like to tell you what I think …" (here the teacher briefly notes the behaviour under discussion) or "Can I suggest why you call out a lot (or butt in, and so on)?" or "Could it be that you call out like that … because you want your classmates to notice you a lot?" I've never had a student say "no" to these sorts of "disclosures" (though they are naturally inquisitive). These questions preface what we-then-disclose as our calculated guess as to why the student engages in such behaviours (see later). Dreikurs call this 'goal-disclosure'.

> Dreikurs et al. caution us that:

> We must be careful not to confront the child with an accusation such as "You do it to get attention", because the child will resent this and deny it. "*Could it be …*" is not an accusation; it is only a guess that may be correct or incorrect. If it is incorrect we should guess again. …

> There is no harm in guessing since if you guess incorrectly, it is merely shrugged off. In the moment that you guess correctly the child feels understood. (1982: 31f.)

If the child says "No" to the "guess" we suggest, we make another "guess". Dreikurs et al. point out that if the child says "Maybe" to our guess, then we are "getting close" (1982: 31). Some children will say "Yes", almost compulsively, when we disclose *their* goal. However, the most common/typical response to such questions is the *recognition reflex*. Dreikurs et al. note that, "the recognition reflex and the teacher's own reaction to the child's misbehaviour are the best guides to an understanding of the child's goal" (ibid.).

The recognition reflex

This refers to the typical sorts of responses a child/young person makes to the sorts of questions (as above) that the teacher/counsellor uses to raise awareness of the child's probable behaviour goal. This "recognition reflex" is often non-verbal: the smile, the quirky look, the eyes looking up and away (as it were), the twitching mouth, the overtapping of fingers, the over- adjustment of their seating. As Dreikurs et al. (1982) note, they give themselves away [sic] through some facial or bodily mannerism that we term the *recognition reflex*. This recognition reflex usually expresses itself through a smile, a grin, an embarrassed laughter or a twinkle in the eye …

I recently had such a chat with a very bright grade three student about his acting out aggressive behaviour of kicking furniture and refusing to come when his teacher called him over (for example) in class time. When I chatted with him one-to-one (away from his class peers) I talked with him about the throwing of things, the kicking of the classroom wall, the rough pushing and, at times, kicking of the furniture … I then asked some questions about attention and power. "Could it be that when you (here I referred to the throwing … the kicking) you are trying to show your teacher – and me – that you can do what you want and we can't stop you …?" He smirked and then grinned. He didn't say "yes" or "no" (in response to the questions); the child's body language signals had indicated where the question had struck an awareness "chord" as it were.

We had noticed that when he couldn't "get his own way" (as his teacher termed it), he would aggress by slamming down his books, kicking at his chair and walking away defiantly from his teacher. This behaviour is a "learned" pattern or response (also at home) *and* it enables (in the child's private logic) his "goal".

My colleagues and I would never ever say a student is bad (in any way) for having angry feelings. Anger (itself) is neither good or bad, it is a feeling, an emotion; it is how we learn to react/respond *when* we feel frustration and anger that is important in social contexts. As adults we know, too well, how intense such feelings can be, and how hard it is for young children to learn to constructively express their emotions. However, what we characteristically think and do (our behaviour) when we have such feelings is part of our learning. As teachers we try to help our students be more self-aware of what goes on – in our body and our behaviour – when we're very frustrated or angry and learn better, more constructive, ways of dealing with such emotions in relationship to others. It is neither appropriate nor acceptable to allow a child to throw books, kick furniture, swear at their teacher or simply run off … when they are frustrated or angry. We have to address such behaviours in the public areas of the classroom, and with necessary consequences (such as time-out and restitution, p. 180f).

We often develop personal behaviour plans with such children (one-to-one), to teach self-awareness skills and ways to understand and communicate frustration and anger, and also manage it, without resorting to reactive aggression. These skills can be learned, even with young children (see Rogers 2003a, 2009; McPherson and Rogers, 2014; and see later, p. 228f).

This approach of "goal disclosure" was a helpful starting point as part of the process where we were able to teach this young child (above) better ways to understand, communicate and manage his feelings of frustration in non-destructive ways.

Goal-disclosure

Some suggested *goal disclosures* include:

- "Could it be that when you call out a lot you want the class to look at you and notice you?"
- Or, if the issue is clownish behaviour, "Could it be that when you say things like … [be specific] you want the class to look at you and laugh?"

If the student's goal is some sort of power exchange (refusal to comply with teacher requests/directions; frequent answering back in front of peers; walking away while the teacher is talking; harassing others, including the teacher), the disclosure would focus on this aspect of the student's behaviour:[3]

- "Could it be that when you refuse to do the work you're wanting to "show" me that you can do what you want and that I can't stop you …?" This assumes that the student *can* do the work and that their behaviour, regarding task refusal, is a display of attentional power. It further assumes that the teacher knows the student well enough and has a positive working relationship with them for them to engage in dialogue in this way.
- "Could it be that you want to do what you want, when you want – and that you believe no one can really stop you …?"
- "Could it be that you want to be the boss, call the shots …?"

Most students respond to a disclosure of their "goal" in non-verbal ways (as noted earlier): raised eyes, a slight grin, a shoulder shrug. This "recognition reflex" (as Dreikurs terms it) is often the student's assent; their acknowledgement that the teacher is "on to something here". If the student says "no" (in response to the disclosure – "Could *it be that* …?") it can help to ask, "If that's not the reason, can you suggest why you call out lots of times (or refuse to do the work when I know you can do it …)?"

It will also help to point out to the student that they have *learned* to behave *like this* at school. Somewhere, sometime, somehow, they *chose* to behave this way. They *choose* to behave like this now. The teacher suggests that the student has *learned* that certain ways of behaving get them the kinds of attention, or the kinds of attentional power they seek. We might well admit to the student that we cannot *make* them learn, or (in fact) do anything. Only they can *make* themself do things. They do not, however, have the right to do *whatever* they want, *whenever* they want. They will have to face the consequences. The teacher is seeking – through this process – to engage a cooperative understanding. They are encouraging the student to learn to *change* their behaviour – and for good, worthwhile, cooperative reasons.

Teachers can work with the student to refocus attentional, power-seeking behaviours into more cooperative opportunities so that the student can gain a sense of social belonging in purposeful ways, such as in positions of responsibility (monitor roles, peer-monitoring, cross-age tutoring) – this positive role is often taken up with some enthusiasm.

In light of the "goal-disclosure", the teacher invites the student to work on a behaviour plan. A key feature of this plan will involve the teacher consciously working with the student on these behaviours enable *cooperative* belonging (see later p. 228f).

An approach that involves the wider class group – through a whole-class discussion – can highlight (for the student) what their peers think of behaviours such as frequent interruption, distracting and clowning (and why).

In conducting such meetings it is important that we do not *name* an individual student (although no doubt particular names will be uppermost in most students' thinking!).

I have even conducted such meetings with infant-age children. The basic rules for such meetings are: "One at a time"; "We're here to discuss issues that affect us all"; "We do not put anyone (or anyone's ideas) down"; "We listen to everyone's contribution"; "If we make any decisions as a result of our meeting those decisions have to fit with our classroom behaviour agreement".

For example, there may be a decision – from the group – that students who *persistently* disrupt learning should have to work away from others or even face time-out (if they do not respond to the teacher's reminder, or directions). Students (as a group) also can learn to *tactically* ignore non-physical, attentional behaviours of an individual student. This strategy is particularly effective at early years level but must be balanced by the teacher's respectful support of the student at other times (including individual behaviour plans).

Consequences like those noted above would need to be consistent with the classroom behaviour agreement, would need to *relate* to the behaviour in question and be *respectful* in their application.

Basic "steps" in the one-to-one discussion using "goal disclosure" questions:

- *Raise behaviour awareness* by "revisiting" the *frequent* distracting/disruptive behaviours. Behaviour mirroring and brief "picture cues" can assist here. Picture cues with primary-aged children can be as simple as a stick-figure drawing illustrating (for example) the child – in question – calling out and the teacher and other children looking upset (illustrating both upsetness and "social disapproval"). These simple, stick-figure illustrations are a powerful visual cue to the child about how his disruptive behaviour appears to his teacher (and class peers).
- *Using the above as the starting point for self-awareness,* we then ask the question: "Do you know why you ...?" (be briefly specific to the behaviour(s) revisited above). This "why" question is designed to trigger the student's initial behaviour self-awareness. Allow a little time for the student to respond. As noted, most students shrug their shoulders or indicate by facial/bodily expressions that they don't know "why" ...
- *We then "suggest" why* we think they behave that way ...
  "Could it be that ...?" (we then add the "suggested" goal/reason for their behaviour) or "I think that ..." (in a respectful questioning tone) and then add the "suggested" goal/reason for their behaviour. "Could it be when you argue and refuse to do the work (when we know you can ...) (always give a *specific* example) you are ..." (here we suggest/disclose the "goal" of such behaviours).
- *Allow take-up time* – even a brief "tactical silence" – to enable the "disclosure" to sink in ...
- If a student says "No" or, "Not really", we move on to the next "goal disclosure". For example, we might start with a disclosure about attention and get no clear response. We then move on to disclosure about "power" to see if the student "connects". This is where we look for the "recognition reflex" (a student will often "look away", grin, shuffle in their seat ...).

  It is crucial that our tone and manner (in this one-to-one meeting) is respectful; we do not seek to impose or "score". Another brief "tactical" silence here (on the teacher/counsellor's part) adding, "I thought so ...", "I thought that's why you e.g.: call out lots of times in class ..." (here a *brief* reference about the behaviour under discussion).

  Again, it is important to stress that our tone needs to be respectful and "invitational" when we say : "I *thought* so ...".

- Having "disclosed" the goal, we can now talk with the student about constructive and cooperative ways of enjoying/having social/relational attention/power within classroom/school life. We, obviously, do not use those terms; we talk about the need to work on a plan together so that the student can learn to cooperate (positive attention and power) without having to resort to the distracting/disruptive behaviours discussed. (For a detailed discussion on how such individual support plans can be developed, see Rogers 2003a, 2006b (Chapter 7); and Rogers and McPherson 2014.)

Of course we can't make the student cooperate with any such "plan", particularly with established patterns of power or revenge. The key is always to work *with* the student and not re-engage in yet another power struggle. The student will, of course, need to know that the school's behaviour consequences will continue if he *continues* to behave in the ways (maladaptive behaviours) noted; however, a plan can always change things for the better – "the door is always open".

Working with challenging children and children diagnosed with emotional, behavioural disorders

James (grade one) was sitting on the carpet in front of his teacher (and myself), we were about to begin morning sharing time. James started to extend his hands outwards to touch the children either side of him. As he did so he laughed very loudly. My colleague told him to "stop that" and "sit up properly". He did – for a while. He started again, my colleague warned him, "James, leave the other children alone and sit properly or I'll have to move you." I was – yet again – surprised how tolerant the other children were of James's vigorous touching and poking and loud laughing. Although it did not seem at all malicious (he certainly seemed to derive some "attentional" satisfaction from the "touching"). It was very disruptive and (of course) unacceptable.

I whispered to my colleague to ask if I could have a word with the class (we were team-teaching). While I was "resettling" the class James started again. I cued him by name; after several calls he turned to look at me frowning. I said to the class "... excuse me a moment everyone. I need to speak to James."

"James (...), James (...) I want you to look this way (...) so I know you're listening." I then hopped off my chair at the front of the room and *briefly* modelled appropriate sitting. ... "James (...) I want you to cross your legs like this (I modelled it) (...). Hands in your lap, like this ... and eyes and ears looking this way. That's it." I resumed my seat in front of the class and thanked the class for waiting, re-engaging a class discussion. Twice I had to remind James of how to sit. Each time with brief, behavioural directions (p. 97f).

An individual behaviour plan

Later my colleague and I developed a plan for James involving the *explicit* teaching of sitting-on-the-mat-together-behaviour. We did this with James at lunchtime. My colleague and I set up 10–15 minutes "Behaviour Recovery" sessions (one-to-one) with James twice a week to teach him the necessary behaviours for "carpet time" and "table group learning time". Using a simple stick-figure drawing showing James sitting like the other children (their faces and the teacher's face were shown as looking happy). Using the pictures as a basic "social story" we identified the helping behaviours we all use together during whole-class teaching time:

  o *Where* to sit – during "carpet time" – with the whole class (we later appointed a "mat-buddy" to sit with James during whole-class teaching time).
  o We *discussed how* to sit (and keep your hands and feet safe).
  o We explained how to listen with eyes and ears; hands up (without calling out if you want to share or ask a question).
  o We explained how to wait for the teacher to call on you (*when* you've got your hand up and want to share ...).
  o We explained how to use your "inside voice" (instead of a loud voice) when you share in whole-class teaching/learning time. We described the behaviours (using the picture cards) (see p. 235f).
     We then modelled each of the behaviours and – crucially – we encouraged James to practise each of the behaviours above within the one-to-one behaviour recovery session. This was – in effect – his plan.
     We had top-up sessions twice times a week (initially) to discuss how his "plan" was going. In class time we used the picture cue to briefly act as a visual *aide-mémoire*. We also fine-tuned the practising of the plan in subsequent one-to-one sessions. When working with children diagnosed with ASD (particularly younger children like James) it does not help to simply tell them to "sit properly" – properly is (in a sense) too general; perhaps even "meaningless". They find a sense of security in clear, specific, direct speech (focused on specific behaviours). This verbal cueing gives a secure and supportive framework for behaviour in class-time, within the student's overall behaviour plan.

The key, though, (in this plan) was the specificity of behaviours, the routines, the practice sessions and specific encouragement in class time (p. 152f).

The responsibility and input of the class were also very positive as James started to change his behaviour. Later we developed a similar plan for time-on-task behaviours at his table group.

This approach can work at any age-level at primary (even middle-school years) (see Rogers and McPherson 2014; Rogers, in Clough et al. 2005).

Reasonable expectations for fair and safe behaviour with children with diagnosed or symptomatic behaviour disorders.

Some teachers will respond to children with diagnosed behaviour disorders as "uniquely different" and will tolerate behaviours they would never tolerate in other students. I believe this is misguided. Even if a child has been diagnosed with ASD (for example), we should not (in my view) ignore extremes of behaviour such as "poking", "pushing", "hitting out" or disrupting children's work time or *any* aggressive behaviour.

Of course there is a range of cognitive activity and social awareness in the ASD and ADHD range. However, when we effectively ignore, play down or excuse a student's disruptive or hurtful behaviour (*because* of their disorder) we effectively say to the other students that his behaviour is "OK"; that this is *so* different from other children that the normal rules and expectations do not apply – it conveys an unhelpful and unhealthy message to the class as a group. Cooperative learning, and social behaviours can be *taught* to children diagnosed with behaviour disorders (like James). They need (of course) one-to-one support for this learning and that is the important key – teaching children with diagnosed behaviour disorders the academic and social skills needed to cope, manage and even enjoy day-to-day schooling (Rogers 2003a; Rogers and McPherson 2014).

As noted earlier, there are many aspects of a child's life, temperament, home and background circumstances and environment that we have little, or no, control over; that contribute to and affect a child's behaviour in a school context. The way some children are treated at home – dysfunctionality in the home environment; domestic violence and abusive relationships; structural and generational poverty and parental long-term unemployment; lack of positive guidance; discipline; "values" and "role models" that are the opposite of what we emphasise at school; the amount and kind of television that even very young children watch; poor nutrition; substance abuse of parent(s) (or siblings) – are all aspects of a child's life that have a significant, and debilitating, impact on the child's behaviour at school. We obviously cannot *control* those influences, structural factors and impacting relationships in a child's home environment. It took me a while as a younger teacher to really appreciate this frustrating truth. It is also of little help to keep whinging about these factors: "If only …".

Our emphasis and energy is better placed supporting the student, in their ongoing welfare and learning while they *are with us at school*. Where, and when, we can support their welfare out of school we will (particularly if the child is "at risk"). This does not mean we are unsympathetic to those factors noted above. Indeed, there are occasions when we can hardly imagine how some of our students cope; how they stay as sane as they do. It means we avoid:

- *blaming* home environments for the child's disruptive behaviour at school
- too easily *excusing* the child's disruptive behaviour because "he comes from a difficult home"
- too easily making the child the "victim" of what we may believe are *causative* pathologies; that is, "he *is this way because* he comes from a difficult home and has a dysfunctional parent, and dysfunctional siblings and … therefore he *can't really help* his behaviour or *can't really change*".

It is important to recognise that while significant disruptive, and challenging, patterns of behaviour clearly have a contribution from those factors noted above (how could they not?), a student's disruptive behaviour at school *is also learned in context*. Negative behaviour is also reinforced when parents and teachers easily "excuse", over-service or reinforce significant patterns of disruptive and challenging behaviour. It is hard not to get impatient with such students or even get angry and shout at such students. In a kind of reinforcing, "socially cybernetic loop", adult behaviour can so easily reinforce the child's attentional and power-seeking behaviour.

Yes, it is understandable that some teachers will shout or even yell at students who frequently roll around on the mat; who make animal noises; or who walk away while the teacher is talking to them; or call out "all the time"; or hide under tables and refuse to join in, or task-avoid and task-refuse ("It's rubbish!!"; "I hate it!!"; "Can't make me!!"; "It's shit!!"); or swear and yell at their teachers; or push and shove and hassle other children in order to get adult attention.

It is hard, as a busy teacher – with 25 *other* students – to take time to reflect on what we currently do when we manage and seek to guide such children, or what we can do to help such children *learn* to behave more thoughtfully, positively and cooperatively. Yet that is what we need to do, but we cannot take on this onerous aspect of behaviour support unless it is a whole-school approach.

A team approach to developing individual behaviour support plans

The key elements of any team approach to working with students who present with SEBD include the following:

- Develop a case supervision approach with the student. A "case supervisor" is a teacher who works with the child one-to-one on their behaviour by developing an *individual behaviour plan*. This plan is then communicated to, and utilised by, all the colleagues who teach (or support) that student.

  At primary level such "case supervision" is normally conducted by the grade (the class) teacher. At secondary level "case supervisors" are normally senior teachers who are given dedicated time-release – and who have responsibility – for working with students who present with SEBD behaviours. Such teachers will be selected for their ability and skill in rapport building, communication and behaviour therapy and support. They also need to be colleagues who are well respected by staff and students alike (Rogers 2006b).

  It is also important to consider the ethical probity of any one-to-one settings where such a teacher spends some time working one-to-one with a student. If the student concerned is a female, it is wise to appoint a female teacher as the ongoing case supervisor, and a male case supervisor for a male student.

- There should be a well-established time-out plan (p. 180f). There are students who can easily, even quickly, "hold a class to ransom" (p. 184f). When a pattern of behaviour is significantly affecting fundamental rights in the classroom a teacher needs *immediate* time-out support (as does the rest of the class). While we often think of the disruptive child as taking time-out, the teacher (and class) also need their cool-off time, and calming time, from such insistent, or even dangerous behaviour. In a crisis, such time-out can also include a senior colleague withdrawing several disruptive students from the classroom to calm and settle the rest of the students (see p. 277).
- With very disruptive – and challenging – students we have found it helpful to "relocate" the child in another class for one or two periods a week to give the regular class teacher a breather. This is a practice more common at primary-age level. This "relocation" involves the child having a set time period, with set work, in another teacher's room. It is to be distinguished from time-out as a behaviour consequence.

Case supervision: working with the child on behaviour support

In working with students described (or diagnosed) as SEBD, it is unhelpful to leave each teacher to come up with their own strategies and approaches; in fact this is impractical at secondary level. If a student is *frequently* presenting with disruptive behaviour across a year group it is in everyone's interests to have a *year-level* approach to behaviour support for that student. I have seen, far too often, *ad hoc* responses across a year level, sometimes with little communication between subject teachers, coordinators and special needs colleagues. Or, worse, "competing" plans for behaviour support between subject teachers and special needs. Case supervision can increase collegial consistency by having one key colleague who works with the student one-to-one on the behaviour/learning plan and liaises with subject colleagues, special needs colleagues, psychologists, teaching assistants and parent(s).

Behaviour profiling

When considering case supervision we begin with a *behaviour profile* of the student with contributions from all adults who work with the student in the school setting. This "behaviour profile" takes into account any child's *diagnosed* (or symptomatic) behaviour disorder. However, notwithstanding diagnosed disorders, it is at the *school level*, hourly, daily, that teachers have to constructively, supportively and *realistically* work with such students.

A behaviour profile needs to include how *frequently* a student is distracting/disruptive in their classes; how often a child calls out, butts in, wanders, pushes in line, exhibits low-frustration tolerance behaviours, and so on; how *intensively* he calls out, butts in, wanders ...; and how *generally* he exhibits such frequently disruptive behaviour *across all teachers and all classes*. It is also important to determine if the behaviour is *durable* (all lessons, every day?) or is it more a "bad-day syndrome" pattern, occurring *some* days more than others?

In working with such students, early intervention is crucial. As soon as a "pattern" of disruptive behaviour is clearly present (in terms of *frequency, generality, durability* and *intensity* of distracting/disruptive behaviour) the senior staff will need to support teachers in developing a collegial plan. This plan will involve both structural colleague support and case supervision. *Structural support* involves time-out plans, even classroom rotation (see "relocation" above p. 231) and timetabling meetings for case supervisors and teachers to discuss and plan.

Case supervision involves a key teacher working with the child, one-to-one, on a long-term basis. These one-to-one sessions generally occur in non-classroom time *at primary* level. At primary-age level the grade/class teacher sets aside 10–15 minutes once or twice a week, normally at lunchtimes. This is a labour-intensive approach for any busy class teacher; however in most primary schools the grade teacher does not have the luxury of dedicated time-release to work with high-risk/high-needs students. Sometimes such individual plans can be developed (one-to-one) by a teaching assistant (TA), or special needs colleague, although it is the grade/class teacher who has to *enable* any such plan at the day-to-day classroom level.

At secondary level the case supervisor's role involves (in the main) developing a personal – individual – behaviour plan with the student. The case supervisor also communicates that plan to all teachers (and teaching assistants) in the team who teach/support the student in question. They will communicate the purpose and elements of the plan, discussing discipline, encouragement and time-out options within the plan. The case supervisor also liaises with parents to explain how this plan will support their child's learning at school, inviting parental understanding, cooperation and support. This *individual* plan emphasises key behaviours that will enable the child to improve their social interaction (and acceptance by their peers) and their on-task learning.

The plan further involves teaching and reinforcing those behaviours with the child through individualised modelling, rehearsal and encouragement in those one-to-one meetings with their case supervisor. As an example, the case supervisor *teaches* the child behaviours such as:

- how to enter the room thoughtfully (without loudness, pushing, shoving, or "grandstanding")
- going to their seat (or sitting on the carpet space early years), without hassling others' personal space
- how to contribute in class discussions (without calling out, talking over others ...)
- how to organise the workspace (table/desk) thoughtfully to enable their on-task learning time
- how to *focus* on a learning task and progress a learning task (within a given lesson) (237f)
- how to better manage their frustration, tolerance and anger.

It is the teaching of these *specific* expressions of positive behaviour that are – in effect – the student's plan. The case supervisor's role is to discuss the child's present disruptive behaviours in light of their expected behaviour and then *teach* the student – through the plan – to be self-aware and self-monitoring within the new and appropriate behaviours.

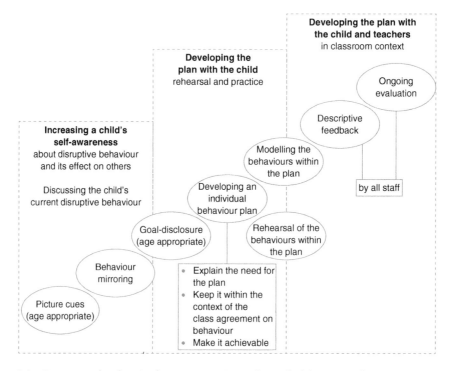

Figure 6.1   Key entry points in behaviour recovery: developing an individual behaviour management plan

Key elements in developing individual behaviour management plans

Case supervision involves a dedicated, one-to-one approach with the student over time. The key elements are set out in Figure 6.1.

- *Picture cues* are often used in individual plans at early years and middle primary level, and with older students on a case-by-case basis. To help the student's self-awareness about their behaviour, and to enhance dialogue with the student about their behaviour, the case supervisor prepares simple drawings of the child's disruptive behaviour and also the expected, appropriate behaviour. "Have a look at this picture ... *Who do you think this is, Nicky?*" Students almost always nominate the picture of the student (rolling on the mat, or calling out, or being loud ...) as themselves.

  The teacher then asks the child what they (the child in question) are *doing* in the picture. The teacher avoids asking the child, at this point, why they are calling out, or rolling on the carpet, or.... In the background of this picture the teacher will have drawn (in smaller figures) other children with

sad, or concerned faces and also an adult's face (the teacher) with similarly sad or concerned face to indicate social concern, disapproval and being upset. If the student won't talk about their behaviour (as illustrated in the picture) the teacher will calmly, briefly, describe the child's distracting/disruptive behaviour – again cueing to the picture.

As noted earlier, these drawings of students being disruptive (in such plans) can be simple stick-figure drawings. The student will often still nominate himself as the disrupting student. The teacher can then refer to the "social disapproval" displayed in the picture cue (the sad or concerned faces of teacher and students), and discuss, briefly, the effect of the child's disruptive behaviour on other students and the teacher. "What can you tell me about my face, the faces of the other students in this picture?"

- *Mirroring* has been discussed earlier (p. 128). The teacher *briefly* displays the child's typical distracting/disruptive behaviour and invites the student to see what their *behaviour* looks like when they call out, or push and shove or are talking loudly, or are leaning back in their seats and so on. My colleagues and I have used "mirroring" approaches with every age group. As noted earlier, it is important to use such an approach with the child's permission ("Do you mind if I …?" or "I'd like to show you what it looks like when you …", or – with older students – "Can I give you a demo? – It will be clearer if I do").

If the child is uncomfortable with us "showing" him what his (disruptive) behaviour looks/sounds like, we will need to respect how they feel and utilise the focus given by the picture cues. The picture cues (and "mirroring") are utilised to enable

the child's behaviour self-awareness. As noted earlier, we need to keep any "mirroring" *brief*; physically *step away* (having shown the student what the disruptive behaviour looks or sounds like) and *refer back* to the beha*viour*: "That's what it looks like when you ...". Many boys (particularly) will laugh when teachers mirror the student's typically disruptive behaviour; that is normal (and natural!).

There are, I believe, some limits to mirroring. Personally, I never mirror back to a student who is hostile and aggressive or swearing, or throwing furniture. In these cases it is enough to pick up a chair, pretend to throw and put it down. That is ample. A simulated "f" (a forceful, fricative, *sound)*, without the *full swearing, t*o "illustrate" what we mean by swearing is sufficient.[3]

- With older children (upper primary age on) *goal disclosure* can help raise self-awareness about behaviour. The teacher will then discuss the student's disruptive behaviour in terms of their attentional or power-seeking goals (p. 217f).
- The second picture illustrates the expected, desired, appropriate behaviour (as contrasted to the first picture). This will become the focus for the child's/student's plan.

The teacher discusses what is different in this picture. For infants and middle primary-age children, simple pictures keep the attentional focus in the discussion. "So, what are you doing in *this* picture?" or "What's *different*, here, in this picture? What are you *doing* here?" The teacher then draws the discussion around to the appropriate behaviour.

Pictures (as an *aide-mémoire* on a small postcard-sized sheet) can be used with older children, too, where appropriate to the child, age and context.

Above is a plan I developed with a Year 8 student who was frequently loud, distracting and restless at his desk area. He had a habit of clicking his knuckles, in part to get attention and, probably, in part because he was struggling with the work; a task-avoidance behaviour.

I had drawn a simple drawing (prior to our meeting) and we discussed his behaviour in terms of possible attention (p. 217f). He rather liked the drawing and asked me if he could have a copy. The actual plan for behaviour change involved:

- keeping his hands "quiet" and using them to work (with writing)
- a modified work-task – he struggled with particular subjects and we were able to negotiate some goal-based learning tasks with the teachers concerned (and the heads of department in his core subjects)
- a small *table pencil case*, which helped him have a less cluttered desk. Instead of a large pencil case full of bits and pieces, such as small toys, football cards (etc.) (as well as defunct pens) we gave him a smaller pencil case to house a blue pen, a red pen, a pencil (no sharpener), an eraser and a small ruler.
- the (postcard-sized) drawing (the bottom half of the 2-part drawing) acted as his *aide-mémoire*, as well as a record of his plan. He kept a copy in his school diary. Each subject teacher who taught him also had a copy of his plan and was encouraged to give him descriptive feedback (privately) during the lesson, and at the end of the lesson wherever possible.
- a twice weekly meeting between the case supervisor and the student to talk about his progress with *his* plan – we always emphasise the plan as the *student's* plan.

It is also important that the case supervisor *models* to the student the behaviour expressed in the plan (in the one-to-one sessions). In the countless one-to-one sessions my colleagues and I have had with students over the years we have sat on the floor (with early years children) and modelled *how* to have eyes and ears facing to the front of the room; we have modelled partner-voice; personal space awareness; how to put your hand up without calling out; and even how to manage feelings of frustration and anger when they come (Rogers and McPherson 2014).

The case supervisor then encourages the student to *practise* the behaviour (within the plan); this involves rehearsing the behaviours several times (during the one-to-one sessions with their case supervisor). Such rehearsal strengthens what my colleagues and I call the student's "kinaesthetic memory".

During such rehearsals the teacher can fine-tune aspects of behaviour such as "personal space", "hands in lap", "keeping hands and feet to yourself when sitting on the mat", "partner-voice", "how to line up", "how to move through the room without annoying others", "how to focus, and pursue, the learning task ...", "how to get teacher assistance during on-task time" (without calling out ...).

Each teacher in the year team who teaches the student (in question) needs to be made aware of the student's plan and any special verbal or non-verbal cues in supporting the student's behaviour self-awareness. For example, for a student who is particularly loud: in helping the child to focus on partner-voice the case supervisor will rehearse simple, non-verbal, reminder cues – perhaps the teacher simulating the turning down of volume. This minimises class teachers having to over-use *verbal* disciplinary reminders.

Each subject, or specialist teacher also has the same copy of the plan as the student (the visual *aide-mémoire*). If the student is disruptive in class time, teachers are asked to positively remind the student (particularly during on-task learning time) about their plan: "Remember your plan", or even "What should you be doing now in *your plan*?" It can help as both a disciplinary *and* encouragement focus.

The student's behaviour is monitored and tracked – within the plan – across the year level. All teachers working with the student are encouraged to give the student descriptive feedback at several points in the lesson, particularly during the on-task phase of the lesson (as a typical plan will often involve "time-on-task behaviours"). This encourages the student when they are behaving thoughtfully within their plan.

Such encouragement is best given "privately", or as a quiet aside, where possible (that is, out of direct hearing of others): "You remembered your plan; you used your partner-voice ...". "You organised your desk space carefully; you took time to read through the work with your reading partner ..." The *descriptive* feedback focuses on what the child did that made a difference in terms of their behaviour, "their plan". Sometimes a brief non-verbal cue will encourage a child back on-task: a smile when the child is working within the plan; a thumbs-up; an OK sign. Once (even twice) a week the case supervisor will meet with the student (one-to-one) to go over their plan (or any new plans), particularly focusing on: "What part of the plan is easiest (for the student) and *why*?"; "What part is hardest and *why?*" The *why* question, in this case, helps the child to be more self-reflective and increase their self-monitoring behaviour.

Plans can be adapted, developed and fine-tuned in these meetings.

Any such plan is a means to an end, the end being to help the child become self-aware of their behaviour and to take ownership for their behaviour. The behaviour support plan can then enable the student to be more self-regulating in respect of their behaviour as it affects others around them (including the teachers).

In *evaluating* any such behaviour support plans, case supervisors work with their collegial peers to determine if there is any positive change in frequency and intensity of disruptive behaviour; whether the student is still needing any time-out; and if there is any stability and generalising of the expected behaviours.

Teacher assistants

The role of teacher aides is always helpful in *any* behaviour support. They spend a lot of time one-to-one with students with behaviour and learning needs; they often build a trusting, supportive, relationship. They learn to "read" mood/temperament and will often intervene supportively to redirect, refocus students when they are having a particularly difficult time at school. They can often take on the role of adult-mentor or "case supervisor" when developing a personal behaviour programme with at-risk students. It is crucial, too, that teachers work with TAs *collegially* (I have worked with some teachers who treat TAs with less professional regard than a fellow teacher).

When nothing seems to help ...

There are some students for whom no amount of one-to-one time or behaviour therapy seems to help or affect changes in their disruptive behaviour at the school. In these cases we will have to work at alternatives to their schooling outside a mainstream school setting. No student can be allowed to continually, persistently, disrupt the learning and safety of others in a school. Alternatives to mainstream schooling in such cases are not only important for the welfare of the other children in the school; they are also important for the welfare of staff.

Inappropriate or "bad" language and swearing

In a press article on swearing it was reported that "90% of Britons are not offended by swearing". "The average Briton utters fourteen expletives a day ...." (one wonders how they get such an exact number). It was perhaps no surprise that " … men admitted to being the more foul-mouthed gender …", though the article goes on to state that "83% of women" swore on a daily basis. The journalist concludes that the British are not so conservative in their public discourse as – perhaps – they once were (Manchester, 2009).

Not all "bad" language or swearing is the same. Even adults sometimes (sometimes?) swear out of frustration. Even teachers (teachers?) swear in staff rooms, in the photocopy room or after the hostile parent has finally left. Whether we like it or not, swearing, as it has been traditionally understood (or sometimes, "bad" language), is more common today in schools than in times past. For some people swearing is even passé. Certainly in many films, books and television shows it has become a "norm" in descriptive dialogue, 'humour' as well as in expressions of frustration and anger.

I was discussing issues of playground behaviour with some "dinner ladies" (mid-day supervisors) and the issue of swearing cropped up, as it often does.

"What kind of swearing?", I asked.

"What do you mean?", they said, initially puzzled.

"Do the students swear at you or each other?"

"Sometimes at each other – rarely at us", they noted.

"So, what is the most frequent kind of swearing?"

It turned out that students were using swearing (for example, "shit", "f—ing", "a—hole") mainly in conversations, or frustration outbursts in game-playing. Should we then distinguish between "kinds" of swearing – or "bad" language? If so, why and how? Thoughtful teachers distinguish between a child who mutters "shit" (*sotto voce*) out of frustration and a student who swears *at* a fellow student or teacher. Some swearing is also "quietly" muttered, in passing, when the student walks past, or away from the teacher ("wanker", "a—hole", "dick-head", "bastard") – do they want us to hear such swearing? They may well want their *classmates* to hear.

Swearing as hostile intent directed at another person (student or teacher) needs to be dealt with immediately by the teacher – firmly, without aggression (this only feeds the latent hostility or anger or even attentional "showing off"…): "That language is unacceptable here. When you've calmed down we'll sort this issue out"; or "Michael (…), we don't swear *at anyone* here. Full stop." Block any argumentative appeals as to *why* they swore at so and so (or even why they swore at you!). Avoid pointing, gesticulating and hostile hand movements. An open – blocking – hand movement helps to assert the firm voice without aggressive intent. Direct the student to take informal, or formal, cool-off time if necessary. It is pointless asking (or demanding from) the student *reasons* why they swore (at you, the teacher, or at a fellow student). In the *immediate, emotional, moment* the teacher needs to communicate (and enable) calmness alongside appropriate assertion.

I have known teachers appeal to a swearing student with comments like: "Why are you swearing at me? I'm not nasty to you am I? What have I done to hurt you?" This non-assertive stance, often with an unhelpfully "reasoning" voice, is counter-productive and often feeds latent student attention and power; there's always an audience.

In the immediate emotional arousal, when hostile swearing is present, it is important to keep the assertive statement brief; focus on the issue or rule (about language or respect then); direct the student to take some cool-off time and follow the issue up *later* with a third party (a colleague) for support if necessary.

Younger children will need a direct, immediate rule reminder: "We don't swear like that in our class." Such behaviour may need to occasion time-out in the room, or out of the room if the child is physically hostile or aggressive.

In the immediate emotional moment we avoid long explanations about *why* the language is unacceptable and resist the moral lecture, "Is that the kind of language you use at home?!" I've actually heard teachers say that *and* I've heard students reply in the affirmative.

It is also pointless to force an apology from the student – in the heat of the moment, in front of their peer audience. If a student swears *sotto voce* ("on the run", as it were, "under their breath"), such swearing can sometimes be tactically ignored in the immediate, emotional, moment and followed-up later when the student has calmed down. It depends, in part, on how *sotto* the *voce* was (did we really hear a frustrated, loud, whispered "wanker"?) and in part on the audience reaction. It is often enough to say something like: "Paul" (always use the child's first name because it gains some attentional focus and personalises the adult–child discipline role) "I heard what you said. I know you're feeling annoyed (or upset). I don't speak about you like that. I don't expect you to speak about me like that." If he argues what he said was not said *to* you, quietly remind him of the rule. Then direct the child back to the task or to what he should be doing now or to cool-off time if necessary.

If we can direct the student aside for a brief chat (using similar language to above), even better. If other students have heard the muttered swearing they need to see us do something. This brief "aside" is not an extended discussion; it is *acknowledging* and briefly *clarifying*.

We can sometimes add – in the one-to-one aside – "David, I heard you swear at Paul earlier …". I've had students look puzzled here (because they don't always think what they say is swearing). I sometimes add in the swearword they used, or even write it down. "Look, I know you were uptight with Craig before (this briefly tunes in to how the student was probably feeling) but we have a class rule about respectful language …".

In a particularly challenging high school in the western suburbs of Melbourne I was teaching a Year 9 English class. As I was moving around the room (in the on-task phase of the lesson) I overheard one of the more vocal (and time-wasting) lads call a girl near him a "f—ing bitch", just above *sotto voce*. I knew they were friends but I could hear the frustration in his voice. I went over and said something like, "Look, Adam, I heard what you said to Belinda …". I pushed the piece of paper on which I had written down his swearing language across to him.

"I didn't say that!" He sounded annoyed.

I added, "I heard you Adam …"

He explained, "I tell you I didn't say that. I said f— off, you bitch. I didn't say f—ing bitch!" He was upset that I'd got the words wrong not that he'd used such offensive language!

The annoying thing was that when I called them both back later (after class) to discuss the issue and offer support to Belinda, she seemed unfazed. She shrugged her shoulders and said, "… it's just Adam … that's how he is …". (Adam had given a cursory apology…).

Part of the challenge of addressing swearing with some students (adolescents most notably) is the "no-big-dealness" of it all. It can often help to raise the issue of swearing and offensive language more widely with the whole-class group through a classroom meeting (Rogers 2006b). Ideally, class teachers should have covered the issue of interpersonal communication; mutual respect and careless, thoughtless, disrespectful and abusive language within the classroom agreement (p. 39f). A classroom meeting can *reaffirm* the issue of respectful language and reassess "how we communicate with one another here".

Swearing, at infant level, may sometimes mean something quite different to a child's perception. One of my colleagues recounts the occasion when a 5-year-old student came up to him with a most serious look on her face and said, quietly, "Sir … Con said the F word."

"Did he Maria – really?"

"Yes he did."

"Are you sure?"

"Yes … the F word."

The teacher thought he would check and very quietly asked, "Maria … what did he say?"

Maria replied, with the utmost seriousness, in a struggling and embarrassed whisper "He said, he said – stewpid!"; and covered her mouth as if to say "sorry I had to tell you he used the F word [stewpid]". The "F" word meant, to her, any "bad" word (!)

Conversational swearing

It is not uncommon, even in primary schools, to hear "conversational swearing"; I hear it sometimes in classrooms (and staffrooms): "Did you see that fantastic f—ing game the other f—ing day. Shit! How was the f—ing score they got, eh? The other team; they're rat shit!" Should we ignore this kind of "swearing" in the, classroom and playground? Should we relegate it to the argument of, "… that's the reality now. That's how it is today – it's just 'street language' …"? I have heard this argument many times now – principally from non-educators. However, a school is not a "street"; nor is a classroom a "street".

Ignoring such language (when we hear it on playground duty or even in the classroom as a *sotto voce* exchange) can easily send the message that we do not care how our students speak, or that such language is OK; or is even the norm (as a conversational exchange). For example, do we distinguish between shit and f___? Is one more "acceptable" than the other?

Of course such language is "street-language", but acceptance can easily excuse, even ratify, language norming. The issue for educators is how can we encourage our students to converse without lazy recourse to "f—ing and blinding …"?

A group of students are discussing the latest "f—ing film" they saw recently; some action-packed thriller with serious maiming, gore and gratuitous … (well, *gratuitous anything* really). You can hear the descriptive qualifiers quite clearly, several yards away. It won't help if the teacher charges in moralising: "Oi!! I could hear *every* word you said!! Is that the kind of disgusting language you use at home – is it?" It may well be they use such language at home, but a judgemental appeal to "home environment" is inappropriate and unnecessary and may, in fact, get a hostile reaction.

The issue of "conversational swearing" can be addressed by a quiet, firm, acknowledgement, followed by a rule reminder about use of language at our school (assuming the issue of thoughtful and respectful language has been explored across the school).

Sometimes a humourous question, or aside, can give a bit of self-checking. The teacher walks over and casually greets the students.

"How's it going?"

The returned, non-verbal body language suggests, "Well, we were going kind of OK till you walked over – really." Their *actual* reply is, "OK." Do they sense their "swearing" is heard? Will they – now – have to "put up" with a teacher's reminder about language probity …?

The teacher leans a little towards them (as if to suggest he doesn't want others to hear) and asks a question about the "*eff*ing film" they had momentarily been discussing (without using the actual words they used). "Seen any interesting films lately beginning with 'F'?"

A couple of the students catch on with a weary smile and sigh. The teacher walks off with a pleasant "goodbye for now". Relaxed vigilance.

If some students habitually, and loudly, converse with strong swearing it is worth following up with these students at a later stage (one-to-one) to discuss their behaviour and engage their responsibility for the way they communicate in our school.

Most conversational swearing is an *unreflective habit*; some (of course) is peer-group, positional, posturing, "Listen to me being 'tough', 'with-it', 'cool', 'just like everybody else' …".

If the issue of conversational or banter swearing is typically frequent (particularly at upper primary and secondary level) it can help to run classroom meetings in tutor groups (or grade classes) to raise the issue: define what is meant by inappropriate or disrespectful language and swearing; discuss how feelings are affected by what we say and how we say it; and readdress core rights and responsibilities as they impact on what we say in relationships. We emphasise that words are powerful for good or ill. Such meetings can be very constructive in raising *shared* consciousness and values about the link between language and how people feel … (Rogers 2006b). If you're not confident in conducting such a meeting, or if it is outside your experience, ask a colleague to discuss, plan and conduct the meeting with you.

Most of all it is getting a balance between language probity, and usage, thoughtful discipline and education and modelling. Our own modelling (as teachers) will go a long way in demonstrating that one can communicate frustration, even anger, without resorting to the lowest, "common", language denominator.

Reflection

- We have all worked with students who procrastinate and argue … How aware are you of how you engage argumentative students – particularly when they display "secondary behaviours"? (p. 12f)
- How aware are you of how you typically communicate with challenging students – in the heat of the moment?
- Do you always follow up with challenging students (say beyond time-out referral, or referral to senior or SENCO colleague)?
- How does the discussion on "attentional" and "power-seeking" behaviours help in the understanding of challenging behaviours? How does it inform your practice?

- Within the support opportunities available for working with and supporting challenging students and students with behaviour disorders in your school, what provision is made for case supervision (as explored in this chapter)?
- How does the discussion on swearing (within the distinctions noted in the text) inform and shape your practice? Do you distinguish the "distinctions" or "types" of swearing in your school? What is your school's policy regarding bad language and swearing? How do we "raise" and "discuss" this issue with students generally? And one-to-one?
- Are there stated consequences for *any* abusive swearing (particularly *to* a teacher)? Does the school advocate restitutional possibilities for a student who has used abusive language, say, to a teacher? How?

Notes

1 In a major research study (by H. Rudolph Schaffer) the point is made that, "… the *potential* of children to recover from early environmental stresses of a quite severe and lasting nature has been underestimated in the past and that a self-righting tendency analogous to that found in physical growth can, under certain circumstances at least, be seen in psychological development too …" (Schaffer 2000: 8, my emphasis).

2 The literature addressing challenging behaviours, and emotional-behavioural disorders, is increasingly using terms – now – such as attention deficit *spectrum* disorder; so too, autism *spectrum* disorder. This (obviously) acknowledges *degrees of symptomatic behaviours* within a diagnosed behaviour disorder.

   A helpful text that addresses a wide range of related issues regarding antisocial as well as challenging behaviour and behaviour disorders in schools is the *Handbook of Emotional and Behavioural Difficulties* (Clough et al. 2005).

   In an essay on "The influences of the school contexts and processes on violence in American schools" (Furlong et al. 2005, cited in Clough et al. 2005) the point is made that we need to distinguish between "violence" and "disruption" and the reality that "school is a place where aggressive, antisocial youth congregate …" (p. 123). We also need to ascertain in what ways aggression "is, at least in part, caused by the dynamics of the school" (Clough et al. 2005: 123). Furlong et al. give a summary of school violence trends, indicating that there has been a trend towards a "decrease of weapon possession and physical fights on school campuses" (ibid.: 125).

   There are a number of strategies in place in American, British, European and Australian schools that address bullying and aggressive and antisocial behaviours.

These programmes range from welfare, breakfast clubs, and social skills, to mentoring programmes for disenchanted and at-risk young men and women. Some of these programmes are explored in Clough et al. (2005). There is, obviously, no single or simple solution to addressing challenging behaviour in schools – its genesis and likely expression is affected by many factors. We do know – from the research – that supportive school environments can, and do, provide *a sane – normally safe – secure local learning community* that can support and enable at-risk students (Rogers 2006a).

A wonderful and very encouraging book for those engaged in supporting young adolescent males in schools is Celia Lashlie's *"He'll Be OK": Growing Gorgeous Boys into Good Men* (2005) (a silver medal winner).

For a teachers' text that utilises case studies – in very practical (and often very moving) ways – see *How to Manage Children's Challenging Behaviour* (Rogers 2009). It comprises a series of essays written by English and Australian teachers working with very challenging children and classes (www.sagepublications.com).

3 My colleagues and I do not normally use mirroring approaches with children diagnosed with ASD. Such mirroring may unhelpfully confuse or upset them. We focus on directly teaching the required, necessary behaviours.

Visit https://study.sagepub.com/rogers4e for additional resources to help you better manage classroom behaviour. You'll be able to hear from Bill himself as he talks you through common behaviour management scenarios.

Managing anger in ourselves and others

"That carries anger as the flint bears fire; who, much enforced, shows a hasty spark."

William Shakespeare, *Julius Caesar* **(4, iii)**

Managing anger

England is full of roundabouts – or so it seems to me. On one of my trips to the UK, some years back, I hired a car at Heathrow airport and was beetling down towards a town in Essex (and a hotel). I had a map, but I was lost. At one of the large roundabouts I sat, idling the engine, and waited to get into the circling mass of cars. To my right an old car pulled up; and with a brief glance I noticed two young lads, both drinking large cans of lager and smoking roll-ups. The lad nearest to my right-hand window wound his window down and said, "Oi – get going alright!" Apparently he could see it was "easy" for me to race into the traffic throng from the cusp of this roundabout. Sitting in this new car, with cars speeding past me, I was much more cautious.

My caution seemed to really annoy them; I was closer to the entry of the roundabout than they were. He called out again, "Just go; f–ing go, alright!!"

I thought their anger was disproportionate to the 20–30 seconds of caution on my part. I looked at him and shrugged (as if to say, "be fair, fellas – I'm waiting for a break in the traffic ...").

"F– you!" was the last I heard from the two lads and they shot off (having "gunned" the car) into the roundabout. But as they shot past my car they hit my right-hand-side mirror, the mirror swivelled 360° but hung on ...

Having entered the roundabout – at last – I took a turn off to what I hoped would be Basildon. As I motored on I saw the two lads on the hard shoulder, standing looking at the damage to their car (where they had hit my mirror). I pulled over and parked about 20 yards in front of them, and got out (hoping I might get their number for potential insurance purposes ... an unwise move perhaps, but ...).

As I was "casually" examining my twisted side mirror, I noted (out of the corner of my eye) one of the lads walking towards me, with his can of lager. He looked tense; perhaps he thought I was going to create a scene. I turned side on (as casually as I could) and said (still looking as if I was examining my mirror) "You OK?"

He said, surprised, "Yeah."

"I'm glad." I replied. "Your car OK?"

"Yeah." Still sounding surprised, even wary.

"My mirror is jammed." I didn't verbally attack him, or judge him, or blame him (notwithstanding the fact that he'd arrogantly hit the mirror although I'm sure he didn't "mean" it).

He looked at the mirror — "It's jammed!"

"Course it's bleedin' jammed!", I felt like saying. I didn't. A bit of "partial agreement", I thought might be apposite — "You're not wrong, it's jammed."

I was conscious of keeping my voice calm, relaxed, not too much direct eye contact.

He seemed less tense now. I was hoping my calmness would trigger some calmness in him.

"You can fix that easy," he said.

"Can you?" I wasn't too sure.

By this time the other lad had come over to see "what was happening". I said "Hi." He grunted something. I added "I'm checking my mirror ...". He also noted the "bleedin obvious".

"It's jammed ..."

The other lad chipped in, "They're a spring — mounted — you just pull it out and it goes back in the housing right. I can fix it if you like." They seemed marginally affable now. I hadn't referred to what they had done back at the roundabout and there was no point (or need) to verbally "attack" them ... It was as if we both had some basic human needs going at this point; we were beginning to see each other as more than a mere hindrance on the road.

He pulled at the mirror, groaned and grunted. I was hoping he wouldn't pull it out of its socket! He let go. It clanked back into place.

"Shit! Fixed it!" He seemed surprised and pleased.

Neither had admitted blame or even apologised. I didn't force it either. I looked at the fixed mirror — a few scratches on the plastic housing. No sweat!

"Good on you, fellas — thanks." They must have picked up on the Aussie accent. The first smile from the two lads.

"You an Australian?"

"Yes." I felt like singing the theme song from *Neighbours*. I didn't. "Fellas, wonder if I could ask a favour." I noticed a little tenseness (perhaps I was going to ask for their licence number). "I'm trying to find a hotel in Basildon." I explained where I was seeking to go.

"I know where that is!" He ground his ciggie on the gravel. "It's ..." he started to explain.

"Could you draw me a map, fellas?"

"Nope — we'll take you there. You follow us — we'll show you where to go".

I had a momentary thought they might lead me up the garden path. But no — they didn't. They went out of their way to help.

While I'd never advise stopping in such a situation, I know the situation could have been worse had I simply let vent with some Alpha male posturing.

I followed them to the hotel. As our cars parted on their different paths they bipped their car horn. I think this was their version of "we're sorry".

While there is never any guarantee that our behaviour can positively affect another's in tense situations like this, I believe that it helps if we consciously calm ourselves before we seek to calm the other person, and take some thought of how we communicate with tense, frustrated or angry (or, potentially, angry) people.

Understanding frustration and anger – in ourselves and others

Anger is an extremely powerful emotion. It can disturb, even destroy, positive working relationships between ourselves and our colleagues, and ourselves and our students. At times it can lead to destructive and dangerous behaviours.

I have seen, and heard, teachers yelling, even screaming, at individuals and whole classes as their frustration, then anger reaches boiling point. I have seen teachers so eaten up with anger that they behave in hostile and aggressive ways to peers and students alike. I have intervened between teachers and students when I have sensed that the teacher could be a few seconds away from getting into a self-defeating conflict or even hitting out at a student. Anger, however, can also validate our feelings and needs – particularly our feelings for justice –and it can help communicate those feelings and needs.

It is important to *understand* our own frustration and anger; to understand those situations, circumstances and people who lower our tolerance to frustration; to understand what we *characteristically* do in such situations, how we react and respond and manage our anger as well as seeking to help others to manage their anger. We can hardly do such reflection in the heat of the emotional moment. It is, however, worth generally reflecting on the emotion of frustration and anger in terms of our role and relationships as teachers.

Aristotle (in his *Ethics*) has taught us that "we must not forget that it is human to be painfully affected by anger and to find revenge sweet" (Thompson's translation 1969: I, 100). He is not saying we should find revenge sweet; he is talking about the human tendency expressed by the familiar (and destructive) epithet, "Don't get angry, get even". A teacher with such a view of retributive justice is doomed to a short career!

Aristotle (in his *Ethics*) goes on, "Neither are we praised or blamed for the way we feel. A man is not praised or blamed for being angry; it is for *being angry in a particular way* …". (1969: II, 63, my italics). He makes clear what we know in our more reflective moments: anger (or at least frustration) is a feeling we often *can't help*; it "just comes" – often when we're tired, hassled or trying to do ten things at once. It also "comes" when we feel a situation, or another's behaviour is unfair, or unjust.

He also distinguishes between the *feeling* of frustration and anger, which we can't help or stop (like when we're in a traffic jam on the M25 and we're in a hurry and we forgot how useless a road system it is at peak times, and so on) and the *behaviour* that results from our anger. He adds, "Being angry, or frightened, is something we can't help but our virtues are in a manner expressions of our will; at any rate there is *an element of will* in their formation" (1969: 81–2, my italics).

The *learned* aspect in our anger is what we do *when* we're angry. We have learned to get angry in certain ways; perhaps we have unhelpful habits of anger-behaviour, but we've learned these habits over time, even though such learning may not be readily conscious. Aristotle goes further and argues that there is an element of "will" in our angry "behaviour". He links the exercise of our will to how helpful or unhelpful, how constructively or destructively, we express our anger. Frustration and anger lie on a continuum from irritation through to temper, rage and even aggressive anger. It is an emotion we have to learn to live with whatever the contributing causes. The "element of will", the "expression of our will" can occasion any "virtue"[1] in what we do when we're angry.

Anger may be produced by a variety of causes – but, however that may be, it is the man who is angry on the right occasions and with the right people at the right moment and for the right length of time who wins our commendation. (1969: 127–8)

For Aristotle, there is a "rightness", an appropriateness, even a virtue in how we manage and communicate our anger. Is this a tall order? Of course! Aristotle never denies the humanity of our anger. What he is saying is that there are some fundamentals about the "rightness" of anger and how we express it.

The psychiatrist Scott-Peck makes the point that to "function successfully" in this complex world of ours we need to "possess the capacity not only to express our anger but also not to express it" (1978: 67).

Frustration-tolerance is a necessary life "skill": traffic jams; queues; the phone on-hold time (press 1 for …, press 2 for …, press 10 for …); hospital emergency wards. OFSTED… *Learning* how to moderate, manage and communicate our concerns, frustrations and anger is a skill. Some people may be more phlegmatic and sanguine rather than choleric ("Get out of the way you b——!! Drive properly!!"). The rest of us probably have had to *learn* how better to manage our frustration and anger.

We are well aware, for example, of those occasions where a verbal outburst would (in hindsight) send the "right" message at the wrong time and, perhaps, severely damage a relationship with a friend, colleague or student. While there are times when an immediate brief, passionate expression of anger is right and just, at other times it is better, wiser, says Scott-Peck, "to express it only after much deliberation and self-evaluation" (1978: 67); as when we write an 'angry letter'.

Anger as drive

Anger seems to *simply* drive us; we're *doing something in its release*: the shouting, the yelling and screaming, the brandishing of a waving finger or fist, the physical encroachment, the throwing of something, the kicking of furniture or walls ...

These behaviours are familiar to children and adults alike. The mobilising drive of anger, though, can never tell us what to do when (and while) the emotion is so intense. It is in the immediacy of the emotional arousal that anger behaviour can be so damaging, so destructive – the arousal seems to just take over. It can however be directed to assert and more constructively address the issue at hand. Then there is the self-justification of our anger, as age, language, even habit reinforce anger behaviours: "He *made* me ... (!)", "It's not *my* fault ...", "I *can't help* it (!)", "He *shouldn't* have said (done ...)!", "He *made* me ...". How did he *make* us angry? This is only partly true; we – too – have a responsibility concerning how we respond:

"I *can't help* it", "I can't help my feelings ..." We often can't help our feelings (particularly when we are frustrated or angry). What we can do is to learn to understand our feelings as they relate to those occasions, contexts, and people who lower our tolerance to frustration (and there will be students and – at times – colleagues and parents who do just that!).

Self-awareness, regarding *feelings* of anger, can enable us to better decide what to do and say in anger arousing situations (Rogers 2012). If such self-reinforcing, self-justifying talk (as that above) is characteristic, it can lead to poor, disturbing – even destructive – patterns of ongoing anger behaviour.

" ... anger carried my mind away." Virgil, *The Aeneid*, Book II

The emotion of anger, when intense, can overtake any guiding rationality and focused direction of will. It is more likely to do this if one's *characteristic beliefs are highly demanding* ... "These children *should* respect me ... they *should not* answer back and be disrespectful ...(!)", "My problems with this class *are the fault of* ...", "I *can't help* my feelings about ... I *can't* control them ...", "I'll *never* be able to ...", "It *shouldn't* be this way ...!", "I *must be in control* of this class at all times ...".

If a teacher frequently – and characteristically – speaks about challenging students and classes this way, it will have a direct – self-justifying – effect during anger episodes. The *demanding nature* of the mind-set ("*must* ...!", "*mustn't* ...!", "*should*/shouldn't!", "*can't* ...", "*never* ...") is itself stressful, making unrealistic demands on the social reality we have to face in day-to-day teaching.

Simply *demanding* respect from our students – for example – is self-defeating; the resulting anger we feel at not being given respect is not simply due to the student's behaviour. The *demanding mind-set* of a teacher will significantly affect the degree of emotion at that point. Later – on "reflection" or rumination – the teacher's belief ("*should*/shouldn't") becomes self-reinforcing in a negatively stressful way. If our demanding belief is not "satisfied" in "social reality" it is (there-fore) not our fault – such a self-justification is affected by an insistent and unrealistic belief perpetuating self-defeating expressions of anger ("It's not *my* fault", "It's *all their fault* ...!") when directly under pressure and stress. Further, it hampers more effective ways of addressing the distracting and disruptive behaviours we have to deal with.

A *preferential* belief is grounded in social reality; it doesn't simply *demand* "Must/mustn't!", "should/shouldn't". "I *don't like* it when students are disrespect-ful, *however*, ..." is different in kind, not just degree (as a belief statement). The "however ..." part is what we can do, and say, instead of the reactive "fight/flight" expression of anger.

When we learn to (characteristically) cognitively reframe – when under emo-tional pressure – this can be a positive form of self-reinforcing. "Yes this *is* a difficult class ... *however* ..." The acknowledgement of social reality – *what* is – is balanced by the "however ..." that follows; the way we have learned to address or assert as the need arises.

This requires, of course, an awareness of our characteristic self-talk; learning to tune-in and dispute erroneous and self-defeating demands and reaffecting realis-tic and supportive self-talk (p. 24f). This is not a denial of stressful reality; it is the awareness that what we *characteristically say to ourselves* when under pressure and – later – when we ruminate and reflect has a *direct and significant effect on our emotions as well as our behaviour when under pressure.*

And when we fail – as we will – we will not lock into self-blame, or other blame, "I'll *never* get it right ...", "It will *always* be like this ...", "It's *all my fault* ...", "It's *all their fault* ...". We will learn to avoid easy cognitive slippage into "global" ("*all* ...", *"always ...", "can't ...", "never ..."*) descriptions of stressful reality or *unrealistic demands* (*"should/shouldn't"*, *"must/mustn't"*) and to redirect our thinking under pressure. This is a healthy cognitive habit that can enable us to utilise our frustration and anger more constructively.

> **NB   "I lost my temper!"**
>
> A frequently used phrase expressed by adults and young persons alike is, "I just lost my temper; that's all!!" We say this – later – to explain the high arousal that occurred at the time we were angry and to explain why we expressed our anger by shouting, yelling or being nasty or vindictive ...
>
>   It's an interesting choice of words. We don't actually "lose" our temper; we "find" it. The issue, really, is how "consciously" do we "find" our temper and *what we do when* we've – very quickly – found it.
>
>   Mind you, it doesn't help to say this to someone when they are angry; it is on isight but reserved later when were in a calmer state of mind!

- Anger is normal; at times it's more than normal, it is *right*. There are occasions when justice demands that we clearly, unequivocally, communicate our anger to others. When we hear someone say "I have a right to be angry ..." they are appealing to what they strongly believe is the justice at stake for them. In this sense, anger drives the thought–emotion–behaviour sequence .... In the heat of the moment, though, the "thinking" aspect of anger arousal is the least dominant. We are in a profession where we simply cannot allow the emotion of anger to "dictate" reactive, uncontrolled, responses to the challenges inherent in our day-to-day leadership. Like any aspect of our leadership, those situations that are particularly stressful, challenging and demanding are likely to occasion frustration and anger. It behoves us to learn to both address – even assertively confront – such situations in ways that legitimise our feelings still while addressing injustice.

Anger awareness

On many occasions our anger is more typically the outcome of life's frustrations, irritations and what Lazarus (1981) calls "daily hassles"; or what Shakespeare (in *Hamlet*) called "the thousand natural shocks that flesh is heir to". Shakespeare wrote "natural" shocks – and who wouldn't get frustrated (even angry) at intransigent, lazy, rude or arrogant student behaviour? Why wouldn't we get angry with an insensitive, unfeeling, "ill-considered" report from an OFSTED inspector?

It is important to be aware of the situations, circumstances and people that lower our tolerance to frustration. The issue of "secondary behaviours" (noted in Chapter 1) is typical of an annoying, even stressful, irritant for most teachers: when students speak in sulky, pouty, insouciant tones of voice; when their body language indicates they don't care (the shrugged shoulders, the eyes to the ceiling, the drawn out sighs). Awareness helps; so does skill. We can develop more effective ways to manage and communicate our anger and to help others when they are angry.

I've talked with young men who say they "can't help getting [aggressively] angry when …". What they mean is that they can't help *characteristically* shouting, yelling, threatening … being immature, or mean-spirited or aggressive *when* they're angry – as if men are somehow "hard-wired" in their social biology to only get angry in loud or aggressively physical ways. Angry *behaviour* is learned. Within our social, and emotional, biology our evolution (particularly in language) has enabled us to utilise language beyond the merely – or only – fight/flight mechanism. Unhelpful, self-defeating even destructive angry *thinking* and angry *behaviour* is learned; it can be unlearned, and other (more helpful and appropriate and constructive) anger behaviours can be learned.

•   It is important to distinguish between anger as an emotion and the behaviour that comes from anger – particularly *impulse behaviour*. Anger is not of itself bad – how can it be? Anger is an emotion inherent in our evolutionary biology. We ought not to convey to children that they are somehow "bad" for having angry feelings or emotions, or "getting angry". As Conrad Baars points out, "it is necessary to realise that the high intensity of an emotion does not make it 'bad', even though its consequences may not be beneficial for that person or others around him" (1979: 68). As Aristotle has said, "We can't help *getting* angry …" (emphasis mine). Instrumentally, and *potentially*, the emotion of anger can serve a constructive purpose in the fight/flight dynamic. While evolution may have equipped the fight/flight/anger arousal, such is not – normally – constructive in the social context of behaviour leadership.

Learning to understand and guide our emotions with thought and skill will, in good part, help determine any constructive behaviour that proceeds from our anger. If we find this a challenge, how difficult must this be for children? (See Rogers and McPherson 2014.)

- It can be helpful to distinguish between annoyance, irritation, being "cheesed off" and frustration; and between frustration, high frustration and anger; and between anger and aggression. Anger is at the very high end of emotional arousal. Imagine, for example, saying to a student "I'm angry that you haven't finished your homework!" or "I'm angry because you're late!" Such behaviours (in students) might merit *annoyance*, or even annoyed concern from teachers, but do they merit *anger?* If we easily, quickly and characteristically get angry over such minor issues, then when we *really* need to communicate anger we lose the emotional weight (or even the moral weight) of that which we might need appropriately to get angry about. Overuse of the word *angry*, or *anger*, will tend to devalue its social, relational meaning and behavioural currency.
- Allied to the previous point is the notion of "getting angry" on issues that matter, or issues that count. In this way students can see, and hear, the relative justice in our expressed passion and behaviour.

For example, if a supply teacher is badly treated by your class, and on your return from the flu you hear a litany of serious complaints from the head-teacher about "your class" or "your students"; this is an occasion where a clear, unambiguous communication of our anger is appropriate as we address the class on our return.

"I am *extremely* disappointed and angry about what I've heard from the principal today about members of our class and the way some students here behaved towards the relief teacher [name the teacher]. I cannot believe *anyone* in our class, or school, would say and do the sort of things some of you did when you …. In fact I was disgusted by some of the things reported to me about the behaviour of some members of our class!"

In communicating our anger we need to be specific and clear about, *what* we are angry *about*.

"I know it wasn't all of you. (This is an important qualifier … it is rarely *all* … The cooperative students will latch on to this and take heart …). Those who said those things will be meeting with me, and the principal, soon (one at a time). I'm also appalled that many of you let others – *in our class* – behave in the way they did. I think of you as responsible, capable, people."

Whenever I've had to speak like this to a class (thankfully rarely) it is said with passion – with a firm and *unambiguously* serious voice; the students sit quietly with a look of perceptible chagrin. They can hear, and see, our anger – and the "justice" driving it. In a case like this it is important that the teacher makes clear that it is the *behaviour* that is totally unacceptable and that we, as their teacher, will be "having a classroom meeting later to see if we can repair and rebuild the damage created by your behaviour yesterday".

When speaking to a *group* of students like this it is important that we:

- are specific and as brief as possible.
- make clear that you are not angry with *all* the members of "our class".
- do not attack them: "You pack of animals, you're no better than animals!!" Tempting as such an attack might be (and I've heard worse), that is hardly going to win their understanding and cooperation or address their *behaviour.* They need to *hear*, feel, our anger without simply vilifying them.
- work for some group restitution *and* an understanding that next time a supply teacher comes I expect that "We (all of us) will …". Then develop with the class a normative "convention" about working with supply teachers.
- follow-up with the suspected/known ringleaders.
- direct the class (as well as key individuals) to – at least – write an apology to the teacher concerned.
- support supply teachers who have to cover known hard-to-manage classes. This can be done with some senior teacher staying (for a while), dropping back in (later), even coming in at the last 5–10 minutes. It is the willingness of the senior teacher to be available (particularly if there is significant and ongoing disruption in the classroom) that gives confidence to supply teachers (or cover teachers) in particularly challenging classes (see Rogers 2003b).

Communicating our anger: some fundamental understandings

It is difficult, very difficult, in the heat of the moment to decide what we might do or say when we're angry. Some prior reflection and general anger management awareness can help.

- We briefly calm ourself before we seek to communicate to the other person *what* it is we are angry about and why. This sounds deceptively easy; it isn't. Take a few calming breaths, but not too deep because the other party may think you're hyperventilating! Count a few seconds in your head, then communicate what is necessary. It may be helpful – then – to take cool-off-time (withdraw) and, later, work with that person on the issue that triggered the anger. It is unproductive to try to resolve the anger-arousing issues or concepts *at the point one is feeling intensely angry.* It is enough to briefly communicate how we feel about …

Mere cathartic expression of anger can increase habituation of angry or aggressive behaviour (Rogers 2012).

- Focus *briefly* on the issue, circumstance, behaviour we are angry about: "I am angry *because* you …"; "I get angry *when* …". If we are only annoyed, or irritated, use that word rather than "angry".
- Address the issue, rather than attacking the other person. This is particularly important when dealing with angry children or their parents. ("Who the hell do you think you are!! Don't you ever speak to me like that …!!").[2] If we need to use assertive language, our assertion needs to focus on the behaviour, or issue, we are angry about. We do this briefly and unambiguously: "I don't *ever* make comments about your body or clothes. I don't expect you *ever* to make comments about mine. It stops *now*!" This to a student who has made a gutless, sexist or sexual, racist, homophobic comment. The first time any student uses sexist or racist language we do not ignore it; we will address it swiftly, briefly, unambiguously and assertively. When we are assertive we need to look the other person in the eye (but not stand too close) and avoid the wagging, pointing, finger. Extend an open, and "blocking", hand and use a clear, firm, confidently strong voice: "I don't swear at you. *That language is totally unacceptable here.* If you're uptight with me find another way of saying it." This to a student who has sworn at a teacher (unprovoked).

  Assertive language is to be distinguished from hostile or aggressive language, as when a person says, "Who the hell do you think you are, you x!!z!!" "You made me so angry with your stupid whining …!!". In contrast, by communicating with an "I" statement we let the other person know how we feel (or are affected by) their behaviour. Our non-verbal behaviour needs to be decisive without being hostile or aggressive. We also do not ask a student why they are using such language … we do not want reasons, or discussion; nor do we want to create too much "theatre" – remember there is always an audience of peers. We model control (of ourselves) *while* communicating our fundamental right and at the same time addressing the other person's unacceptable behaviour.
- De-escalate the voice and the residual tension quickly. We may need to raise our voice (not shout) to initiate attention and assert a point. It is important then to drop the voice to a firm, controlled, more measured tone. Children are rarely adept at de-escalating emotional arousal when a situation is very tense. We, as adults, have to take the lead.

- Having communicated our anger, some cool-off time enables both parties to calm down; perhaps even think and reflect. They may – then – be more amenable to work for resolution.
- It is incumbent – professionally and morally – for the teacher (as adult) to initiate some repairing and rebuilding after the anger-arousing incident. Few children will come to their teachers and say, "Look, I'm sorry, sir. I've been tossing that incident around in my mind – you know when I lashed out at you and said … well … I'd like to repair and rebuild with you … to re-effect that working relationship".
- As the adult – even if our anger was justified in the emotional moment – we will still need to "reach out with the olive branch" later to model the repairing and rebuilding behaviour that we hope they will exercise (perhaps one day).

We need to "repair and rebuild" because it is the right thing to do. Unresolved, residual, feelings of animosity unnecessarily impair the teacher–student relationship (or collegial relationships(!)). When we repair and rebuild we give the student the opportunity to share their feelings about the issue that led to the anger episode. Someone has to make the first move.

After cool-off time we can sit down with the student and:

- explain, briefly, what it was we were angry about at the time, and why.
- invite the student's right of reply.
- tune into their perception and feelings but refer back to the fundamental right affected by the student's behaviour.
- avoid forcing the student to share their feelings. If they choose not to share how they felt, or how they are feeling now. It can help to briefly suggest, "Perhaps you're feeling really annoyed about what happened the other day because or/when …". At times it is enough that we simply communicate that no grudges are held and "we move on from here".
- discuss how "we" might handle a similar incident "next time".
- separate amicably; well, as amicably as possible. (See also p. 132.)

For a male teacher speaking with a female student one-to-one it will be important to have a female colleague present for ethical probity.

Frustrated and angry parents

If you have ever had an angry parent storm into your office (even your classroom!), or try to "buttonhole" you in the playground you will know how stressful such an encounter can be. There are parents who are hostile, who simply *demand*, who refuse to accept the sometimes appalling behaviour of their children – it's *always* and *only* the school's fault(!). Each year I read similar articles from many countries. Fortunately the number of very hostile and aggressive parents is – generally – small, although the perception is that this issue is an increasing one (Rogers 2009). Nonetheless we have to deal with such parents professionally and supportively.

Thankfully most parents are reasonable when they present to the school with concerns and problems relating to their children. They moderate, or curb, or focus their feelings of frustration at what they perceive as being unfair, inappropriate or unacceptable treatment of their child. They do not merely go, immediately, "on the attack".

When working with frustrated and angry parents it is crucial to acknowledge and affirm how they feel and what they (initially) perceive as "the problem". Their perception may not be the same as ours and may (in fact) be incorrect, but it is *how they feel and perceive* "things to be" at this point.

- Allow the parent some time to explain how they feel; avoid the temptation to immediately butt in and defend the school. Allowing the parent to have their say may mean letting them – initially – "run out of steam" as it well.
- Invite the parent to sit down (it's harder to be overly physiologically angry when sitting down).
- Listen first, then reflect back: "I can see you're really upset or angry about …", "So you seem to be saying that …", or "As you see it …". So, for example, if a parent believes their child is being harassed or bullied, one should be able to acknowledge and understand parental anger as well as refocusing energy towards clarifying the actual details and *then* working towards appropriate mediation and consequences.
- Assure them (briefly) that you know they (and the school) care. "I know you care about Justin – you wouldn't be here now if you didn't care. We care too – and we are here to support your son …"
- Be sure to have the facts (about the student/issue) as the school sees them, and invite the parent to view the problems within the school's policy and due processes. It is within the rights and responsibilities (and rules) that we need to discuss and address their issue of concern.
- Honesty is crucial: about how things are, what has happened and the need to – then – work on the most workable, sensible and fair options open to all "parties". At times reasonable compromise may be necessary without the school making promises or commitments they can't keep, and without

compromising the school's behaviour policy on rights, responsibilities, rules and consequences.

• Early support given to parents can often eliminate messy, and often inaccurate, disclosures in the public domain (parental gossip, the media).

I've taught with a number of colleagues over the years who have been reduced to tears by bombastic, arrogant and angry parents who bring no self-control to the wild, ill-formed accusations, and even threats, delivered in a barrage of invective and of four-letter words.

A colleague of mine, a principal (in Australia) had suspended a girl (Year 8) for punching another girl in the face. The victim had bad bruising around the jaw and face and a broken tooth. The principal had given the other girl a non-negotiable suspension for three days, pending an accountability conference involving some mediation and restitution with the victim of this bashing.

The morning after the girl was suspended her mother stormed into his office (bypassing the school secretary).

"What did you suspend my daughter for? Eh?! Anybody calls my daughter a slut I tell her to f—ing punch her f—ing lights out …!!" The mother was hopping around, finger wagging and waving in the air. Spraying saliva flashing around the office in the early morning sun.

By this time a few senior colleagues are hovering near the door ready to give moral support. "And you can all p— off!!" yelled the mother …

I asked my colleague what he did to manage this fracas. "I know what I'd like to have said," he smiled wearily, I'd liked to have said… "'No wonder your daughter is off her tree with a mother like you!! Who the hell do you think you are, storming in here yelling, screaming and abusing me you stupid ———!! Now get out of this school! Go home. Take a valium sandwich and come back if and when you calm down. And don't you ever storm in here without making an appointment! Do you understand!?' But I can't say all that can I? Tempting as it may be. If I do that I'm on the television news that night. The mother is standing there, now calm, looking seriously hard done by this cruel and heartless school. She faces the camera, dressed for the part, and says, 'You go to the school because you're concerned about your daughter. She was bullied you know — I can't repeat what she was called — and what did I get — no help at all but abuse, and from a school principal!'"

"So what did you do then?" I asked, although I'd already guessed. He said, "I let her 'run out of steam' as it were. She jumped around, yelled at me, 'effing and blinding'. Eventually she calmed down. I was offering no 'resistance'. Nor did I try, at this stage, to defend what I'd done. She stood there, somewhat 'out of breath'. I asked her if she'd like to take a seat. She sat, arms folded. I said, "I can see you're really upset about Chantelle — about what's happened. I know you care about Chantelle, so do we. If we talk this through, without attacking each other, we can support your daughter. After all, that's why you're here. I won't yell and swear at you, Ms —. I expect you not to swear at me. Thanks. Now …"

He then talked about the incident, getting the facts clear and straight. "No, I'm not calling your daughter a liar, Ms —," in response to her accusation that the witness reports were from liars in contrast to her daughter's "ever so honest" account.

Eventually he got some understanding and assurance that the due process of mediation would help (in three days' time – after cool-off time for all). He didn't "defend" the school's policy on violence; just explained and reaffirmed it as non-negotiable and supportive to *all* parties.

It is hard to stay calm and professional in such situations. Indeed, sometimes the parent will fly off the handle again as the discussion of the problem challenges their view of rough justice. In these cases *continual* yelling and swearing by the angry and hostile parent is best dealt with by a firm verbal assertion: "This meeting is over. It's not working Ms —." He holds up a blocking hand. "It's not working. I've asked you to discuss this calmly. You're swearing and yelling at me and threatening – I'm not prepared to continue. Leave now; when you've had a chance to calm down please make an appointment and I'll be happy to talk with you – anytime." The principal then walks towards to door (conveying take-up time) showing the parent to the door. If they refuse to leave (it happens!), it is better to leave yourself. They may harangue you all the way down the corridor, "You bastard!! You've never cared about our Chantelle. You're all a bunch of gutless …!!"

Meanwhile one of our colleagues will direct the parent to leave or warn them that the police will have to be called. These sorts of scenarios are rare (thank goodness) but they do happen, and in most cases teachers are incredibly professional in the way they handle such incidents.

In such situations:

- Calm yourself before consciously helping the other person to calm down. This will include consciously unclenching fists, and presenting open body language (easier said than done).
- It may help to let them "run out of steam" (as it were) to aid their own calming.
- Invite them to sit down.
- Tune into how they may be feeling at this point.
- Make sure you have the facts (in writing) beforehand – hopefully from accurate, reliable, records. This is what we, now, focus on …
- Give an appropriate right of reply; listen, reflect back briefly.
- Emphasise that we're there to work on the problem – not attack each other.
- Work on a solution (if possible) or refer the issue to the due process that needs to be followed. The focus should move to a solution that is mutually workable

wherever possible. Always keep the focus on the *core rights and responsibilities of the school policy* as it relates to the parent's complaint and to the issue as we know it at school.

- Separate as amicably as possible with an assurance that the parent can ring and make another appointment if necessary.

It is crucial that the colleague who has been on the receiving end of such parent behaviour has some debriefing later that day with their peers. I've seen teachers unnecessarily blame themselves for the anger episode created by "bolshie" parents. A debriefing can allow the teacher's pent-up frustration, or anxiety, to be shared and provides the opportunity to validate their feelings and move on – hopefully learning something.

Many schools now have an internal procedural policy for managing complaining and angry parents. Such a policy needs practical in-servicing, reflection and review.

When the other person is angry

There are times when we have to manage a very frustrated or angry student. In a Year 8 class I taught, some years ago, a student had taken massive umbrage that I'd "taken over the class from another teacher". Within a few minutes of me being in the classroom Lisa stood up (in the front row) and in a raised voice, leaning forward, nearly shouting, she said, "What did you have to come into our class for?! We don't need you!! This class was alright till you came!!" That was probably true! I'd come into this class as a mentor-teacher to help refocus their noisy, unfocused pattern of behaviour and now Lisa's power position was under *perceived* threat.

In such cases yelling back would be pointless (if tempting). I chose (in the emotional moment) to let her "run out of steam". In a sense this "took the wind out of her sails". A thankfully unexpected thing happened. The student next to her pulled down on Lisa's jumper and said, "At least he's listening to you!!"

While I was letting Lisa "run out of steam" (as it were) I was scanning the eyes of the other students to non-verbally communicate to them that "you are part of 'this' too – as an audience you have a part to play". I also sought to convey (non-verbally) a sense of "calmness" and assurance to the rest of the class that in letting Lisa "run out of steam" that I was still "in control" (as much as anyone can be) of the *situation*. I can't control the angry student; I can control my responses to her and her peer audience. Fortunately the rest of the class was "with me". Lisa sat down, folded her arms, slumped back in her seat with a frown, a pursed mouth, muttering f—s (!) The class was basically quiet now; some nervous laughter. I thanked the student next to her, "Thanks, Carmel". Turning to Lisa I said, "I *was* listening to you, Lisa; however I'm not yelling at you. I don't expect you to yell at me". I wasn't nasty; just clear, brief and assertive.

When the other person is angry, and we have a management responsibility to lead (and even "control"), we need to assist the other person to reclaim some sense of self-control. At times this may involve a dignified time-out (calm-down) option. On this occasion the student settled (if sulkily) back into her seat.

"OK, everyone" (this to the class), "Let's get back to what we need to be doing ..." We carried on with the class discussion and the lesson. I organised a meeting, later that day, to speak with Lisa (and a senior female colleague) about what had happened in class. Over several sessions (following that first class) my colleague and I worked with the class to help them refocus how the class was (and wasn't) working and what we needed to do to change things. I also found out (later) that Lisa had an alcoholic father who had come to school on several occasions and embarrassed her publicly, and that she had had run-ins with other male teachers. Having explained (to her) why I was the "new teacher", and also that I thought I understood a little of how she might be feeling about having a new teacher in the class we then discussed other ways of making one's feelings and concerns known in constructive ways. We made some progress.

In time Lisa and I got on reasonably well. She learned to moderate her more "bolshie" communication style and when I finished my time with her class we parted amicably, with some residual goodwill.

Anger and aggression

There are some situations when an assertive command is necessary, as when two students are engaged in serious fighting. The sharp, brief, command "Oi! (…) or use of student's name (whenever known) Stop that! Move away *now*!" needs to make unambiguously clear that such behaviour must stop. The sharp tone is then reduced to a firm, controlled, assertive and calmer voice: "Move away (…) *now*." We'll often need to repeat the command: "Move away (…) *now*." The dropping of the voice communicates a sense of calmness and control and *expected* compliance. If the voice is *kept* sharp and high it can create too much arousal. If the fighting students don't move apart we will need to decide whether to physically intervene (a risky course of action). Whatever we do in a fight situation we should *always* send for a senior colleague (for practical support and as witness) and direct the peer audience away (often the audience are just waiting for "adult permission" to leave the fight scene in a face-saving sense).

Most schools have a policy for managing crisis situations such as "fights" (see Rogers 2006a, *Behaviour Management: A Whole-School Approach*).

In the rare circumstance where a student physically threatens a teacher (with a weapon, a chair or a fist) an assertive *command* may not be appropriate. Nor will it be appropriate to let them run out of steam! It is essential in such situations to use decisively *calm assertion*. It is also crucial to send for senior colleague support immediately.

A colleague of mine had a student walk into her high school class with a large knife. He was clearly, visibly, angry; breathing heavily, rapidly. His eyes darted around the room. He was looking for someone. My colleague knew this lad quite well; that helped. She looked him in the eyes and in a calm voice, amazingly controlled, said, "Ahmed (...), Ahmed (...), I can see you're really upset ... I know you don't want to hurt me or anyone else here. I can see you're very angry." She tuned into his feelings quickly, *calmly*, making a reference to herself in the situation. "I know you don't want to hurt me or anyone else here ...". She said she never took her eyes off him; as if by *calm, sustained eye contact* and the calm (reassuring) voice she could communicate calmness to him. "Put the knife over there, Ahmed. Come on. We'll go outside now and we can talk. Come on." She walked slowly, with her arm beckoning gently *but not touching him* ... He put the knife down and followed her out. Thank God.

The class was sitting in stunned silence; many students visibly shocked and anxious, some even fearful ... By this time the principal had heard what was going on and rushed down to help. He saw the teacher walking with Ahmed towards the office area. Wisely, he too responded calmly, walking with the student and teacher towards the office. Halfway down the corridor my colleague collapsed – she had fainted. She had, she said later, used "all her emotional energy up" and just collapsed. The class and teacher had some debriefing, and counselling – later. Ahmed, too, received counselling (after a formal suspension of two weeks). Apparently the knife was to scare another boy whom he had accused of stealing his girlfriend. The police were also involved at a later stage.

While there is never a guarantee that the *way* my colleague acted will see a safe outcome the behaviour she evidenced in a crisis (like this) is likely to increase rather than exacerbate the anger arousal of the other person.

You may never have had, or will ever have, such an experience (I hope you don't). If you teach in EBD schools, or Pupil Referral Units or schools within prisons hopefully you will receive training for appropriate, professional, responses in crisis-management situations (including "restraint procedures"). In mainstream schools such scenarios are – fortunately – rare. Spare a thought for teachers who regularly have to manage tense, hostile, aggressive students (and parents) like that of my colleague noted here (though without weapons).

At the end of the day I share nothing here – about anger and anger management – that I do not struggle with as a teacher. These comments and understandings about anger are an attempt to engage some reflection and, hopefully, more thoughtful behaviour in our professional role as teachers.

Reflection

- When did you last get angry – really angry? Reflect – just for a moment – how difficult it can be for a child to manage their anger when we – as adults – struggle with this emotion at times. We distinguish between anger (the emotion) and what we do when we're angry (the behaviour).
- How aware are you of your *characteristic* anger behaviour? What do you do and say when you are very frustrated or angry?
- It is not easy to express our feelings at times and our feelings are natural; we cannot often help feeling a given way, and it never helps to deny or merely suppress them. How do the suggestions on "communicating our anger" enable your experience and reflection?
- Do you have an internal school policy on dealing with hostile and angry parents? How do the suggestions noted in this chapter inform that policy/practice? (It is always harder to think of "what to say/do" in the heat of the emotional moment!)
- What restorative practices inform, and enable, post-anger repairing and rebuilding in your school?

Notes

1 Virtue (in this sense) means the characteristic direction of one's moral will. Aristotle also speaks of virtues as habits of mind (in the *Nichomachean Ethics*). *Cardinal* virtues are those recognised in the earliest writing by philosophers (such as Plato and Aristotle):

Prudence: circumspection, care, appropriate to the situation … how we make judgements between, at times, competing demands.

Justice: *how* we seek to work for what is right and fair …

Temperance: (moderation) effectively this "old-fashioned" word addresses self-control, "to temper …" It is crucial in anger management.

Courage: our fortitude under the "slings and arrows …". How we bear up in the day-to-day as well as in the extremes that come our way.

Virtues are our habits of mind and will, as Aristotle writes in his *Ethics*.

2   In the second edition of *How to Manage Children's Challenging Behaviour* (Rogers 2009), my colleagues and I have devoted a chapter to exploring how we work with (and try to support) hostile and angry parents.

Visit https://study.sagepub.com/rogers4e for additional resources to help you better manage classroom behaviour. You'll be able to hear from Bill himself as he talks you through common behaviour management scenarios.

When things get difficult: hard class, hard times

"What you cannot enforce – do not command."

Sophocles, (496–406 BC)

Struggling teachers – the hard class

> A few years back I was struggling with a really hard class. I'd tried being kind, I'd tried the "power-struggle" [*sic*] approach … I'd kept kids back – even the whole class … yet I was also too proud and naive to attempt to discuss my problems with any of my colleagues who seemed to be handling things so well. (Secondary teacher, cited in Rogers 2002a)

From time to time a difficult class, like this (noted above), comes our way; a class that seems to sap and drain our energy, erode our goodwill and makes *that* time-table slot, or *each* day, a struggle. In the case of the colleague speaking above it was a seemingly recalcitrant Year 7.

All that we would normally do, and more, to manage such a class, still saw my colleague struggling, halfway through Term One: residual noise levels coming from loudly "chatting" students; students frequently off-task; calling out; talking while the teacher was trying to teach; students engaged infrequent task avoidance; a few very "mouthy" students … A class like this can shake the confidence of even experienced teachers. I've worked with teachers who have felt they are a failure because they cannot manage *this* class, *this* year. Rather than seeing their failure as the annoying natural mix of challenging students and classroom dynamics, some teachers (struggling with such a class) will tend to blame themselves.

The term "struggling teacher" should not be a simple pejorative label. When teachers experience a hard class, or several difficult-to-manage students, they sometimes feel that admitting that they are struggling or having a problem indicates that they are not able to cope (which is actually true but not a bad thing in itself). When teachers feel less effective (in their role) they may also feel that an admission of their struggle means they will be evaluated or judged in some way. Hopefully, this attitude is not present in your school. If a teacher perceives any opportunity for (or offer of) colleague support as having an implied judgement – or "strings attached" – it may well constrain them from asking for early, valuable and necessary support.

Colleague support is crucial when coming to terms with the management of a harder than average class. That support, in the first instance, needs to be offered and expressed in a way that does not communicate simple blame or mere fault.

Offering support

> There's this ludicrous idea that when someone is really struggling we have this hands-off mentality – just in case we do, or say, the wrong thing. It's stupid really especially when we *know* they need help. (Senior teacher, cited in Rogers 2002a)

The Elton Report (1989) has outlined this ambivalence about directly offered colleague support as it relates to behaviour management and discipline issues. On the one hand, the offer of support may seem that one implies that a colleague is not coping; so, too, the request for support by a struggling colleague may imply (or "telegraph") that they cannot cope. So a teacher who is struggling with a hard-to-manage class may struggle on alone – unassisted.

Teachers have tended to stay out of each others' classrooms and not talk about their own discipline problems. Too often teachers do not seek help because it feels like an admission of incompetence and they do not offer it because it feels like accusing a colleague of incompetence. As a result, the tradition of classroom isolation persists in many schools (Elton Report 1989: 69).

This ambivalence, however, depends on how collegially supportive the school is (as a whole) and on how the school enables colleague support (Rogers 2002a, 2011). Such support includes moral support as well as "structural" expressions (and forms) of support that can meet colleague needs. "Structural support" includes specific plans and processes – from a clear time-out plan to on-going mentoring support (see later).

"I don't have a problem with ..."

I've been in many, many meetings with colleagues to discuss issues relating to behaviour management and discipline concerns and someone will say, "but I don't have a problem with ... [a particular student or class ...]". Even if what they say is true it hardly helps a struggling teacher. What can often result from such a comment is that the colleague is engaged in negative self-rating: the struggling teacher unrealistically, unhelpfully, rates themselves against the "better" or more able colleague.

The sad thing is that the "more able" colleague who "may not [really] have a problem" may well be able to understand, support and give valuable assistance. The struggling teacher is, however, unlikely to listen when hearing that others "don't have a problem ..." with the class (and students) they struggle with.

Tim O'Brien describes a typical scene where a teacher has had a hard time with a difficult student, comes into the staff room for a caffeine fix and bravely (and professionally) shares his or her struggle: "in the hope that empathy or advice will ensue. The response (sometimes) given is the verbal equivalent of a swift kick in the groin. 'He's alright with me ...'." Tim goes on to suggest (tongue in cheek?) that we should "ban the singular and plural versions of this morale wrecking phrase from our schools" (O'Brien 1998: 90).

Some teachers may say, "I don't have a problem ..." because they are anxious that if they speak up about management or discipline concerns they will be seen (or judged) to be "ineffective" or "weak" teachers; perhaps even incompetent. The masked assurance ("I don't have a problem ...") may also indicate the teacher's belief that a request for support from senior colleagues may invoke offers of support with "strings attached" and the request will be remembered in the teacher's ongoing service review. This kind of unprofessional culture tends to breed a degrading survivalism rather than professional empowerment (Rogers 2002a, 2012).

Colleague support: stress and coping provision

The kind, and degree, of colleague support in a school can affect stress levels and coping resources in a number of ways:

- In their research on job-related stress, Russell et al. (1987) note that social support can significantly affect stress – even burnout – in positive, "buffering", ways. (see also Rogers 2012)

Job-related stress, and feelings of stress and de-personalisation, decreased as the level of *supportive* supervision increased. Individuals who have supportive collegial relationships are able to rely on others to aid and support them in dealing with stressful situations.

Schools that consciously seek to address colleague support are aware that stress *and* burnout have a relational, social causation as well as individual psychological causation. *How* we relate to, and consciously seek to support, one another enables the *social* dimension of support. It enables that sense of social and professional belonging. It is unfair to merely ascribe a person's stress simply as having individual psychological causation, that they (alone) need to (merely) address their concerns as an individual. Stress, in the workplace, has a social dimension that can significantly affect one's *personal* perception, experience of and response to stress in that workplace (Rogers 2002a; see also Hobfoll 1998).

- Positive support from supervisors is consistently cited as predictive of measures of physical and mental health (see Rogers, 2002a, 2012). Teachers who indicate that when others (particularly senior staff) in their school acknowledge and affirm *their* skills and abilities there is a greater sense of personal and team accomplishment and that feelings of depersonalisation were lessened (Rogers 2012; see also Bernard 1990).

- Supportive collegiality (within a school) consciously seeks to address the normative stress of day-to-day teaching by enhancing the "ecology of support" and strengthening the sense of supportive interdependency within the school. That "ecology" needs to provide formal opportunities (as well as informal ones) for airing concerns and problems (without censure) and enable realistic opportunities to work through those concerns. We also need "structures" to support colleagues in their naturally stressful role, particularly in challenging classroom contexts. A clear example of this is the school's time-out policy. No teacher should have to feel they cannot ask for that kind of support for fear they will be seen as "weak", unable to manage significally disruptive behaviours. The degree to which a school *consciously* acknowledges colleague support is an integrating factor in a school's culture (as well as its normative work), and the degree to which a school leadership seeks to address the needs of its staff, will significantly affect the *dependability* and *reliability* of any ongoing support.

- The "buffering" and "coping" aspects of colleague support are enhanced when such support is given in a non-blaming, non-judgemental way; where the "ecology of support" in a given school consciously seeks to meet colleagues' basic human needs as well as their professional needs (Rogers 2012).

In collegially supportive schools "reliable alliances" are nurtured through informal, and formal, sharing and teaming. These alliances can be informal, transitional and dyadic as well as expressed in more formal and systemic expressions such as teaming, mentoring and policy imperatives.

Colleague support can:

- lessen the feelings of isolation ("I'm not alone here …"; "It's not all my fault …"; "I'm not totally responsible for all that happens …")
- provide fundamental moral support – even in the many brief collegial transactions within a school day (sharing a coffee, offloading a concern, seeking reassurance about a lesson activity, or coping with the follow-up of a difficult student …)
- empower staff through the sort of teamwork that promotes committed and caring relationships among staff. Such teamwork can also increase an individual's confidence and risk-taking as they grow professionally
- provide assurance that one is on the right track, at least "the best track at the moment …" (in terms of one's teaching resources, strategies, approaches)
- provide a forum, a *collegial* forum, for problem sharing, problem analysis, problem solving and coping resources. This, in turn, reduces negative feelings of inadequacy (as one accesses wider resources beyond oneself)
- enable the essential stress-relieving support in the management of attentional, disturbing and challenging student behaviours (Rogers 2012).

Senior administration can also address stress in the workplace by allowing genuine needs-analysis on those structural, organisational and role factors that contribute to stress in the workplace day-to-day, even so-called "minor" irritants like fluorescent lights not working; poor photocopier facilities (or access to same); inadequate staffroom facilities, particularly toilet/restroom facilities; communication processes; procedures and systems (particularly unfair timetabling); broken furniture in classrooms and so on. After all, this is "our place of work" day after day after…

A stress audit, conducted each year, is a positive and practical way of legitimising genuine concerns or complaints of staff and enabling action planning to reduce the stress associated with such concerns (Rogers 2002a). When staff believe their needs are being allowed expression and are being realistically (and reasonably) addressed they feel better (acknowledged and affirmed) and tend to engage in their work less stressfully. (Rogers 2002a)

Moral, structural and professional support

Colleague support can range from normative whinging to active and constructive problem solving. Teachers need to "offload" – to whinge – to complain about individual children and classes that they find difficult. However, if that is all colleagues do it will be of little long-term help with hard-to-manage students and hard-to-manage classes. Colleague support, in such situations, needs to be professional and "structural" in its ongoing application *as well as* giving the moral support we all need to be reassured and encouraged.

"Structural support" in this sense, refers to those dependable "forms", "processes", "procedures", "action plans" and "policies" that can be depended on by colleagues when under pressure.

Professional support refers to the way we enable our colleagues to reflect on, and appraise, their professional obligations *and needs*, in light of the aims and objectives of their role in the school.

No one *expression* of colleague support stands alone, or is sufficient in or of itself. All expressions of support seek to meet colleague needs. When addressing the management of a hard class, a *collegial* action plan seeks to meet colleague needs with emotional and practical support through shared action planning.

Developing a collegial action plan for re-establishing a difficult-to-manage class

A collegial action plan provides a forum and a process for meeting the moral, practical and professional needs of a colleague struggling with a hard-to-manage class, or several hard-to-manage students within a class. It can also enable those students in class whose "silent" voice of concern is not always heard. When such a process is effected early in the cycle of concern, it can often re-engage the necessary hope, goodwill and energy of teachers and students alike.

• This process begins with a year-level team meeting as early as possible before the hard-class issue becomes a habituated problem drifting into Term Two. Early intervention is crucial. Once a profile of *group* and individual behaviour is clear it will be important to have a meeting with *all* the teachers who work with the class in question.

Issues to be addressed will include:

○ How many (and which) students are disruptive and in what ways?
○ How frequent and intense are the disruptive behaviours?

- ○ Who are the ring leaders? the highly attentional? The "power-brokers"?
- ○ Is the class "hard" to manage for all teachers who teach this group (and the 'catalytic' core)? Is this class difficult "only" for one or a few teachers who teach this particular class? Even if it is only *one* teacher struggling with a given class we still need to offer early colleague support. As noted, a typical – disconcerting – obstacle in supporting struggling teachers is the common perception that it is a sign of weakness to admit there is a significant problem with the management and leadership of a given class (or individual students). The non-judgemental collegial approach and constructive offer of support can help minimise negative and self-defeating perceptions. In time – of course – trust invested (we hope) will be trust rewarded.

No doubt there will be some whinging in such a meeting. This can be cathartic; up to a point. It can be healthy to affirm our common struggle and validate common feelings about such students, as long as colleagues avoid the easy "I don't have any problems with that particular student, or class" or, conversely, blaming all the students and categorising them as "impossible to work with". Any whinging will need to go beyond just the whinging itself to problem analysis and shared action planning.

It is also true that *some* teachers, by the way they *characteristically* treat individuals and groups, contribute to the "hard class" phenomenon. This needs to be acknowledged. For example, I've worked with teachers who use whole-class detention to punish the whole class for the disruptive behaviour of the catalytic half-dozen. This is unfair to the majority who – given the opportunity – will always respond positively to respectful, confident behaviour leadership. At this first meeting it is important to allow some focused collegial attention to this reality. Teachers need to acknowledge and address their own *characteristic* behaviour and attitudes *as well as that of their students.*

- Develop a year-level plan based on thoughtful year-level needs analysis utilising the questions noted above. Some of the issues that will need to be reassessed in such a plan are:
  - ○ a reassessment of how colleagues established the class group in their first meetings, including basics such as: establishment of routines like seating plans (or lack thereof); classroom entry, settling and calming; noise levels; routines for asking questions and obtaining teacher assistance; classroom rules for behaviour and organisation for learning and so on (see Chapter 2). The way a class is initially established has a significant effect on group behaviour norms as the term progresses. I recently worked (as mentor) in a challenging grade

four class. In my first meeting with the class they were noisy, unfocused, with several "catalytic" students whose attentional and power-seeking behaviours were making teaching and learning very difficult. One significant factor we addressed in re-establishing the class was the inappropriate seating arrangements. Table groups were – at times – attentionally distracting cliques, and the physical layout was also a problem – one could not move without bumping chair to chair, there was little "through space". We should never underestimate this aspect of organisation. We changed the seating arrangements, including who sits with whom, and that – along with the sorts of changes noted later – had a significant impact on how the class re-established a sense of what it means to be a learning community.

   ○ a discussion of short-term options for immediate colleague support in areas such as time-out options for *persistently* disruptive students or even time-out options for the teacher (see p. 277f on colleague-assisted time-out).

   ○ a clarification of procedures for tracking particularly difficult, challenging and "at risk" students, including how colleagues currently follow up with such students beyond classroom settings (p. 122f). This includes some students needing individual behavior support (see Chapter 6).

   ○ a discussion of *any* issues of harassment of teachers (p. 280f).

- Decide on possible approaches in enacting the plan. A common approach we've used – for example – is to begin with a classroom meeting with all the students of a given class group to discuss issues of common concern. We then use student, and teacher, feedback to develop a shared plan to *re-establish the class*. In this sense, the students are given a degree of ownership in the re-establishment or "fresh start" process (see below).

   In developing any collegial action plan, it is essential to elicit and engage the understanding and support of the senior leadership team.

Classroom meetings to re-establish a difficult class

Any such meeting should address: the common behaviours of students currently causing concern to teachers and most probably causing concern to the cooperative students in the class; the rights being affected by disruptive behaviour (that is, the right to *basic respect*; the right to *learn and teach* without undue distraction/disruption; the right to *feel safe* in this class group); the responsibilities being ignored by some students – at present, and what needs to happen (as a class group) to address these issues.

In a more "open" classroom meeting the teacher can direct the class focus to questions such as:

1. What is working well – activities, our work, our physical place/space ... (in our class) – at this stage in our class journey? Why do you think these aspects (as we've noted in response to this question) of our class are working well?
2. What isn't working well – and why? If an issue or concern is too personal, or likely to cause embarrassment to the "respondent"/student, it can be written down (anonymously by the student) and read by the teacher at a later stage (assure confidentiality).
3. What can we do to change things in our classroom and how? This question addresses individual, and group, behaviour to the goal that everyone's rights are enjoyed (and protected) and we take our individual and shared responsibilities seriously.

When we conduct such an open classroom meeting there is always the possibility that some mean-spirited students will use such an open forum to "have a go" at the teacher. If conducting an "open meeting", it will be helpful to have a colleague sit in to assist; one with experience in conducting such class meetings. If there is any suspicion overly negative behaviour will occur in an open meeting, these questions can (and should) be asked through a questionnaire format (as above). Students respond to the questions (noted earlier) through an individual questionnaire.

The emphasis behind such questions addresses how we (teacher and students) consciously address the positive development of a learning community: "we *all* share the same place, time, space, needs, resources here; and that is why we need to work on these concerns and issues together. We also share the same basic feelings and needs." The questionnaire gives *all* students a voice, and an appropriate right of reply.

It is crucial after such a meeting that teachers (at a later stage) give feedback to the class on their responses and work with the class on developing a shared plan for key aspects of behaviour and learning – a re-establishing and a basis for a "fresh-start" as a class. (See the DVD, *Cracking The Challenging Class*. In this DVD, my colleagues and I conduct such a meeting with the year and class. SAGE Publ.) (see Bibiliography).

In a re-establishment plan we always refocus the class back to:

○ their core rights and responsibilities (p. 41f).
○ the *rules* for classroom behaviours that affect, and protect, those core rights and responsibilities, such as the way we treat one another; the way we learn

here and how we create a safe classroom/school community (see also Appendix A). A "safe" classroom always needs to address "psychological" as well as physical safety (that is, teasing, put-downs, hassling and bullying). Some rules may need some specific focus (for example, use of shared equipment and property, movement around the room)

○ the *routines* for the smooth running of the class, particularly procedural routines (Chapter 2)

○ the *consequences* for affecting others' rights. These consequences will range from obvious rule reminders through to time-out options and even detention. Students need to know the consequences in advance. They also need to know that these consequences are fair and relate back to protection of our common rights (Chapter 5)

○ students also need to know the positive outcomes that will flow from students supporting each other, and their teacher, within such a plan. This is a crucial feature of any "fresh start" approach with a whole class. If the meeting is simply another opportunity to growl, or moan, at the class group it will further alienate the goodwill of the majority of the class who are probably quite cooperative and – when given a chance to engage a fresh start – will support positive, and respectful teacher leadership.

It is helpful to publish the essential elements of the plan on a couple of large posters with headings emphasising the central features of our "fresh start". These posters are displayed in the classroom and referred to wherever necessary. It is also important to utilise positive language wherever possible in the published outcome. The plan can also be published on A4 sheets and made available to all students (see Appendix A).

As noted earlier, any such meeting, involving students, is best developed by those colleagues in the team who are both experienced and "comfortable" in conducting classroom meetings to support the struggling teacher(s).

The development of any fresh-start approach with a class will include ongoing shared collegial feedback and can also include cross-class visits (in our rare non-contact time) to see how "our" students are behaving and learning in other subject areas/settings with other teachers. It can even involve some elective team-teaching, observational feedback and mentoring (see later, p. 288f).

Have a review meeting with the colleague team a few weeks into the *re-establishment phase of the plan* and discuss what is working well, what isn't, and work on those areas where fine-tuning or change is necessary. It may be helpful to look at: how the time-out referrals have operated; how individual case supervision (of students with challenging behaviour) is affecting the class dynamic; and how teachers' perceptions about noise levels, time on-task, general student motivation, enthusiasm and cooperation have changed (if at all). Any such review may also need to include possibilities such as changing the structure and student placement in groups and even possible teacher rotation across groups. If, for example, one or two students are, effectively, holding the class to ransom, it will often be necessary to re-enrol those students to other classes (even "enrolling" such students in classes above their year-level with set work on a regular basis). This may be necessary both for the welfare of other students as well as the teacher. While this is a somewhat difficult organisational option, it will need to be considered. Where feasible we will give such students a clear, directed and consequential choice before such "re-enrolling", making clear that if their disruptive behaviour (be specific) continues then … This needs to be conducted as a *directed* and *consequential choice* rather than a threat.

The fact that the senior administration have been a supportive part of this process will significantly affect how such an option is considered and realised.

Time-out for the teacher (colleague safety valve)

Walking past a classroom in the corridor one day I saw (and heard), through the corridor windows, some serious "catalytic conversion" going on: loud yelling, excited voices and raucous laughter. Looking through the window I saw a student standing on a table with his arm in an overhead rotating fan. He was laughing, his "mates" egging him on. The teacher looked quite stressed. Should I intervene? As a senior teacher in the school if I do intervene – how should I do it in a way that minimises embarrassment to my colleague while giving immediate support?

One *short-term* supportive strategy in such a situation is for the "passing" colleague, or even a colleague teaching nearby, to knock on the door and offer either to withdraw one or two students (the ringleaders) or (on occasion) give the teacher an opportunity for a dignified "exit". It is particularly important that any senior teacher intervention observe basic protocols of collegial dignity and respect.

- If a senior teacher walks past a classroom situation where a colleague is clearly struggling, rather than staring through the window with a look of implied judgement, or simply walking past, or (worse) walking in and shouting the class down, the support colleague knocks, enters and walks across to the teacher and quietly says – for example – "Excuse me, Mr Smith (…), I wonder if I could borrow one or two students?" This is "code" for "I'll take the two or three most difficult 'ringleaders' or 'power-brokers' off your hands for the rest of the class period". The teacher may feel like saying "One or two would be fine but eight would be better!"

The support colleague escorts the trouble-makers away to a time-out situation and talks through with them their inappropriate and unacceptable behaviour. A follow-through consequence will also need to be organised for those students later that day. The support colleague may even escort the students to another classroom for some "time-out". This option will need to have been discussed, with colleagues, as a viable school-wide option.

This approach is preferred to a teacher walking in and shouting at the class, "Who the hell do you think you are!! I can hear you all from my office!! I'm sick and tired of your stupid behaviour. Just shut it – alright?! You make me sick!!" *Of course* the students may well go "*stumm*", especially if the harangue is given by a senior teacher. As the senior teacher walks out – on the now 'quiet' class – his non-verbal demeanour says, in effect, "*That's* how you deal with them." The class teacher may well feel unsupported, even undermined. Of course if a senior teacher "shouts a class down" for five minutes, they will probably "go silent", even stay "quiet", for the next five minutes or so however they will soon re-habituate … The five-minute "shout down" has done nothing *effectively* (longer term) for the class teacher.

- *Teacher time-out.* There are situations in the classroom where 'loss of control' by the teacher is so serious that the best short-term support we can give the teacher is time-out for the teacher. This is what I did in the instance of the boy with his arm in the fan. I need to add that his arm was in plaster; he was having a lot of "fun" using it as a brake in the fan … and, of course, getting plenty of peer attention. The supporting teacher knocks on the door (loudly – it needs to be loud to be heard). "Sorry to bother you, Mr Smith", with an "excuse me" to the whole class (as the supporting teacher briefly scans the faces of the students …). "There's a message for you at the office." This is code to the class teacher for "Leave the classroom … I'll take over for now and I'll catch up with you later …". The "message" at the office is simply, "Who's got your class?" This is carried through calm by, decisively respectfully.

The supporting teacher then stays with the class (as I did in this case) to refocus the students for the rest of that class period. It took me a good 5–10 minutes to settle and refocus the class. I also let them know I would be having a meeting (later) with them – as a class – to discuss their behaviour. I pointed out what I'd seen and heard as I approached their class. I also pointed out that it wasn't all of them. I let them know – too – I would be following up with several students individually. Our colleague who has left then has a breather, regains some composure and – perhaps – takes stock of what happened. The supporting teacher's action is not merely some "white-knight" routine: it is a dignified collegial option in a crisis.

The supporting teacher then meets with their colleague – later that day – to debrief and offer longer-term support. Our first thought though (in an immediate crisis) is for the emotional welfare of our colleague, followed – of course – by the safety and welfare of the students. When we "take over" in such a situation, it is important not to convey the message to the students that the regular teacher is ineffective, or can't cope: that is, "OK!! The *real* teacher is here *now*. The one who *has it all sorted* (unlike the teacher who has just left …)!"

Fortunately situations like this are rare in most schools. Any such "colleague safety-valve" support (like this) must be followed up by longer-term needs analysis and strategic planning with the supported colleague and the class (p. 228f).

There is a big difference between a testy class or bad-day syndrome and a class where there is a loss of control and a feeling of panic that order, purpose and focus cannot be regained by the teacher. It is one of the most unpleasant, stressful, feelings in teaching.

If you have ever had such experiences then early acknowledgement that there *is* a problem is not a sign (or symptom) of weakness; it is a professional acknowledgement that you need colleague support. I've worked with teachers who have struggled for weeks on end with such classes and end up "breaking-down":

○ "I didn't want people to think I couldn't cope …"

   Well, you couldn't. That's not a sin; it's a recognition that something is wrong and you need support to reassess "where?", "why?", "how?" and so on.

   "What will others think of me? Will it be a black mark against my career …?"
○ Not in a supportive school …

I can understand why some teachers are reluctant to disclose their anxieties and struggles, but hopefully it shouldn't take a crisis issue like that noted here to begin a process of support.

In some situations the only long-term recourse will be to reassign the teacher to another class. This is not the most elegant solution but it may be the necessary one.

Where colleague support (including ongoing mentoring) has seen no real changes in a teacher's ability to successfully work with a class it will be necessary to re-establish the class with a new teacher. The educational welfare of the students needs to be considered as well as the welfare of the current classroom teacher.

When passing the leadership of the class group to another teacher it will be important that the "new" teacher does not convey, or impute, that their previous teacher was a "failure" or was incompetent. A brief acknowledgement that it's time for *us* to move on is enough.

Harassment in the workplace

A provocative newspaper headline reads "Workplace is a war zone ..." (Perore 2000). A closer reading of that research (from the Australian Institute of Criminology), conducted among police, doctors, nurses, taxi-drivers and teachers, indicates that these professions face the greatest risk of verbal attacks and even assaults; at least teachers are last on the list! The article used a broad term, "workplace violence" to include: "injury through employer negligence, physical and verbal abuse, racial abuse, bullying, sexual harassment and even malicious gossip" (Perore 2000: 8). The article goes on to say that "we should not countenance such behaviours as a permissible, systematic work-related risk'" (Perore 2000: 8). Harassment of any kind is a workplace health and safety issue. It should never be trivialised or minimised – or given the gutless "wink-wink/nudge-nudge" that it is somehow "the victim's fault"! In such a climate teachers often feel scared to speak up (scared of even losing their job because they "can't manage these kids"). Harassment, and lack of acknowledgment and support, can (and does) affect health, wellbeing and confidence. Teachers will even say they feel somehow unworthy, even "blamed"(!). (See also House of Representatives Standing Commitee, *Workplace Bullying: We Just Want It to Stop* 2013.)

When the harassment *of teachers* is raised as an issue, particularly in more "challenging" schools, there is sometimes a tacit acceptance of some expressions of hostile or verbally challenging behaviour as *only* "boys being boys", or "this is the way kids are around here", or "some classes here are just difficult". Such statements may minimise or even tacitly accept what is – in effect – psychological harassment by a small group of students. Worse, if we categorise harassing behaviour as merely "disruptive behaviour" that the teacher *cannot control*, we may then – too easily – blame the teacher for the harassing behaviour of the students.

Harassment is more than merely unacceptable – it is wrong. It is an abuse of fundamental rights: the right to feel safe and the right to be treated with basic respect. Such harassing behaviours also significantly affect the right to teach and the right to learn.

Blaming the victim is not an uncommon feature of bullying/harassing students: "yeah, well, he [the teacher] deserve it. He's a useless teacher". This global, quick labelling then ratifies and even excuses the students' behaviour when they call out such things as, "don't listen to him", " he's rubbish", and "this is boring – boooring!!" Harassing behaviour can include the non-verbal suggestions that students use to refer to a teacher's sexual preference, or body shape, or clothing or "anything" they can pick on that will ratify and – gutlessly gratify – their exercise of social power. There has recently been a spate of Facebook incidents of students vilifying, harassing, teachers in "web-space", as reported on Australian television and in the press.

I'm not talking here about "reactive student behaviour" and the occasional silly, stupid, unthinking behaviour of some students, or even the outbursts of challenging students (Chapter 6). That kind of behaviour needs to be addressed for what it is – it is not bullying. There are occasions when a teacher's behaviour sees understandable reactions from students. A teacher walks past a student's open bag on the floor, by the chair, and spies a packet of cigarettes in the bag. The teacher takes them stating, "You're *not* supposed to smoke here – I'll take *them*!!" The student's reaction is immediate, "Hey!! They're mine … don't you f—ing touch them!" The *student's* behaviour here is not harassment; it is an understandable reaction to a piece of unthinking, unnecessary, behaviour by a teacher. What did the teacher think? Did she really think the student would just acquiesce? Did she care?

Harassment – addressing the issue

This is not an easy issue to write about. I have done so because I have observed it in some schools and have been involved in supporting colleagues to address it wherever it occurs.

- Harassment is not occasional bad-day syndrome behaviour. Some students will sometimes take the risk of "having a bit of fun" with a teacher (particularly a new teacher or a supply teacher). Most teachers recognise such behaviour for what it is; point out quickly that the student has gone too far and the teacher will rein it in. Such behaviour will also necessitate the teacher conducting some follow-up (p. 122f) to make the point clearly about the limits of "fun" (as the student perceives it). Harassment involves those *intentional*, *selective* and *repeated* behaviours of an individual, or a group, designed to hurt or abuse their victim. Bullies "select" people they perceive as weaker than they are (psychologically and physically weaker) and use bullying behaviour to confirm (and continue to ratify) their social power (Rogers 2012).

- Bullies rely on collusive acceptance of, or acquiescence by, other students in their bullying/harassing behaviour. *Collusive bullies* may not directly harass a teacher but they do silently approve of, or give a non-verbal chorus to, the bullies' behaviour (the "clapping", the whistling, the muted cheer …). Unintended collusion can also occur when students who are afraid of the bully go silent and will not speak out in (or out of) class. Bullies accept such collusion as confirmation of their social power.

  Bullies also trade in secrecy – not from their peers (they need their "collusion") but from adults. They don't want to be "found out". It is important to crack this "secrecy code" early.

- As noted earlier, one of the problems inherent in any workplace harassment is that some teachers feel insecure about admitting that they are "having problems in a given class"; they believe that an admission that some students are "making their life hell" is a sign of their own weakness; that they can't cope; that they just *should* be able to cope.

  "I didn't want people to think I couldn't cope …"; I've heard this so many times – sometimes too late in the day. The point is that sometimes a teacher cannot cope with such harassing behaviour on their own; *nor should they have to.*

  A more disturbing issue arises when teachers feel that if they do "speak out" about harassment then nothing (effectively) will be done; that such student behaviour will not actually be seen as harassment.

  It is important to address any harassment as early as possible in its cycle – to crack the "secrecy code", confront the main perpetrators and the active collusive perpetrators (where necessary) and support the victim (the teacher) and perhaps other students who are witness to bullying behaviour.

  If you are ever in this situation or circumstance of knowing that the behaviour you are experiencing is more than merely a disruptive class on a bad day; that you are going home significantly disturbed, anxious or even angry about repeated disruptive or personally abusive behaviour; or you virtually hate coming to school when you have to teach a particular class, then you need to speak to a senior colleague *as early as possible* to address and confront the issue (see later).

  If you are a senior colleague who senses that something is clearly wrong with a teacher's class, and suspect that harassment is a factor, it will be important to speak supportively with your colleague about your concerns and offer immediate support.

  At such a meeting with a colleague it will be crucial to allay any anxiety about perceived judgement, or that in coming forward with their concerns they are a weak and ineffective teacher. A sharing of what you suspect about the class concerned (and the behaviour of some of its members) and an invitation to talk

It through should lead to an early reassurance of support and the development of a plan to confront the perpetrators.

Ideally, the first incidence or suggestions of harassment by any students should have been nipped in the bud with an assertive comment by the teacher and immediate follow-up beyond the classroom (p. 122f). However, some teachers who lack assertive skills let such early behaviour go in the belief that it will go away in time. It rarely does – it needs to be confronted decisively.

Accountability conferencing

The concept of "accountability conferencing" can be utilised for any significant issue of concern that a teacher has about the way a student has behaved towards an adult (in or out of a classroom setting) – particularly here, though, it is discussed relative to harassment/bullying.

Early intervention should include the teacher directly confronting the student with their harassing behaviours. Such an intervention needs the support of a senior colleague and thoughtful prior planning. By "confronting" I mean setting aside "one-to-one" meeting time with the student (the perpetrator of the harassment), where the senior teacher (and the teacher who is the victim of such harassment) makes *clear* to the student what it is they have *specifically* been doing, saying or suggesting (or writing/texting) that constitutes the harassing/bullying behaviour. Such confrontation needs to be respectful, truthful and non-laboured. An opportunity is then given to the student to reply and account for their behaviour. The student is then expected to give a clear assurance and commitment that such behaviour will cease.

It is crucial that the facilitator (a senior teacher) plans this meeting with the teacher concerned beforehand. It is essential to get the facts clear (and written down). The *specific* nature, frequency, occasions and context(s) of the bullying behaviour will be noted; the specific language used; the non-verbal posturing and also the behaviour of the collusive bullies. The senior colleague will also enable their colleague to think through the order of the meeting and how the different stages of the meeting might develop towards the desired outcome.

Any student who bullies others needs some collusive support of other students to applaud, to "confirm" and "consolidate" their behaviour within their peer audience. It will also be crucial to conduct a meeting between each collusive bully and the teacher concerned (separately not together). We will need to discuss with each suspected collusive perpetrator (one at a time) what they know about *what has been going on* with regard to the main perpetrator's behaviour with regard to the teacher who is the victim of the bullying. While collusive bullies do not regard themselves as *bullies,* they need it to be made clear that "laughing along with …", "goading" and "cheering" and "desk-banging" are all forms of harassment for which they are responsible and accountable. They also need to give a clear *assurance* of what they will do to make these behaviours stop.

Conducting an accountability conference with a bullying student

Such a meeting can reawaken quite emotional issues and concerns for the teacher, so it will be important to discuss what they will say and how they might respond to "discounting" and "avoidance" behaviours by the student at such a meeting. If the perpetrator is a female student and the "victim" a male teacher it will be wise to have a female senior colleague facilitate the process (for perceived ethical probity).

• The facilitator (a senior teacher) calls a meeting between the teacher and the student (the perpetrator of the harassment). The meeting is obligatory for the perpetrator.
• At the outset of the meeting the facilitator (senior teacher) explains why this meeting has been called. The tone of the meeting is serious; formal but respectful. If the tenor of the meeting is vindictive and merely an opportunity to attack the student, it will not work for the desired outcome. Nor should the meeting suggest that "this is *just* a little chat about a few problems in class".

  "I've called this meeting between you, Troy [the student], and Mr Smith because we are really concerned about …". Here the facilitator (the senior teacher) briefly outlines the facts that relate to the student's *behaviours*. It is not an attack on the student as a person (tempting as that might be). The facilitator makes the rules of the meeting clear. We each listen to the other without interruption, giving assurance that there will be a right of reply for the student. The aim of the meeting is to determine what has been happening (in the classroom or wherever) and to make sure that the upholding of the rights and *responsibilities* of the individual – and of a safe, respectful classroom – are the expected outcome.
• The teacher who has been the recipient of this harassing behaviour is now given the opportunity to address their issues of concern about the student's behaviour, *directly* to the student. The teacher outlines the behaviours that the student has been engaged in, *briefly* and *specifically*. It will help to have the typical incidents recorded (with a copy for the student/s) to refer to during this meeting. It can sometimes help if the facilitator "models" some of the

non-verbal harassing behaviour to increase clarity and understanding. This possibility needs to be discussed beforehand with the teacher concerned. The student(s) needs to understand that *repeated* gestures and postural cues are also forms of harassment.

- The teacher *briefly* explains how such behaviour affects the teaching and learning in "our class …" and how it affects "the teacher's right to respect and fair treatment …". Avoid talking *too much* about personal feelings. Such admissions may be unhelpful "grist to the bully's power-seeking mill."

- The teacher (who has been the victim of harassment) points out that the behaviours detailed are *harassing/bullying behaviours* and must stop: "This behaviour (beckon to the list) has to stop so that I can get on with the job of teaching and the students in *our* class can get on with their learning … and so that I can feel safe here and have that basic respect I seek to give to you …".

- The facilitator then invites the student to respond and explain what they will do to "Make these behaviours stop …" (specifically described and noted on the list). Many students (in response to the invited right of reply) will disclaim, discount or minimise their harassing behaviour: "I was only mucking about …!"; "I was just joking …"; "Just having a bit of fun …!"; "Other kids said stuff too!!"; "I wasn't the only one …!"; "C'mon, it's no big deal is it?!"

The facilitator (or teacher) will reframe these discounting and avoidance behaviours: "Maybe you thought it was a joke, Troy, but it clearly *wasn't* for Mr Smith *because* …"; "*That* kind of joke or mucking-around is *never* acceptable in our school – even if half the class laughed with you …" (and they didn't!); "Maybe you were not the only one who said and did these things … *I'll be speaking to other students in our class too* … At the moment I'm talking about *what you did … and about your responsibility* …". This lets the student know that the "secrecy code" will be cracked across the classroom group – one-by-one, as necessary. Sometimes students claim a kind of "right to silence" – refusing to speak. If they refuse to respond verbally, the facilitator can suggest to the student what they might be saying: "Perhaps you're saying in your head, Troy (because you're not speaking to us) … perhaps you're saying that it is no big deal because you were just mucking around. It is a big deal *because* … – it is extremely serious *because* …". Here the facilitator reframes why such behaviour cannot be minimised, "laughed off" or excused. The tone and manner (as stated earlier) is very important; firm but respectful.

"Troy, what do you need to do *now*, and in the future to change this behaviour?" Here the teacher invites an apology and an assurance of behaviour change from the student. A brief reminder about the fundamental rights and responsibilities expected in the student's behaviour is outlined.

Some students will benefit from having a provisional plan about *the specific behaviours they need to stop* (and the obvious *why*) *and the behaviours they need to start* and the obvious, supportive, *why* … so that all of us can learn without distraction/disruption, feel safe here … enjoy respect/fairness here …). This provisional plan can form the basis for a discussion with the student/s about behaviour change.

The key messages emphasised by the facilitator (the senior teacher) are:

- "You own your own behaviour; nobody makes you do, say X, Y and Z."
- "It's your choice – every time you go into our classroom – to decide whether you'll support fair rights and responsibilities or not."
- "It's all about what *you choose to do say* …". The facilitator will emphasise that the class/grade teacher is wanting to work these issues through with the student in a way that does not need to involve the student's parent(s) *at this stage* but does need the understanding, the accountability and cooperation of the student now and in the future.

If, however, the meeting sees no appropriate response at all from the student, or sees a defiant unwillingness to acknowledge any responsibility, or accountability, the issue will need to be referred to a more formal harassment due process – within the school's harassment policy. The student will need to understand what the more formal due process will involve – including parent contact. Point out, if necessary, the consequences of a refusal to acknowledge, and change, their current pattern of behaviour.

- If the student has grudgingly (or even cooperatively) acknowledged their harassing behaviour, apologised and agreed to change, assure them there will be a review meeting (in a week's time) "to see how things are going back in your classroom [or wherever the harassing behaviour has been occurring]". This puts the student "on notice", but does so with the belief communicated that, "You can make things change … You can support the rights and responsibilities here." Students need to know the difference between "sorry words" and "sorry behaviour": *what behaviours* will show that you are sorry? It is crucial to keep accurate records of the student's behaviour during that week.
- Separate amicably at the close of the meeting. Avoid any telegraphing of animosity, "pay-back" or threat. The relative success of this accountability– mediatory approach relies on early intervention; senior colleague support, thoughtful planning and teacher goodwill to work with the perpetrators to

expose and confront the behaviour while inviting understanding and cooperation and necessary change in behaviour.

At the review meeting, if there is no change in the behaviour (during that week), formal due process will need to be entered into quickly. We should give no indication that we will continue to tolerate such behaviour. If necessary, due process may necessitate suspension and even (on some occasions) expulsion.

Special areas of focus for colleague support

Colleague support in some schools can often be incidental, based on loose (one-to-one) associations as well as more formal expressions (such as meetings and ongoing collegial teams). There are key areas, however, where colleague support cannot be left to mere goodwill, chance association or even formal teaming, (faculty/grade-teams).

Induction of new staff to a school

Each school has its own, unique, idiosyncratic culture and practices. A new teacher to a school can be assisted by having a "teaching buddy", to help induct even experienced teachers into a new school. Such 'induction' is not patronising to an experienced colleague; it is the offer of support from someone who can help make sense (through their availability) of the essentials one needs to know and be aware of when starting out in a *new school* (in *this* school). It is also important to introduce and welcome the new colleague formally at assembly – to the whole school – and even to their new classes. I have been in schools where this normal, cordial, collegial convention has been ignored.

First-year teachers

I have heard too many accounts of newly qualified teachers having to engage their first year of teaching, and the new culture of their first school, without focused colleague support.

- Provision needs to be made for a "mentor" – an experienced colleague – to support the new teacher during their first term. Such support will involve regularly meeting with the new teacher to discuss any concerns, as well as being available at other times. Issues such as lesson planning, classroom management and follow-up of students are typical concerns that will need to be addressed. The mentoring role may also involve in-class teaming to give the "mentee" an opportunity to observe a senior colleague's teaching practice and conversely gain supportive feedback from the mentor observing the "mentee's" classroom teaching and management (see later).

- An in-school peer-support group can be formed to act as an "emotional clearing house" (without it being a total whinge session). Such groups can be a forum for needs identification, ideas generation, problem-solving, professional development and suggested action-planning (Rogers 2011).

- A network forum with other first-year teachers (across several schools) to discuss common concerns, needs, experiences and strategies is also an extremely useful peer-support option. It is also important to assist first-year teachers with basic essentials such as: a decent map of the school; the published discipline/behaviour policy; time-out practice (particularly who to call on for escorted time-out); detention policy; referral procedures and the responsibility of follow-up with students one-to-one; and playground management procedures. These "basics" are often so well entrenched in the organisational culture of a school that senior colleagues may forget how different, even strange, the first few weeks in a new school culture can seem for a newly qualified teacher or a teacher new to that school.

Again, a "teaching buddy" can give valuable assistance in coming to terms with these fundamentals.

Supply teachers

On the law of averages, supply teachers often take over the more difficult classes for one or several days. In some classes supply teachers are sometimes treated as "fair game" by students. They will need support similar to that offered to new teachers, even if such support is "only" needed for a day's teaching cover (map, break times, and so on). It can also help if a senior teacher introduces the supply teacher to the staff *and* their new classes to enhance the link between the administration and the "new" teacher and have a "collegial buddy" for the day who they can call on in break times. (See particularly, *Effective Supply Teaching*, Rogers 2003b.)

Elective mentoring

Elective mentoring can provide the opportunity for a teacher to work with a trusted, supportive colleague over a period of time, providing a basis for ongoing professional reflection; review of *characteristic* teaching and behaviour leadership and exploring opportunities for skill development.

Mentoring has to be elective if a colleague is going to feel that they have some professional ownership of the support offered through such mentoring. Obviously, the normative opportunity for such mentoring needs to be present in a school for colleagues to take it up as an professional development option.

The emphasis of such mentoring needs to be construed within a supportive, professional development context rather than "struggling-teacher context". Mentoring, in this sense, does not imply a superior–inferior relationship or an implied imputation of failure in one's teaching and management practice.

Any mentoring, even with a trusted colleague, has some natural "risk" attached. Inviting a colleague to work with you, over time, particularly in a difficult class means exposing one's personal, and professional, self-esteem to another. Collegial goodwill and professional trust can minimise any perceived sense of inadequacy as both mentor and "mentee" focus on (the) common aims and needs as the basis for mentoring support.

For example, the "mentee" may be unaware of some of the factors in the classroom dynamics that their classroom management – or even their normative teaching practice – may be affecting. A key aspect of the mentor's role will be to enable a colleague's awareness of what is actually, and characteristically, going on in their classroom. That awareness will involve supportive feedback that addresses such teacher behaviour where necessary. Supportive feedback enables *professional self-awareness* as the precursor to encouraging change. Any feedback needs to be given with conscious sensitivity to a colleague's professional self-esteem.

> **NB** In using the terms "mentor" and "mentee" there is no imputation of superiority by the more experienced mentor colleague. The terms are used here to distinguish roles within the colleagial relationship. In the schools where I work as a mentor (and in training and supporting mentor programmes) we are careful to select colleagues who are clearly able to invite and engage collegial trust, goodwill and respect. "Mentees" can self-elect to work with a mentor through their head of department. Colleagues who are clearly struggling in their management of a class and who may be reluctant to seek mentoring support can be approached by their head of department (respectfully, privately, professionally) and invited to consider in-class mentoring.

Before any feedback is given, however, the mentor will need to discuss the purpose of feedback, how it is likely to be given (supportively and non-judgementally)

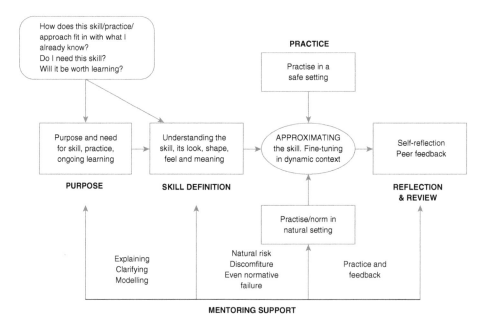

Figure 8.1   Skill development within a mentoring model

and how such feedback might be utilised in ongoing action-planning, particularly the development of one's teaching and management practice.

There are a number of "stages" in the ongoing professional journey of mentor and mentee. These are set out in Figure 8.1. Any mentoring will need to begin from a basis of perceived need on the mentee's part and a willingness to work in a professionally supportive way with a colleague-mentor.

Normative whinging: "hearing" a teacher's frustration and concern

"Whinging" can range from the occasional grizzle and moan to an ongoing state of being! At its most typical, it is frustration battling with goodwill and the constraints of time in our day to day teaching and management. It can also be a way of bonding with another ("in the same boat ... leaking, rusty, but roughly going in the same direction"). It can enable a reframing of built-up tension, particularly through shared humour, giving a little "coping edge" or "momentary uplift" in one's day. It can also ratify a view of one's struggle: "you're not the only one".

Some whinging, though, can be ongoing, laboured and even resilient to reframing and problem-solving. It can also be destructive to collegial goodwill and an "avoidance strategy" by the whinger (Rogers 2002a). When sharing with a colleague who frequently, even consistently, moans and complains it is important to:

- listen and acknowledge (first) before offering possible suggestions – *unsolicited* advice is not always well (or easily) received. Such listening is an affirmation of their feelings and needs; it doesn't have to validate all they are saying about a given incident or concern
- be aware that sometimes the whinging is enough, acting as a kind of "offloading" (even if you're the one who has been cornered for the offloading)
- if the whinging is a recurrent pattern – or keeps raising a recurrent theme – suggest a more focused form of support that includes some needs analysis; problem-solving; conflict-resolution (if necessary); or some kind of *workable plan* to address the recurrent concern.

If whinging descends into a destructive moaning, inaction, destructive blame or dissenting behaviour that stymies any effective change or resolution options, make it clear to the colleague what it is they are doing *through* their whinging, and let them know that productive support will always help if the problem, issue or concern is actually confronted and addressed. Some colleagues, it seems, would rather keep whinging about X, Y and Z than do something (anything!) about X, Y and Z. This sort of constant whinging behaviour can sap at the goodwill of supportive colleagues.

These professional discussions are never easy for a senior colleague. There are some colleagues whose lack of professionalism in their characteristic practice and their resistance to support and change will need to be addressed through review and professional accountability protocols.

Support, professional, mentoring

The particular approach (see Figure. 8.1)

The particular mentoring model – addressed here – is one my colleagues and I utilise for a teacher's reflection on their characteristic behaviour leadership in classroom contexts. It is primarily a coaching approach based in episodic team-teaching opportunities. By being with a colleague, teaching with them – *in their class* – we can see, hear and feel the normative classroom dynamics and *characteristic* features of a teacher's behaviour leadership and teaching practice. One can go for years in our profession without having the opportunity of working directly with a colleague in their more challenging class(es). Once a week, mentor and "mentee" team-teach in class(es) nominated by the mentee and, later both will reflect on and review one another's behaviour characteristic leadership practice. All feedback and review is based in the sorts of practices and skills notes in Chapters 2–4 of this text.

Any such visits, by a mentor to a mentee's class, need to be well planned, particularly in respect to: how the mentor is introduced to the class (briefly); the mentor's role during team-teaching times; how any behaviour management issues might be addressed by the mentor during the course of any lesson; and any cues or signals the mentor and mentee can use to indicate when (for example) the mentor could take a management lead during the course of a lesson. I have (on many occasions) chosen to calm a disturbingly noisy class and refocus their attention during a colleague's struggle to manage whole-class behaviour. The collegial cue for this (verbal or non-verbal) needs to be planned prior to any exercise of "direct classroom control" by the mentor. The last thing a supportive colleague needs to do is convey, publicly (to their class), that the supported colleague is an ineffective, incompetent teacher. The approach I normally use is to give a brief, verbal cue at such an appropriate time: "Excuse me, Mr Smith, do you mind if I (have a word with …) …?" and then address the behaviour *within the framework of the joint-teaching focus* for that lesson.

This form of mentor-coaching is – naturally – a labour-intensive approach to professional development but highly valued by colleagues because it is based in *elective* colleague trust. It also sees mentor-teachers often naturally struggling with challenging behaviour concerns typically experienced by their mentee colleague.

"It's not just me, is it?"

In my mentoring work in schools I have had many highly attentional and power-seeking students seek to exercise their "social place" through their disruptive behaviour. While I'll often deal with such behaviours (see the many case studies in this text) differently from my mentee colleague, they can see *their* students' distracting and disruptive behaviour *with another teacher*. Many, many times I've stood in front of such restless classes, initiating and sustaining whole-class attention and focus, dealing with calling out, butting in, talking while I'm seeking to teach …, and the strident student who says, "Why are you here!? You're not our normal teacher." (I've been tempted to reply, "There aren't any normal teachers …"). The students who walk in late, who see the "new" teacher in their class, adding, "Who are you?" again, often in a stridently inquisitive voice … My colleague, standing a metre or so away, has the opportunity to see how another teacher (their colleagial mentor) leads *their* class. It is in that shared existentiality that collegial trust is earned.

I have no "status" (as such) with these students; yes I am an older, senior, teacher but I have no long-term role (within the school) as – say – a head-teacher. Like any new teacher I have to "earn" my status through how I lead, guide, support and discipline, and encourage in *that* class. The students do not change their behaviour simply because an older teacher is in shared leadership of the class. All that I've shared in Chapters 2–4 is what I seek to do as if it were "my" class in "my establishing phase" as it were.

Because my colleague has seen my "natural struggle" to lead, direct, manage the behaviour in *their* class, the most common response I get – over coffee – is "It's not *just* me, is it ...?"

"So that's what you mean ...?"

When my colleagues and I debrief after team-teaching a particularly challenging class, we discuss the behaviour of the more catalytic students, how we sought to address and focus behaviour and learning together. It is within this shared, and focused, teaming my colleagues will acutely notice features of behaviour leadership such as *tactical* ignoring; *selective* attention; *positive corrective language*; take-up time; how a teacher moves around the room, micro-teaching, giving descriptive feedback and encouragement ... My colleagues often say things like, "So *that's* what you mean by 'take-up time' ...; *tactical* ignoring; focused encouragement ..." because they have seen it in their class(es), with their students; again, that shared existentiality enables trust and focus.

Seeing core practices and skills *in situ* under the natural constraints and pressures of day-to-day teaching is a powerful way of identifying, and teaching, behaviour leadership skills *contextually*.

The word "mentor" comes from Homer's *Odyssey*. In this epic Greek myth, Mentor (the long-time loyal friend of Odysseus) is entrusted with the support of Odysseus' and Penelope's son, Telemachus. He carried out this role so well that the word "mentor" has come down to us today as meaning "wise advisor and guide – one who gives support and encouragement". Odysseus, king of Ithaca, was one of the heroes of the Trojan War. (The Romans named him Ulysses.)

Goal setting

Mentor and "mentee" discuss and develop goals for the mentee to work on. These goals may include (for example) a particular approach to management say, establishing whole-class attention more thoughtfully or more effectively, or particular skills in the language of discipline, or even particular approaches to classroom teaching (see Chapters 3 and 4).

This approach to mentoring does not merely watch a colleague from the back of the classroom but directly team-teaches with their colleague. This gives the mentee the opportunity to directly see how their mentor-colleague addresses distracting and disruptive behaviours and engages the teaching and learning dynamic. It also gives a basis for the ongoing coaching.

It is always important to remember that what seems patently obvious, and clear, to the mentor (as a "skill") may appear difficult or even confusing to the mentee. It will be important to clarify and discuss a particular behaviour management approach or skill; even practise the skill in a "safe", non-classroom, environment. It will also be important to reassure one's colleague that skill development takes time, consciously focused effort and even *normative* failure and that normative failure is OK. Any goals regarding teaching or management practice need to be developed collegially; they also need to be realistic, behaviourally focused, *incremental* and supported with ongoing feedback by the mentor.

Feedback

For feedback to be supportive and effective it needs to focus on targeted areas and goals and particular skills. When giving feedback, mentor and mentee should focus on the present *behaviour* and the present issues observed in the natural setting of the classroom. While it is helpful to *generally* note that a certain class is particularly noisy and difficult to settle, it also helps if the mentor *specifically* notes what they believe contributes to the noise level and restlessness (in that class); even if the mentee's behaviour (as the class teacher) is a significant "factor". Before any feedback session it is essential for mentor and mentee to discuss the purpose and nature of colleague feedback by mentor to mentee and vice versa.

The mentor will keep any feedback *descriptive* and be sure to focus the feedback on *characteristic* aspects of teacher behaviour (including discipline language).

A teacher may be unaware of their *characteristic* language usage in discipline contexts; they may also be unaware of their non-verbal behaviour – how they "come across" to their students; they may be unaware of how they address particular aspects of disruptive behaviour ... In giving *descriptive* feedback the mentor is describing what they see, hear and perceive as a basis for shared reflection and shared action planning. Before developing any new skill repertoire a colleague will need to be aware of their *current characteristic behaviour leadership behaviour*.

Descriptive feedback, supportively and sensitively shared, enables that professional self-awareness. Examples of the typical questions used to raise mentee awareness in feedback sessions are: "Were you *aware* that (specific examples are given…) …?"; "Did you *hear* yourself say …?"; "Were you *conscious* of …?"; "How did you *feel* when …?"

- We should also avoid giving feedback that is too extensive or wide-ranging as it can easily dissuade or discourage a colleague. Overloaded feedback that covers too many factors about a colleague's teaching and management behaviour may make change look difficult, even insurmountable. One can cope with incremental, *supported*, changes.
- Keep any feedback non-judgemental. The feedback should avoid any criticism of "personality" factors.
- Encourage, develop and affirm a colleague's skill development *within and from the feedback*. Professional feedback, of any kind, is most useful, valued and effective when linked to common needs, aims and objectives.
- Some changes will be relatively easy, such as *physical organisation of the* classroom (seating/movement, see also p. 52f). Routines such as management of noise level, student time on-task, how students get teacher assistance require management skill in communication to the class as a group and to individual students, and skills of behaviour leadership in terms of discipline language, even using descriptive encouragement, are more challenging skill areas for teachers to develop.

Disengagement

There will come a time when the mentor will need to separate from the ongoing, supportive, journey with their "mentee" colleague, though occasional visits by the mentor to their mentee colleague's class(es) are often common practice and greatly appreciated. This does not mean a lack of further support; it means the professional mentoring journey now focuses the mentee on *generalising* their skills and adapting their skills into their own teacher leadership practice. A school should have its own normative opportunities for ongoing professional sharing, professional development and appraisal. Ideally, all such opportunities are geared to enabling and encouraging personal and shared reflection on one's teaching and management in a spirit of professional collegial goodwill and trust.

Colleague support

Not all colleagues want or feel they need support from their peers; even in supportive schools. Some teachers will give support because the culture in the school makes the giving of such support easier, or perhaps because one perceives it as a personal or professional duty arising from "mutual regard" and shared perspective-taking or even our fundamental shared humanity. Within a school culture there are complex relationships that exist between personalities, structures and the demands of one's role. Those who do give – and give unstintingly – of their time and energy to support their colleagues speak about the stress of *giving* support as well as the benefits of support enjoyed by the recipients (Rogers 2002a).[1] It is important for school leadership to acknowledge these natural, creative, tensions.

Colleague support cannot simply be mandated. Like any feature of school culture and practice, *the things that really matter cannot be mandated or forced on others* (McLaughlin 1990; Fullan 1993; Rogers 2002a, 2012). Teachers generally acknowledge that they want, need and benefit from colleague support, yet a school administration cannot simply mandate that colleagues give and receive support, or that it *will* operate. This does not negate external direction, policy initiatives, and the establishing of "forms" or planned expressions of support, but it does mean that what colleagues say they value and need cannot *simply* be built by policy imperative. Thoughtful procedures, plans and policies – while subject to the constraints of fallibility – can, however, be vehicles for human support and action. They can give a sense of shared purpose, dependable organisational structure, "back-up" and reciprocal interdependency. Of course such "structures" or "forms" need to be broadly and characteristically worthy of our trust. Time and usage will give the confirmation or refutation of such assurance and trust.[2]

When a school leadership seeks to address colleague support, such support needs to focus on how the school – as a collegial community – can meet colleague needs; their need to be accepted and acknowledged *as a professional*; to be treated with respect and fairness and without discrimination (selective support/cliques/favourites …). In this sense "form" always follows function. The question we always need to ask is: *does the colleague support we offer (or "plan", for) actually meet colleagues' needs?*

Collegially supportive structures, "forms", processes, mentoring opportunities, "teaming structures", and so on can be enhanced by periodic colleague review. Such a review proceeds from the affirmation that the school values mutual regard and supportive collegial interdependency.

> **NB   Needs analysis and colleague support**
>
> - How acknowledged are the individual and collective needs of colleagues at your school? In what ways are they acknowledged? What current "forms", (structures, processes or policies) seek to address these needs?
> - Where would you regard your school, now, in terms of a general "consciousness of colleague support"? This in part will be perceived within your current role. As a senior teacher – of course – the responsibility (and limitations) of giving support will range from the incidental, daily, moral support we give through to more involved support, such as back-up in discipline contexts (like time-out); follow-up (with the teacher) of challenging students; supporting positive labour-intensive programmes like colleague mentoring.
> - Have colleagues been asked to identify areas of need relative to colleague support? Have colleagues been given a genuine opportunity for needs analysis such as that noted earlier (for example, the stress audit, p. 271)?
> - What changes will need to be made (or are functionally able to be made) to address and seek to meet identified colleague needs – particularly in the area of behaviour leadership?
> - What changes to current "forms", structures, plans, policies and procedures will need to be made to enable the meeting of identified needs? (Rogers 2002a). Critical areas of review will involve the "reality link" between stated behaviour policy and daily practice.

Commitment to an "ecology of support" (Rogers 2002a) depends on how a community of professionals chooses to operate, and cooperate. Choices that enhance and *enable* colleague support are more likely to occur when the school culture consciously endorses, and encourages, colleague support, particularly from a supportive leadership team. That kind of colleague support can only be based (fundamentally) in a sense of mutual regard, colleague watchfulness and shared humanity.

Reflection

- If you are struggling with a difficult-to-manage class, how confident are you of obtaining colleague support? What support would you – realistically – want need? Who would you seek support from? Or expect support from? How (for example) would you approach a senior colleague for support if you were struggling with behaviour concerns.
- If you are a senior teacher and are aware of a teacher clearly having significant management/discipline problems, how would you approach a colleague to offer support?

- How are teachers struggling with challenging students/classes "identified" and supported in your school?
- If such teachers do not "come forward" to ask for support how do we extend/offer/process such support?
- How do you respond to the concept of short-term – immediate – support with a class where the teacher is "losing control" (p. 277)?
- What forms/processes exist for assisting a teacher to develop a fresh start with a hard-to-manage class (p. 272f)?
- Are classroom meetings used to help refocus challenging classes? How? (p. 274f)
- How do you respond to the issue of harassment (of teachers)? Are there any colleagues you are aware of who may be experiencing harassment (of any kind) from students? How is the issue of such harassment addressed in your school?
- The behaviour leadership skills noted in Chapters 3 and 4 can provide a basis for professional review and development. In what ways can such professional development (in behaviour leadership/discipline) be pursued and developed in your school, your faculty, your grade team?
- What mentoring opportunities does your school offer/provide? (For first-year teachers; for "buddy" systems; for mentor-coaching?)
- What professional feedback opportunities exist in your school (apart from formal and summative approaches like Ofsted)?

Notes

1   In his autobiography, *Clinging to the Wreckage* (1989), John Mortimer notes that the world is roughly divided into "nurses" and "patients". Does this ring a bell(?).
2   Hargreaves (1994) notes that trust can be invested in persons or processes, in the qualities and conduct of individuals, or the expertise and performance of abstract systems. It can be an outcome of meaningful face-to-face relationships or a *condition* of their existence (italics are mine).

   In this sense policies *and practices* for behaviour management and discipline need to bridge that "reality gap" between stated policy imperative and direction and what we actually do (or seek to do!) in the day-to-day of behaviour leadership in classroom and non-classroom settings.

 Visit **https://study.sagepub.com/rogers4e** for additional resources to help you better manage classroom behaviour. You'll also be able to hear from Bill himself as he talks you through common behaviour management scenarios.

Epilogue

No doubt, like me, you went into teaching because you believed you could make a difference to the lives of your students in their educational journey. This is a profession that takes up a good deal of our time in and out of the classroom. We spend time outside classroom teaching, supporting our students by sharing time and assistance, being part of special events, and keeping on top of the ever-present marking and feedback. Our profession is more than a job – it is a challenging and chosen *noblesse oblige*.

This book has a parallel text, beyond classroom management, discipline and effective teaching: that of colleague support. Without colleague support – reasonable, basic support – our profession is made more difficult and more stressful.

Colleague support can meet our basic needs for belonging and affiliation as well as our professional needs for affirmation, assurance, shared professional identity and supportive feedback (Rogers, 2002a, 2012).

From the transitional whinge and offloading to the brief assurance that we're on the right track, from the sense of shared identity through to shared teaming and appraisal, colleague support affirms and enables our daily coping, our morale and our professionalism.

To some of you (if you've read this far) I will have said more than enough about the sorts of management, discipline and teaching issues you face each day as a teacher; to others I will not have said enough. There is always more that can be said to qualify, extend and clarify. I hope that what I have shared has helped your personal reflection on your day-to-day teaching and management.

I wish you well in your teaching journey – all sanity and grace, day-to-day.

Kind regards, Bill Rogers

Our daughter, Sarah, did this drawing when she was 11 years old (many years back now ...). I had been chatting with her about what I was writing on colleague support. "What's a colleague?" she had asked. I did my best to explain (my wife and I, and our eldest daughter are teachers). We chatted about colleagues (and support) and she then did this drawing. The rings under the eyes were her observation; that these are teachers. She has tried to demonstrate colleague support: note the long, collegial arms; that shared humanity that has to reach across, and encompass, any formal expression of support we seek to build in school.

Appendix A – Poster formats

These "poster formats" are used by many of my colleagues (and myself) as visual reminders to students of our classroom rules. We developed these some years back and have fine-tuned them since.

The three rules are derived from the core non-negotiable rights:

- **the right to feel safe here …;**
- **the right to learn here;**
- **the right to respect and fair treatment.**

In subject areas such as Food Tech., Materials Design/Tech., Art, Physical Education, we would have a specific rule poster/s for safety concerns attenuating more specific aspects of safety relevant in that subject and learning space.

We suggest that when making the rule posters they be neatly written in bold lettering *large enough* to be seen from the back of the classroom. The headings need to be bolder in format. It can help to laminate them. Some schools get them professionally printed.

These rules are discussed with each form group/tutor group/pastoral group in the establishment phase of the year.

A class works well, learns well, when *each* class member makes an effort to

COOPERATE with others.

IN ORDER TO COOPERATE WE HAVE TO LEARN TO GET ON WITH EACH OTHER HERE. IT'S OUR PLACE.

− WE *ALL* HAVE RIGHTS (to feel safe here, to learn without distraction from others, and to show and give respect and fairness).
− WE HAVE RESPONSIBILITIES SO WE CAN ENJOY THOSE RIGHTS.

(we) TAKE TURNS IN CLASS DISCUSSION.

(we) ARE WILLING TO HAVE OUR VIEWS AND OPINIONS CHALLENGED.

(we) DISAGREE RESPECTFULLY AND GIVE *REASONS* FOR WHY WE DISAGREE.

(we) ARE WILLING TO HELP/SUPPORT AND ENCOURAGE EACH OTHER IN OUR LEARNING HERE.

WE ALL HAVE A RIGHT TO LEARN

TO LEARN WELL HERE WE:

(1) Get to class on time (entry);   (2) Settle/relax/prepare ...;

(3) Appropriate materials;   (4) Hands up ...   **FGFA**

(5) Partner-voice/Cooperative talk;   (6) If you need TA remember:

Check first ⟶ classmate ⟶ ⟨THB⟩ ⟶ ⟨OW⟩

Mr Rogers: English   (Ta)

NB **FGFA = fair go for all THB = Teacher help board OW = go on with other work until teacher comes (e.g. class novel/worksheet options ...)**

WE ALL HAVE A RIGHT TO RESPECT

To enjoy one another's respect here we remember that:

- **We all share the same place, space and reason for being *here*.**
- **We all share the same fundamental feelings** – it's all about the way we treat one another here.
- **Safety is more than physical safety** (people's feelings, personal space, property).
- **Considered language** (no put-downs, cheap shots).
- Bullying is totally unacceptable in our school.
- **Courtesy, consideration, manners. Thanks.**

Mr Rogers: English   'Ta!'   Courtesy is catching!

Appendix B – Confronting and bullying behaviour

The typical excuses that children make regarding confronting and bullying behaviour

Whenever a teacher addresses confronting and bullying behaviour with a student there are common responses made, by the bully, to discount, minimise or mitigate their behaviour, all of which seek to avoid taking responsibility for their behaviour; *learned* avoidance behaviours. The excuses and avoidance language used by bullies need to be countered and reframed as part of the process of accountability, mediation and due process.

- *"It was only a joke!"* How many times have we heard this from a student who has pushed, shoved, tripped or hit another student. *"My fist slipped!"* (a student actually said that to me!)
  "So, who was laughing? Was the victim laughing? Even if you and some of your mates were laughing, that didn't make it a joke. It is not funny. Not in *our* school. *And*, tripping others, pushing them, throwing their school bag in the bushes is just an excuse to hurt someone."
  "I was only playing!" is similar to the above.
  "But you left the person (always use the first name of the victim) bruised, hurt, frightened, crying …"

"… It was the same yesterday when you gate-crashed the footy game … That's not 'playing', it's *invading* others' games and activities without asking or being invited."

- *"It was an accident."*
  "So Michael is hurt, bruised, tripped up – by you – in the corridor … His bag is thrown on the floor … his things all spilled out. Did you stay to help? That's what people *normally* do when there is 'an accident'. They stop and help, or they report to a teacher, they apologise … You didn't. That's wrong – it was done on purpose. That's bullying."
- *"I didn't mean it."*
  "You were there, you were seen, you even tried to get others to laugh, and tease, and putdown with you …" "You chose." While some children may not have 'meant' their behaviour to end up (at times) so hurtfully (in outcome) they need to know they *started* what ended up as a hurtful outcome.
- *"Anyway I found it."* How many times has this one been trotted out? Money, toys, that expensive pen, watch, phone, jewellery … etc.
  "It's someone else's. It doesn't belong to you. If you find something like … (name the item) you would *at least* take it to the office, or to a teacher. *You* kept it …"
- *"But I only borrowed it!"* I have found students in possession of items/objects, and amounts of money, clearly not theirs. There are students who will "grapevine" the information (particularly if they are scared of the student who is confronting or bullying others …). When challenged the perpetrator will often say " … *but I only borrowed it!*" This, again, is similar: the money, watch, pen, toy, phone … is 'borrowed'. We need to ask the perpetrator: "Who did you borrow it from? When? What's their name? What class are they in? Michael (the victim) was crying and hurt; we don't go around borrowing money, or phones, or … from someone who is a 'stranger' and someone who *never* gave permission. That's mugging and thieving." It will almost always help if we can encourage the victim to face their perpetrator (with an adult mediator) and say what really happened (see p. 201f).
  It is important we address our questions, and responses, to their avoidance behaviour in a calm way. Allow for pausing (we do not rush the dialogue); it is not a police investigation (yet).

We are teachers helping a student become aware of, accountable and then responsible for their confronting and harassing behaviours. Ideally it will help if the victim has an opportunity to face their perpetrator *with* a teacher who has experience and skill in mediation. The teacher conducting such a meeting will need to get the facts clear beforehand and plan the meeting with the victim before they face their "perpetrator". There are also, often, witnesses to harassing behaviour. Bullies trade in secrecy *from adults*, not from their peers; they seek attention and power – that collusive peer approval of their "power". (p 217f).

The aim of any such meeting is to make clear to the perpetrator that they made a choice to do what they did. No one *made* them do it. It is also important to have the incident (a clear account of what the perpetrator did and said) written down from the victim's perspective. The victim in any such a meeting is encouraged to face their perpetrator to make clear:

- *what* happened regarding the confronting and harassing behaviour (and when) and how
- how they feel about what happened
- what they want to happen now *and in the future*.

Most victims want assurance that it won't happen again – an apology is always requested. We also need to make clear the difference between sorry *words* and sorry *behaviour*. What will show to _____ (the victim), and others, that you are sorry for what you did? We call the bully to account for *their behaviour*. It is at this point the excuses (noted earlier) are often routinely trotted out. We need to calmly, clearly, address such avoidance language and refocus the perpetrator to the fact that they chose to do what they did to this fellow student in *our school*.

We need to ask them *what* they need to do to make amends, to fix things up. This may, at times, involve restitution as well.

It will also help to let the perpetrator know that "... we will have another meeting in a week's time to see how things are going in the playground ..." or wherever (most harassing behaviour occurs in non-classroom settings). This review meeting puts the perpetrator "on notice", as it were, to monitor their own behaviour. The hardest feature of harassing behaviour to address, however, is the *attitude* and stance of attentional power exercised by bullies. Attitudes are affected by education, culture, experiences – all of which a school can address for positive good. In the meantime we will always call the perpetrator to account and we will not accept their excuses.

Grateful thanks are extended to my colleagues at *North Walsham High School* (England) to draw on some of the material from their school policy on bullying.

See also:

Rogers, B. (2006) *Behaviour Management: A Whole-School Approach* (2nd edn). London: Sage.

Further reading

Important websites

Carer Support and Schools: www.sofweb.vic.edu.au

The Children, Youth and Family Act 2005, which became law in April 2007, is the legislative base for current reforms to child protection and family services. See www.office-for-children-vic.gov.au/ece

A helpful website address for attention deficit spectrum disorder:

www.bigpond.com/addiss

Some websites that address bullying are:

www.education.unisa.edu.au/bullying

www.antibullying.net

www.bullystoppers.com

www.kidscape.org.uk

www.dfes.gov.uk/bullying

www.bbc.co.uk/schools/ bullying

The Nurture Group: www.nurture.groups.org

See also: www.education.gov.uk for advice to governing bodies, head-teachers and staff on legal "power" and guidelines for appropriate and legal use of force to control/restrain (my inverted commas around the word "power" used in this web note – see p. 144/192 in this text) www.edfac.unimelb.edu.au/swap/wellbe ing/teachers/environment/restorative.html-this website address student well bcing restroactive practices.

Also see: School discipline and exclusions at www.gov.uk/school.../discipline and www.publicnet.co.uk.features/2010/03/05/improving-pupil-behaviour-through-a-restorative-process

On the United Nations Conventions in *The Rights of the Child*, see particularly the UNICEF web-site UK and Australia. Since the 1924 Declaration of Geneva, the rights of the child have emphasised provision, protection and participation. These have led, in subsequent declarations, to give form to non-discrimination laws that will heighten children's protection (from harm) and strengthen their participation (particularly in education). This has included the right to *fair treatment* and the *right to be heard*. All these have had a significant effect on how schools educate and manage.

Resources for autism (autism spectrum disorder)

Some very helpful resources are:

- The National Autism Hotline (UK 0845 070 4004): www.nas.org.uk
- The Centre for Social and Communication Disorders: www.patient.co.uk
- The Interact Centre: www.interactcentre.com
- Haddon, Mark (2004) *The Curious Incident of the Dog in the Night-Time*. London: Vintage Random House. This is a unique kind of novel about an 18-year-old with Asperger's Syndrome – written by someone clearly able to see inside the mind and perceptual world of Asperger's within the context of a thoroughly good read!
- *Olane Sara'sburry (2009) Martian in the Playground: Understanding the School Child with Asperger's Syndrome.* London: Sage. This should be a seminal text in schools.
- Attwood, T.C. (2008) *The Complete Guide to Asperger's Syndrome.* London: Jessica Kingsley.
- Ben-Arich, J. and Miller, H.J. (2009) *The Educator's Guide to Teaching Students with Autism Spectrum Disorders.* California: Corwin Press.
- See also www.acer.edu.au/autism

Resources for extreme situations (including restraint)

- HMSO (1974) *Health and Safety at Work Act.* London: HMSO.
- Department for Education and Skills (2007) *School Discipline and Behaviour Policies.* London: DES.
- HMSO (2005) *5 Steps to Risk Assessment.* London: HMSO.
- Department for Education and Employment (1998) Section 550A (Education Act 1996) *The Use of Force to Control or Restrain Pupils.* London: DFEE.
- Department of Health and Department for Education and Skills (2002) *Guidance for Restrictive Physical Interventions: How to Provide Safe Services for People with Learning Disabilities and Autism Spectrum Disorder.* London: Department of Health.
- Department for Education and Skills (2003) *Guidance on the Use of Restrictive Physical Interventions for Pupils with Severe Behavioural Difficulties.* London: DFES.
- Department for Children, Schools and Families (2007) *The Use of Force to Control or Restrain Pupils.* London: DCSF.

Other resources

- Cracking the Challenging Class. The two-part DVD series (developed and filmed in a UK school) addresses the common challenges teachers face with hard-to-manage and challenging classes. It is available in the UK from London: Sage Publications.
- Thody, A., Gray, B. and Bowden, D. (2000) *The Teacher's Survival Guide.* London: Continuum. This book contains a useful and very practical guide to voice management. Graham Welch's *essay* is very helpful for those enabling mentoring support or professional development generally.
- House of Representatives Standing Committee (2013) *Workplace Bullying: We Just Want It to Stop.* Report by House of Representatives Standing Committee on Education and Employment (February). Available at: www.aph.gov.au. This report outlines the nature of workplace bullying and details major recommendations to address such behaviour. They note that "Bullying, harassment or victimisation means repeated, unreasonable behaviour directed towards a worker or group of workers that creates a risk to health and safety. Bullying does not include reasonable management practices including performance management conducted in a reasonable manner.

See also:

Guide for Preventing and Responding to Workplace Bullying. www.safeworkaustralia.gov.au

Preventing and Managing Bullying at Work: A Guide for Employers: www.comcare.gov.au

Glossary

Assertive behaviour   Communicating with a firm, resolute, unambiguous tone of voice and manner, matched by confident but non-aggressive body language.

Behaviour agreement   An agreed set of rules and routines that emerge from discussions with the students about behaviour and learning.

Behavioural consequences   What happens after certain behaviour; they can be an attempt to teach responsibility and accountability, for example, the teacher links a consequential outcome to a student's disruptive behaviour.

Case supervision   This involves a key teacher working with the child, one-to-one, on a long-term basis. The case supervisor's role would include developing a personal, individual behaviour plan with the student, and communicating the plan to all teachers working with the student and to the student's parents.

Collegial action plan   Provides a forum and a process for meeting the moral, practical and professional needs of a colleague struggling with a hard-to-manage class, or several hard-to-manage students.

Deferred consequence   You explain what will happen if the student doesn't comply with your directed choice of behaviour, but you don't dwell on this (you move on with the lesson).

Establishment phase   The beginning of your relationship with a class, and a period when rights, rules, responsibilities, expected behaviours can be established.

Partial agreement   You might agree with the statement the student makes, but not the way they react to it.

Primary behaviour   The student behaviour that is the cause of the disruption.

Relaxed vigilance   The teacher's confident, assured, firm expectations about cooperative compliance when engaged in behaviour management.

Secondary behaviour   The student behaviour that contributes to the primary behaviour, for example, tone of voice, body language.

Case studies and examples index

Bibliography

Adler, A. (1979a) *Superiority and Social Interest: A Collection*. New York: W.W. Norton.

Adler, A. (1979b) *The Problem Child*. New York: G.P. Putnam and Sons.

Adler, A. (1981) *Understanding Human Nature*. St Paul, MN: Fawcett Press. (First published 1927)

Aristotle (1969) *The Ethics of Aristotle: The Nichomachean Ethics*. Trans. J.A.K. Thompson. London: Penguin.

Attwood, T. (2006) *The Complete Guide to Asperger's Syndrome*. London: Tessian Kingsley Publications.

Baars, C.W. (1979) *Feeling and Healing Your Emotions*. Plainfield, NJ: Logos International.

Beck, A.T. (1976) *Cognitive Therapy and the Emotional Disorders*. New York: International Universities Press.

Bernard, M. (1990) *Taking the Stress out of Teaching*. Melbourne: Collins Dove.

Campbell, D. (2000) *The Mozart Effect for Children*. Sydney: Hodder.

Carr, W. (ed.) (1989) *Quality in Teaching: Arguments for a Reflective Profession*. London: Falmer.

Charles, C.M. (2005) *Building Classroom Discipline: From Models to Practice* (8th edn). Boston, MA: Allyn and Bacon.

Clark, M. (1991) *The Quest for Grace*. Ringwood, Victoria: Penguin.

Clarke, D. and Murray, A. (eds) (1996) *Developing and Implementing a Whole-School Behaviour Policy*. London: David Fulton.

Clough, P., Garner, P., Pardeck, J.T. and Yuen, F. (eds) (2005) *Handbook of Emotional and Behavioural Difficulties*. London: SAGE.

Cornett, C.E. (1986) *Learning through Laughter: Humour in the Classroom*. Bloomington, IN: Phi Delta Kappa Educational Foundation.

Cummings, C. (1989) *Managing to Teach*. Edmonds, WA: Teaching Inc.

Denenberg, V.H. and Zarrow, M.J. (1970) "Rat pax". *Psychology Today*, 3(12): 45–7, 66–7.

Dewey, J. (1897) "My pedagogic creed". *The School Journal*, 55(3), 16 January: 77–80. In P. Nash (1968), *Models of Men: Explorations in the Western Education Tradition*. New York: John Wiley and Sons.

Dodge, K.A. (1981) "Social competence and aggressive behaviour in children". Paper presented at Midwestern Psychological Association, Detroit, Michigan, USA, May.

Dodge, K.A. (1985) "Attributional bias in aggressive children". In P.C. Kendall (ed.), *Advances in Cognitive Behavioural Research and Therapy* (Vol. 4). Orlando, FL: Academic Press.

Doyle, W. (1986) "Classroom organisation and management". In M.C. Whitrock (ed.), *Handbook of Research on Teaching*. New York: Macmillan.

Dreikurs, R. (1968) *Psychology in the Classroom* (2nd edn). New York: Harper & Row.

Dreikurs, R., Grunwald, B. and Pepper, E. (1982) *Maintaining Sanity in the Classroom* (2nd edn). New York: Harper & Row.

Edwards, C. (1997) "RET in high school". *Rational Living*, 12: 10–12.

Edwards, C.H. and Watts, V. (2008) *Classroom Discipline and Management* (2nd Australian edn). Stafford, Queensland: John Wiley and Sons.

Ellis, A. (1977) *Anger: How to Live With It and Without It*. Melbourne: Sun Books.

Elton Report (1989) *Discipline in Schools: Report of the Committee of Inquiry* (The Elton Report). London: HMSO.

Faber, A. and Mazlish, E. (1982) *How to Talk so Kids will Listen and Listen so Kids will Talk*. New York: Avon Books.

Farrell, P. and Tsakalidou, K. (1999) "Recent trends in the reintegration of pupils with emotional behavioural difficulties in the UK". *School Psychology International*, 20(4): 323–37.

Frankl, V. (1963) *Man's Search for Meaning: An Introduction to Logotherapy*. New York: Simon & Schuster.

Fullan, M. (1993) *Change Processes: Probing the Depths of Educational Reform*. London: Falmer.

Fullan, M. and Hargreaves, A. (1991) *What's Worth Fighting for? Working Together for your School*. Toronto: Ontario Public School Teachers' Federation.

Geffner, R. and Brians, S. (1993) *Effective Teaching Approaches for ADHD Children*. Texas: ADHD Association of Texas.

Gillborn, D., Nixon, J. and Rudduck, J. (1993) *Dimensions of Discipline: Rethinking Practice in Secondary Schools*. London: HMSO.

Ginott, H. (1971) *Teacher and Child*. New York: Macmillan.

Glasser, W. (1986) *Control Theory in Classrooms*. New York: Harper & Row.

Glasser, W. (1992) *The Quality School*. New York: HarperCollins.

Goffman, M. (1972) *The Presentation of Self in Everyday Life*. Harmondsworth: Penguin.

Green, C. and Chee, K. (1995) *Understanding ADD*. Sydney: Doubleday.

Groom, B. (2006) "Supporting the return of pupils with EBD to mainstream school from specialist provision". *Reach: Journal of Special Needs Education in Ireland*, 20(1): 61–9.

Guskey, T.R. (1986) "Staff development and the process of teacher change". *Educational Review*, 15(5): 5–12.

Hargreaves, A. (1994) "Restructuring restructuring: postmodernity and the prospects for individual change". *Journal of Education Policy*, 9(1): 47–65.

Hart, P.M. (1994) "Teacher quality of life: integrating work experiences, psychological distress and morale". *Journal of Occupational and Organisational Psychology*, 67: 109–39.

Hart, P.M., Wearing, A.J. and Conn, M. (1995) "Wisdom is a poor predictor of the relationship between discipline policy, student misbehaviour and teacher stress". *British Journal of Educational Psychology*, 1195(65): 27–48.

Hattie, J. (2009) *Visible Learning: A Synthesis of over 800 Meta-Analyses Relating to Achievement*. London: Routledge.

Hattie, J. (2012) *Distinguishing Expert Teachers from Novice and Experienced Teachers: Teachers Make a Difference*. Australian Council for Educational Research (ACER).

Hattie, J. and Timperley, H. (2007) *The Power of Feedback Review of Educational Research*, 77(1): 81–112.

Hobfoll, S.E. (1998) *Stress, Culture, and Community: The Psychology and Philosophy of Stress*. New York: Plenum Press.

House of Representatives Standing Committee (2013) *Workplace Bullying*: We Just Want it to Stop. Report by House of Representatives Standing Committee on Education and Employment (February). Available at: www.aph.gov.au.

Howell, K. (1993) "Eligibility and need: is there a difference between being disturbed and being disturbing?" In D. Evans, M. Myhill and J. Izard (eds), *Student Behaviour Problems: Positive Initiatives and New Frontiers*. Camberwell, Victoria: ACER.

Jarman, E.C. (1992) "Management of hyperactivity: multi model interventions". *Practical Therapeutics*, August: 31–8.

Johnson, D.W. (1972) *Reaching Out: Interpersonal Effectiveness and Self-Actualisation* (5th edn). Boston, MA: Allyn and Bacon.

Johnson, D.W. and Johnson, R.T. (1989) *Leading the Cooperative School*. Edina, MN: Interaction Book Co.

Jons, P. and Tucker, E. (eds) (1990) *Mixed Ability Teaching: Classroom Experiences in English, ESL, Mathematics and Science*. Roseberry, NSW: St Clair Press.

Kounin, J. (1971) *Discipline and Group Management in Classrooms*. New York: Holt, Rinehart and Winston.

Kyriacou, C. (1981) "Social support and occupational stress among school teachers". *Educational Studies*, 7: 55–60.

Kyriacou, C. (1986) *Effective Teaching in Schools*. Oxford: Blackwell.

Kyriacou, C. (1991) *Essential Teaching Skills*. Oxford: Blackwell.

Labi, N. (2001) "Let bullies beware". *Time Magazine*, 2 April: 44–45.

Lashlie, C. (2005) *"He'll Be Ok": Growing Gorgeous Boys into Good Men*. Auckland: HarperCollins.

Lazarus, R.S. (1981) "Little hassles can be hazardous to health". *Psychology Today*, July: 58–62.

Lee, C. (2004) *Preventing Bullying in Schools*. London: SAGE.

Lee, C. (2007) *Resolving Behaviour Issues in Your School*. London: SAGE.

Leiberman, A. (ed.) (1990) *School as Collaborative Cultures: Creating the Future Now*. London: Falmer Press.

Magnusson, M. (2004) *Keeping My Words: An Anthology from Cradle to Grave*. Hodder and Stoughton. London. The headquote on p300 (ch.6) is from this book: Green, G. *The Power and the Glory* (1940) Chapter 1.Magnusson quotes this.

Manchester, D. (2009) "Cursing? Britons swear by it… 14times a day", *Daily Mail*, 16 January 2009. Available at: www.dailymail.co.uk/news/article-1118386/Cursing-Britons-swear-14-times-day. html (accessed 6 February 2015

McGough, R. (1993) *Defying Gravity*. London: Penguin.

McGrath, H. and Francey, S. (1993) *Friendly Kids, Friendly Classrooms*. Melbourne: Longman.

McInerney, D.M. and McInerney, V. (1998) *Educational Psychology: Constructing Learning* (2nd edn). Sydney: Prentice-Hall.

McLaughlin, M. W. *Educational Researcher is the Journal. The Rand Change Agent Study Revisited*. American Educational Research Association. Washington, DC.

Miller, A. (1996) *Pupil Behaviour and Teacher Culture*. London: Cassell.

Mortimer, J. (1984) *In Character*. London: Penguin.

Mortimer, J. (1989) *Clinging to the Wreckage*. London: Penguin.

Nias, J., Southworth, G. and Yeomans, R. (1989) *Staff Relationships in the Primary School*. London and New York: Cassell.

Nelsen, J. (1987) *Positive Discipline*. New York: Ballantine Books..

O'Brien, T. (1998) *Promoting Positive Behaviour*. London: David Fulton.

Ofsted (1999) *Principles into Practice: Effective Education for Pupils with Emotional and Behavioural Difficulties*. London: Ofsted Publications.

Ofsted (2004) *Special Educational Needs and Behavioural Difficulties*. London: Ofsted Publications.

Pearce, H. (1997) "Groupwork in the classroom". Unpublished notes.

Perore, S. (2000) "Workplace is a war zone", *The Age* (newspaper), 22 February: 8.

Relf, P., Hirst, R., Richardson, J. and Youdell, G. (1998) *Best Behaviour: Starting Points for Effective Behaviour Management*. Stafford: Network Educational Press.

Rickard, J. (1994) *Relaxed Activities for Children*. Melbourne: ACER.

Robertson, J. (1997) *Effective Classroom Control: Understanding Teacher–Pupil Relationships* (3rd edn). London: Hodder and Stoughton.

Rogers, B. (1998) *You Know the Fair Rule and More*. London: Pitman.

Rogers, B. (2002a) *"I Get by with a Little Help": Colleague Support in Schools*. London: SAGE.

Rogers, B. (Ed.) (2002b) *Teacher Leadership and Behaviour Management*. London: SAGE.

Rogers, B. (2003a) *Behaviour Recovery* (2nd edn). London: SAGE. pp. 135–186.

Rogers, B. (2003b) *Effective Supply Teaching*. London: Paul Chapman.

Rogers, B. (2006a) *Behaviour Management: A Whole-School Approach* (2nd edn). London: SAGE.

Rogers, B. (2006b) *Cracking the Hard Class: Strategies for Managing the Harder than Average Class* (2nd edn). London: SAGE.

Rogers, B. (ed.) (2009) *How to Manage Children's Challenging Behaviour* (2nd edn). London: SAGE.

Rogers, B. (2011) *You Know the Fair Rule* (3rd edn). Melbourne: ACER; London: Pearson Education.

Rogers, B. (2012) *The Essential Guide to Managing Teacher Stress*. London: Pearson Education.

Rogers, B. and McPherson, E. (2014) *Behaviour Management with Young Children: Crucial First Steps with Children 3–7 Years* (2nd edn). London: SAGE.

Rosenthal, R. and Jacobson, L.F. (1968) "Teacher Expectations for the Disadvantaged", *Readings from Scientific America*. San Francisco: W.F. Freeman & Co.

Russell, D.W., Altimaier, E. and Van Velzen D. (1987) "Job related stress, social support and burnout among classroom teachers". *Journal of Applied Psychology*, 72(2): 269–74.

Rutter, M., Maughan, B., Mortimer, P. and Ousten, J. (1979) *Fifteen Thousand Hours: Secondary Schools and their Effects on Children*. London: Open Books.

Sacks, O. (1990) *Awakenings*. London: HarperCollins.

Schaffer, H.R. (2000) "The early experience assumption: post, present and future". *International Journal of Behavioural Development*, 24(1): 5–14.

Schwab, R.L. and Iwanicki, E.E. (1982) "Who are our burned out teachers?" *Educational Research Quarterly*, 7(2): 5–16.

Scott-Peck, M. (1978) *The Road Less Travelled*. London: Arrow Books.

Seligman, M. (1991) *Learned Optimism*. Sydney: Random House.

Smith, P.K. and Thompson, D. (1991) *Practical Approaches to Bullying*. London: David Fulton.

Stoll, L. (1998) "Supporting school improvement". Paper presented at the OECD conference "Combating Failure at School", Christchurch, New Zealand, 1–5 February.

Tauber, R.T. (1995) *Classroom Management Theory and Practice* (2nd edn). New York: Harcourt Brace.

Thody, A., Gray, B. and Bowden, D. (2000) *The Teacher's Survival Guide*. London: Continuum.

Thorsborne, M. and Vinegrad, D. (2009) *Restorative Practices in Schools: Rethinking Behaviour Management*. Bodenin Old: Incentive Plus (Inyahead Press).

Tolstoy, L. (1964) *Childhood, Boyhood, Youth*. Trans. R. Edmonds. London: Penguin Classics.

UNICEF (UK) (1989) *UN Convention of the Rights of the Child*. Resolution 44/25, 20 November.

Virgil (1985) *The Aeneid*. Trans. C.H. Sisson. London: Everyman Classics.

Wolfgang, C.H. (1999) *Solving Discipline Problems: Methods and Models for Today's Teachers*. Boston, MA: Allyn and Bacon.

Woodhouse, D.A., Hall, E. and Wooster, A.D. (1985) "Taking control of stress in teaching". *British Journal of Educational Psychology*, 55: 119–23.

Woolfolk, A., Margetts, K., Godintion, S., Frydenberg, E., LoBianco, J., Freeman, E. and Munro, J. (eds) (2007) *A Restorative Approach to Behaviour Management*. Frenchs Forest, NSW: Pearson Education Australia.

Index